THE SUPREME COURT
AND
THE SECOND BILL OF RIGHTS

THE SUPREME COURT
AND
THE SECOND BILL
OF RIGHTS

The Fourteenth Amendment
and the Nationalization of Civil Liberties

Richard C. Cortner

THE UNIVERSITY OF WISCONSIN PRESS

Published 1981

The University of Wisconsin Press
114 North Murray Street
Madison, Wisconsin 53715

The University of Wisconsin Press, Ltd.
1 Gower Street
London WC1E 6HA, England

First printing

Printed in the United States of America

For LC CIP information see the colophon

ISBN 0-299-08390-X

For
Hanna O

Contents

Preface

Most Americans are aware—albeit vaguely—of the existence of the Bill of Rights and its guarantees of the fundamental liberties of the individual, and undoubtedly most would agree that the adoption of the Bill of Rights in 1791 was an important event in the history of human freedom. Even otherwise well informed Americans, however, are often unaware that, until recently, the rights guaranteed in the Bill of Rights were restrictive of the powers of the national government alone, and did not limit the powers of state and local governments. The application of most of the rights in the Bill of Rights as restrictions upon the powers of state and local governments occurred only after the adoption of the Fourteenth Amendment in 1868, and has, by and large, been a constitutional development of the last sixty years.

Had this application of most of the Bill of Rights as restrictions on state power—the nationalization of the Bill of Rights—been accomplished through the formal process of constitutional amendment, as was the adoption of the Bill of Rights itself, such a fundamental change in the nature of the American constitutional system no doubt would have engendered intense public debate and scholarly inquiry. The nationalization of the Bill of Rights occurred, however, not through formal amendment of the Constitution but rather incrementally, through decisions of the United States Supreme Court interpreting the Due Process Clause of the Fourteenth Amendment over a period of a hundred years. The creation of a second American bill of rights, by the application of most of the original Bill of Rights to the states via the Due Process Clause of the Fourteenth Amendment, therefore took place with little public notice, and only certain aspects of this dramatic constitutional development have been subjected to intensive scholarly inquiry. It is the purpose of this work to subject to in-depth analysis the litigation that resulted in the nationalization of the Bill of Rights and the fundamental alteration that thus occurred in the constitutional protection afforded political and civil liberties in the United States.

In analyzing the litigation that produced the nationalization of the Bill

of Rights, I have tried to communicate the essentials of the decisions
through which the Supreme Court applied incrementally most of the Bill
of Rights to the states. And since the Court has been responsible for this
fundamental alteration in our constitutional system, I have focused additionally upon the theoretical justifications offered by the Court or individual justices in support of, or opposition to, the nationalization process.

Constitutional development as it occurs in Supreme Court litigation also
has, however, a very human dimension beyond the exposition of constitutional doctrine and theory in the decisions of the Court. I have therefore
also looked at the individual litigants who were caught up in the most important cases involving the nationalization of the Bill of Rights and have
examined the impact of the litigation upon their lives. The legal problems
of murderers, thieves, bookies, Communists, Jehovah's Witnesses, university professors, narcotics addicts, and others are thus an integral part of
the story that follows.

Great constitutional causes nonetheless tend to overshadow the particular individuals whose difficulties with the law happen to be involved, and
larger issues of constitutional policy are often shaped in crucial ways by
the lawyers participating in the litigation and, quite often, by the interest
groups that perceive constitutional litigation as a means of advancing their
interests. This was no less true of the nationalization of the Bill of Rights,
and I have therefore analyzed the roles in the nationalization process
played by such groups as the American Civil Liberties Union, the International Labor Defense, the American Newspaper Publishers' Association,
the Industrial Workers of the World, etc., and have examined the contributions, as well as the mistakes, of individual lawyers who played important roles in the litigation I have covered.

During the years that my work on this study proceeded, I received help,
criticism, and encouragement from numerous individuals. I especially
thank Professor David Fellman of the Department of Political Science at
the University of Wisconsin–Madison for his advice and criticism regarding my manuscript. And my colleague Professor Clifford M. Lytle of the
Department of Political Science at the University of Arizona was generous
with both his time and advice regarding various parts of the manuscript as
my work progressed. I also was aided in the later stages of my research by
a research grant from Project '87, sponsored jointly by the American Historical Association and the American Political Science Association. This
grant was crucial to the completion of my research, and I express my gratitude to Project '87 for its support.

I hope that this study of the nationalization of the Bill of Rights will
contribute to our knowledge and understanding of the process of Supreme
Court litigation as a vehicle of constitutional change in the United States.
More important, however, I hope that the study will result in a greater un-

derstanding and appreciation of what is the most important modern development in the constitutional protection of political and civil liberties in the United States—the creation of a second bill of rights through the Due Process Clause of the Fourteenth Amendment.

R. C. C.

Spring, 1980
Washington, D.C.

THE SUPREME COURT
AND
THE SECOND BILL OF RIGHTS

1

The Bill of Rights
and the Fourteenth Amendment

As it emerged from the Philadelphia convention in the fall of 1787, the Constitution did not contain a bill of rights.[1] George Mason's motion that the convention appoint a committee to draft a bill of rights was unanimously defeated by the delegates, voting as state units. A bill of rights was unnecessary, it was argued, since the rights of the people were adequately secured by state constitutions that generally contained bills of rights. Subsequent arguments against attaching a bill of rights to the Constitution were that the powers of the national government were limited to those clearly delegated to it, and no delegation of power to the national government involved the power to invade basic individual liberties. And, it was also argued, a bill of rights was dangerous, since the listing of certain rights in a bill of rights might be construed as indicating that other basic rights of the people were not protected.[2]

George Mason had declared during the Philadelphia convention, however, that he wished the Constitution "had been prefaced with a Bill of Rights, & would second a Motion if made for that purpose—It would give great quiet to the people. . . . "[3] Mason's views were vindicated in the state ratifying conventions, when it became clear that the lack of a bill of rights in the Constitution was indeed well-nigh universally regarded as one of its most disquieting features. Despite the arguments of the Federalists that a bill of rights was unnecessary and even dangerous, they were constrained to promise consideration of amendments to the Constitution as the price of its ratification in key state ratifying conventions.[4]

Although James Madison was initially among those who considered bills of rights to be mere "parchment barriers" against governmental power, he was finally converted to Jefferson's view "that a bill of rights is what the people are entitled to against every government on earth, general or particular; and what no just government should refuse, or rest on inference."[5] A bill of rights, Madison also came to perceive, would undermine the still-powerful opposition to the new constitutional system and the demands of some Anti-Federalists for amendments to the Constitution that

3

would substantially reduce the power of the national government. Responding somewhat reluctantly to Madison's initiatives, Congress finally referred twelve amendments to the states for ratification in September of 1789. Ten of these amendments were adopted by the requisite three-fourths of the states by December of 1791, and the Bill of Rights (usually regarded as the first eight amendments) was born.[6]

It was clear from the history of the adoption of the Bill of Rights that it was intended to restrain the power of the national government to interfere with basic individual liberties, and was not intended as a limitation on the powers of the states. Madison had proposed that Congress adopt an amendment prohibiting the states from infringing upon the rights of conscience, free press, and trial by jury, and he had declared that this amendment was "the most valuable on the whole list."[7] The amendment was rejected by Congress, however, and the Bill of Rights became exclusively a limitation on the power of the federal government.

Chief Justice Marshall confirmed that the Bill of Rights applied exclusively to the federal government in *Barron* v. *Baltimore*, decided by the Supreme Court in 1833.[8] Counsel for Barron argued that the Fifth Amendment's guarantee of just compensation for private property taken for a public use applied not only to exercises of federal power but also to exercises of the powers of the states. Writing for a unanimous Court, Marshall found the *Barron* case to present an issue of "great importance, but not of much difficulty." Pointing to the history of the ratification of the Bill of Rights, Marshall noted that there had been "immense opposition" to the ratification of the Constitution and that serious "fears were extensively entertained that those powers which the patriot statesmen who then watched over the interests of our country, deemed essential to union, and to the attainment of those invaluable objects for which union was sought, might be exercised in a manner dangerous to liberty." In almost all of the state ratifying conventions, he noted, amendments to "guard against the abuse of power were recommended" not against the state governments, but against "the apprehended encroachments of the general government. . . ." In compliance with the wishes of the ratifying conventions, Marshall concluded, the Bill of Rights had been adopted, and it contained "no expression indicating an intention to apply them to the State governments. This court cannot so apply them."[9]

The Supreme Court reaffirmed the principle of *Barron* v. *Baltimore*, that the Bill of Rights restricted national but not state power, in *Permoli* v. *New Orleans*, decided in 1845. In order to halt the spread of yellow fever, the city of New Orleans had enacted an ordinance prohibiting funerals in Catholic churches and confining funerals to one chapel. Permoli, a Catholic priest, was fined for violating the ordinance by performing funeral services in a Catholic church other than the designated chapel, and he appealed his conviction to the Supreme Court, arguing that the New Orleans ordinance violated the free exercise of religion guaranteed by the First Amendment of the Bill of Rights. The Court, however, dismissed the case for lack of jurisdiction. "The [federal] Constitution makes no provision for protecting the citizens of the respective States in their religious liberties," Justice Catron said; "this is left to State constitutions and laws; nor is there any inhibition imposed by the Constitution of the United States in this respect on the States."[10]

The Bill of Rights was thus confined to being a limitation only upon the power of the federal government and played a very limited role in American constitutional adjudication prior to the Civil War. For the protection of their most basic political and civil liberties from invasion by the states, Americans were required to look to their state constitutions and state bills of rights and not to the federal Bill of Rights.

The Civil War, however, led to the adoption of the Civil War Amendments to the Constitution—the Thirteenth, Fourteenth, and Fifteenth Amendments—and as a consequence, the federal system was significantly altered. This alteration was most forcefully symbolized by the Fourteenth Amendment, which was ratified in 1868. Unlike the Bill of Rights, the first section of the Fourteenth Amendment was directed at restraining the exercise of power by the states. "No State shall," the first section declared, "make or enforce any law which shall abridge the privileges or immunities of citizens of the United States; nor shall any State deprive any person of life, liberty, or property, without due process of law; nor deny to any person within its jurisdiction the equal protection of the laws." These clauses —the Privileges and Immunities, Due Process, and Equal Protection Clauses, respectively—opened up broad new avenues of potential appeals to the federal Constitution against exercises of power by the states.[11]

From the outset, however, there was confusion and conflict over what kinds of restrictions upon the exercise of state power the vague generalities of the first section of the Fourteenth Amendment would impose. The principal managers of the proposed Fourteenth Amendment in the Congress, Congressman John A. Bingham of Ohio and Senator Jacob M. Howard of Michigan, expounded upon the meaning of the proposed amendment, but their statements were hardly clear. Nonetheless, both Bingham and Howard did make statements that have been construed to support the view that one of the purposes of the Fourteenth Amendment was to apply the Bill of Rights to the states. The clearest statement in this regard was made by Senator Howard during the Senate debates on the proposed amendment. The purpose of the amendment, he said, was to protect various privileges and immunities guaranteed by the Constitution against interference by the states, including "the personal rights guaranteed and secured by the first eight amendments of the Constitution. . . ."[12]

Despite such statements, the problem has been whether or not the rest of the Congress that proposed the Fourteenth Amendment, and the members of the state legislatures that ratified it, understood that amendment to apply the Bill of Rights to the states. If this was their understanding, as Professor Charles Fairman has shown, precious little was said about such a purpose of the Fourteenth Amendment, aside from the statements by Bingham and Howard.[13]

However the debate over the true intentions of the framers and ratifiers of the Fourteenth Amendment is ultimately resolved, the fact is that the operational meaning of the Amendment lay in the hands of the Supreme Court, which had the power to give content to the new restrictions on state power contained in the first section. And in the first test of the meaning of the Fourteenth Amendment, the *Slaughter House Cases* of 1873, the Court by a five-to-four vote set its face against a latitudinarian interpretation of the Amendment's new restrictions on the traditional powers of the states.[14]

At issue in the *Slaughter House Cases* was the validity of a statute enacted by the carpetbag legislature of Louisiana conferring a monopoly upon one company for the maintenance of facilities for the landing and butchering of livestock in New Orleans. A result of wholesale bribery of the legislature, the statute required the largely French-speaking, Cajun butchers of New Orleans to utilize the monopoly's facilities and to pay a fee for such use. The irate butchers retained counsel—the most prominent of whom was former United States Supreme Court Justice John A. Campbell—and a constitutional attack on the statute was launched. Campbell's principal argument against the statute was that it interfered unreasonably with the right of the New Orleans butchers to pursue their lawful callings. The right to pursue a lawful calling, free from unreasonable and particularly monopolistic interferences, he argued, was a privilege and immunity of United States citizenship protected by the Privileges and Immunities Clause of the Fourteenth Amendment. Subsidiary arguments by Campbell were that the Louisiana statute deprived the butchers of their liberty and property in violation of the Due Process Clause, denied the equal protection of the laws in violation of the Equal Protection Clause, and imposed involuntary servitude in violation of the Thirteenth Amendment.[15]

Writing for a majority of five in the *Slaughter House Cases*, Justice Samuel F. Miller held that the police powers of the states, under which the health, welfare, and safety of the community could be protected, clearly justified the regulation of slaughterhouse facilities in a large metropolitan area such as New Orleans. The New Orleans butchers had not been deprived of their right to pursue their callings by the Louisiana statute, Miller also held, since they could still continue their occupations, subject only to the qualification that they land and slaughter their livestock at the facilities of the slaughterhouse company and pay a reasonable fee for the use of the company's property.[16]

Miller could have stopped at this point and simply held that whatever the ultimate content of the Privileges and Immunities Clause might be, it did not protect a right to pursue a calling free of state regulations such as those embodied in the Louisiana statute. Instead, he undertook a general exploration of the meaning of the Civil War Amendments and explored in particular the ultimate meaning of the Privileges and Immunities Clause. The result was an opinion for the Court that held in general that the Civil War Amendments were not intended to modify profoundly the nature of the federal system as it had existed prior to the Civil War and, more specifically, a ruling that the Privileges and Immunities Clause of the Fourteenth Amendment protected only a very narrow spectrum of rights against interference by the states.

Reviewing the history of the Civil War, Miller concluded that the principal purpose of the Civil War Amendments had been to declare the freedom of the slaves and to raise blacks to a plane of equality in the enjoyment of civil rights. The primary purpose of the amendments, he said, had been "the freedom of the slave race, the security and firm establishment of that freedom, and the protection of the newly made freeman and citizen from the oppressions of those who had formerly exercised dominion over him." Although Miller refused to say that "no one else but the negro can share in this protection" afforded by the Civil War Amendments, he concluded that in "any fair and just construction of any section or phrase of these amendments, it is necessary to look to the purpose which we have said was the pervading spirit of them all, the evil which they were designed to remedy, and the process of continued addition to the Constitution until that purpose was supposed to be accomplished, as far as constitutional law can accomplish."[17]

Counsel for the New Orleans butchers had called to the Court's attention the comments in Congress to the effect that the Fourteenth Amendment was intended to apply the Bill of Rights to the states. The Court's narrow interpretation of the Civil War Amendments, and especially the Privileges and Immunities Clause, in the *Slaughter House Cases*, however, precluded the possibility that the Fourteenth Amendment would be held to embrace such a broad spectrum of rights.[18]

The Fourteenth Amendment, Justice Miller said, recognized two distinct citizenships in the United States. By declaring that all persons were citizens of the United States who were born or naturalized in the United States and subject to the jurisdiction thereof, the Fourteenth Amendment was interpreted to define national citizenship. Distinct from this United States citizenship was state citizenship, which was acquired by an individual through residing within a particular state. Under the dual citizenship thus recognized under American law, Miller continued, the individual possessed two sets of rights—one deriving from state citizenship and the other deriving from United States citizenship. Most of the fundamental rights one enjoyed derived from one's state citizenship, Miller held, and such rights were secured by state law and not by the federal Constitution. The rights derived from state citizenship embraced "nearly every civil right for the establishment and protection of which organized government is instituted."[19]

The privileges and immunities possessed by the individual as a consequence of United States citizenship, and protected by the Privileges and Immunities Clause of the Fourteenth Amendment, were, in contrast, held to be relatively limited in importance and scope. Among the privileges and immunities of U.S. citizenship listed by Miller was the right of the individual to have access to the seat of the U.S. government, "to assert any claim he may have upon that government, to transact any business he may have with it, to seek its protection, to share its offices, to engage in administering its functions." Also protected as privileges and immunities of U.S. citizenship was the right to access to seaports, to subtreasuries, land offices, and courts of justice of the United States and the right to demand the protection of the national government when on the high seas or in a foreign country. Finally, Miller also included under the protection of the Privileges and Immunities Clause the right to assemble and petition the national government for redress of grievances, the right to the writ of habeas corpus, the right to use the navigable waters of the United States, and the rights secured by treaties with foreign countries.[20]

Beyond this, however, the most basic political and civil liberties of individuals remained, as they had prior to the Civil War, guarantees of state laws and state constitutions. To expand the list of rights protected by the Privileges and Immunities Clause to include those contended for by John A. Campbell, Justice Miller held, would be "to fetter and degrade the state governments. . . ." And certainly not included among the rights protected by the Privileges and Immunities Clause, he concluded, was the right to pursue a lawful calling. The Louisiana statute was thus held to be free from any constitutional defect under the Privileges and Immunities Clause.[21]

The contentions that the Louisiana statute imposed involuntary servitude, deprived the butchers of their liberty and property without due process of law, or denied them the equal protection of the laws were given short shrift by the Court. The statute clearly did not impose involuntary servitude in violation of the Thirteenth Amendment, Miller said. The Due Process Clause argument, he noted, had not "been much pressed," but in any case under no interpretation of due process "that we have seen, or any that we deem admissible, can the restraint imposed by the State of Louisiana upon the exercise of their trade by the butchers of New Orleans be held to be a deprivation of property within the meaning of that provision." And, finally, Miller expressed doubt that "any action of a State not directed by way of discrimination against the negroes as a class, or on account of their race, will ever be held to come within the purview of" the Equal Protection Clause. He concluded, therefore, that Louisiana had not denied the butchers the equal protection of the laws.[22]

Chief Justice Chase and Justices Field, Bradley, and Swayne dissented from the majority's narrow reading of the Fourteenth Amendment in the *Slaughter House Cases*. The Court's reading of the Privileges and Immunities Clause, Justice Field declared in dissent, had made it "a vain and idle enactment, which accomplished nothing, and most unnecessarily excited Congress and the people on its passage," and Justice Bradley indicated that he would have construed the Privileges and Immunities Clause to embrace the rights in the Bill of Rights. Justice Swayne perhaps best summed up the feelings of the dissenters toward the Court's narrow reading of the Fourteenth Amendment, and especially the Privileges and Immunities Clause: the Court had, he said, turned "what was meant for bread into a stone."[23]

In the first major test of its meaning, the Fourteenth Amendment was thus given a very narrow interpretation by the Court. The justices who constituted the Court that decided the *Slaughter House Cases* had experienced the travail of the Civil War, had seen a president narrowly miss conviction on impeachment charges, and had seen the Court itself attacked by a dominant Congress that had removed part of its appellate jurisdiction to prevent it from passing on the constitutionality of military reconstruction in the South. The same justices had witnessed the forces of nationalism that were unleashed by the Civil War undermine the status of the states within the federal system and had seen the concomitant strengthening of the power of the national government. Against this background, the votes of the majority of the Court in the *Slaughter House Cases* expressed a desire to restore stability in American constitutional law and politics and to turn away from the turbulence of the Civil War and its aftermath. A similar mood in the country as a whole was soon expressed in the Compromise of 1876, which marked the end of reconstruction efforts in the South.[24]

Perhaps the key words in Justice Miller's opinion in the *Slaughter House Cases* therefore related to the effect of the Civil War Amendments, and particularly the Fourteenth Amendment, on the federal system as it had existed prior to the Civil War. If Campbell's arguments were accepted, Miller said, the result would be a decision that "radically changes the whole theory of the relations of the state and Federal Governments to each other and of both these governments to the people. . . ." And at the conclusion of his opinion, Miller returned to the theme that the Civil War Amendments had not impaired the essential features of the federal system existing prior to the Civil War. The Court could not, he said, "see in [the Civil War Amendments] any purpose to destroy the main features of the general system."[25]

The majority of the Court in the *Slaughter House Cases* thus sought to temper the nationalizing forces produced by the war through construing the constitutional changes wrought by the war in a manner that would minimize their impact upon the constitutional system. The most immediate casualty of this approach to the interpretation of the Fourteenth Amendment was, of course, the Privileges and Immunities Clause. Under the doctrine of dual citizenship as enunciated by Justice Miller in the *Slaughter House Cases*, the Privileges and Immunities Clause was reduced to insignificance as a vehicle by which important civil liberties might be protected against impairment by the states. The most important rights of the individual, Miller had said, derived from state citizenship and were not among the rights of United States citizenship protected by the Privileges and Immunities Clause. Despite the Privileges and Immunities Clause, therefore, the individual was still dependent upon state laws and state constitutions for the protection of most of his basic rights, as had been the case prior to the Civil War.

Writing of the *Slaughter House Cases* in 1890, John W. Burgess criticized the Court for overreacting to the nationalism generated by the Civil War in its decision in those cases. The Court had, he said, attempted a "restoration of that particularism in the domain of civil liberty, from which we suffered so severely before 1861. . . . " The Court's decision in the *Slaughter House Cases*, Burgess continued, threw away the "great gain in the domain of civil liberty won by the terrible exertions of the nation in the appeal to arms. I have perfect confidence that the day will come, when it will be seen to be intensely reactionary and will be overturned."[26]

Despite Burgess's "perfect confidence," a reversal of the *Slaughter House Cases* in regard to the interpretation of the Privileges and Immunities Clause was not to be. Although litigants time and again appealed to the clause in challenging state policies, the Court stood firm in refusing to give the clause any significant content. As the Court's obdurate position on the Privileges and Immunities Clause was slowly perceived by the bar, however, challenges to state policies were increasingly based upon the clause in the Fourteenth Amendment that had not "been much pressed" in the *Slaughter House Cases*—the Due Process Clause.

The Due Process Clause, of course, prohibited the states from depriving any person "of life, liberty, or property, without due process of law. . . ." As civil liberties litigation came to focus on the Due Process Clause, litigants pressed the Court time and again to interpret the terms *liberty, prop-*

erty, and *due process of law* to embrace the substantive and procedural rights listed in the Bill of Rights, an interpretation that would convert the Due Process Clause of the Fourteenth Amendment into a second bill of rights applicable to exercises of state power.

The Bill of Rights itself had been proposed by Congress and ratified by the states within a span of two years. The conversion of the Due Process Clause of the Fourteenth Amendment into a second bill of rights applicable to the states, on the other hand, occurred in a slow, incremental process involving almost a century of Supreme Court litigation. As this process was reaching its culmination, however, a critic declared, with little exaggeration, that he could "think of nothing in the history of our constitutional law which has gone so far since John Marshall and the Supreme Court decided *Marbury* v. *Madison* in 1803."[27] Despite Justice Miller's strictures in the *Slaughter House Cases*, therefore, the nature of the American constitutional system was profoundly altered by the Fourteenth Amendment, which ultimately became a guarantee of individual liberty second only to the Bill of Rights itself. It is to an analysis of the litigation that produced this nationalization of the Bill of Rights that we now turn.

2

From the *Slaughter House Cases* to *Maxwell* v. *Dow*
A Study in Contradiction

The *Slaughter House Cases* ended the possibility that the nationalization of the Bill of Rights—the application of all or parts of the Bill of Rights as restrictions on state power—could be accomplished via the Privileges and Immunities Clause of the Fourteenth Amendment. The Due Process Clause therefore eventually became the focus of litigation in the Supreme Court through which the nationalization of the Bill of Rights was sought. In its decision in *Hurtado* v. *California* in 1884, however, the Court indicated that a nationalization of the Bill of Rights could also not be accomplished via the Due Process Clause.[1]

The *Hurtado* Case and the Doctrine of Nonsuperfluousness

The *Hurtado* case began with what appeared to be a simple brawl in the Bank Exchange Saloon in Sacramento, California, on Saturday, February 4, 1882. Joseph Hurtado assaulted José Antonio Estuardo.[2] Hurtado was arrested for battery, and the case was scheduled to be tried in the Sacramento police court on the following Monday morning. On the morning of the scheduled trial, however, the city attorney was unable to appear, and the trial was postponed for three days. Estuardo had in the meantime attempted to persuade the authorities to charge Hurtado with the more serious offense of assault with intent to commit murder and had argued that Hurtado should be held in jail on such a charge without bail because of his dangerous nature.

After the postponement of the police court case, the witnesses, court officials, Hurtado, and Estuardo left the courtroom. Hurtado proceeded to a saloon located on the corner of Front and I streets. As Estuardo also approached the saloon, Hurtado came out, approached Estuardo to within six to eight feet, and shot him in the chest. Estuardo turned and fled, but Hurtado shot him again in the back, and he fell to the ground. Hurtado then shot Estuardo a third time as he was lying on the ground, and then bludgeoned him with his pistol. Deputy Sheriff George Rider dragged

Hurtado away from the mortally wounded Estuardo. The Sacramento *Daily Bee* reported that as he was taken to jail, Hurtado was "as cool as though he had but just called on a social errand."[3]

As the facts leading to this violent episode subsequently unfolded, it was learned that the murder of José Estuardo was the culmination of a tragedy that was to follow Hurtado to the end of his life. Hurtado had been a resident of Sacramento for thirteen years and had married his wife, Susie, in 1879. A year later, they became the parents of a child. José Estuardo was a native of Chile and had arrived in Sacramento with his wife and three young children three years before his death. Estuardo's wife soon died, and he was forced to place his children in the Protestant Orphan Asylum. In the meantime, Estuardo and Hurtado had become friends, and Estuardo was a frequent visitor in the Hurtado household.

Hurtado subsequently discovered that his wife and Estuardo were having an affair, and when he confronted his wife, she admitted her involvement with Estuardo. Hurtado also confronted Estuardo, who was reported to have said, "I am the meat and you are the knife, kill me if you like." Hurtado instead demanded that Estuardo leave Sacramento, and Estuardo promised to do so as soon as he had earned enough money. He reneged on his promise, however, and instead continued to pursue Susie Hurtado.

Hurtado then sent his wife to her parents in La Paz, Mexico, in January of 1882. Hurtado was reported by his relatives and friends to have wept frequently, and one relative subsequently said that in discussing the situation, he "raved and tore his hair." He was also reported to have surrendered his pistol to a friend for fear of what he might do. Susie Hurtado returned to Sacramento about a week before the murder, but Estuardo still pursued her. Hurtado then assaulted Estuardo in the Bank Exchange Saloon; he was charged with battery; and after that case was postponed in police court on February 6, he shot Estuardo down in the street.[4]

Interviewed in jail, Hurtado related the events that had led to the crime, but public opinion apparently regarded it as a particularly cold-blooded killing. In addition, Estuardo had been the secretary of the Chilean Benevolent Society, and his fellow countrymen were much aroused by the crime. "I expect no sympathy," Hurtado told an interviewer, "all I ask is justice; God has me in His hands and will decree my fate as He thinks best." He indicated that when Estuardo attempted to have him charged with assault with the intent to commit murder and held without bail, "that was too much for me." He then decided, he said, to kill Estuardo and to commit suicide. Hurtado was clearly no stranger to violence. In 1880, he had shot and killed one man and had seriously wounded another in a saloon brawl, but he had been acquitted by a jury on a plea of self-defense.[5]

In the federal courts, and in most state courts at the time, Hurtado would have been indicted by a grand jury. Under the California Constitution of 1879, and legislation implementing its provisions, however, criminal defendants could be proceeded against by way of information rather than by indictment by grand jury. California criminal practice thus deviated from the practice in the federal courts, where the Fifth Amendment's Grand Jury Clause required indictment by grand jury in capital, or otherwise infamous, crimes.[6]

Without an indictment by a grand jury, therefore, a preliminary hearing was held in the Sacramento police court on February 15 to determine if there was probable cause to hold Hurtado in jail pending a formal charge. The case attracted intense public attention, and the courtroom and the surrounding area were "densely crowded with an eager throng, and there was much jostling and pushing required on the part of the officers to get through the packed passages with the prisoner." Hurtado continued to be "as calm and composed as if no such serious charge was hanging over him, and watched the entire proceedings with a wonderful coolness." The prosecutor easily demonstrated probable cause to hold Hurtado in custody, given the numerous eyewitnesses to the shooting. The police court judge ordered Hurtado held without bail on the charge of murder. On February 20, H. L. Buckley, District Attorney of Sacramento County, filed an information charging that Hurtado did "willfully, unlawfully, feloniously, and with malice aforethought, kill and murder a certain human being, to wit, José Antonio Estuardo." Represented by counsel, Hurtado was arraigned on this charge on March 22, and he entered a plea of not guilty.[7]

Hurtado's case came on for trial on May 2 in Department Two of the Superior Court of Sacramento County before Judge S. C. Denson and a jury. The courtroom was again crowded, and Hurtado was described as being "cool and self-possessed, as he has from the first." He also expressed his "anxiety for immediate trial, saying he would rather have it all ended some way than be cooped up in a little cell any longer." Given the number of eyewitnesses to the shooting, the prosecution easily proved that Hurtado had killed Estuardo. The defense argued that Hurtado had been suffering from "emotional insanity" at the time of the crime. As his defense was outlined, and his wife testified to her infidelity in his defense, Hurtado's demeanor changed, and he became "suffused with tears" and ultimately gave way to "audible sobs." During the latter part of the trial, he was described as sitting beside his attorney "but never lifts his head or raises his eyes from the floor, and keeps perfectly quiet, never making a suggestion to the counsel."[8]

After instructions from Judge Denson, the jury retired for deliberations just before midnight on Saturday, May 6. A verdict was reached by the jury early on Sunday morning; it found Hurtado guilty of murder in the first degree. Hurtado was said to have "betrayed no emotion," but he indicated to reporters that he felt that he had been right in killing Estuardo and was confident that his conviction would be reversed by the California Supreme Court. Judge Denson nevertheless sentenced Hurtado to "be hung by the neck until he is dead" on July 26.[9]

Despite Hurtado's expectations, the California Supreme Court on March 18, 1883, affirmed his conviction, rejecting all arguments that reversible error had occurred at the trial.[10] The Superior Court of Sacramento County then proceeded to set a new execution date, but counsel for Hurtado filed a bill of exceptions to the execution of the sentence. In this bill of exceptions, it was for the first time argued in the *Hurtado* case that the state, in proceeding against Hurtado by way of information rather than by an indictment by a grand jury, had violated the Fifth and Fourteenth Amendments of the federal Constitution. The superior court, however, rejected this contention, and resentenced Hurtado to be hanged on August 30, 1883.[11]

Counsel for Hurtado again appealed his conviction and sentence to the California Supreme Court, but that court reaffirmed the conviction and sentence in the *Hurtado* case on September 18.[12] The decision of the California Supreme Court was in turn appealed by writ of error to the United States Supreme Court, and the Court granted the writ on September 29, 1883.[13] Whether the states were required by the Due Process Clause of the Fourteenth Amendment to indict criminal defendants by grand juries would now be authoritatively determined.

In relying on due process as the basis for a reversal of Hurtado's conviction, counsel for Hurtado were invoking a concept that had hitherto been only vaguely defined by the Supreme Court. In an 1856 decision interpreting the Fifth Amendment's Due Process Clause, for example, the Court had held that in ascertaining whether a particular procedure violated due process, the Constitution itself had to be examined, to determine if the challenged procedure violated any of its provisions. If this was not the case, the Court said, then "we must look to those settled usages and modes of proceeding existing in the common and statute law of England, before the emigration of our ancestors, and which are shown not to have been unsuited to their civil and political condition by having been acted on by them after the settlement of this country." Due process, the Court concluded, generally required "regular allegations, opportunity to answer, and a trial according to some settled course of judicial proceedings, . . . yet this is not universally true."[14]

Such a vague definition of due process was typical of judicial attempts to give content to one of the most elusive concepts in American constitutional law, and the inclusion of a Due Process Clause in the Fourteenth Amendment increased the pressure on the Court to further define due process, since due process challenges to state policies proliferated rapidly after the Civil War. In *Davidson* v. *New Orleans*,[15] decided in 1878, the Court indicated that it was not a little vexed and perplexed by the numerous cases that were being appealed to it under the Fourteenth Amendment's Due Process Clause, and it undertook a major effort to explain the meaning of due process.

Writing for the Court, Justice Miller noted that the "docket of this court is crowded with cases in which we are asked to hold that State Courts and State Legislatures have deprived their own citizens of life, liberty or property without due process of law." This indicated, he said, that "there exists some strange misconception of the scope of this provision as found in the XIVth Amendment." While the specific meaning of the Due Process Clause would be supplied on a case-by-case basis, "by the gradual process of judicial inclusion and exclusion," Miller continued, an attempt would be made to dispel the "strange misconception" of litigants before the Court as to the meaning of due process.[16]

Although due process generally guaranteed fair procedure, Miller said, a state legislature could not simply declare by statute that a particular procedure conformed to due process. If a legislature attempted to transfer A's land to B, he pointed out, such action would deprive A of his property "without due process of law, within the meaning of the constitutional provision."[17] Despite this implication that the Due Process Clause might protect certain substantive rights, Miller's principal emphasis was upon the procedural limitations imposed upon the states by the clause. Even when property was taken, he said, if state laws "provide for a mode of confirming or contesting the charge thus imposed, in the ordinary courts of justice, with such notice to the person, or such proceeding in regard to the property as is appropriate to the nature of the case, the judgment in such proceedings cannot be said to deprive the owner of his property without due process of law, however obnoxious it may be to other objections." If, under the laws of a state, he concluded, "the party aggrieved has, as regards the issues affecting his property, a fair trial in a court of justice, according to the modes of proceeding applicable to such case," the Court could not hold that there had been a violation of due process.[18]

Miller's emphasis on the flexibility of procedure allowed the states under the Due Process Clause gave small comfort, of course, to counsel for Hurtado in their arguments before the Court. Due process, they argued, should not be so narrowly construed as to embrace only "the right to be heard in a proceeding conducted according to general laws applicable to all alike." Such a narrow construction of due process would allow state legislatures "to pass any kind of laws, providing for the most arbitrary proceedings, which they might deem wise. . . ." The Due Process Clause, they contended, was rather intended to preserve the "ancient common law rights" that Americans had inherited from England. And among these ancient rights was the right to be indicted by a grand jury in a criminal case, since indictment by grand jury had been universally recognized at the time of our separation from England as being among "the fundamental rights of trial according to the ancient principles of the common law."[19]

The right to indictment by grand jury, counsel for Hurtado argued, was an invaluable right of the individual, since it was a barrier to unjustified prosecutions by hostile or overzealous prosecutors. Yet in California, they said, because of the abolition of grand jury indictments, "the only thing left to protect the individual against the loss of reputation and jeopardy involved in a final and public trial for an infamous offense, at the option of a hostile prosecutor, is the determination of a common Justice of the Peace" that there was probable cause to bind an individual over for trial. Counsel for Hurtado thus urged the Court to preserve the right to indictment by grand jury as an inherent and essential element of due process, and because California had not so indicted Hurtado, to reverse his conviction under the Due Process Clause.[20]

In making this argument before the Court, counsel for Hurtado were not only urging more stringent due process standards than the *Davidson* decision had indicated were applicable to the states, but in urging the court to hold that a right in the Bill of Rights was a guarantee also of the Due Process Clause, they were also asking the court to adopt a policy that it had rejected in two recent cases. For in *Walker* v. *Sauvinet* and *United States* v. *Cruikshank*,[21] both decided in 1876, the Court had rejected arguments that the Due Process Clause required jury trials in state civil cases (as the Seventh Amendment required in federal civil cases), or that the right to assemble and petition and the right to bear arms (rights guaranteed by the First and Second Amendments) were also guaranteed by the Due Process Clause.

In addition to this demonstrated reluctance of the Court to apply any of the Bill of Rights to the states via the Due Process Clause, another major hurdle for Hurtado's counsel was the argument made on behalf of the state of California by John T. Carey, District Attorney of Sacramento County. Since the *Hurtado* case turned on the meaning of the Due Process Clause of the Fourteenth Amendment, Carey told the Court, the first inquiry should be whether the phrase was used "elsewhere in the Constitution, and, if so, what is its meaning? The answer is, we find it in the Fifth Article of Amendment to the Constitution of the United States." Counsel for Hurtado, Carey argued, had in effect contended that the phrase "due process of law" in the Fourteenth Amendment "is convertable into the expression 'unless on the presentment or indictment by a grand jury.'" This, however, according to Carey could not be correct. The Fifth Amendment, he noted, contained a Due Process Clause, yet it also contained a guarantee of the right to indictment by grand jury, as well as guarantees of freedom from double jeopardy, the right to just compensation, and the right against self-incrimination. If the phrase "due process of law" included the right to indictment by grand jury, Carey said, then the listing of the right to indictment by grand jury along with the Due Process Clause in the Fifth Amendment was "surplusage and mere verbiage"[22]

If, on the other hand, Carey argued, one accepted the idea that the framers of the Fifth Amendment had not been repetitive in their use of language, then the phrase "due process of law" in the Fifth Amendment had not been intended to include the right to indictment by grand jury. "Then if 'due process of law' in the Fifth Article of Amendment does not mean 'unless on presentment or indictment by a grand jury,'" he continued, "why should it be given such a meaning or construction as it appears in the Fourteenth Article of Amendment? Is there anything in the Fourteenth Article rendering such a construction warrantable? Is it not more rational to conclude that the people or the States adopted and accepted it with the meaning and construction that it had in the Fifth Article of Amendment, that it had received by the judiciary and law writers?"[23]

If Carey's premises were accepted, his argument on this point not only refuted the claim that the Due Process Clause of the Fourteenth Amendment protected the right to grand jury indictment, but it also could be utilized to deny that any right in the Bill of Rights was protected by the Due Process Clause. That is, based on Carey's premises, any of the rights guaranteed specifically in any of the first eight amendments could not be said to be protected by due process, since if this were so, the framers of the Bill of Rights would not have listed them separately but would have assumed their protection by the Due Process Clause of the Fifth Amendment. And since the words in the Due Process Clause of the Fourteenth Amendment were essentially the same as that in the Fifth, the Due Process Clause of the Fourteenth Amendment also could not be said to protect any of the rights in the Bill of Rights against state action.

Carey proposed instead that due process only guaranteed the right to be heard in an appropriate proceeding under general laws applicable to all alike. He also noted that fully nine states had modified or abandoned grand jury indictments as the method of initiating criminal proceedings— a clear indication, he said, that due process was not felt to require indictment by grand jury. And finally, he argued that in proceedings involving the initiation of criminal charges, a defendant was protected as much or more by information as by indictment by grand jury. The right to indictment by grand jury was the right to be indicted in secrecy on the basis of evidence supplied by the prosecutor alone. "No one, it seems to me," Carey said, "familiar with the manner of investigations by grand juries would complain because he had been deprived of a hearing before a secret tribunal, constituted and constructed as it is." A hearing before a magistrate on the charges contained in an information, he concluded, offered more protection to the individual than the secrecy of grand jury proceedings.[24]

The Supreme Court decided *Hurtado* v. *California* on March 3, 1884, and affirmed the decision of the California Supreme Court.[25] In an opinion by Justice Matthews, the Court explored more extensively than ever before the relationship between the Due Process Clause of the Fourteenth Amendment and the Bill of Rights. The Court examined the question of whether the right to an indictment was a part of the "law of the land" clause of Magna Charta and whether it should be considered an essential element of due process of law. Due process, the Court admitted, meant that "a process of law, which is not otherwise forbidden, must be taken to be due process of law, if it can show the sanction of settled usage both in England and in this country; but it by no means follows, that nothing else can be due process of law." To define due process as embracing only those procedures sanctioned by the past, the Court said, "would be to deny every quality of the law but its age, and to render it incapable of progress or improvement. It would be to stamp upon our jurisprudence the unchangeableness attributed to the laws of the Medes and Persians."[26]

The Constitution, and the concept of due process, the Court said, "was made for an undefined and expanding future, and for a people gathered and to be gathered from many Nations and of many tongues." And since the common law had always drawn "its inspiration from every fountain of justice, we are not to assume that the sources of its supply have been exhausted. On the contrary, we should expect that the new and various experiences of our own situation and system will mold and shape it into new and not less useful forms." The Due Process Clause was therefore not intended, the Court continued, to freeze all traditional common law procedures and to impose them upon the states. The states were to remain free to modify traditional procedures and to adapt the common law system to the exigencies of modern times.[27]

The Court presented yet another reason for rejecting the claim that the Due Process Clause required the states to indict by grand jury. It accepted John Carey's argument that the meaning of the Fifth and the Fourteenth Amendments' Due Process Clauses was the same, and that this meant that the Fourteenth Amendment's Due Process Clause could not logically guarantee the right to indictment by grand jury. Since the Fifth Amendment contained a guarantee of indictment by grand jury as well as a Due Process Clause, the Court held, the framers of the Bill of Rights must have felt that the right to indictment by grand jury was not contained in the conception of due process, or otherwise they would not have provided separately for grand jury indictments in the Fifth Amendment.

"According to a recognized canon of interpretation, especially applicable to formal and solemn instruments of constitutional law," the Court said, "we are forbidden to assume, without clear reason to the contrary, that any part of this most important [Fifth] Amendment is superfluous. The natural and obvious inference is, that in the sense of the Constitution, 'due process of law' was not meant or intended to include, *ex vi termini*, the institution and procedure of a grand jury in any case." The conclusion was therefore irresistible, the Court continued, "that when the same phrase was employed in the 14th Amendment to restrain the action of the States, it was used in the same sense and with no greater extent; and that if in the adoption of that Amendment it had been part of its purpose to perpetuate the institution of the grand jury in all the States, it would have embodied, as did the 5th Amendment, express declarations to that effect."[28]

Due process did impose important limitations upon the exercise of governmental power, the Court conceded. No state could interfere with "those fundamental principles of liberty and justice which lie at the base of all our civil and political institutions. . . ." But "any legal proceeding enforced by public authority, whether sanctioned by age and custom, or newly devised in the discretion of the legislative power, in furtherance of the general public good, which regards and preserves these principles of liberty and justice, must be held to be due process of law." Dispensing with grand jury indictments did not interfere with these "fundamental principles of liberty and justice," the Court concluded, since it was impossible to say that for a state to proceed by information, "after examination and commitment by a magistrate, certifying to the probable guilt of the defendant, with the right on his part to the aid of counsel, and to the cross-examination of the witnesses produced for the prosecution, is not due process of law."[29]

Justice John Marshall Harlan was the only dissenter from the judgment of the Court in the *Hurtado* case, and he argued that the purpose of the Fourteenth Amendment had been to apply to the states all of the rights in the Bill of Rights. Harlan was a six-foot three-inch, tobacco-chewing Kentuckian, who had been appointed to the Court in 1877 at the age of forty-four by President Hayes. He would serve on the Court for almost thirty-four years and die in harness in 1911. It is one of the ironies of history that Harlan's grandson, John Marshall Harlan II, following his appointment to the Court in 1955, became one of the strongest critics of the position that the Fourteenth Amendment applied the Bill of Rights to the states.[30]

Harlan had earlier charged that the Court had sacrificed the "substance and spirit" of the Civil War Amendments "by a subtle and ingenious verbal criticism,"[31] and he declared in dissent in the *Hurtado* case that the Due Process Clause of the Fourteenth Amendment was intended "to impose upon the States the same restrictions, in respect of proceedings involving life, liberty and property, which had been imposed upon the general government."[32] Indictment by grand jury, he said, had always been considered an essential element in the mode of proceeding in criminal cases at the common law, and should therefore be held to be a requirement of due process.

Harlan also attacked the Court's assertion that the Due Process Clauses in the Fifth and Fourteenth Amendments must have identical meanings, and therefore that due process did not embrace a right to grand jury indictment, since such a right was listed separately from the Due Process Clause of the Fifth Amendment. This doctrine of nonsuperfluousness, he argued, would necessarily lead to the conclusion that no right in the Bill of Rights could be protected against state action by the Due Process Clause of the Fourteenth Amendment. "This line of argument, it seems to me," he said, "would lead to results which are inconsistent with the vital principles of republican government."[33]

On the other hand, Harlan noted, the Court had held that the Due Process Clause protects "those fundamental principles of liberty and justice which lie at the base of all our civil and political institutions." Since the right to indictment by grand jury had been traditionally recognized as an important right at common law, in the federal Constitution, and in the constitutions of the states, how could the Court, he asked, fail to consider it to be a "fundamental principle of liberty and justice?"[34]

As Harlan correctly noted in his dissent, the doctrine of nonsuperfluousness asserted by the Court in the *Hurtado* case seemed to end any prospect that the Due Process Clause of the Fourteenth Amendment could be the vehicle for applying the Bill of Rights to the states. The same reasoning could as easily be applied to hold that since such rights as freedom of speech or of religion, or the right against unreasonable searches and seizures, or the right to counsel, were listed separately from the Due Process Clause of the Fifth Amendment in the Bill of Rights, such rights could not be protected by the Due Process Clause of the Fourteenth Amendment against state action. The Court's acceptance of John Carey's argument in the *Hurtado* case thus seemed to end any possibility that the nationalization of the Bill of Rights might be accomplished via the Due Process Clause of the Fourteenth Amendment, just as the *Slaughter House Cases* had ended such a possibility via the Privileges and Immunities Clause.

Yet the Court had held in *Hurtado* that the Due Process Clause did protect against state encroachment those "fundamental principles of liberty and justice which lie at the base of all our civil and political institutions." The question that remained after the *Hurtado* decision, despite the Court's apparent acceptance of the doctrine of nonsuperfluousness, was whether or not at least some of these "fundamental principles of liberty and justice" were listed in the Bill of Rights. It would seem difficult indeed for the Court to maintain that the Bill of Rights listed no rights that could be said to be defined in this manner.

Aside from the long range theoretical impact of the *Hurtado* decision, its more immediate effect was, of course, to affirm that the unfortunate Joseph Hurtado would be hanged in an appropriately solemn ceremony by the state of California. Hurtado received the news of the Court's decision calmly in his jail cell in Sacramento. He told an interviewer that he would meet his fate manfully and bravely and that he realized that all that remained for him was to await the executioner. He insisted, however, that his shooting of Estuardo had been in keeping with the unwritten law that permitted a man to protect his wife and his domestic life.

Hurtado had contracted tuberculosis in jail, and he was reported to be "a wreck of his former self," with sunken cheeks and a hollow chest. Almost every breath he took was followed by a "cough and expectoration of blood." One month after the Supreme Court's decision in his case, on the evening of April 3, 1884, Hurtado died in his cell of a hemorrhage of the lungs. His mother, wife, and daughter were permitted to be with him, and he died affirming his Catholic faith to two priests who attended him. He was thirty-three years old.[35]

District Attorney John Carey communicated the fact of Hurtado's death to the clerk of the United States Supreme Court on April 6. "If there is any thing further to be done on the part of the State in the *Hurtado* case," Carey wrote, "please inform me what it is and I will attend to it in order that further delay may be avoided." "Hurtado," he added, "died a few days since and this ended the further history of his case."[36]

While Carey was correct in reporting that Hurtado's death ended the history of his case in the immediate sense, the doctrine of nonsuperfluousness that the Court embraced in the *Hurtado* case continued for many years to be a roadblock to the nationalization of the Bill of Rights. Given the reasoning in the *Hurtado* case, it is not surprising that in 1886 the Court again rejected an argument that the Second Amendment applied to the states via the Due Process Clause of the Fourteenth Amendment. And in 1887, the Court also dismissed a case in which John Randolph Tucker, a leader of the bar, argued that all of the Bill of Rights applied to the states through the Fourteenth Amendment.[37]

The Court's resistance to the nationalization of the Bill of Rights continued into the early 1890s, when on three occasions it rejected arguments that the Cruel and Unusual Punishment Clause of the Eighth Amendment applied to the states via the Fourteenth Amendment.[38] In *O'Neil* v. *Vermont*, the last of the Cruel and Unusual Punishment Clause cases, Justices Stephen Field and David Brewer joined Justice Harlan's dissenting argument that the purpose of the Fourteenth Amendment had been to apply all of the Bill of Rights to the states.[39] Justice Field resigned from the Court in 1897, however, and Justice Brewer apparently later recanted his views. Justice Harlan was therefore left to further the "total incorporation" (as his position would later be called) of the Bill of Rights into the Fourteenth Amendment in a manner to which he was accustomed—alone.

In contrast to its refusal during this period to interpret the Due Process Clause as applying all or parts of the Bill of Rights to the states, the Court was rapidly transforming the clause into a bastion of strength against state interferences with property rights. In 1886, the Court held that corporations were "persons" within the meaning of the Due Process Clause, and thus converted the clause into a protector of corporate property rights against interferences by the states.[40] And by the 1890s, the Court had jettisoned the idea that the Due Process Clause was essentially a procedural guarantee and had accepted the concept of substantive due process—that is, the concept that the Due Process Clause protected certain substantive rights against governmental impairment regardless of the procedure involved.[41]

The "liberty" protected by the Due Process Clause, the Court thus held, embraced more than the negative concept of an absence of physical restraint, and instead insured to the individual positive rights that were beyond state interference. This new liberty under the Due Process Clause, the Court held in 1897, meant "not only the right of the citizen to be free from the mere physical restraint of his person, as by incarceration, but the term is deemed to embrace the right of the citizen to be free in the enjoyment of all his faculties; to be free to use them in all lawful ways; to live and work where he will; to earn his livelihood by any lawful calling; to pursue any livelihood or avocation, and for that purpose to enter into all contracts which may be proper, necessary and essential to his carrying out to a successful conclusion the purposes above mentioned."[42]

By the 1890s, therefore, the Court had interpreted the Due Process Clause to guarantee rights that the Court had earlier rejected under the Privileges and Immunities Clause in the *Slaughter House Cases*. In the field of the substantive due process rights it had now recognized, the Court's emphasis was upon the rights of property and contract, and indeed the most important substantive due process right to emerge during this period was that of liberty of contract. In *Lochner* v. *New York*, decided in 1905, the Court thus invalidated a statute setting a ten-hour day for bakers as an interference with liberty of contract, and the doctrine of liberty of contract would continue to be a major obstacle to labor reform legislation until the 1930s.[43]

Although the new substantive rights the Court was carving out under the Due Process Clause related primarily to property rights, the recognition that the Due Process Clause protected such substantive rights would ultimately have a profound effect upon the nationalization of the Bill of Rights. For if the "liberty" protected by the Due Process Clause embraced the right to be free to use one's faculties, the argument could and would be made that in addition to acquiring and possessing property, such a broad right should also embrace the rights of free speech, freedom of the press, and freedom of religion, as well as other substantive liberties guaranteed in the Bill of Rights. While the most immediate consequence of the acceptance of substantive due process by the Court was to strengthen the constitutional protection of property rights, the development of substantive due process ultimately laid the basis for the application of the substantive guarantees in the Bill of Rights to the states via the Due Process Clause.[44]

For the time being, however, the "fundamental principles of liberty and justice" which lay "at the base of all our civil and political institutions" continued to involve, in the decisions of the Court, essentially property rights. It is not surprising, therefore, that property rights were involved when the first significant breakthrough regarding the nationalization of the Bill of Rights occurred—in *Chicago, Burlington & Quincy Railroad Co.* v. *Chicago*, decided by the Court in 1897.[45]

The *Chicago, Burlington & Quincy Railroad* Case

With the railroads revolutionizing the transportation system of the country, Chicago became the great railroad center of the Midwest following the Civil War. Railway tracks crisscrossed the city, and the railroad companies owned substantial parts of the property located in the expanding metropolis. The pressure of growth in Chicago rather naturally led to conflicts between the railroads and the city.

One such conflict arose when the city began, under the power of eminent domain, to condemn railroad properties for the purpose of street expansion. The railroads argued that if their property was to be taken for the public purpose of street expansion, they were entitled to just compensation measured by the value their property might have if it were used for any suitable commercial purpose. Since the extension of a street across railroad tracks did not prevent the railroad company from continuing to use its roadbed, and impaired the roadbed's usefulness only minimally, the city maintained that the railroads were entitled to only nominal compensation for their property.

These differences between the city of Chicago and the railroads came to a head when the city council passed ordinances in 1889 and 1890 providing for the extension of several streets within the city. The city had been given the power of eminent domain under a state statute of 1872, and under the procedure outlined in the statute, any person or corporation whose property would be condemned was entitled to just compensation. And if the monetary offer for the property condemned was not acceptable, a trial of the issue could be obtained in the Circuit Court of Cook County.

In addition to property belonging to several individuals, the extension of streets proposed by the city council involved the condemnation of certain property owned by the Chicago, Burlington & Quincy Railroad Co. and the Chicago & Northwestern Railroad Co. To settle disputes over the value of several parcels of land to be condemned, including land owned by the railroad companies, trials were held in the Cook County Circuit Court to determine the compensation to be paid by the city.

A total of 30,335 square feet of Chicago, Burlington & Quincy Railroad property was involved in two separate cases, while the Chicago & Northwestern Railroad had 6600 square feet of its land involved in another case. In the trial of each of these cases, the court adopted the position that the railroad companies were entitled to compensation only to the extent that their property was impaired for use for railroad purposes. The court excluded offers of proof by the railroads relating to other factors by which the value of the property being condemned would have been substantially increased. And in each case, the railroad companies were awarded only one dollar in compensation, while substantial amounts were awarded to the other parties whose property was also being condemned. For example, in the two cases involving the Chicago, Burlington & Quincy Railroad Co., the juries awarded a total of $12,762.75 in compensation to the other parties, but in each case awarded only one dollar in compensation to the railroad company.[46]

Given the substantial amounts of railroad property in the city of Chicago, and the likelihood of railroad involvement in such condemnation proceedings in the future, the railroads had a major stake in reversing the interpretation of just compensation adopted by the Cook County Circuit Court. Both the Chicago, Burlington & Quincy and the Chicago & Northwestern railroad companies appealed the verdict rendered in the circuit court to the Supreme Court of Illinois. That court, however, rejected the railroads' contention that they should have been compensated on the basis of the value of their properties for a variety of possible commercial purposes rather than on the basis of the extent to which the railroad functions of their properties had been impaired by the Chicago street expansion.[47]

As a result of this loss in the Supreme Court of Illinois, the stakes for the railroads in the litigation had risen. It was now the law of Illinois that railroads need only be compensated for their property condemned for street improvements to the extent that its use for railroad purposes was impaired. The railroads therefore understandably continued to controvert the Illinois compensation policy by filing writs of error in the United States Supreme Court seeking reversals of the decisions of the Illinois courts.

Having failed to prevail on the compensation point under Illinois law, the railroads now argued that the Due Process Clause of the Fourteenth Amendment applied the Just Compensation Clause of the Fifth Amendment to the states, and that a proper interpretation of the federal guarantee would sustain their contentions. The assignment of errors filed by the

Chicago, Burlington & Quincy Railroad in the Supreme Court thus asserted that the property of the railroad had been taken "for public use without just compensation, contrary to the Fifth Amendment to the Constitution of the United States."[48] Counsel for the Chicago & Northwestern Railroad, however, had failed to raise such a federal issue in the Supreme Court of Illinois, and as a consequence the *Chicago & Northwestern Railroad Co.* case was dismissed by the United States Supreme Court on November 30, 1896.[49]

John J. Herrick was the principal attorney for the Chicago, Burlington & Quincy Railroad, and he argued before the Supreme Court that a right to just compensation was guaranteed by the Due Process Clause of the Fourteenth Amendment. He went further in his argument, however, and asserted that the Fourteenth Amendment had been intended to apply all of the Bill of Rights to the states, including the Just Compensation Clause of the Fifth Amendment. He conceded that the Bill of Rights had originally been intended to apply only to the federal government, with the result that it "fell short of giving to the citizen the full protection to which he was entitled in respect to his life, liberty and property, so far as state action was concerned." But the Fourteenth Amendment, Herrick told the Court, "was adopted to remedy and correct this defect in the supreme organic law of the land" and was therefore intended "to place the same limitation upon the power of the states which the Fifth Amendment had placed upon the authority of the Federal Government."[50]

Since the Just Compensation Clause applied to the states, Herrick argued that the railroad was entitled to much more substantial compensation for its property than the one dollar awarded by the Illinois courts. He renewed his argument that the railroad was entitled to compensation measured by the commercial value of its property. Even if this measure of just compensation were not accepted, he argued, the railroad company should at least have been compensated to the extent the property's usefulness for railroad purposes had been impaired, and for any additional expenses the company incurred in insuring the safety of its operations across public streets.[51]

Counsel for the state of Illinois, on the other hand, pointed out to the Court that the Chicago, Burlington & Quincy Railroad had received a fair trial on the issue of compensation in the Illinois courts, and that under the Court's interpretation of the Due Process Clause in *Davidson* v. *New Orleans* this was all that was required of the state. The railroad company had had notice of the condemnation proceedings, they said, had appeared at trial represented by counsel, and had received a fair hearing under the mode of proceeding in such cases under the law of Illinois. The "condemnation suit in which the [Chicago, Burlington & Quincy Railroad] was summoned, and appeared and urged its contentions," counsel for the state therefore argued, "was none the less due process of law, even if the rulings of the state court were erroneous."[52]

If the Court accepted Herrick's argument that the Fourteenth Amendment applied all of the Bill of Rights to the states, Illinois counsel continued, the result would be the destruction of the federal system. "Put to it by the stress of his case," they said, Herrick had so defined the meaning of the Fourteenth Amendment as to "make it very difficult to deny the jurisdiction of this court of a writ of error to review the judgments of the courts of a state in any case involving life, liberty or property, and would leave nothing of the sovereignty of the states."[53]

The Chicago, Burlington & Quincy Railroad, Illinois counsel concluded, had received a hearing in full conformity with the Due Process Clause, and the trial court had properly excluded all evidence of the value of the railroad's property except that which related to the impairment of the value of the property for railroad purposes. And since the extension of streets across railroad tracks and rights-of-way interfered only minimally with railroad operations, the nominal compensation awarded the railroad had been just compensation.[54]

Chicago, Burlington & Quincy Railroad Co. v. *Chicago* was finally decided by the Court on March 1, 1897. As was to happen more than once in the history of the nationalization of the Bill of Rights, the railroad company won the battle but lost the war. Speaking through Justice John Marshall Harlan, the Court unanimously held that the Due Process Clause of the Fourteenth Amendment did require the states to give just compensation for private property taken for public uses. "In our opinion," the Court said, "a judgment of a state court, even if it be authorized by statute, whereby private property is taken for the state or under its direction for public use, without compensation made or secured to the owner, is, upon principle and authority, wanting in the due process of law required by the 14th Amendment of the Constitution of the United States, and the affirmance of such judgment by the highest court of the state is a denial by that state of a right secured to the owner by that instrument."[55]

The question then became one of determining if the railroad had been denied just compensation and thus due process by the courts of Illinois. It could not, the Court held, pass upon the facts upon which the jury had based its verdict. The Seventh Amendment, which provides in part that "no fact tried by a jury shall be otherwise re-examined in any court of the United States than according to the rules of the common law" prohibited the Court from reexamining the facts upon which the jury had relied.

The Court did, however, pass upon the rulings of law made by the trial court on the admissibility of evidence offered by the railroad to prove the value of its property. The trial court, the Court said, properly excluded from consideration by the jury evidence offered by the railroad indicating the value of its property for nonrailroad purposes, the extent to which the property would be impaired for future railroad purposes, and the costs to the railroad of operating safely across public streets. The Court accepted the argument that the compensation due to the railroad should be measured by the extent to which its property was impaired for present railroad purposes by the extension of streets across it, an impairment that the Court held it was reasonable to conclude was minimal. The nominal award to the railroad, the Court concluded, had therefore been just compensation and had not violated the Due Process Clause and its newly found requirement of just compensation.[56]

Chief Justice Fuller did not participate in the decision of the Court, and only Justice Brewer dissented on the point of whether the railroad had received just compensation, while agreeing that the Due Process Clause did impose such a requirement upon the states.[57] Unanimously, and one might even say casually, the Court thus held for the first time that a right in the Bill of Rights was also a right protected against state action by the Due Process Clause of the Fourteenth Amendment.

The *Chicago, Burlington & Quincy Railroad Co.* case, however, left the theory under which the Court was approaching the interpretation of the Due Process Clause rather unclear. In the *Hurtado* case, the Court had concluded that the Due Process Clauses in the Fifth and Fourteenth Amendments were identical in meaning. And utilizing the doctrine of nonsuperfluousness, it had indicated that no right, that was also guaranteed in the Bill of Rights could logically be guaranteed against state action by the Due Process Clause of the Fourteenth Amendment. Now, in the *Chicago, Burlington & Quincy Railroad Co.* case, the Court had held that a right of just compensation was, after all, guaranteed by the Due Process Clause. Since the Fifth Amendment contained a Just Compensation Clause, a Grand Jury Clause, and a Due Process Clause, the *Hurtado* doctrine of nonsuperfluousness would have precluded the Court's recognition of the just-compensation claim in the *Chicago, Burlington & Quincy Railroad Co.* case, just as it had led the Court to reject the proposition that the Due Process Clause guaranteed grand jury indictments in the *Hurtado* case.

Despite these contradictions, the Court made no attempt to reconcile its rulings in the *Hurtado* and the *Chicago, Burlington & Quincy Railroad Co.* cases. And as a consequence, its theoretical approach to the relationship between the Bill of Rights and the Due Process Clause was left unclear.

The *Chicago, Burlington & Quincy Railroad Co.* case, however, did appear to substantially undermine the nonsuperfluousness doctrine of the *Hurtado* case, and this perhaps encouraged disappointed litigants in the state courts to continue to press upon the Court the argument that some, if not all, of the rights in the Bill of Rights were also guaranteed by the Fourteenth Amendment. Litigants also received encouragement on this point with the publication in 1898 of William D. Guthrie's *Lectures on the Fourteenth Article of Amendment to the Constitution of the United States.*[58]

Guthrie had been a largely unknown young lawyer of thirty-five in the Seward firm in New York when, in 1895, he successfully guided the *Income Tax Case* to the Supreme Court. As one of the attorneys who had persuaded the Court to invalidate the income tax, Guthrie was immediately elevated "to the front rank of the legal profession."[59] Ignoring the Supreme Court's decision in the *Slaughter House Cases* and similar decisions in subsequent cases, Guthrie maintained in his *Lectures on the Fourteenth Amendment* that the Privileges and Immunities Clause prohibited the states from impairing "the fundamental rights of the individual which are mentioned in the first eight amendments to the Constitution. These early amendments are known as the Federal Bill of Rights." He supported this assertion by citing Senator Howard's statement on the meaning of the Privileges and Immunities Clause and the argument by John Randolph Tucker before the Supreme Court in the 1880s that all of the Bill of Rights applied to the states. Cases such as the *Hurtado* case, Guthrie argued, would have been decided differently "if the clear intention of the framers of the Fourteenth Amendment had been called to the attention of the Court. . . ."[60]

The *Lectures* became an oft-cited source in briefs and arguments before the Supreme Court,[61] and given Guthrie's prominence at the bar, his *Lectures* undoubtedly encouraged litigants to continue to argue that the Fourteenth Amendment applied all or parts of the Bill of Rights to the states. Despite Guthrie's views, however, the Court again pointed out in *Brown* v. *New Jersey*, decided in 1899, that the "first ten Amendments to the Federal Constitution contain no restrictions on the powers of the states, but were intended to operate solely on the Federal government."[62] Such discouraging words from the Court nevertheless appeared to have little effect on litigants, since in 1900, a major effort was made in *Maxwell* v. *Dow* to convince it that the Fourteenth Amendment required the common law jury of twelve to be utilized in state criminal trials, just as the Sixth Amendment required such juries in federal criminal cases.[63]

"Gunplay" Maxwell's Case

The right to trial by jury was one of the few civil liberties contained in the Constitution before the addition of the Bill of Rights. Article III provides that the trial of all crimes, except impeachments, shall be by jury. With the ratification of the Bill of Rights, two additional jury-trial provisions were added to the Constitution. The Sixth Amendment provides that in "all criminal prosecutions, the accused shall enjoy the right to a speedy and public trial, by an impartial jury," and the Seventh Amendment requires jury trials in all civil cases involving more than twenty dollars.

By the eighteenth century, the definition of what constituted a common-law jury had become well established. A trial, or petit, jury was composed of twelve jurors in both criminal and civil cases. It had also been established that the verdict of a common law jury must be unanimous. And until the 1960s and 1970s, this common law definition of a jury trial was accepted by the Supreme Court as defining the constitutional right to trial by jury.[64]

The jury-trial provisions of the federal Constitution, however, applied only to federal proceedings, and some states modified the twelve-juror, unanimous-verdict characteristics of the common law jury.[65] Even as a territory, for example, Utah began to experiment with deviations from the common law requirements for juries. The Utah territorial legislature thus provided for less-than-unanimous verdicts in civil cases, and this legislation was upheld by the territorial supreme court. When the issue reached the United States Supreme Court, however, it was held that the Seventh Amendment applied to the territories and required unanimous verdicts by juries of twelve in civil cases involving more than twenty dollars. The Court limited its holding to federal proceedings where the Seventh Amendment applied. Citing *Walker* v. *Sauvinet*—where it had held that the Seventh Amendment did not apply to the states—the Court was careful to note that "the power of a state to change the rule in respect to unanimity of juries is not before us for consideration.[66]

After becoming a state in 1896, Utah continued to experiment with the jury system. The Utah Constitution provided that in other than capital cases, criminal cases could be tried by juries composed of fewer than twelve persons. It therefore became the practice in Utah to try noncapital felonies with juries of eight.

An attorney from Provo, J. W. N. Whitecotton, soon became a persistent challenger, however, of Utah's tampering with the common-law requirements for juries. Whitecotton was counsel for Lars Thompson, who was accused of stealing a calf. Thompson had been tried and found guilty by a twelve-man jury prior to Utah's admission to the Union. A new trial was ordered, however, and Thompson was retried—after Utah achieved statehood—by the then-prevailing eight-man jury. He was again convicted, and his conviction was affirmed by the Utah Supreme Court.[67]

Whitecotton pursued the issue on writ of error to the United States Supreme Court. He argued that to subject Thompson to a new trial by a jury of eight, when he had been entitled to a jury of twelve when the crime was committed, violated the prohibition against ex-post-facto laws in the federal Constitution. The Court agreed with Whitecotton's argument in *Thompson* v. *Utah*, decided in 1898. Since Utah was still a territory when

Thompson had committed the crime for which he was tried, the Court said, the Sixth Amendment applied to his case. His later subjection to a trial by eight jurors was held to violate the constitutional prohibition against ex-post-facto laws. The question in the *Thompson* case, the Court held, was "whether the jury referred to in the original Constitution and in the 6th Amendment is a jury constituted, as it was at common law, of twelve persons, neither more nor less." The question, it continued, "must be answered in the affirmative." Since the Sixth Amendment requirement of juries of twelve applied to all crimes committed while Utah was a territory, the state could therefore not subject those accused of such crimes to trial before its poststatehood eight-juror system without violating the ex-post-facto prohibition.[68]

Utah conformed to the Supreme Court's ruling in the *Thompson* case, and indeed the charges against Thompson were dismissed on remand from the Court, since there were no state statutes providing for a retrial in his case by a twelve-person jury.[69] But in regard to noncapital crimes committed after it became a state, Utah continued to utilize the eight-person jury. Although conceding that the Sixth Amendment's jury-trial provision applied while it was still a territory, Utah contended that it no longer applied after statehood was achieved, and juries were subject to regulation by the state constitution and the state legislature and not by the federal Constitution. J. W. N. Whitecotton, however, soon again disputed the state's contention on this point.

The Springville bank opened as usual at ten o'clock on the morning of May 28, 1898. About 10:45 A.M., the cashier stepped out for a few moments, leaving the bookkeeper, A. O. Packard, alone in the bank. Two men then entered and presented a note that indicated that they should be paid two hundred dollars from the account of C. H. Carter. When Packard turned to examine the deposit books, the men pulled revolvers and ordered him to keep his hands up. While Packard was covered by one of the bandits, the other scooped up $3,020 in gold coins.

The bank had an alarm connected to Reynolds's store across the street, however, and Packard was able to push the alarm button. Reynolds assumed that the alarm was a false one, since there had been several in the past. He thus telephoned the bank, but when there was no answer, he grabbed two Winchester rifles and ran to the bank. The robbers, in the meantime, had fled in a horse and buggy that had been waiting outside, and they headed east to Hobble Creek Canyon. They stopped their flight only momentarily to take a horse at gunpoint from a rider they encountered, throwing forty-six dollars on the ground in payment.

Many of the residents of Springville quickly formed a posse and pursued the robbers, with Reynolds in the lead. As the posse closed in, the robbers abandoned their horses and buggy and fled into the brush at the mouth of

Hobble Creek Canyon. Members of the posse began a search of the brush, and soon encountered one of the robbers, who turned out to be Charles L. "Gunplay" Maxwell. In his attempt to escape, Maxwell had been wading in the creek, and when ordered to surrender, he replied, "Well, partner, I am pretty cold," and gave up without a fight. When part of the bank loot was found on him, Maxwell said, "Let me count that boodle; I haven't had a chance yet. I'd like to see how much we got."[70]

Maxwell's partner in crime was not so fortunate. A member of the posse, Joseph W. Allen, spotted the second robber, and ordered him to surrender. The robber instead began shooting, wounding Allen in the leg. "The ball struck me in the thigh, breaking my leg and causing me to fall on my knees," Allen said later. "I cried out, 'My God, he's got me,' but collected myself, took deliberate aim and fired, killing him instantly. The only sound he made was a heavy gurgling in his throat."[71] The name of this second robber was never discovered, since "Gunplay" Maxwell consistently refused to identify him. He had a wife and family, Maxwell said, "and when he does not return to them in a certain length of time they will think he died a natural death, and there is no need of having them think anything else."[72]

At the time of his arrest, Maxwell claimed to be John Carter, but his true identity was soon established. He had only recently escaped from custody in Wyoming, where he had been charged with stealing horses, and a Wyoming sheriff telegraphed the Provo sheriff advising him to "keep a close watch on" Maxwell, "for he is certainly a bad man and will try to get away if he gets the least opportunity. He will not hesitate to kill you. . . ."[73]

The governor of Utah had also posted a five-hundred-dollar reward for the arrest of Maxwell. Maxwell had stolen most of the cattle belonging to Alfred Starr in the Robber's Roost area in Utah and had threatened to kill Starr after he had sworn out warrants for Maxwell's arrest. Because of his threats against Starr and his notorious cattle-rustling activities, Maxwell was almost lynched when he was captured. He nevertheless appeared cool and collected and was described as being "without doubt the sharpest and brightest criminal local officers ever handled." At his preliminary hearing on May 28, Maxwell's bond was set at $5,000, and the district attorney asked him if he could raise that amount. "If I was out a little while," Maxwell replied, "I guess I could."[74]

Maxwell pleaded not guilty to a charge of armed robbery and was tried on September 19, 1898, in the Fourth Judicial District Court in Provo before Judge Warren N. Dusenberry and a jury of eight men. Maxwell was reported to have enjoyed the trial "as any disinterested spectator might," but while his attorney objected to the eight-man jury, no defense was offered to the charges. After the presentation of the prosecution's case, therefore, the jury deliberated for about an hour, and returned a verdict of guilty. Judge Dusenberry sentenced Maxwell on the afternoon of the day of the trial to eighteen years in the state prison, and Maxwell was delivered into the custody of George N. Dow, the warden of the prison, later the same evening.[75]

Maxwell apparently did not enjoy the Utah prison as much as his trial, since he retained J. W. N. Whitecotton, who filed a petition with the Utah Supreme Court for a writ of habeas corpus seeking Maxwell's release. In the petition, Whitecotton argued that Maxwell had been denied the right to be indicted by a grand jury and the right to be tried by a jury of twelve persons, rather than the jury of eight that had returned the verdict against him. The Utah Supreme Court, however, dismissed the petition for a writ of habeas corpus in June of 1899. Neither the Privileges and Immunities Clause nor the Due Process Clause of the Fourteenth Amendment, the Utah Supreme Court said, required the states to either indict by grand jury or to try criminal defendants by the common law jury of twelve.[76]

Whitecotton again pursued his battle against the Utah eight-person jury system, as well as the grand jury issue, by filing a writ of error in the United States Supreme Court. The appeal of *Maxwell* v. *Dow* to the Court, however, posed financial problems. Maxwell was incarcerated and had no funds with which to take an appeal to the Court. Whitecotton thus advised the clerk of the Supreme Court, James McKenney, that Maxwell "has no money with which to pay any fees of any kind, and I do not now know how we will get his case record printed unless I pay for it." He was willing to pay for the printing of the record, Whitecotton said, "rather than have him fail of a hearing, but the other fees he cannot pay nor give security for." Would McKenney let him know, Whitecotton continued, "the practice of your office in such cases, and if he may have the benefit of the 'poor litigant's oath' in this class of case, and if you have special blanks for this purpose, will you kindly send me one."[77]

Contemporary practice before the Supreme Court rather freely allows criminal defendants to proceed *in forma pauperis*. The Court's rules now waive most technical and printing requirements for indigent criminal defendants, and if an *in-forma-pauperis* petition is granted, an attorney is appointed to represent such defendants without cost. The result is that at present criminal defendants who are indigent have relatively ready access to the Court in the raising of their claims.

At the time of the *Maxwell* case, however, the practice concerning indigent defendants was considerably different, as McKenney's reply to Whitecotton's letter indicated. The Supreme Court, McKenney replied, "does not encourage proceedings *in forma pauperis* and rarely grants such applications except in capital cases. Such applications are hardly ever made and there are no special blanks for use in making them. A printed motion, supported by affidavit, should be presented to the Court in open session." The requirements of a printed motion presented in an open session of the Court by an attorney, of course, effectively precluded prisoners who, like Maxwell, were indigent, from proceeding *in forma pauperis* in the Supreme Court.[78]

Whitecotton therefore informed McKenney that he would "pay personally all the costs incurred in this case, but trust you will let me divide it up a little, as it will not hurt so badly, part at a time."[79] But Whitecotton complained about the long delay before the *Maxwell* case could be heard by the Court, since the issues in the case were matters "of supreme importance to many men who are situated the same as Maxwell, and all are in prison 'without benefit of clergy.' "[80] On McKenney's advice, Whitecotton filed a motion to advance the *Maxwell* case on the Court's docket, and the case was finally argued on December 4, 1899.

Although Whitecotton argued before the Court that Maxwell had been entitled to both an indictment by a grand jury and a trial by a common law jury of twelve, his principal emphasis in his argument was on the right to trial by a jury of twelve. He caustically criticized the Utah deviations from the common law jury system, which, he said, had begun when "a wild and untamed spirit of innovation in respect to juries took possession of the legislature of the Territory of Utah, and the same frenzy invaded the sacred precincts of the Territorial Supreme Court." This aberrant behavior on the part of Utah had continued after the state's admission to the Union, he said, indicating that everyone "in the United States outside of Utah seems to know what a jury is, while here we do not seem to know, nor to have the ability to learn."[81]

The right to an indictment by a grand jury and to a trial by a jury of twelve—rather than by a jury of eight, as in Utah—Whitecotton argued, was guaranteed in state proceedings by the Privileges and Immunities Clause, as well as the Due Process Clause, of the Fourteenth Amendment. His emphasis was primarily on the Privileges and Immunities Clause, and in his argument he "respectfully invited" the Court to examine Senator Howard's statement on the meaning of the Privileges and Immunities Clause during the consideration of the Fourteenth Amendment by Congress. In arguing that the Grand Jury Clause of the Fifth Amendment and the Jury Trial Clause of the Sixth Amendment were also guarantees of the Due Process Clause, he additionally cited William D. Guthrie's *Lectures on the Fourteenth Amendment* and Justice Harlan's dissent in the *Hurtado* case. Whitecotton concluded that because Maxwell had not been indicted by a grand jury, and because he had been tried by a jury of eight rather than a jury of twelve, as required by the federal Constitution, the Court should reverse his conviction.[82]

Counsel for the state of Utah, on the other hand, cited the *Slaughter House Cases* as ample authority for the Court to reject Whitecotton's claim that the Privileges and Immunities Clause guaranteed either the right to a grand jury indictment or to a jury trial in a state proceeding. Additionally, Utah counsel noted, the Court had held in *Walker* v. *Sauvinet* that the Seventh Amendment's requirement of a jury trial in a civil case did not apply to the states via the Fourteenth Amendment, and the same reasoning would deny that the Jury Trial Clause of the Sixth Amendment applied to the states. And, finally, counsel for Utah argued that the *Hurtado* case not only completely refuted Whitecotton's argument that the Due Process Clause guaranteed a right to indictment by grand jury in a state proceeding but also indicated that none of the rights in the Bill of Rights were applicable to the states via the Due Process Clause.[83]

Utah had a considerable stake in obtaining a judgment upholding Maxwell's conviction in the Supreme Court, since of the 158 prisoners in the state prison, fully 133 had been convicted by juries of eight.[84] The Court relieved the state's anxiety in this regard, however, when it decided *Maxwell* v. *Dow* on February 26, 1900, and upheld the state's eight-juror system.[85]

In an opinion written by Justice Peckham, the Court gave short shrift to the argument that the Due Process Clause guaranteed the right of indictment by grand jury in state proceedings. On this point, the Court said, the *Hurtado* case was "a complete and conclusive answer." The Court then turned to the principal argument advanced by Whitecotton—that the Privileges and Immunities Clause guaranteed against state action the right to a grand jury indictment and the right to be tried by a jury of twelve.

The Court conceded that "there can be no doubt" that the Jury Trial Clause of the Sixth Amendment required a common law jury of twelve in federal criminal proceedings, and that the Seventh Amendment's guarantee of jury trials in civil cases required that "there shall be a unanimous verdict of twelve jurors in all Federal courts where a jury trial is held." The question in the *Maxwell* case, the Court nonetheless said, was whether the Privileges and Immunities Clause imposed these jury-trial requirements and the right to indictment by grand jury on the states.[86]

Relying on the *Slaughter House Cases* and their progeny, the Court reaffirmed the proposition that the Privileges and Immunities Clause did not impose significant new restrictions, such as the rights in the Bill of Rights, upon the states. And taking notice of Whitecotton's quotation of Senator Howard's remarks on the meaning of the Privileges and Immunities Clause, the Court also refused to interpret the remarks as having much significance. The meaning of a proposed constitutional amendment, it said, "is one to be determined by the language actually therein used, and not by the speeches made regarding it."[87]

A constitutional amendment, the Court continued, is not only debated and proposed by the Congress but must also be debated and ratified by three-fourths of the states. Rather than accepting what was said in Congress on the meaning of a constitutional amendment as authoritative, the Court held, the safer course was to read the language of the amendment "in connection with the known condition of affairs out of which the occasion for its adoption may have arisen, and then to construe it, if there be any doubtful expressions, in a way, so far as is reasonably possible, to forward the known purpose or object for which the amendment was adopted."[88]

Having thus denied that Senator Howard's remarks were authoritative as to the meaning of the Privileges and Immunities Clause, the Court held that the clause guaranteed neither the right to trial by a common law jury of twelve nor the right to an indictment by a grand jury in a state proceeding. This conclusion left the Court with Whitecotton's argument that juries of twelve were required by the Due Process Clause, but this argument had been, the Court held, "substantially answered by the reasoning of the opinion in the *Hurtado Case.* . . ." If the states could abolish indictments by grand jury without violating the Due Process Clause, it noted, "the same course of reasoning which establishes that right will and does establish the right to alter the number of the petit jury from that provided by the common law." Trial by jury, the Court concluded, has "never been affirmed to be a necessary requisite of due process of law."[89]

Once again, as in the *Hurtado* case, Justice Harlan dissented alone from the judgment of the Court. He again argued that the Privileges and Immunities and Due Process Clauses applied all of the Bill of Rights to the states. Under the Court's reasoning, he declared, it would be impossible to escape the conclusion "that a state may abolish trial by jury altogether in a criminal case, however grave the offense charged, and authorize trial of a case of felony before a single judge. I cannot assent to this interpretation, because it is opposed to the plain words of the Constitution, and defeats the manifest object of the Fourteenth Amendment."[90]

Harlan also made a telling point in regard to the Due Process Clause. Citing the *Chicago, Burlington & Quincy Railroad Co.* case, he pointed out that the Court had there held that the Due Process Clause embraced a right to just compensation, despite the fact that the Fifth Amendment guaranteed just compensation separately from its Due Process Clause. If the Due Process Clause of the Fourteenth Amendment guaranteed just compensation, he continued, "but does allow the life or liberty of the citizen to be taken in a mode that is repugnant to the settled usages and modes of proceeding authorized at the time the Constitution was adopted and which was expressly forbidden in the national Bill of Rights, it would seem that the protection of private property is of more consequence than the protection of the life and liberty of the citizen."[91]

Despite Harlan's protest, "Gunplay" Maxwell's trial by a jury of eight rather than by a common law jury of twelve had been upheld by the Court, and he seemed condemned to serve his eighteen-year term in the Utah state prison. Had the Court not affirmed Maxwell's conviction, the Utah attorney general said, "it would have reduced this state to practically a reign of anarchy and at the same time necessarily placed the state at a great expense as over two-thirds of the prisoners at the penitentiary would apply for habeas corpus proceedings." Maxwell, on the other hand, was shaken by the news of the Court's decision. It was reported that he had written a history of his life and that he would soon take some action that would force the prison guards to kill him.[92]

Maxwell instead wrote to the governor and offered to lead an expedition against the outlaws in the Robber's Roost area in exchange for his freedom. His offer was not accepted, but his sentence was commuted on November 21, 1903, reportedly in response to pressure brought by influential friends. Maxwell's freedom was short-lived, however, since he was soon killed in a gunfight in the streets of Price, Utah, with another outlaw known as "Shoot-em-up Bill."[93]

The meaning of Maxwell's case in the Supreme Court, on the other hand, was not as clear as was his ultimate fate. The Court had failed in the *Maxwell* case to reconcile its contradictory rulings in the *Hurtado* and *Chicago, Burlington & Quincy Railroad Co.* cases. And the *Hurtado* case had been cited and relied on by the Court in *Maxwell* v. *Dow*, even though the doctrine of nonsuperfluousness could not be reconciled with its later holding in the *Chicago, Burlington & Quincy Railroad Co.* case.

At the turn of the century, therefore, the Court had left in doubt whether its holding in the *Chicago, Burlington & Quincy Railroad Co.* case had been a temporary aberration or a significant breakthrough in regard to the nationalization of the Bill of Rights via the Due Process Clause. At the same time, its heavy reliance on the *Hurtado* case in *Maxwell* v. *Dow* had revived the possibility that the Court was reverting to the doctrine of nonsuperfluousness as the proper interpretation of the Due Process Clause, an interpretation that denied that any of the Bill of Rights could apply to the states. Some clarification of the Court's contradictory approaches to the relationship between the Due Process Clause and the Bill of Rights would finally come, however, in its 1908 decision in *Twining* v. *New Jersey*, a decision that would open the door to the nationalization of the Bill of Rights.[94]

3

From the
Twining Case to the *Gitlow* Case
The Door Opens

The Asbury Park Bank-Fraud Case: *Twining* v. *New Jersey*

Friday, February 13, 1903, turned out to be an especially unlucky day for
those citizens of Asbury Park, New Jersey, who had accounts in the First
National Bank and the Monmouth Trust and Safe Deposit Company.
The bank, organized in 1886 as the first national bank in Asbury Park,
was under the supervision of the United States government through the
Comptroller of the Currency. On February 13, J. W. Scholfield, a national
bank examiner, posted a notice to the public that the First National Bank
was "closed and in the hands of the Comptroller of the Currency." This
notice was the first indication that depositors in the bank had received that
it was in difficulty, and the news "fell like a thunderbolt on the business
community."[1]

The First National Bank was located in the Monmouth Building, where
the Monmouth Trust and Safe Deposit Company was also located. When
the bank closed, many depositors of the trust company demanded that
their deposits be returned. Officers of the trust company assured them
that the trust company was in no way affected by the closing of the bank,
but this failed to satisfy the anxious depositors. Albert C. Twining, the
president of the trust company, was constrained to post a notice at noon
on February 13 that because of the "closing of the First National Bank,
the Monmouth Trust and Safe Deposit Company will close its doors temporarily."

Albert Twining also issued a statement that the directors of the trust
company had decided to close its doors "to avoid any run which might be
occasioned through a misapprehension on the part of the public concerning any connection between the trust company and the First National
Bank." He assured the public that the trust company's offices would be
open on Saturday, February 14, "to afford its depositors an opportunity to
serve notice of their intention to withdraw their funds within a specified
length of time." The temporary closing of the trust company, Twining

said, "was taken to protect the company from the effects of a concerted run or one due to public excitement, the Trust Company's affairs being in an entirely satisfactory and solvent condition."

Upon being reassured by Twining, the depositors dispersed, but on the following day they began gathering in the corridor of the Monmouth Building outside the trust company's office at eight o'clock in the morning. By nine o'clock the corridor was filled with depositors demanding their money. Contrary to Albert Twining's assurances the day before, the trust company did not open its doors. The angry depositors finally dispersed at noon, when Larue R. Vreedenberg, a state bank examiner with the New Jersey State Banking Commission, arrived to investigate the trust company's books.[2]

Upon the closing of the trust company, Albert Twining commented that he had "nothing to say, further than this: Things are not nearly as dark as they have been represented." And Larue Vreedenberg said that until the examination of the books of the company was completed in two or three days, "no statement of the condition of the trust company will be issued."[3]

As the conditions of both the First National Bank and the Monmouth Trust Company unfolded, it was revealed that their affairs were considerably interwoven through interlocking directors and officers. Albert Twining had been an organizer of the First National Bank and had served as its second president, but had resigned to become president of the trust company. Twining continued as a director on the boards of both the bank and the trust company. The president of the bank at the time of its closing, George Fred Kroehl, was also a member of both the bank's board of directors and the trust company's board.[4]

The First National Bank went into a receivership administered by the United States Comptroller of the Currency, and by assessing the shareholders of the bank heavily, 97 percent of the money owed the bank's depositors would ultimately be returned to them. As a result of the examination of the trust company's books by Larue Vreedenberg, the company was permanently closed on February 16 and the New Jersey Attorney General petitioned for the appointment of a receiver to administer the company.[5]

Vreedenberg's report on the condition of the trust company was devastating, and it implicated Albert Twining, George Kroehl, and David C. Cornell, the treasurer and a director in the company, in several suspicious transactions. The company had engaged in "illegal and unsafe" investments, Vreedenberg's report said, and its liabilities were over $44,000 more than its assets. The liabilities of the directors of the trust company, he reported, were in excess of $139,000. Some of the directors were capable of paying their liabilities, but some were clearly not able to shoulder such large debts. "Mr. Twining's liability is so large [$12,401]," Vreedenberg said, "in comparison with his own resources, that his ability to pay is doubtful."[6]

Vreedenberg also revealed that Twining, Kroehl, and Cornell had used the trust company's money for their own personal purposes. David Cornell had, for example, endorsed a note under which his brother had been loaned over $5,000. This loan, Vreedenberg found, was an "unsafe investment" of the company's funds. Albert Twining and George Kroehl had also borrowed money from the company. Vreedenberg criticized this on the grounds that accepting notes from Kroehl and Twining "in such large amounts was hazardous and unsafe, as the known assets available to both Mr. Twining and Mr. Kroehl did not make their paper a safe investment."[7]

Albert Twining, however, appeared to be the worst offender in using the trust company's funds for his own purposes. He owned $90,000 worth of shares in the Fraser Mountain Copper Company of New Mexico, and he had been a leading promoter of the copper company when the trust company loaned the copper company over $22,000. In his report, Vreedenberg concluded that "to loan money to an enterprise of that character without the endorsement upon the paper of names of men of known responsibility was imprudent and the notes are an unsafe investment."[8]

On the day the First National Bank was forced to close, Twining also was involved in the trust company's purchase of $44,875 of the bank's stock. The trust company paid $117 per share, yet the bank's stock was selling at that time for only $60 per share on the open market, and it was probably worthless as a result of the bank's failure. Vreedenberg stated in his report that it was this purchase of the bank's stock by the trust company that brought about the company's collapse, leaving it with only $14,000 on hand to meet obligations of more than $60,000.

Vreedenberg's report on the condition of the trust company was released on February 17, 1903, and it created a "sensation" in Asbury Park. No one there, it was reported, had "dreamed that the affairs of the company were in anything like the state the Examiner represents." On the night of February 17, Twining and Kroehl left town on their way to New York City, but warrants charging Twining, Kroehl, and David Cornell with violations of the state banking laws were issued before the end of the month. All three were arrested in Asbury Park in late February, and they posted bonds pending their trials. When arrested, George Kroehl appeared to be near collapse and remarked to reporters, "This disgrace is awful. Make it as light as possible for me, for I have done nothing wrong."[9]

Thus began a series of prosecutions of Twining, Cornell, and Kroehl on both federal and state charges growing out of the financial problems of the First National Bank and the trust company. As the most ubiquitous defendant in these prosecutions, Twining had amazing luck, and probably even better attorneys. Twining and Cornell were first tried and convicted for misappropriating funds from an estate administered by the trust company. Their convictions were overturned by the New Jersey Supreme Court, however, because of a faulty indictment.[10] Twining and George Kroehl were also prosecuted in United States district court on charges arising out of the collapse of the First National Bank. Both were charged with misappropriation of the bank's funds, but a jury acquitted both men on February 4, 1905.[11]

Twining was subjected to another prosecution in United States district court on an indictment charging him with making false entries on the books of the First National Bank. He was convicted on three counts and sentenced to six years in prison. The United States Court of Appeals for the Third Circuit, however, reversed Twining's conviction on December 11, 1905. The entries in the bank's books had been made by the bank's treasurer, the court of appeals held, and the evidence did not support the government's theory that the treasurer had only acted under the direction of Twining. In addition, the court held, the entries in the bank's books at issue in Twining's case truthfully reported fraudulent transactions and therefore were not "false entries" within the meaning of the federal statute.[12]

Twining had won again, but his luck was not to last. When Larue Vreedenberg had inquired regarding the suspicious purchase of the First National Bank's stock by the trust company for such an inflated price, David Cornell and Twining had showed him the minutes of a meeting of the trust company's board of directors at which the purchase of the bank's stock had been approved. The minutes indicated that a meeting of the company's board of directors had occurred on February 9, 1903, four days before the collapse of the bank, and was attended by five directors, including Twining and Cornell. At this meeting, the minutes indicated, a resolution to purchase 381 shares of the bank's stock had been approved. The state of New Jersey later proved that this meeting never occurred and that such a resolution was never approved by the trust company's board of directors.[13]

This transaction appears to have been undertaken by Twining with the connivance of Cornell, because, with the collapse of the First National Bank, the shareholders of the bank were liable for any shortages in the bank under the federal banking laws. Twining and the other shareholders in the bank were thus likely to be required to make up the shortages found in the bank. If, however, the shares in the bank possessed by Twining and others were purchased by the trust company, the company—and not Twining and the others as individuals—would be liable for any assessments to make up the shortages in the bank. Twining and others had thus enriched themselves by selling their bank stock to the trust company at the inflated price of $44,000, and at the same time had transferred to the trust company any liability for the shortages in the bank.[14]

Ironically, it was not this highly fraudulent transaction itself that spelled the worst trouble for Twining and Cornell. Under the Trust Company Act of 1899, the legislature of New Jersey had made it a criminal offense for any director, officer, agent, or clerk of a trust company to willfully and knowingly exhibit any false paper with the intent to deceive any person authorized to examine the condition of a trust company. David Cornell and Albert Twining were indicted under this statute for showing Vreedenberg the document that falsely reported that the trust company's board of directors had approved the bank-stock deal. Both men pleaded not guilty to the charge in the indictment on February 4, 1904.[15]

The trial of Twining and Cornell began on March 1 in the Monmouth County Court of Quarter Sessions before Judge Wilbur A. Heisley and a jury. Larue Vreedenberg was, of course, the principal witness for the prosecution, and he described how Twining and Cornell had shown him the false document reporting the approval of the bank-stock deal by the trust company's board of directors. Two directors of the trust company also testified that the alleged meeting of the board of directors never occurred, and a secretary of the company testified that Twining had dictated the minutes of the alleged meeting to her for typing.

The attorneys for Twining and Cornell vigorously cross-examined the prosecution's witnesses, but no witnesses were presented for the defense. Twining and Cornell did not take the stand to testify in their own behalf, and at the close of the state's case, Judge Heisley denied a defense motion for a directed verdict of acquittal.[16]

At this point in the trial, events occurred that were to form the basis for an appeal to the United States Supreme Court and to make the *Twining* case an important episode in the nationalization of the Bill of Rights. In summing up the state's case before the jury, the prosecutor commented upon the failure of both Twining and Cornell to take the stand and refute the charges against them. The state had introduced evidence indicating their guilt, the prosecutor told the jury, yet Twining and Cornell had remained mute and made no attempt to rebut the state's evidence.[17]

In charging the jury, Judge Heisley also commented extensively upon the failure of Twining and Cornell to testify in their own behalf. It was not necessary for the defendants to prove their innocence, the judge told the jury, but "the fact that they stay off the stand, having heard testimony which might be prejudicial to them, without availing themselves of the right to go upon the stand and contradict it, is sometimes a matter of significance." Neither defendant was required to take the stand and testify in his own behalf, Judge Heisley told the jury, but the state had produced testimony that the approval of the bank-stock deal had never occurred in a meeting of the board of directors, and neither Twining nor Cornell had "gone upon the stand to deny that they were present, or to show that the meeting was held."[18]

Counsel for Twining took "a general exception to the whole charge" to the jury by Judge Heisley, and the attorney for Cornell excepted to the charge to the jury in regard to "what the Court said about the defendants not going upon the stand. . . ."[19] After only an hour's deliberations, however, the jury returned verdicts of guilty against both Twining and Cornell. And on May 3, 1904, Judge Heisley sentenced Twining to six years and Cornell to four years in prison, both sentences to be served at hard labor.[20]

The *Twining* case was appealed to the New Jersey appellate courts, with counsel for Twining and Cornell challenging the validity of the comments by the prosecutor and the judge upon the failure of the defendants to testify. Such comments, it was argued, violated the right of Twining and Cornell to be free from compulsory self-incrimination under both the law of New Jersey and the Fifth and Fourteenth Amendments of the United States Constitution.

During the first half of the nineteenth century, defendants had been unable to testify in their own behalf under the common law rules of evidence enforced in most American jurisdictions. The presumption of the common law rules was that witnesses with interests in the outcome of trials, such as criminal defendants, were likely to lie and should therefore not be allowed to testify.[21] The common law rules prohibiting defendant testimony because of interest were adopted by the English courts at approximately the same time that they were also recognizing the right against self-incrimination. And the rules disqualifying defendants as witnesses reinforced the right against self-incrimination by excluding the possibility that a defendant might reveal incriminating information while under cross-examination as a witness. Most states, however, abolished the common law rule prohibiting the testimony of defendants after the Civil War, and Congress also abolished the common-law rule for criminal trials in the federal courts in 1878. Most of the American legislation abrogating the common-law rule additionally provided that no presumption against defendants should be entertained by reason of their failure to use their new right to testify in their own behalf.

Such a provision was contained in the congressional legislation of 1878 making defendants competent witnesses in federal criminal trials, and in 1893 the United States Supreme Court interpreted this legislation to mean that comment upon the failure of defendants to testify was prohibited in the federal courts. Most state legislation on the subject of defendant testimony was similar to the federal statute, and most state courts also banned comment on the defendant's failure to testify.[22]

The New Jersey legislature enacted a statute in 1871 abolishing the rule prohibiting defendants from testifying, but the New Jersey statute did not bar presumptions or comment upon the failure of a defendant to use the right to testify. And the New Jersey courts interpreted the statute and the state's guarantee against compulsory self-incrimination as permitting comment by prosecutors and judges upon the failure of a defendant to testify in his own behalf when direct evidence of his guilt had been presented by the prosecution.[23] The New Jersey Supreme Court therefore affirmed the convictions of Twining and Cornell on November 13, 1905, and the court of errors and appeals, the highest appellate court in the state, followed suit on November 19, 1906. When the "evidence given on the part of the state, in the presence of the defendant," the court of errors and appeals said, "directly showed acts of his, in respect to which he had been given the privilege of testifying, it was not error to direct the attention of the jury to his failure to avail himself of the opportunity of contradicting such direct evidence."[24]

Although neither counsel for Twining nor for Cornell had pressed the argument that the Self-Incrimination Clause of the Fifth Amendment applied to the states via the Fourteenth Amendment before the New Jersey courts,[25] such an argument became the basis for an appeal of the *Twining* case to the United States Supreme Court. Given the Court's steadfast refusal to modify the narrow interpretation of the Privileges and Immunities Clause it had pronounced in the *Slaughter House Cases*, counsel for Twining understandably devoted most of their argument to the proposition that the Self-Incrimination Clause of the Fifth Amendment applied to the states via the Due Process Clause of the Fourteenth Amendment. Citing William D. Guthrie's *Lectures on the Fourteenth Amendment*, they did, however, briefly argue that the right against self-incrimination was a privilege and immunity of national citizenship. Whether the Self-Incrimination Clause applied to the states as a privilege and immunity of U.S. citizenship, they told the Court, "is still an open question undecided by this Court," and the "power of the States to abridge [the rights in the Bill of Rights] can never be conceded until the Court shall expressly so decide in a case involving the exact question and adequately argued."[26]

In their argument based on the Due Process Clause, counsel for Twining contended that the clause was intended to preserve the traditional common law rules of evidence that had been in force in England for centuries. The right against self-incrimination was among such rules, they argued, and was therefore protected against invasion by the states by the Due Process Clause. The right against self-incrimination, they continued, guaranteed to the criminal defendant the right to remain silent at his trial, and for a state to allow comment upon the defendant's silence was tantamount to penalizing the exercise of the right against self-incrimination. The fact that comment upon the failure of an accused to testify was prohibited in all of the states except New Jersey, and was banned in the federal courts, it was argued, indicated almost universal agreement that such comment was considered to violate the right against self-incrimination.[27]

In New Jersey, counsel for Twining also noted, a defendant's prior criminal record could be revealed to the jury if he testified in his own behalf. And Twining's conviction in federal court, for making false entries in the books of the First National Bank, had not yet been reversed at the time of his trial on the exhibition of false-papers charge. Twining was therefore "forced to take either one or the other horn of the dilemma. Remain silent and have his silence taken as a presumption of guilt. Take the stand and be forced to strengthen the weak record already adduced by the prosecution by the fact that he was then an adjudged criminal." New Jersey's comment practice, Twining's counsel concluded, had thus resulted in an especially grievous violation of the right against self-incrimination and due process at Twining's trial, justifying a reversal of his conviction by the Court.[28]

In contrast to the argument on behalf of Twining, counsel for David Cornell relied almost exclusively on the Privileges and Immunities Clause in arguing that the Self-Incrimination Clause applied to the states. Indeed, relying heavily upon William D. Guthrie's *Lectures* and Senator Howard's statement on the meaning of the Privileges and Immunities Clause, counsel for Cornell argued that all of the rights in the Bill of Rights applied to the states via the Fourteenth Amendment.[29]

Counsel for New Jersey of course denied that there was a federal right against self-incrimination guaranteed by the Privileges and Immunities Clause and invoked the dual-citizenship doctrine of the *Slaughter House Cases* in support of their contention. The rulings of the New Jersey courts on the self-incrimination issue in the *Twining* case had been final, they argued, since there was in the federal Constitution "no guarantee of a privilege against compulsory self-incrimination which is binding upon the courts of New Jersey, or the abridgment of which by the State courts would give corrective jurisdiction in the Federal Supreme Court." And citing *Barron* v. *Baltimore*, state counsel pointed out that the Court had always held that the rights in the Bill of Rights applied only to the federal government and not to the states. "The only right against compulsory self-incrimination guaranteed to citizens of the United States," they said, "is a right and immunity operative in federal courts, or in any sphere of federal influence, but there is no such right guaranteed as such to citizens of the United States by the Constitution of the United States or its amendments, which the State of New Jersey is obliged to consider."[30] Since the state had not violated the federal constitutional rights of either Twining or Cornell, New Jersey counsel concluded, their convictions should be affirmed by the Court.

The Court handed a victory to New Jersey counsel when on November 9, 1908, it decided *Twining* v. *New Jersey* and affirmed the convictions of Twining and Cornell.[31] Speaking for the Court, Justice William Moody addressed the contention that the right against self-incrimination was included among those rights of national citizenship protected from invasion by the states by the Privileges and Immunities Clause of the Fourteenth Amendment. Such a contention, Moody said, had been answered in the negative by the decision in the *Slaughter House Cases*. While acknowledging that "criticism of this case has never entirely ceased, nor has it ever received universal assent by members of this court," Moody nonetheless said that a contrary decision would have resulted in the subjection of all state "legislative and judicial acts to correction by the legislative and review by the judicial branch of the national government." The contention that the Bill of Rights was applied to the states by the Privileges and Immunities Clause, Moody continued, had been uniformly rejected by the Court in a long line of decisions since the *Slaughter House Cases*, and the question "is no longer open in this court." The Court therefore concluded, he said, "that the exemption from compulsory self-incrimination is not a privilege or immunity of national citizenship guaranteed by this clause of the 14th Amendment against abridgment by the states."[32]

Turning to the arguments based on the Due Process Clause, Moody implicitly acknowledged that the Court's decision in the *Chicago, Burlington & Quincy Railroad Co.* case, holding that the Due Process Clause guaranteed a right of just compensation, gave support to arguments that the Due Process Clause protected rights like those in the Bill of Rights. Citing the *Chicago, Burlington & Quincy Railroad Co.* case, Moody thus agreed that the due process contentions in the *Twining* case deserved separate consideration, since "it is possible that some of the personal rights safeguarded by the first eight Amendments against national action may also be safeguarded against state action, because a denial of them would be a denial of due process of law." If this were so, he continued, "it is not because those rights are enumerated in the first eight Amendments, but because they are of such a nature that they are included in the conception of due process of law."[33]

The question in the *Twining* case thus became whether or not the right against self-incrimination was considered by the Court to be a part of the "conception of due process of law." The Court had determined the meaning of due process, Moody said, by a process of "inclusion and exclusion," and it had held that due process embraced "those settled usages and modes of proceeding existing in the common and statute law of England before the emigration of our ancestors, and shown not to have been unsuited to their civil and political condition by having been acted on by them after the settlement of this country." Due process, on the other hand, did not embrace all such common law procedure, but was adaptable to new and changed conditions, since otherwise "the procedure of the first half of the seventeenth century would be fastened upon the American jurisprudence like a straight jacket, only to be unloosed by constitutional amendment." Due process nevertheless did prohibit any change in procedure, Moody continued, "which disregards those fundamental principles, to be ascertained from time to time by judicial action, which have relation to process of law, and protect the citizen in his private right, and guard him against the arbitrary action of government." The test of whether a right was protected by due process, he said, was this: "Is it a fundamental principle of liberty and justice which inheres in the very idea of free government and is the inalienable right of a citizen of such a government?"[34]

In determining whether or not the right against self-incrimination was such a "fundamental principle of liberty and justice," Moody admitted that the right was "universal in American law," that it distinguished the common law "from all other systems of jurisprudence," and that it was recognized as "a privilege of great value, a protection to the innocent, though a shelter to the guilty, and a safeguard against heedless, unfounded, or tyrannical prosecutions."[35] But after exploring the origins of the right against self-incrimination in English law, he concluded that it had not been regarded "as a part of the law of the land of Magna Charta or the due process of law, which had been deemed an equivalent expression, but, on the contrary, is regarded as separate from and independent of due process." The right against self-incrimination had come "into existence not as an essential part of due process, but as a wise and beneficent rule of evidence developed in the courts in the course of judicial decision."[36]

The history of the right against self-incrimination up to the time of the drafting of the first American constitutions pointed in the same direction, Moody concluded. The right was not at that time "ranked among the fundamental and inalienable rights of mankind," and was not "conceived to be inherent in due process of law, but, on the other hand, a right separate, independent, and outside due process." The right against self-incrimination, Moody therefore held, "is not fundamental in due process of law, nor an essential part of it," and the convictions of Twining and Cornell were affirmed on the ground that "the exemption from compulsory self-incrimination in the courts of the states is not secured by any part of the Federal Constitution."[37]

Justice John Marshall Harlan was again the only dissenter from the judgment of the Court, and he again argued that all of the Bill of Rights applied to the states via the Fourteenth Amendment. New Jersey had violated a federal right against self-incrimination, he said, and in an attack on the Court's historical analysis, he declared that if, "at the beginning of the Revolutionary War, any lawyer had claimed that one accused of crime could lawfully be compelled to testify against himself, he would have been laughed at by his brethren of the bar, both in England and America."[38]

Albert Twining had come to Washington to hear his case argued and had been impatient for a decision. On March 22, 1908, he had written to the clerk of the Court, saying that he had "omitted, before my departure from Washington this past week, to ask you the time of a possible or probable decision in my case just argued, #187." If it was not asking too much, he said, "I would be pleased to have your version of the subject." Twining now had his answer, but he was undoubtedly not pleased with the prospect of six years in prison at hard labor. His remarkable luck in the judicial process had finally run out.[39]

Justice Felix Frankfurter later characterized *Twining* v. *New Jersey* as showing "the judicial process at its best—comprehensive briefs and powerful arguments on both sides, followed by long deliberation, resulting in an opinion by Mr. Justice Moody which at once gained and has ever since retained recognition as one of the outstanding opinions in the history of the Court."[40] Certainly the Court's decision in the *Twining* case was a major benchmark in the development of the Due Process Clause. The Court's holding that the Due Process Clause did not protect a right against self-incrimination in state proceedings was to stand for almost sixty years until its repudiation in 1964.[41] And the Court also made it clear in *Twining* that arguments invoking the Privileges and Immunities Clause in the future were doomed to failure. While the Court acknowledged the dissatisfaction with the decision in the *Slaughter House Cases*, it forthrightly affirmed the conclusion of the Court in those cases. While Privileges and Immunities Clause claims would be pressed upon the Court after *Twining*, the doctrine of the *Slaughter House Cases* would continue unimpaired.[42]

The *Twining* case was most important, however, for the discussion by the Court of the meaning of due process. The Court conceded that the Due Process Clause of the Fourteenth Amendment might protect against state action some rights similar to those in the Bill of Rights. But the Court had also said that if rights similar to those in the Bill of Rights were protected by the Due Process Clause, they were protected "not because those rights are enumerated in the first eight Amendments, but because they are of such a nature that they are included in the conception of due process of law." The Court thus seemed to be indicating that if the Due Process Clause protected rights similar to some of those in the Bill of Rights, such rights would be only similar and not identical in scope and meaning to their counterparts in the Bill of Rights.

The Court therefore did not reverse *Barron* v. *Baltimore* in the *Twining* case and hold that some of the rights in the Bill of Rights might directly apply to the states via the Due Process Clause. In the future, the Court instead indicated, rights similar to some of those in the Bill of Rights might be guaranteed by the Due Process Clause because they were thought to be inherent in the terms *liberty* and *due process of law*.

This interpretation of the Due Process Clause had of course been foreshadowed by the Court's decision in the *Chicago, Burlington & Quincy Railroad Co.* case that the Due Process Clause protected a right to just compensation. Unfortunately, however, the interpretation of due process in the *Twining* case did not fully clarify the Court's due process theory as it related to the nationalization of the Bill of Rights. The *Twining* theory of due process was logically irreconcilable with the doctrine of nonsuperfluousness as enunciated in the *Hurtado* case, since the *Hurtado* doctrine would not have permitted a holding that the Due Process Clause guaranteed rights either identical or similar to those in the Bill of Rights. The Court's interpretation of the Due Process Clause in the *Twining* case—as its earlier decision in the *Chicago, Burlington & Quincy Railroad Co.* case —therefore necessarily involved an implicit repudiation of the *Hurtado* doctrine of nonsuperfluousness, yet the repudiation was only implicit and was not openly acknowledged by the Court. The result was that the *Hurtado* doctrine remained officially alive and available to cause theoretical difficulties as the nationalization of the Bill of Rights proceeded.

Despite the Court's unsatisfactory resolution of its due process problems, the *Twining* case did open the door to the possibility that future decisions defining *liberty* and *due process of law* in the Due Process Clause would include rights at least similar to some of those in the Bill of Rights. The Court's statement on the meaning of the Due Process Clause in the *Twining* case had thus taken the form of a blank check, the value of which was to be filled in by the future course of constitutional litigation.

Despite this promise of the *Twining* case, however, term after term of the Court passed without any further developments regarding the nationalization of the Bill of Rights. The Court had not moved beyond the *Twining* case when the nation entered World War I, and the postwar era appeared to be inhospitable to any expansion of civil liberties. The social and economic dislocations of the war and a general disillusionment with its results, added to the fear of the alien, foreign-born, and radical elements engendered by the Bolshevik revolution in Russia, led to the so-called Red Scare during the postwar period. State legislatures responded to the fear of radical elements by enacting criminal syndicalism legislation that prohibited the advocacy of force, violence, or other unlawful means to bring about political or industrial change, and at the national level mass arrests and deportations of alien "radicals" were undertaken. Predictions of attempts to overthrow the government by the radical, Bolshevik element by U.S. Attorney General A. Mitchell Palmer only served to increase the national hysteria.[43]

The Red Scare and the *Gitlow* Case

In New York, the legislature created the Lusk Committee to investigate subversive activities in the state, and on Saturday, November 8, 1919, the committee organized seven hundred policemen to stage raids on radical centers in New York City. Large quantities of radical literature were seized in the raids, and over five hundred persons were arrested. The raids were conducted according to the prevailing procedure of the period, generally without valid arrest or search warrants and with little discrimination as to who was arrested or what was seized. Among those arrested in the raids were the leaders of the left-wing faction of the Socialist party—those who would soon organize the American Communist party. Included in this group were Benjamin Gitlow, Charles Ruthenberg, Isaac A. Ferguson, Harry Winitsky, and "Big Jim" Larkin.

Benjamin Gitlow was the most prominent of the group. He had been born on December 21, 1891, at Elizabethport, New Jersey, the son of poverty-stricken Russian-Jewish immigrants. He joined the Socialist party at the age of eighteen, and after high school, he studied law for two years and was elected a member of the New York legislature on the Socialist ticket in 1918. The success of the Bolshevik revolution in Russia convinced Gitlow that the time was ripe for revolution in the United States, and he became a prominent leader of the left wing of the Socialist party, which was instrumental in creating the Communist party in the United States. When he was arrested in the Lusk Committee raid, Gitlow was twenty-eight years old.[44]

With the Red Scare dominating the country, the arrest of Gitlow and his fellow radicals was applauded in New York. New York City Mayor John F. Hylan congratulated the police commissioner on the raids, offering his compliments "on the way you handled the 'Reds' on Saturday." He was very pleased, the mayor said, "and I think all New York is also, although it is easier to deal with bomb throwers than it is for you to defend yourself against some of the people whose chief stock in trade is in knocking the Police Department."[45] Gitlow and his comrades were also not unhappy about their arrests. "We were in the best of spirits," Gitlow said later. "We were, after all, revolutionists, ready to sacrifice all for the revolution, so that a mere arrest and a ride in a patrol wagon was a trifling incident."[46]

On the day of Gitlow's arraignment, it was reported in the press that "Lenin himself had dictated the Bolshevik operations in this city," and that the evidence was in "the hands of agents of the Lusk Committee."

Chief City Magistrate William McAdoo set Gitlow's bond at $15,000. When Gitlow's attorney, Charles Recht, protested this amount, McAdoo refused to reduce it, saying that the Communist party "is intended to destroy organized government" and had "declared a state of war against the United States and the Government of the State of New York, and the establishment of the Communist Party in the State of New York is the highest crime known to our law, and I will not reduce the bail one dollar." A few days later in binding Gitlow over for the grand jury, McAdoo also declared that a "few years back, if anyone had said that in this year of grace, 1919, there would be, in the City of New York, known to the authorities, between seventy and eighty official headquarters of a criminal organization like this, well equipped with money and the rooms bulging with literature, more dangerous to civilization than microbes of disease are to the human body, he would have been laughed at." Failure to enforce the law in such circumstances, he continued, would be "a species of treason against the State itself," and only "dilettante parlor socialists" and "pseudo anarchists" appeared to be critical of the "zeal of the officers" in pursuing radicals like Gitlow.[47]

Gitlow was charged with violating the New York Criminal Anarchy Act of 1902. Unlike the criminal syndicalism legislation that was passed by many states during and after World War I in response to the Red Scare, the New York act had been passed in reaction to the assassination of President McKinley by a reputed anarchist at the Pan American Exposition in Buffalo. The Criminal Anarchy Act thus defined criminal anarchy as "the doctrine that organized government should be overthrown by force or violence, or by assassination of the executive head or of any of the executive officials of government, or by any unlawful means." Any person, the act provided, who by "word of mouth or writing advocates, advises or teaches the duty, necessity or propriety" of criminal anarchism, or who "prints, publishes, edits, issues or knowingly circulates, sells, distributes or publicly displays any book, paper, document, or written or printed matter in any form" advocating criminal anarchy, was guilty of a felony.[48]

Four months before the Lusk Committee raids, Gitlow had been involved in the publication of *Revolutionary Age*, which served as the organ of the left-wing Socialists in their attacks on the more moderate Socialists who did not favor revolutionary tactics. As a part of this factional fight, *Revolutionary Age* published a denunciation of the moderate Socialists as well as a statement of the principles of the left wing. This "Left Wing Manifesto" proclaimed that humanity could be saved "from its last excesses only by the Communist Revolution." The manifesto attacked the belief of the moderate Socialists that socialism could be achieved through parliamentary democracy and proclaimed that it was necessary "to destroy the parliamentary state, and construct a new state of organized producers, which will deprive the bourgeoisie of political power, and function as a revolutionary dictatorship of the proletariat. . . ."[49]

This was to be achieved, the manifesto continued, by organizing the unorganized industrial workers and using mass strikes to capture control of the means of production and to destroy the capitalist, parliamentary system. "The final objective of mass action is the conquest of the power of the state," the manifesto declared, "the annihilation of the bourgeois parliamentary state, and the introduction of the transition proletarian state, functioning as a revolutionary dictatorship of the proletariat. . . ." The old order was in decay and civilization collapsing, the manifesto concluded. "The proletarian revolution and the Communist reconstruction of society —*the struggle for these*—is now indispensable. This is the message of the Communist International to the workers of the world. The Communist International calls the proletariat of the world to the final struggle."[50]

Revolutionary Age was already defunct, but because of his involvement in the publication of the Left Wing Manifesto, Gitlow was charged with advocating the violent overthrow of the government and with having printed and circulated a document advocating criminal anarchism. He was tried in the Supreme Court (Criminal Branch) of New York County before Judge Bartow S. Weeks and a jury. Clarence Darrow was persuaded to join the defense team, while Assistant District Attorney Alexander I. Rorke led the prosecution.[51]

The state proved that Gitlow had been the business manager of the *Revolutionary Age* and had been directly involved in the writing, printing, and distribution of the Left Wing Manifesto. Darrow objected that Gitlow was being prosecuted for exercising his freedom of speech and that the state had not shown that any overt illegal acts had occurred or were likely to occur as a result of Gitlow's expression of views. In overruling Darrow's objection, however, Judge Weeks ruled that the only lawful means of change in the United States was through the ballot box and that demonstrations and strikes for political purposes were criminal acts.

The defense did not call any witnesses, but Darrow made one of his rousing arguments to the jury. "For a man to be afraid of revolution in America, would be to be ashamed of his own mother," Darrow declared. "Nothing else. Revolution? There is not a drop of honest blood in a single man that does not look back to some revolution for which he would thank his God that those who revolted won." If Lincoln were alive, he said, "Mr. Palmer, the Attorney General of the United States, would send his night riders to invade his office and the privacy of his home and send him to jail."[52]

Darrow, however, had never been optimistic about the possibility of an acquittal in the case. "Oh, I know you are innocent," he told Gitlow, "but they have the country steamed up. Everybody is against the Reds." He was also unenthusiastic when Gitlow insisted upon making a statement to the jury defending his Communist principles. "Well," Darrow said, "I suppose a revolutionist must have his say in court even if it kills him." And in an address to the jury, Gitlow declared his allegiance to the principles stated in the Left Wing Manifesto. His whole life was dedicated to the Communist movement, he told the jury, and no "jails will change my opinion in this respect. I ask no clemency. . . . Regardless of what your verdict may be, I maintain that the principles of the Left Wing Manifesto and Program on the whole are correct. . . ."[53]

The jury took only forty-five minutes on February 5, 1920, to find Gitlow guilty as charged. Justice Weeks congratulated the jury on its work, saying the verdict was a "distinct benefit to the country and the State." Benjamin Gitlow was "a striking example of the educational opportunity of the country," Weeks continued. "He has enjoyed high honors. He earned $41 a week, yet he confesses he has not even accumulated any property. Is that in harmony with the idea of ambition of those who come from foreign lands to this land of opportunity?" The only way one could keep one's "feet on the ground," he concluded, "is to stand on something substantial—to stand by the Government. I hope the verdict will reach out and act as a deterrent to others." On February 11, Justice Weeks gave Gitlow the maximum sentence, five to ten years in prison.[54]

The verdict in the *Gitlow* case was praised editorially by the *New York Times*. The criminal-anarchy statute under which Gitlow had been convicted, the *Times* said, had nothing to do with free speech. The freedom of speech "so often and so wearisomely appealed to by the men and women who seek to overthrow freedom and free government by physical force, had nothing to do with the case." Communism, the editorial continued, was a plan to destroy the government, and for "abetting that plan Gitlow has justly been found guilty of criminal anarchy. A few convictions like this may cool the ferocity of the thousands of Communists now in the United States."[55]

When Justice Weeks pronounced sentence, Gitlow was immediately escorted to jail. As he said later, when he was locked in his cell, "I was in a daze. I sat down on the cot. I was certain I would spend the entire ten years in prison, for I knew that the hysteria against the Reds was in full force and I did not expect it to abate soon." He was later transferred to Sing Sing prison, but after serving over two years in various New York prisons, he was freed on bail on April 22, 1922, pending the outcome of an appeal of his case to the New York Court of Appeals.[56]

When he was released on bail, the appellate division of the supreme court had already affirmed his conviction and had rejected an argument that Gitlow's freedom of speech had been violated. In a decision announced on April 1, 1921, the appellate division held that advocacy of unlawful action could be punished even though there was no clear and present danger of unlawful action resulting from such advocacy. A law so limited, the court held, "might only become effective simultaneously with the overthrow of the government, when there would be neither prosecuting officers nor courts for the prosecution and punishment of crimes." Gitlow had justifiably been found guilty of advocating dangerous doctrines, the court held, and there was no constitutional right on the part of "aliens who are members of the Left Wing," or "naturalized citizens who have sworn to uphold the Constitution," or "native-born citizens of alien parentage, such as [Gitlow] is," to advocate the overthrow of the government. If "immigration is properly supervised and restricted," the court concluded, "the God-fearing, liberty-loving Americans" who "have made and are making sacrifices to improve their condition and that of their families, and to accumulate property for themselves and those who come after them, will see to it these pernicious doctrines are not permitted to take root in America."[57]

The New York Court of Appeals affirmed this decision of the appellate division on July 12, 1922. Freedom of speech, the court of appeals held, could not be utilized to "destroy that freedom which the [federal and state] Constitutions have established." Judge Cuthbert Pound, joined by Judge Benjamin Cardozo, on the other hand, dissented from the court of appeals' decision. The Criminal Anarchy Act, Pound said, applied only to the advocacy of anarchism, not to the advocacy of communism. "The advocate of proletarian class rule," he said, "while advocating a vicious doctrine subversive to our institutions and menacing the orderly rule of law, is advocating not anarchy, but something entirely different."[58]

Although some of his comrades in the Communist party urged him to jump bail and flee to the Soviet Union, Gitlow surrendered to authorities and was returned to prison after the court of appeals affirmed his conviction. He spent only three months in prison, however, since he was again released on bail when the American Civil Liberties Union (ACLU) appealed his case to the United States Supreme Court.

The American Civil Liberties Union began as the Civil Liberties Bureau (CLB) of the American Union against Militarism, a pacificist organization opposed to the United States's entry into World War I. Organized by Roger Nash Baldwin in 1917, the Civil Liberties Bureau was primarily concerned with defending conscientious objectors, but as the suppression of dissidents spread during and after the war, the CLB was inexorably drawn into the defense of a broader spectrum of civil liberties. The CLB became an independent organization, the National Civil Liberties Bureau (NCLB), in October of 1917, and finally in January of 1920, the NCLB was reorganized and renamed the American Civil Liberties Union. Roger Baldwin continued to be the director and driving force behind the ACLU, and in the *Gitlow* case, the organization secured the services of Walter H.

Pollak as Gitlow's principal attorney, while Pollak was assisted in the appeal by Walter Nelles, Charles S. Aschen, and Albert DeSilver. Fundraising for the appeal in the *Gitlow* case, on the other hand, was undertaken by the National Defense Committee of the Workers' [Communist] Party.[59]

Although the appeal of his case to the Supreme Court was thus assured, Benjamin Gitlow could probably have secured a pardon from Governor Al Smith during the winter of 1923, when Smith pardoned other political prisoners serving terms in New York. As Roger Baldwin explained to the ACLU's contact with the governor's office, however, the ACLU did not want Gitlow to be considered for a pardon along with the other political prisoners. "I want to call your particular attention to the application of Benjamin Gitlow whose case is on appeal to the United States Supreme Court," Baldwin said. "We do not want the Governor to act on his case at this time, because it is important to get a decision from the Supreme Court on the constitutional question involved." "Gitlow," Baldwin continued, "who would prefer personally to withdraw his appeal and take a pardon, is willing to subordinate his personal interests to the larger issue involved. His application is transmitted at this time only so that the Governor may have it before him when the Supreme Court decides the case. We ask the Governor [to] hold it until then."[60]

Although the mooting of the *Gitlow* case was thus avoided, Walter Pollak and his ACLU colleagues faced formidable obstacles in attempting to convince the Court that Gitlow had been exercising his legitimate right of free speech. The appointment of William Howard Taft as chief justice in 1921 had signaled a conservative turn in the Court's decisions, since Taft's appointment was followed by similarly conservative additions to the Court. George Sutherland was appointed in 1922, and the appointments of Edward T. Sanford and Pierce Butler followed in 1923. Taft thus presided over a solid conservative majority composed of himself and Justices Sutherland, Van Devanter, McReynolds, Butler, and Sanford. Justice Joseph McKenna was senile and was finally persuaded to retire in 1925, to be replaced by Harlan Fiske Stone. To the disappointment of Chief Justice Taft, Stone soon joined Justices Brandeis and Holmes as a critic of the Taft Court's conservative majority.[61]

For the conservatives of the Taft Court, the primary value protected by the Due Process Clause of the Fourteenth Amendment was the right of property. The broadening of property rights that had occurred in the decisions of the Court after 1890 was therefore reinforced and expanded by the decisions of the Taft Court. And as a consequence, governmental attempts to regulate child labor, to set minimum wages, and to regulate business more extensively fell before the constitutional strictures of the Court.[62]

When confronted with civil-liberties claims such as freedom of speech or of religion, the Taft Court also dealt with them in terms of the general "liberty" and "property" rights protected by the Due Process Clause, and appeared to be consciously avoiding any ruling that the specific rights in the Bill of Rights were guaranteed by the Constitution against interference by the states. Important cases like *Meyer* v. *Nebraska* and *Pierce* v. *Society of Sisters*, which involved significant free-speech and religion challenges to state statutes, were thus disposed of by the Taft Court in terms of the general "liberty" and "property" rights secured by the Due Process Clause without any indication by the Court that the freedoms of speech and religion were in fact guaranteed by the Fourteenth Amendment.[63]

Justices Holmes and Brandeis were often in disagreement with the due process approach of the Taft Court, and both protested the expansive interpretation of the Due Process Clause that imposed severe restrictions upon state economic policy. Holmes and Brandeis, and many progressives in the country at large, saw the Due Process Clause as the vehicle by which the Court was imposing some of its most reactionary decisions on the states. The vagueness of the Due Process Clause, it was felt, allowed the justices to roam at large and to read into it their personal political, social, or economic views as constitutional requirements. And since the majority of the Court was conservative, the result had been an overemphasis upon property rights as the primary constitutional value. It was in reaction to the Court's use of due process to enforce an inflated notion of property rights that Felix Frankfurter, then a contributor to the *New Republic*, exclaimed that the "due process clauses [in the Constitution] ought to go." And at one time Brandeis also apparently believed that the Due Process Clause ought to be repealed because it allowed room for too much judicial policymaking.[64]

The approach of Holmes and Brandeis to the Due Process Clause of the Fourteenth Amendment, therefore, was not necessarily hospitable to the nationalization of the Bill of Rights. Both were opposed to the Court's use of due process to impose restrictions on state economic policies and would have given the states great flexibility in the field of economic policy. As the *Gitlow* case approached the Court, the question was whether they would also oppose a further expansion of the Due Process Clause that would involve the imposition of rights similar to those in the Bill of Rights on the states.

In addition to the problem the composition of the Court presented, counsel for Gitlow faced the problem that the Court had never held that freedom of speech was a right secured by the Due Process Clause. In 1907 the Court had rejected a free-speech argument under the Fourteenth Amendment, while leaving "undecided the question whether there is to be found in the 14th Amendment a prohibition similar to that in the 1st,"[65] and it had subsequently upheld serious restrictions imposed by the states on freedom of expression.[66] As late as 1922 the Court had declared in *Prudential Insurance Co.* v. *Cheek* that "the Constitution of the United States imposes upon the states no obligation to confer upon those within their jurisdiction either the right of free speech or the right of silence." Neither "the 14th Amendment nor any other provision of the Constitution," it said, "imposes upon the states any restrictions about 'freedom of speech' or 'liberty of silence'. . . ."[67]

In spite of such negative comments, however, Walter Pollak argued on behalf of Gitlow before the Court that in "deciding whether a right is protected under the due process clause, the question, as was said in *Twining* v. *New Jersey* . . . , is this: 'Is it a fundamental principle of liberty and justice which inheres in the very idea of free government and is the inalienable right of a citizen of such a government?'" And Pollak insisted that with "regard to freedom of opinion and expression on matters of public concern, the question can be answered in only one way."[68]

Since freedom of speech was a "fundamental right" protected by the Due Process Clause against impairment by the states, Pollak argued that New York could punish Gitlow only upon a showing that his expression of views had created a clear and present danger of unlawful action. Free government, Pollak told the Court, "is premised on the proposition that no human agency other than the ultimate good sense of the whole community can be trusted with the power to gauge the dangerous tendency of mere expression of political doctrine." For a statute like the New York Criminal Anarchy Act to be valid, he said, it must be applied to speech that had "a causal relation with substantive evil, consummated, attempted or likely," but in the *Gitlow* case it had been applied to "a situation involving no element of public danger. In its relation to such a situation the statute is a mere invasion of an express constitutional right."[69]

Pollak thus attempted to convince the Court not only that the Due Process Clause did protect a right of free speech, but also that the proper measure of the scope of free speech was the "clear and present danger" doctrine. This doctrine had been enunciated in 1919 by Justice Holmes, writing for a unanimous Court in *Schenck* v. *United States*. The question in every case involving governmental punishment of speech, Holmes said, "is whether the words used are used in such circumstances and are of such a nature as to create a clear and present danger that they will bring about the substantive evils that Congress has a right to prevent."[70]

The clear-and-present-danger doctrine seemed to suggest that the government must show that advocacy of illegal action might actually cause such action—a showing that had not been made in the *Gitlow* case. There had been no showing by the state of New York that the Left Wing Manifesto had induced anything other than massive yawning among the public of New York, and as Zechariah Chafee has said, any "agitator who read these thirty-four pages [of the Manifesto] to a mob would not stir them to violence, except possibly against himself."[71] Pollak's clear-and-present-danger argument in the *Gitlow* case nonetheless faced an uncertain reception by the Court, since the clear-and-present-danger doctrine was not followed by the Court in *Abrams* v. *United States*, a case decided within months after the *Schenck* case in 1919.[72]

In opposition to Pollak's arguments, both the attorney general of New York and the district attorney of New York County filed briefs urging the Court to affirm Gitlow's conviction. The attorney general forthrightly challenged Pollak's argument that the Due Process Clause protected a right of freedom of speech. "The first amendment of the Constitution," he said, "does not by virtue of the adoption of the Fourteenth Amendment, curtail the rights of the states to limit the freedom of speech and of the press."[73] This argument was not pressed, however, and the attorney general principally addressed the dangers the Criminal Anarchy Act was meant to control. The act had been passed in response to the assassination of President McKinley, he told the Court, and was meant to prohibit any advocacy of the overthrow of the government. If it could only be applied to expressions creating clear and present dangers of unlawful action, he continued, "then of course it could not have accomplished the object for which it was passed; that is, to prevent the dissemination of a doctrine as such, which working insiduously on a perverted mind would cause another tragedy, perhaps not of the same kind, but nevertheless a tragedy which it is the duty of the state to avoid if possible."[74]

In contrast to the attorney general, the New York County District Attorney did not deny that the Due Process Clause protected freedom of speech, but rather told the Court that he would argue "the power of the State to punish abuses of the right of free speech." Except for the half-hearted denial of Pollak's argument by the attorney general, there was thus no extensive argument in the *Gitlow* case against the proposition that the Due Process Clause guaranteed freedom of speech.[75]

Although there were categories of speech that could never be punished and others that could be punished only upon a showing that a clear and present danger of unlawful action resulted from them, the district attorney argued, advocacy of the violent overthrow of the government fell into a third category of speech that could be punished as such. Criminal anarchy, he argued, "is so inherently dangerous that it is competent for the State to forbid the advocacy of that doctrine absolutely, without regard to whether there is imminent danger that the advocacy will result in the taking of actual steps to carry out the doctrine advocated." If the government were required to wait until the advocacy of such doctrines created a clear and present danger of unlawful action, the district attorney concluded, "the Government might perish because of its failure to take reasonable protective measures. The time to kill a snake is when it is young."[76]

Gitlow v. *New York* was appealed to the Court in the summer of 1922 and was argued on April 12, 1923. The Court, however, ordered a reargument in the case on November 23, 1923, and did not announce its decision until June 8, 1925. In the meantime, Benjamin Gitlow remained free on bail and continued to play a prominent role in the Communist party. He was the party's candidate for vice-president in 1924, but was not exactly an electoral success, since the party garnered only slightly over thirty-three thousand votes. Gitlow's Communist party activities had to be suspended once again, however, when the Court affirmed his conviction by a six-to-two vote.[77]

Writing for the majority of the Court, Justice Sanford held that the Left Wing Manifesto had not involved the advocacy of abstract doctrine but had employed the language of direct incitement. "That the jury were warranted," he said, "in finding that the Manifesto advocated not merely the abstract doctrine of overwhelming organized government by force, violence, and unlawful means, but action to that end, is clear."[78]

Then came one of the more important statements of the Court in the process of the nationalization of the Bill of Rights. "For present purposes we may and do assume," Sanford said, "that freedom of speech and of the press—which are protected by the 1st Amendment from abridgment by Congress—are among the fundamental personal rights and 'liberties' protected by the due process clause of the 14th Amendment from impairment by the states." The Court's statement in *Prudential Insurance Co.* v. *Cheek* that the Due Process Clause did not guarantee freedom of speech, Sanford continued, was not regarded by the Court "as determinative of this question."[79]

Having "assumed" that freedom of speech and of the press were protected by the Due Process Clause, the Court had to meet Walter Pollak's argument that the proper measure of the scope of freedom of speech was the clear-and-present-danger doctrine, which would have required a showing by the state of New York that Gitlow's expression of views had created a clear and present danger of unlawful action. The clear-and-present-danger doctrine, Sanford pointed out, was applicable only when a statute prohibited certain acts, and the question was whether the statute applied also to language advocating the acts prohibited by the statute. "In such cases," he said, "it has been held that the general provisions of the statute may be constitutionally applied to the specific utterance of the defendant if its natural tendency and probable effect were to bring about the substantive evil which the legislative body might prevent."[80]

In the Criminal Anarchy Act of 1902—Sanford pointed out, on the other hand—the New York legislature had determined "that utterances advocating the overthrow of organized government by force, violence, and unlawful means, are so inimical to the general welfare, and involve such danger of substantive evil that they may be penalized in the exercise of its police power." Faced with a statute in which the legislature has made such a determination, Sanford continued, the Court's only function was to determine whether the legislative judgment embodied in the statute was an arbitrary or unreasonable one. "In other words," Sanford continued, "when the legislative body has determined generally, in the constitutional exercise of its discretion, that utterances of a certain kind involve such danger of substantive evil that they may be punished, the question whether any specific utterance coming within the prohibited class is likely, in and of itself, to bring about the substantive evil, is not open to consideration. It is sufficient that the statute itself be constitutional, and that the use of the language comes within its prohibition."[81]

The New York legislature's judgment in regard to the danger to the public of the advocacy of violent overthrow of the government was an eminently reasonable one, Sanford said, since such advocacy threatened "breaches of the peace and ultimate revolution. And the immediate danger is none the less real and substantial because the effect of a given utterance cannot be accurately foreseen. The state cannot reasonably be required to measure the danger from every such utterance in the nice balance of a jeweler's scale." "A single revolutionary spark may kindle a fire that, smoldering for a time, may burst into a sweeping and destructive conflagration," Sanford concluded. "We cannot hold that the present statute is an arbitrary or unreasonable exercise of the police power of the state, unwarrantably infringing the freedom of speech or press; and we must and do sustain its constitutionality."[82]

Although dissenting from the judgment of the Court, Justice Holmes, joined by Justice Brandeis, agreed that the "general principle of free speech, it seems to me, must be taken to be included in the 14th Amendment, in view of the scope that has been given to the word 'liberty' as there used, although perhaps it may be accepted with a somewhat larger latitude of interpretation than is allowed to Congress by the sweeping language that governs, or ought to govern, the laws of the United States."[83]

Despite their opposition to the use of the Due Process Clause by the Court to prevent economic experimentation by the states, both Holmes and Brandeis thus accepted the expansion of the Due Process Clause to protect freedom of speech against state action. Holmes also suggested, however, that the freedom of speech protected by the Due Process Clause might not be identical with the freedom of speech protected by the First Amendment against federal action. Under the Due Process Clause, he appeared to suggest, the states might be given a wider latitude in regulating speech than the First Amendment allowed Congress. Holmes therefore appeared to accept the suggestion in the *Twining* case that while the Due

Process Clause might protect rights similar to those in the Bill of Rights, the rights so protected would be only similar, and not necessarily identical, to those in the Bill of Rights.

The proper test of the limits of the freedom of speech protected by the Due Process Clause, Holmes nevertheless insisted, was the clear-and-present-danger doctrine. And under that doctrine, he argued, it could not be held that the Left Wing Manifesto had produced any real danger of an attempt to overthrow the government. The Court had held that the manifesto was an incitement to unlawful action, Holmes continued, but "every idea is an incitement. It offers itself for belief, and, if believed, it is acted on unless some other belief outweighs it, or some failure of energy stifles the movement at its birth. The only difference between the expression of an opinion and an incitement in the narrower sense is the speaker's enthusiasm for the result. Eloquence may set fire to reason." But the Left Wing Manifesto, Holmes concluded, had "no chance of starting a present conflagration. If, in the long run, the beliefs expressed in proletarian dictatorship are destined to be accepted by the dominant forces of the community, the only meaning of free speech is that they should be given their chance and have their way."[84]

When the Court's decision affirming his conviction was announced, Benjamin Gitlow was himself continuing his efforts to see to it that the Communist party had its way. Gitlow again surrendered to the authorities, however, and was returned to prison in November of 1925. Gitlow found that, because of factional differences he had with the leaders of the Communist party, the party met the Court's decision, not with strident denunciation, but merely with indifference. The American Civil Liberties Union, however, appealed to Governor Alfred Smith to pardon Gitlow as he had pardoned others convicted of political crimes during the Red Scare. Smith responded by pardoning Gitlow in December of 1925. He had no doubt that Gitlow had been properly and legally convicted, Smith said, but the question was "whether or not he had been sufficiently punished for a political crime."[85]

After his pardon, Gitlow continued his leadership role in the Communist party and was again the party's vice-presidential candidate in 1928. By 1929 Gitlow was secretary of the executive department of the Communist party, but the leadership of the party was called to Moscow to explain its factional problems. Stalin and the Comintern ordered the Lovestone faction, which included Gitlow, to resign. Gitlow refused and made a defiant speech that prompted Stalin to denounce the Lovestone faction angrily. "Who do you think you are?" Stalin shouted. "Trotsky defied me. Where is he? Zinoviev defied me. Where is he? Bukharin defied me. Where is he? And you? When you get back to America, nobody will stay with you except your wives." And he was reported to have added that the

Russians knew how to handle strikebreakers, noting that there "is plenty of room in our cemeteries."[86]

After having helped found the American Communist party, and having been a member of the ruling executive committee of the party and a member of the executive committee and praesidium of the Communist International, Gitlow discovered in 1929 that he had, on orders from Moscow, no position in the American party. He and the other purged leaders attempted for a time to organize opposition groups to the party, but Gitlow dropped out of the Communist movement in the 1930s. He soon became a strong anti-Communist, writing and lecturing against the movement and serving as a paid witness before national, state, and local investigations of subversive activities. Gitlow died of a heart attack at the age of seventy-three on July 19, 1965, at his home in Compound, New York.[87]

Benjamin Gitlow's prosecution by the state of New York, when taken together with Albert Twining's earlier legal difficulties, had opened the door to the nationalization of the First Amendment of the Bill of Rights. In the *Twining* case, the Court had indicated that the Due Process Clause might guarantee certain "fundamental" rights similar to those in the Bill of Rights, and then in the *Gitlow* case it had assumed "for present purposes" that freedom of speech and of the press were secured against state action by the word *liberty* in the Due Process Clause. The question after the *Gitlow* case, however, was whether the Court's "assumption" had been only for the purpose of deciding Gitlow's case, or whether a major breakthrough with respect to the nationalization of First Amendment rights had occurred. This question would remain unanswered for another six years, but by the early 1930s, the assumption in the *Gitlow* case became a reality in the decisions of the Court.

4

From Assumption to Reality
The *Stromberg, Near,* and *DeJonge* Cases

"We all wanted a decision on the criminal anarchy law and we got it," Roger Baldwin said of the *Gitlow* case, "though it was not what we were looking for."[1] While the *Gitlow* case was pending decision in the Supreme Court, however, the American Civil Liberties Union was in the process of sponsoring the appeal of two other cases, *Whitney* v. *California* and *Burns* v. *United States,* to the Court, both of which challenged the validity of California's criminal syndicalism statute as an unconstitutional restriction of freedom of speech.[2] The ACLU was again disappointed, however, when the Court on May 16, 1927, upheld the validity of the California syndicalism act in the *Burns* and *Whitney* cases and affirmed the convictions in both cases.

In the *Whitney* case, the Court failed to elaborate upon the "assumption" in the *Gitlow* case that freedom of speech and freedom of the press were secured by the Due Process Clause. The Court upheld Charlotte Anita Whitney's conviction for criminal syndicalism because of her participation in a convention of the Communist Labor party, rejecting an argument that her conviction violated her freedom of speech. Justice Sanford held for the majority of the Court that "the freedom of speech which is secured by the Constitution" did not confer an absolute right to speak, but he did not elaborate further on the question of the meaning of the Due Process Clause in relation to freedom of speech.[3]

Justice Brandeis, joined by Justice Holmes, concurred in the result in the *Whitney* case, while eloquently reiterating the contention that the proper measure of the scope of freedom of speech was the clear-and-present-danger test. Because counsel for Charlotte Anita Whitney had not raised the issue of whether a clear and present danger of unlawful action existed in California as a result of her participation in the Communist Labor party convention, and because there was evidence before the jury upon the basis of which it could have found that a clear and present danger of unlawful action did exist, Brandeis and Holmes concurred in the Court's affirmation of Whitney's conviction. Brandeis, however, also appeared to be having some second thoughts about the Court's assumption in the *Gitlow* case that freedom of speech and freedom of the press were substantive due: process guarantees. "Despite arguments to the contrary which had seemed to me persuasive," he said, "it is settled that the due process clause of the 14th Amendment applies to matters of substantive law as well as to matters of procedure."[4]

As in the *Gitlow* case, Walter Pollak had argued the *Whitney* case before the Supreme Court, and he reported to the ACLU that the Court's decision in the *Whitney* case, when taken together with the *Gitlow* decision, was a major blow to the Union's challenge to the validity of criminal-syndicalism statutes. "The decision definitely establishes the validity under the Federal Constitution of criminal syndicalism laws penalizing membership in organizations which advocate violent methods of effecting political or economic change," Pollak said. In the Supreme Court's view, he continued, "the Legislature's power over membership in organizations which the facts disclose to be incendiary is at least as great as its power to prohibit speech which incites to violence. Membership in such organizations is analogized by the Court to participation in a conspiracy."[5]

From the standpoint of the ACLU, the only bright spot in an otherwise gloomy situation was the Court's decision in *Fiske* v. *Kansas*, rendered the same day as the decisions in the *Whitney* and *Burns* cases. Harold Fiske was a twenty-six year old member of the Industrial Workers of the World (IWW), who was arrested on July 2, 1923, in Geneseo, Kansas, while recruiting for the IWW Agricultural Workers Industrial Union. Fiske was described as "a regular walking roll top desk, his pockets serving for pigeon holes. His [IWW] blanks and literature were neatly folded and arranged, being held together with rubber bands."[6]

Along with other IWW literature, Fiske had in his possession upon his arrest a copy of the preamble of the IWW constitution. The preamble declared that the "working class and the employing class have nothing in common" and that "there can be no peace so long as hunger and want are found among millions of the working people and the few who make up the employing class have all the good things of life." Between the employers and the workers, the preamble continued, "a struggle must go on until the workers of the World organize as a class, take possession of the earth, and the machinery of production and abolish the wage system." By organizing industrially, the preamble concluded, the IWW were "forming the structure of the new society within the shell of the old."[7]

The state of Kansas charged that this preamble advocated force, violence, and lawlessness as a means of political or industrial change and that Fiske, in recruiting IWW members, had thus violated the Kansas Criminal Syndicalism Act. The IWW, however, had established a General Defense Committee to defend its members against such charges, and Harold

O. Mulks of Chicago had become the leading counsel for the IWW General Defense Committee during the early 1920s.[8] Soon after his arrest, Harold Fiske therefore telegraphed the IWW headquarters in Chicago, requesting an attorney, and Harold Mulks subsequently represented Fiske at his preliminary hearing. Fiske was nevertheless bound over for trial in the Rice County District Court. After an appeal to the ACLU, that organization advanced $1000 from its National Bail Fund to secure Fiske's release pending trial.[9]

Harold Mulks was also expected to defend Fiske at that trial in September of 1923, but at the time of the trial Mulks was engaged elsewhere and was unable to appear. Charles L. Carroll of Great Bend had previously served as defense counsel for IWW defendants in western Kansas, and when Mulks was unable to appear, Carroll was retained by the IWW to defend Fiske at his trial.[10]

The principal evidence introduced against Fiske by the prosecution was the preamble of the IWW constitution, which, the prosecution argued, proved that the IWW and Fiske advocated violence as a means of political and industrial change. Although the defense denied that either Fiske or the IWW advocated violence, Fiske—in testifying in his own behalf—refused to repudiate the principles of the IWW and declared that the IWW would "in time rule the labor situation and overpower the capitalists of the United States." The jury deliberated only two hours before finding Fiske guilty, and two days later, on September 20, 1923, the trial judge sentenced Fiske to from one to ten years in prison.[11]

With the encouragement of the trial judge and the continued financial support of the IWW General Defense Committee, Charles Carroll appealed Fiske's conviction to the Kansas Supreme Court. Carroll mishandled the appeal, however, and the case was dismissed by the supreme court for failure to follow the court's rules. At this point, Carroll retained Colonel A. M. and Randal C. Harvey of Topeka to undertake the appeal in the *Fiske* case. On November 8, 1924, however, the Kansas Supreme Court affirmed Fiske's conviction, rejecting an argument that Fiske's freedom of speech as guaranteed by the Kansas Constitution and the Due Process Clause of the Fourteenth Amendment had been violated.[12]

Although the ACLU issued a press release following the Kansas Supreme Court's decision stating that efforts "to obtain pardons from the governor are now the only course left in criminal syndicalism cases in Kansas as a result of the [Kansas] Supreme Court's decision," the Union nonetheless posted bond for Harold Fiske, pending an appeal to the United States Supreme Court. The Harveys were again retained by Charles Carroll to handle the appeal to the Court.[13]

In their arguments before the Supreme Court, the Harveys contended that there was nothing in the preamble of the IWW constitution that advocated force or violence or any unlawful acts as means of effecting political or industrial change, and that Fiske's conviction by the Kansas court had violated his freedom of speech. "We assume," they continued, "from the decision in *Gitlow* v. *New York* . . . that freedom of speech and of the press are among the fundamental personal rights and liberties protected by the due process clause of the Fourteenth Amendment from impairment by the states, and therefore have not discussed this question at length."[14]

Since Kansas counsel also assumed freedom of speech to be a guarantee of the Due Process Clause,[15] the *Fiske* case offered the Court a clear opportunity to confirm the assumption of the *Gitlow* case. Speaking for a unanimous Court, Justice Sanford held that the preamble of the IWW constitution did not advocate force, violence, or other unlawful means to bring about political or industrial change. Fiske's conviction under the Kansas Criminal Syndicalism Act, Sanford therefore held, "is an arbitrary and unreasonable exercise of the police power of the State, unwarrantably infringing the liberty of the defendant in violation of the due process clause of the 14th Amendment."[16]

Counsel for Fiske and the IWW General Defense Committee had therefore won a notable victory, and Harold Fiske was a free man. In an analysis of the *Fiske* case for the ACLU, Walter Pollak reported that "this case is noteworthy as the first decision by the Supreme Court of the United States sustaining any constitutional claim—whether directed against Federal or State legislation—squarely rested upon the basic liberties of speech, press, worship or assembly."[17] Contrary to Pollak's evaluation, however, was the fact that not once had Justice Sanford mentioned freedom of speech as a guarantee of the Due Process Clause in his *Fiske* opinion, nor was the assumption of the *Gitlow* case discussed. It was as if the *Gitlow* case had never occurred, and the Court was consciously avoiding a clearcut holding that freedom of speech was indeed a Due Process Clause guarantee. As a consequence, it was not until 1931 that the legal difficulties of such disparate characters as the owners of a Minneapolis scandal sheet and a young California woman Communist led the Court to acknowledge openly that freedom of speech and freedom of the press were guarantees of the Due Process Clause.

The *Stromberg* and *Near* Cases

In September of 1927, J. M. Near and Howard A. Guilford began to publish the *Saturday Press* as a weekly newspaper in Minneapolis, Minnesota. Both Near and Guilford had had stormy careers in Minneapolis. Guilford had been arrested for carrying concealed weapons and had been convicted of criminal libel in 1917. He had been an unsuccessful candidate for mayor in 1918, and two years later he was tried and acquitted for extortion. Near and Guilford had first teamed up to publish the *Twin City Reporter*, but they had sold that weekly to Jack Bevans and Ed Morgan. In the *Saturday Press*, Near and Guilford charged that the *Twin City Reporter* was being used for blackmail purposes and that it was behind the gambling rackets in Minneapolis. They pledged that they would "exterminate the *Twin City Reporter*," despite threats that had been made against them. If anything happened to either of them, Near and Guilford warned, "old Sir John Law will begin stuffing Stillwater penitentiary full of certain gentlemen and before he finishes, that model institution will be so overcrowded that the last few dozen will have to sleep with their legs out the windows."[18]

A few days after the initial issue of the *Saturday Press* appeared, Howard Guilford was shot and seriously wounded, and another attempt was made on his life while he was in the hospital. "I was told when I refused to accept a weekly envelope from the gambling syndicate in Minneapolis sometime ago that I would be 'bumped off,'" he said. "But I'm just started. As soon as I can get my shoes on again I'm going through with it." Two men were indicted for the assault on Guilford, and the *Saturday Press* charged that the same "mills that ground them from school to the penitentiary are the mills the *Saturday Press* is asking you to close: The gambling joints, owned and operated by the *Twin City Reporter* gang and that publication itself."[19]

The "*Twin City Reporter* gang," Near and Guilford charged in the *Saturday Press*, was composed of Mose Barnett, Ed Morgan, Jack Bevans, and "Red" Clare. As leaders of the gang, Mose Barnett was characterized by the *Saturday Press* as a "fatjowled Jew" and a "slimy thing too foul to fight fair," while Ed Morgan was called "a human louse" and a "blackmailer." The Minneapolis chief of police and the head of the Law Enforcement League were part of a conspiracy protecting the gang's gambling rackets, Near and Guilford charged, and even the other Minneapolis newspapers were "cringing in fear of that Jew spawn, Mose Barnett, and that ruddy-faced blackmailer and gangster Ed Morgan and Ed's dirty rag, the *Twin City Reporter*."[20]

County Attorney Floyd Olson—who would later become governor—was not at first attacked by the *Saturday Press*, but in the final issues of the newspaper, Guilford and Near charged that Olson's printing bills as a candidate for governor in 1924 had been paid by the gambling syndicate. Olson, they charged, was also in the "vest pocket of the horse thieves who have been running Minneapolis," and he consistently steered evidence of wrongdoing away from county grand juries. "And now that you are out in the open with the rest of the gang," the *Saturday Press* asked Olson, "what are you going to do?"[21]

The anti-Semitism of the *Saturday Press* grew more blatant with each issue. J. M. Near charged that "ninety percent of the crimes committed against society in this city are committed by Jew gangsters." If law-abiding Jews wanted to "rid themselves of the odium and stigma THE RO-DENTS OF THEIR OWN RACE HAVE BROUGHT UPON THEM," Near declared, "they need only step to the front and help the decent citizens of Minneapolis rid the city of these criminal Jews." Guilford also charged that he had been shot by Jews and as a result had "withdrawn all allegiance to anything with a hook nose that eats herring." The *Saturday Press*, he said, would soon demand a special grand jury and a special prosecutor to ferret out crime in Minneapolis. "Up to the present we have been merely tapping on the window," he warned. "Very soon we shall start smashing glass."[22]

Near and Guilford were unable to "start smashing glass," however, since on November 22, 1927, they were served with an order to show cause why an injunction should not be issued restraining them from "producing, publishing, editing, circulating, having in their possession, selling and giv-ing away a malicious, scandalous, and defamatory publication known as *The Saturday Press*, or known by any other name, in the State of Minne-sota." This order had resulted from a complaint filed by County Attorney Olson in the Hennepin County District Court charging that the *Saturday Press* had printed scandalous, malicious, and defamatory attacks against the head of the Law Enforcement League, the mayor and chief of police of Minneapolis, the *Minneapolis Tribune* and *Minneapolis Journal*, mem-bers of the county grand jury, the "Jewish race," and finally, Olson him-self. Olson's complaint asked the district court to issue a permanent in-junction against the publication of the *Saturday Press*.[23]

Olson's action was based on a statute passed by the Minnesota legisla-ture in 1925. The statute prohibited the publication of obscene, lewd or lascivious, or malicious, scandalous, and defamatory newspapers or other periodicals. The county district courts were authorized to issue injunctions against such publications and to punish violations of their injunctions with one-year jail terms and thousand-dollar fines. During the injunction pro-ceedings under the statute, a publisher could defend himself by proving the truth of his allegations, if published with good motives and for justifi-able ends.

This Minnesota "gag law," as it would be called, had been passed by the legislature in response to complaints by many state politicians that they were being attacked by "scandal sheets." The press of Minnesota generally did not oppose the gag law, and indeed many newspapers de-fended it. Governor Theodore Christianson, who signed the act into law, was himself the owner of a county weekly, the *Dawson Sentinel*, and Her-man Roe, publisher of the *Northfield News* and former president of the National Editorial Association, was a warm defender of the gag law, as were many other publishers of weekly Minnesota newspapers. It is therefore not surprising that the impetus to the attack on the constitutionality of the gag law came from outside the state.[24]

Counsel for Near and Guilford opposed the issuance of an injunction by the Hennepin County District Court and argued that the gag law was a violation of the freedom of the press. Judge Mathias Baldwin rejected this argument on December 9, 1927, however, ruling that the gag law was a "valid exercise of the police power of the State," which was intended to suppress publications that were "harmful to the community at large." Judge Baldwin nevertheless admitted that by its provisions, the gag law provided "for the suppression, in the most drastic manner, of any publication proscribed," and he conceded that there was "some doubt in the court's mind as to the correctness of its holding." He therefore certified to the Minnesota Supreme Court the question of whether the gag law was constitutionally valid.[25]

Unlike Judge Baldwin, the Minnesota Supreme Court expressed no doubts regarding the constitutionality of the gag law. The publication of scandalous materials such as the *Saturday Press,* the court held, was detrimental to public morals and tended to disturb the peace of the community and to provoke "assaults and the commission of crime." There was no constitutional right, it said, "to publish a fact merely because it is a fact," and indulgence in such publications as the *Saturday Press* "would soon deprave the moral taste of society and render it miserable. A business that depends largely for its success upon malicious scandal and defamation can be of no real service to society." The gag law therefore did not violate the right of freedom of the press, the court concluded, but rather was a valid exercise of the police power by the legislature.[26]

The temporary injunction against the publication of the *Saturday Press* was thus sustained by the Minnesota Supreme Court, but J. M. Near refused to accept defeat. In June of 1928, Near sent a copy of the supreme court's decision and other materials in his case to the American Civil Liberties Union with a request for aid. The ACLU in turn had the materials in the *Near* case evaluated by one of its cooperating attorneys, Carol Weiss King. King reported to the Union that the freedom of the press was "seriously menaced" by the Minnesota Supreme Court's decision, since if the gag law was indeed constitutional, "then the 14th Amendment, and inferentially the 1st Amendment, no longer protects the press against previous restraints. . . . I do not feel that the fact that Near and his associate Guilford are fanatics has any bearing on their right to publish whatever they see fit with only the possibility of punishment afterwards if what they have already published violates the criminal law," King continued. The *Saturday Press* had attacked public officials, and the "right to criticize political officials would seem pre-eminently one which the Constitution protected."[27]

"This case," King concluded, "more directly involves essentially civil liberties issues than any case that I have ever had anything to do with; the prospect of a successful termination of the litigation seems to me rather better than in the average case in which the Civil Liberties Union has taken an interest." King noted, however, that the decision of the Minnesota Supreme Court had sustained a temporary injunction against the *Saturday Press*, and that if the ACLU wished to appeal the case to the United States Supreme Court, a permanent injunction constituting a "final decision" of the state courts would have to be entered in the *Near* case before such an appeal would be possible.[28]

The ACLU accordingly informed Near that his case appeared to be "one of the most extraordinary cases that have ever occurred in the United States. It clearly involves issues in which this organization is interested." The ACLU executive committee, Near was informed, recognized "the very great importance of an appeal to the U.S. Supreme Court. We are ready to sponsor such an appeal and are making arrangements to that end." The Union suggested a local Minneapolis attorney to Near as an appropriate person to obtain a final decision in the case in the Minnesota courts as a prelude to an appeal to the U.S. Supreme Court.[29]

Near, however, vehemently rejected the ACLU's suggestion, pointing out that the attorney in question was "a close personal friend and political henchman of our county attorney, Floyd B. Olson," who had invoked the gag law against the *Saturday Press*. In addition, Near charged that the attorney recommended by the ACLU did not have "one fluid ounce of liberalism in his body" and was "[c]old blooded as a fish, crafty and cunning —but never a liberal." The attorney chosen by the ACLU, Near continued, "wouldn't fight for the rights of his great aunt unless the old lady layed [*sic*] down the currency in advance," and "wouldn't defend Christ if the Pilates of our political and official spoils system told him not to." "I never suspected . . . ," Near told the ACLU, "when I wrote those first few issues [of the *Saturday Press*], that the scum of the underworld lapped milk from the same saucer as our law enforcement bodies, city and county —and I am not at all certain that many of our state officials cannot be included." It did not matter to him personally, he said, "whether the infernal injunction law is wiped out or not. I can gouge and bite a living out of the world despite that injunction. . . . " But if the gag law was allowed to stand, he warned, the United States would soon have a "censorship of the press such as we have not had since Star Chamber days." If the ACLU was going to pursue his case, Near concluded, he preferred the attorney who had represented him all along without compensation, Tom Latimer. Latimer had lost the case in the Minnesota Supreme Court "not through any fault of his, but because the pressure of gangland is felt in this state, from highest to the most lowly official."[30]

Because of his closeness to County Attorney Floyd Olson, Near predicted that the Minneapolis attorney favored by the ACLU would not accept the *Near* case, and on this point he was correct. In response to the ACLU's request that he undertake the *Near* case, the attorney replied that the *Saturday Press* "was all that was claimed by the state to be, a scandalous and defamatory sheet." The character of the *Saturday Press* and its "motives and objects, to say [the] least, are so questionable, that it is doubtful that the United States Supreme Court will reverse the holding of the [Minnesota] Supreme Court." "There is an odor about this particular case," the attorney continued, "which is bound to obscure the real issues involved." Floyd Olson was himself a member of the Civil Liberties Union, the attorney said, and he asked, "Will it not be time enough to have this law, or a similar one in another jurisdiction, tested in a case which makes a meritorious appeal to us on the facts as well as the law?"[31]

Given this rejection of the *Near* case by its first choice of Minnesota counsel, the ACLU acquiesced in Near's insistence upon representation by Tom Latimer, while it retained Walter Pollak to pursue the appeal in the U.S. Supreme Court.[32] Near assured the ACLU that he was "staking my faith in your organization and if it fails me, I'll fight on, some way, but damn [if I] will stand to be licked by this gang of outlaws." If the Civil Liberties Union were ever to "hear me say I've quit or sold out," he said, "have me shot at sunrise."[33]

Near, however, was soon suffering the pangs of unemployment, and reported to the ACLU that the "fact of the matter is, I am BROKE. . . ." To extricate himself from his financial predicament, he wanted to resume publishing and to defy "this jackassical court order. . . ." "I don't want to turn gunman; I don't want to become a thief and there's no money in bootlegging! There's too many 'good citizens' engaged in that business as it is." "Tell me what to do," Near asked the ACLU. "Defy the court order or quit eating." Although Roger Baldwin felt Near could take the chance of resuming his publishing career, Carol Weiss King advised him against it. "If contempt proceedings are instituted against you," King informed Near, "it will tend to embarrass us. We should like to have the record in this case completely closed up after the injunction against you has been made permanent without tag ends of contempt tending to [cloud] the main issue."[34]

The role of the ACLU in the *Near* case ended precipitiously, however, when it was informed on November 30, 1928, that Near had turned his case over to attorneys from the *Chicago Tribune*.[35] A representative of the *Tribune* had visited Minneapolis to investigate his case, Near explained later, and "after a long talk, I wrote a letter to the editor of the *Tribune* and told him I would be glad to have them take the case and give it full publicity as well as the necessary legal remedy. They at once sent a battery of attorneys to Minneapolis and opened the fight. . . ." The *Tribune* was prepared to spend ten to fifteen thousand dollars on the case, Near reported, adding that "I simply had to do something and the *Tribune* offered me what seemed to be the only immediate avenue through which I could escape the Olson stranglehold. . . ."[36]

The ACLU informed the *Tribune* that "we could not be in the least unfriendly to sponsorship of the case by anybody else or by any other organization which might feel a similar interest to ours. We are therefore pleased that the *Chicago Tribune* has taken upon itself the rendering of this high public service." "At the same time," the Union added, "we cannot help feeling that there was a clear breach of faith on Mr. Near's part in allowing us to go to expense in this matter before he put it in the hands of the *Chicago Tribune*," and the Union inquired whether the *Tribune* would be willing to reimburse it for its expenses.[37] The managing editor of the *Tribune*, E. S. Beck, replied that the paper was under no obligation either "legal or moral" to reimburse the ACLU, and the *Tribune* subsequently also rejected an offer by the ACLU to file an *amicus curiae* brief in the *Near* case in the Supreme Court. The *Near* case thus proceeded to the Supreme Court under new management.[38]

This new management of the *Near* case consisted of a combination of the *Chicago Tribune* and the American Newspaper Publishers' Association (ANPA). In 1928, the ANPA created a Committee on Freedom of the Press, with Colonel Robert R. McCormick, publisher of the *Tribune*, as its chairman. Through the Freedom of the Press Committee, McCormick declared, the press was "in close touch with the movements menacing it."[39] Thus, the *Tribune*'s attorneys again challenged the gag law in the Minnesota trial court, but their arguments were overruled, and a permanent injunction was issued prohibiting Near from publishing the *Saturday Press* or any other malicious, scandalous, or defamatory publication. The *Tribune* then sponsored another appeal to the Minnesota Supreme Court, but on December 20, 1929, that court again upheld the gag law and ruled that it violated "neither the State nor Federal Constitution."[40]

At this point in the litigation in the *Near* case, Colonel McCormick felt that the case should be formally sponsored by the American Newspaper Publishers' Association, and a poll of the membership of the association resulted in an overwhelming vote in favor of sponsoring the case to the United States Supreme Court. The ANPA, however, was without funds to finance the appeal, and the *Chicago Tribune* continued to finance the litigation. It was vital to the freedom of the press, Colonel McCormick declared, for the Supreme Court to invalidate the gag law, since that law constituted "the greatest attack upon freedom of the press in the history of the republic" and was "tyrannical, despotic, unAmerican and oppressive." No newspaper could withstand the kind of attack that had been launched against the *Saturday Press*, he continued, and the gag law had to be declared unconstitutional "because it is a menace to good government, a shield for official corruption and rascality, and a formidable device for keeping the public in ignorance of facts which it is entitled to know."[41]

McCormick's views of the gag law were seconded by a resolution adopted at the ANPA convention in 1930. The resolution declared that the gag law was "violative of the First and Fourteenth Amendments of the Constitution of the United States, a peril to the right of property, and a menace to republican institutions. . . ." The law was a "dangerous and vicious invasion of personal liberties," the ANPA said, and it pledged to "cause its annulment and to prevent the enactment of similar legislation."[42]

The Supreme Court agreed to hear the appeal of *Near* v. *Minnesota* in the spring of 1930, but while the *Near* case was taking its somewhat tortuous path to the Court, the Red flag case, *Stromberg* v. *California*, had also been proceeding through the California courts. The *Stromberg* case began with a raid in the late summer of 1929 on a Communist-party youth camp in the foothills of the San Bernardino Mountains near Yucaipa. The raid was conducted by the American Legion post at Redlands and was led by the District Attorney of San Bernardino County, George H. Johnson— himself a Legionnaire. The seven adults in charge of the camp were arrested, and the children were sent home, except for three who were detained as witnesses. A red flag and quantities of Communist-party literature were also seized in the raid.

Among the adults arrested in the Yucaipa raid was Yetta Stromberg, who was the nineteen-year-old daughter of Russian immigrant parents. Born in Cleveland, Ohio, she was a graduate of Roosevelt High School in Los Angeles and had attended college for one year at UCLA. Yetta Stromberg's function at the camp had been to conduct a study hour each day for the forty children at the camp. The children were taught economics and history, with emphasis on "class consciousness, the solidarity of the workers, and the theory that the workers of the world are of one blood and brothers all." At seven o'clock each morning, the children under Stromberg's supervision also participated in a flag-raising ceremony. The flag was that of the Soviet Union, and the children recited a pledge of allegiance to "the workers' red flag, and to the cause for which it stands; one aim throughout our lives, freedom for the working class."[43]

Having taken the adults who had run the camp into custody, the San Bernardino authorities puzzled for a time over what offense they should be charged with. Prosecutions under the California Criminal Syndicalism Act had become unpopular, so the possibility of filing charges under that act was rejected. Finally, the authorities discovered the California "Red flag law," which had been enacted in 1919 but never used in a prosecution. The Red flag law made it a felony to display "a red flag, banner or badge, or any flag, badge, banner, or device of any color or form whatever in any public place or in any meeting place or public assembly or from or on any house, building or window as a sign, symbol or emblem of opposition to organized government or as an invitation or stimulus to anarchistic action or as an aid to propaganda that is of a seditious character. . . ."[44]

Although the Communist party youth camp was one mile from the nearest highway and could be reached only by a private road on private property by passing through two gates, the authorities learned of the flag-raising ceremony through questioning the children who had been at the camp. Yetta Stromberg and the other adults at the camp were therefore charged with having raised a red flag in violation of the Red flag law, and for conspiracy to do so, in an information filed by San Bernardino County District Attorney George H. Johnson on August 26, 1929.[45]

The national office of the American Civil Liberties Union was almost immediately notified of the raid on the Yucaipa camp by its Southern California branch, which urged the national office to aid in posting $10,300 in bail for those arrested "since the International Labor Defense guarantees against default."[46] The International Labor Defense (ILD) was a Communist-front organization created in 1925, and it was affiliated with the Comintern's International Red Aid. The ILD was pledged to the legal defense and support of class-war prisoners, and the Communist party was careful to include prominent non-Communists on the ILD's national committee, such as Eugene V. Debs, liberal theologian Robert Whitaker, and feminist Alice Stone Blackwell. The ILD, however, was tightly controlled by the Communist party, and its activities were dictated by Communist tactics and ideology, and it became "the most mature expression of a front thus far achieved by American Communists."[47]

The ILD did not limit itself to the sponsorship of cases involving Communists, but seized opportunities to involve itself in any prominent case that would serve as a propaganda vehicle. Thus, it played a prominent role in the campaign to save the anarchists Nicola Sacco and Bartolomeo Vanzetti, campaigned for the release of labor unionists Tom Mooney, Warren Billings, and J. B. McNamara, and seized control of the litigation in the *Scottsboro* cases in the early 1930s. The ILD also sent five dollars a month to over one hundred class-war prisoners in prisons throughout the United States.

Although the ILD undoubtedly contributed to the defense of radicals and dissidents during the 1920s and 1930s, its tactics often were more harmful than helpful to those being defended. It frequently appeared to be more interested in furthering the Communist party's propaganda purposes than in offering effective legal help to political defendants. And its open hostility to those who did not follow the party line drove away many non-Communists who were opposed to the injustices done in many cases, while making an effective legal defense more difficult in such cases.[48]

The ILD and the ACLU were nonetheless jointly involved in the California Red flag case almost from its inception, since the ACLU posted bail for Yetta Stromberg and the other defendants in the case, while the ILD retained a defense attorney. The attorney retained by the ILD was John Beardsley of Los Angeles, who was a member of the State Committee of the California CLU.[49]

Yetta Stromberg and her codefendants were tried in the Superior Court for San Bernardino County before Judge Charles L. Allison and a jury. The prosecution presented evidence establishing that the youth camp was supported by various Communist groups and that Yetta Stromberg had instructed the children in history and economics and had supervised the flag-raising ceremony. The prosecution also produced the Communist literature seized at the camp, but Yetta Stromberg denied that it had been used in instructing the children. She did, however, assume all responsibility for the flag-raising ceremony, and testified that the flag was the flag of the Soviet Union as well as that of the American Communist party.[50]

At the end of the trial, Judge Allison included a crucial instruction in his charge to the jury. The Red flag law prohibited the displaying of a Red flag as a "sign, symbol or emblem of opposition to organized government," as an "invitation or stimulus to anarchistic action," or as an "aid to propaganda that is of a seditious character," and Judge Allison instructed the jury that it could convict the defendants if it found that they had displayed the red flag at the camp for any one or for all of these purposes. Under these instructions, and without indicating whether the red flag had been displayed at the camp for all or for only one of these purposes, the jury found Yetta Stromberg guilty of unlawfully displaying a red flag and for conspiracy to do so, while also finding all but one of Stromberg's codefendants guilty of conspiracy to display a red flag.[51]

Yetta Stromberg was sentenced by Judge Allison to from twelve months to ten years in San Quentin, while the other defendants were sentenced to from six months to five years imprisonment. The only male defendant arrested at the Yucaipa camp, Isadore Berkowitz, escaped sentencing, however, by committing suicide after the conclusion of the trial.[52] Another rather unusual incident occurred at this time involving Mrs. Kate Crane-Gartz, described as a wealthy humanitarian and resident of Altadena. Mrs. Crane-Gartz wrote to Judge Allison urging leniency for the defendants in the Red flag case. Judge Allison responded by holding Mrs. Crane-Gartz in contempt of court and fining her seventy-five dollars. If "anyone could write a private letter to a judge advising him what to do about a case," Judge Allison said, "there would no longer be respect for our courts." Mrs. Crane-Gartz, however, would be heard from again in the Red flag case.[53]

Yetta Stromberg subsequently charged that the raid on the Yucaipa camp was part of "the brutal, unceasing offensive campaign of the bosses against the working class" and that the raid had been instigated by the "KKK, the Better America Federation and the American Legion who found that instead of the teaching of boy scout principles the children were being guided along the lines of working class solidarity. . . ." The trial in the San Bernardino Superior Court, Stromberg said, "exemplified the capitalist justice doled out to class conscious workers by the capitalist courts."[54]

After the conviction of the defendants in the Red flag case, both the ILD and the ACLU began considering whether to appeal, but the principal problem for both organizations was the financing of an appeal, a problem that was to plague the *Stromberg* case to its conclusion and would cause increasing strains in the relationships among the ACLU, the ILD, and John Beardsley as defense counsel. The ACLU posted appeal bonds for the defendants after their convictions, with the ILD again guaranteeing the bonds against default; financing an appeal, however, was another matter.[55] The executive committee of the Southern California branch of the ACLU voted in early November of 1929 to support an appeal in the Red flag case, but appealed to Roger Baldwin and the ACLU national office to finance the case. Clinton Taft, director of the Southern California branch, thus urged Baldwin to supply the funds "in order to test this law to the fullest extent. This is the first case to be tried under this code section since its enactment ten years ago." "We have difficulty [in raising] sufficient money to carry on our ordinary activities," Taft told Baldwin. "Do your best for us, Roger."[56]

Roger Baldwin and the national office of the ACLU, however, proved to be rather hard-nosed on the question of financing an appeal in the Red flag case. Before any money might be furnished for an appeal, Baldwin informed Taft, "we want to know the grounds on which the appeal is taken and what the chances are of getting results," since the national office was not likely to finance an appeal "in which it is fairly certain you are to be licked." "Also," Baldwin added, "give us a line on what the expenses are for, how much for court costs, how much for attorneys, how much the case has cost you so far and how much has been raised, [and] how much is the share of the ILD."[57]

In November of 1929, John Beardsley responded to Baldwin's inquiries, pointing out that an appeal in the Red flag case had already been filed "and the fight in the appellate court will be vigorous and very difficult." "From the standpoint of the ACLU the principal ground for appeal is that the law is, in our opinion, an infringement of freedom of speech, speaking broadly, in that it punishes the advocacy of communism," Beardsley continued. "The Constitution of California provides that citizens may freely speak, write and publish their emotions on all subjects, and that no law shall be passed restricting the freedom of speech. We take the ground that using a red flag as an emblem of a belief in communism, is a form of publication of belief." The courts, Beardsley admitted, had "hacked away at the constitutional guarantees until there is almost no such thing left as freedom of speech," but the "California [Red flag] law has never been tested and it is vital that it should be resisted strenuously."[58]

He had explained the issues in the Red flag case to Professor Zechariah Chafee of Harvard, Beardsley said, and Chafee expressed "his opinion that we do not have much chance on appeal." Even if he could not prevail on the freedom-of-speech issue, Beardsley argued, he thought he might win a reversal of the convictions of at least some of the defendants on technical grounds and that therefore "as to all but Yetta Stromberg our chances of reversal on appeal and saving the defendants from the penitentiary are good." "Although the ACLU has no particular interest in the technicalities of the law, it does have a very live interest in protecting citizens and non-citizens against imprisonment," Beardsley continued. "If the higher court should sustain the constitutionality of the red flag law but reverse the convictions of some of the defendants on technical grounds, the net result to the Cause of Freedom of Speech would be advantageous, though not so much so as if the law were knocked out. In my opinion the appeal should be pressed and I intend that it shall be pressed."[59]

Regarding the cost of the case, Beardsley informed Baldwin that he had been retained by the ILD as defense counsel at the trial but had been paid less than one-third of the fee promised him by the ILD. "I think the ILD ought to be able to raise its own funds and take care of their own cases . . . ," Beardsley concluded, "but the attack upon this statute concerns all of us as much as it does the radicals. If the attack is not made, and if it is not successful, we may look for a lot of prosecutions and a lot of imprisonments. If the attack should be successful, the cause for which the ACLU stands will be greatly strengthened. I feel that we must not think of lying down before this extremely restrictive statute."[60]

The ACLU national office sought the advice of Arthur Garfield Hays as to whether the Union "should join with the International Labor Defense in the appeal of the Yucaipa (Cal.) 'red flag' case," and Hays responded that he was familiar "with the Yucaipa case. I think we should join in."[61] In response to Beardsley's appeal for help, Roger Baldwin promised to "take it up here and see what we can do to help finance the appeal. I agree with you as to its importance."[62] The ACLU and the ILD subsequently agreed to jointly pay Beardsley's fee for the trial of the Red flag case, and the two organizations also came to a vague understanding that they would be jointly responsible for the cost of the appeal. The execution of this vague agreement, however, turned out to constitute more promise than performance on the part of either organization.[63]

John Beardsley meanwhile had perfected an appeal in the Red flag case to the California District Court of Appeal for the Fourth Appellate District, and on June 27, 1930, the court handed Beardsley a partial victory by reversing the conspiracy convictions of all of the defendants, while affirming Yetta Stromberg's conviction for displaying a red flag. The court admitted that the clause of the Red flag law prohibiting the displaying of a red flag as a "sign, symbol or emblem of opposition to organized government" might be an unconstitutional infringement upon freedom of speech, since the clause might apply to "peaceful and orderly opposition to a government as organized and controlled by one political party by those of another political party equally high minded and patriotic, which did not agree with the one in power." On the other hand, the court upheld the validity of the clauses in the Red flag law prohibiting the displaying of a red flag as "an invitation or stimulus to anarchistic action" or as "an aid to propaganda that is of a seditious character." Since Yetta Stromberg could have been convicted by the jury under these valid clauses of the law, the District Court of Appeal concluded, her conviction for unlawfully displaying a red flag was valid.[64]

"I see you won something at least, if not the main point, in the red flag appeal," Roger Baldwin wrote Beardsley. "Our congratulations to you. . . . What are the conditions on which you will handle Miss Stromberg's appeal to the Supreme Court of California?" Beardsley replied that he was worried that the San Bernardino County District Attorney might retry all of the defendants on the conspiracy charges, and that it appeared "quite likely I could get an agreement from the Prosecutor to drop that charge if I would let up on the appeal as to Yetta Stromberg and my attack on the constitutionality of the [Red flag] law. Personally I am not at all inclined to consider any such arrangement. And I am confident the . . . other women would not want to buy their freedom at the cost of surrendering as to Yetta." "Of course, my main contention is that the law is unconstitutional," Beardsley said. "I'm trying, too, to avoid trying the conspiracy charges again, and to free Yetta Stromberg, whom I have referred to, at times, as Joan of Arc."[65]

Beardsley accordingly filed an appeal of Yetta Stromberg's case in the California Supreme Court, but that court refused to hear the appeal on July 24, 1930. "Please advise if all steps exhausted in Red Flag case," Roger Baldwin telegraphed Beardsley after the California Supreme Court's action. "No," Beardsley replied. "I advise appeal to Federal Supreme Court on constitutionality."[66] Yetta Stromberg had been working as an organizer for the ILD in Seattle while free on appeal bond, but, Beardsley realized, unless he could "get the United States Supreme Court to go into the case, there is nothing more that can be done and Yetta will

have to surrender herself very soon for delivery to San Quentin." Since the
decision of the California District Court of Appeal, Beardsley told Roger
Baldwin, he had spent almost all of his time on the Red flag case, and he
would now have to spend more time on an appeal to the U.S. Supreme
Court. "No arrangement has been made at all for paying me anything," he
concluded. "I let you think about that a little. Meanwhile I am having to
go right ahead."[67]

Despite his growing irritation with both the ACLU and the ILD for
their failure to financially support the *Stromberg* case, Beardsley filed the
appeal to the U.S. Supreme Court, and in order to save costs also petitioned
the Court to allow the appeal to proceed *in forma pauperis*. The Supreme
Court subsequently granted the motion to proceed *in forma pauperis* and
noted probable jurisdiction in the case. Despite this favorable turn of
events, however, Beardsley had tired of fighting a behind-the-scenes battle with both the ACLU and the ILD to obtain some remuneration for his
services in the *Stromberg* case, and he was now at the end of his patience.

Although the ILD had originally retained him as defense counsel for the
trial of the Red flag case, that organization had not yet even paid him his
fee for that trial. And while the ACLU had subsequently agreed to pay
half of the trial fee, Beardsley had not yet been fully paid, despite many
appeals to both the ILD and the ACLU for money. In one of his many appeals for financial support to the ILD, Beardsley pointed out that if the
Red flag law was upheld, "members of the Communist Party, citizens and
non-citizens alike, would be subject to prosecution whenever they might
display the red flag of their Party and of Soviet Russia. Therefore, it seems
to me of very vital importance that your organization should carry to the
highest court possible the fight against the enforcement of that law." "I
haven't any idea," Beardsley told the ILD, "how long you think that a
lawyer can go . . . devoting a large share of his time to your work without
any money at all on account," but it was not, he assured the ILD, "the
pleasantest thing to have to correspond for weeks on end about the matter
of fees."[68]

The ILD's response to such appeals, however, was to pressure Beardsley personally and through the ACLU to reduce his fees for his work in
the *Stromberg* case.[69] The ACLU defended Beardsley's fees as being
"moderate," and when national ACLU personnel resisted attempts by the
ILD to pressure Beardsley on the question of his fees, the ILD responded
testily. "Even though you think that we stand very little chance of getting
a reduction [of Beardsley's fees]," George Mauer of the ILD wrote the
ACLU's Forrest Bailey, "nevertheless an effort should, really must be,
made. Why shouldn't you try to save money for the ILD as well as the
ACLU?" "I do not understand your language when you say that an effort

must be made," Bailey replied to Mauer. "As to the ACLU's willingness to save the ILD's money as well as to save ourselves money, I should think there has been considerable evidence on that point in the past."[70]

The ILD nevertheless continued to resist paying Beardsley's fees for the appeal in the *Stromberg* case, contending that they were "*not* very modest" and that "in view of the nature of the case . . . that Beardsley should have been much more considerate than he is." Beardsley, on the other hand, was complaining to the ACLU that the ILD seemed "always to be short of funds, and no matter how low I make my charges they practically always want me to reduce them. . . ."[71]

Finally, in communications with the ACLU in March of 1931, after the Supreme Court had agreed to review the *Stromberg* case, Beardsley called the hands of both the ILD and the ACLU. Both organizations had failed to pay what had been promised in the case, he pointed out, while there was still "a fighting chance on the appeal. Justices Holmes and Brandeis, in their dissenting opinion in the *Gitlow* case, have gone much farther in upholding the constitutional right of freedom of speech (more broadly freedom of expression) than the Court need go to uphold my contentions in [the *Stromberg*] case." "Of course the case is of importance not only to the ILD, and the Communists, and to Yetta Stromberg, whose personal liberty is at stake, but also to the ACLU," Beardsley continued. "If somebody will provide the expense of a trip to Washington, and I am assured that the fee will be paid, as much as possible now, and the remainder as soon as may be within a reasonable time, I shall of course be glad to go to Washington and make the argument. We have some sort of a fighting chance for a decision upsetting the [Red flag] law on constitutional grounds."[72]

The ill-concealed threat by Beardsley to abandon the case unless he was paid led the ACLU to appeal to the ILD to "pay something immediately and specify intentions and possibilities,"[73] but neither the ILD nor the ACLU ultimately paid John Beardsley's fees for the appeal of the *Stromberg* case to the Supreme Court. Instead, they were paid by Mrs. Kate Crane-Gartz, who had been fined by the trial judge for urging leniency for the defendants in the Red flag case.

Roger Baldwin expressed the ACLU's thanks to Mrs. Crane-Gartz for her "great generosity in paying [Beardsley's] entire fee . . . for the appeal in Yetta Stromberg's case." "As you know," Baldwin said, "we raised half of his original fee and were prepared to raise part of his fee on the appeal. But both the ILD and ourselves felt that it was too high, and certainly beyond our means." The appeal to the Supreme Court, Baldwin continued, "will settle the issue of the Red Flag Laws for the whole country, and while I feel that the decision is going to be adverse, we will at least know one more bad rule of the unhappy game of suppression."[74]

Stromberg v. *California* thus joined the *Near* case before the Supreme Court for consideration during its 1930 term, and the cases raised the twin rights of freedom of speech and freedom of the press, which the Court had assumed in the *Gitlow* case in 1925 to be protected by the Due Process Clause of the Fourteenth Amendment. In both the *Stromberg* and *Near* cases, counsel on both sides largely took this *Gitlow* assumption to be a reality and argued the questions of freedom of speech and of the press on the merits.

Counsel for J. M. Near thus asserted that beginning "with *Gitlow* v. *New York* . . . in 1925, and following with *Whitney* v. *California* . . . and *Fiske* v. *Kansas* . . . in 1927, this court has thrice enunciated the doctrine that the right of free speech and press is protected as a liberty belonging to all persons under the Fourteenth Amendment." Similarly, John Beardsley argued on behalf of Yetta Stromberg that "freedom of speech and of the press—which are protected by the 1st Amendment from abridgment by Congress—are among the fundamental personal rights and 'liberties' protected by the due process clause of the 14th Amendment from impairment by the states."[75]

Counsel for the state of California in the *Stromberg* case did not dispute this argument, but rather assumed that freedom of speech and freedom of the press were guaranteed by the Due Process Clause. Minnesota counsel did assert in the *Near* case that the gag law did not violate either the First or Fourteenth Amendments, since the First Amendment "is a limitation of the right of congress and not on the rights of the states," but this argument was not pressed, and Minnesota counsel quickly turned to the merits.[76]

On the merits, counsel for Near argued that the Minnesota gag law allowed the imposition of a prior restraint upon freedom of the press, a restriction that was outlawed by the constitutional protection of freedom of the press in America. A permanent injunction against the publication of the *Saturday Press* was a form of prior restraint, it was argued, since such a restriction on publication assumed that future issues of the *Press* would be scandalous, malicious, or defamatory, rather than allowing publication of those issues and punishing such offenses if they occurred.

Minnesota counsel, on the other hand, denied that the gag law authorized the imposition of prior restraints on publication. Near was free to publish the *Saturday Press* under the trial court's injunction, it was argued, as long as he did not publish scandalous, malicious, or defamatory materials. In any case, Minnesota counsel continued, the gag law was not aimed at legitimate newspapers, but at "the scandal monger and professional defamer. To such a class the liberty of the press affords no sanctuary. The Constitution of the United States does not safeguard them in the practice of their nefarious trade."[77]

John Beardsley argued that the Red flag law was a violation of the freedom of speech protected by the Due Process Clause, since there was no legislative finding in the law, as there had been in the New York Criminal Anarchy Act in the *Gitlow* case, of a clear and present danger arising from displaying a red flag. It was difficult to imagine, he said, "a time and place or circumstances more remote" than in the circumstances surrounding the display of the red flag in the *Stromberg* case.[78]

Beardsley also noted that the California District Court of Appeal had in effect held the first clause of the Red flag law invalid, but had upheld Yetta Stromberg's conviction on the basis of the last two clauses of the law. Yet, he pointed out, the trial judge had instructed the jury that it could convict if it found the red flag had been displayed for any of the purposes prohibited by the law, and the jury had returned a general verdict of guilty. Beardsley therefore argued that Yetta Stromberg might have been convicted by the jury for displaying a red flag as a symbol "of opposition to organized government," yet this part of the law had been invalidated by the District Court of Appeal. Because there had been no showing of a clear and present danger of unlawful action that might result from Stromberg's display of the red flag, and because she might have been convicted for displaying a red flag for purposes protected by the guarantee of freedom of speech, Beardsley urged the Court to reverse her conviction.[79]

Counsel for the state of California argued, on the other hand, that in passing the Red flag law, the California legislature had obviously concluded that such displays created clear and present dangers of unlawful action. Even if the clause of the law prohibiting the displaying of a Red flag as a symbol of opposition to organized government was invalid, California counsel argued, the state clearly had the power to prohibit such displays to prevent the encouragement of anarchistic action or seditious propaganda, and the Court should not second-guess the jury as to what part of the law the jury had relied on in its verdict. And citing the *Gitlow* case, counsel for the state concluded that while the children Yetta Stromberg was training "would not be likely to commit immediately any acts of violence, yet she was creating in them the spark which, when fanned, might burst into a great conflagration."[80]

The Court that heard the arguments in *Stromberg* v. *California* and *Near* v. *Minnesota* during January and April of 1931 had undergone significant personnel changes during the previous year. Chief Justice Taft had become almost paranoid with concern over what he perceived as dangerously liberal trends both on the Court and in the country at large. Writing privately in 1929, Taft said that "as long as things continue as they are, and I am able to answer in my place, I must stay on the court in order to prevent the Bolsheviki from getting control. . . ." The dissents of Holmes, Brandeis, and Stone from the conservative majority's decisions also increasingly irritated the chief justice, and he especially resented Brandeis's trips to Harvard, where he "communed with Frankfurter and that crowd." Frankfurter, Taft felt, seemed "to be in touch with every Bolshevik, Communist movement in the country."[81]

Taft also wrote to Justice Butler in 1929, expressing the hope that the conservative majority would remain intact and "prevent disastrous reversals of our present attitude." With Butler, Van Devanter, Sutherland, Sanford, and McReynolds on the Court, he said, "there will be five to steady the boat. . . . We must not all give up at once." Within a year, however, deteriorating health forced Taft to retire, and Justice Sanford died in 1930, diminishing the conservative bloc to four—Butler, Sutherland, Van Devanter, and McReynolds.[82]

To replace Taft, President Hoover appointed Charles Evans Hughes as chief justice, and after the Senate rejection of Court of Appeals Judge John J. Parker, Owen Roberts was appointed to the Sanford vacancy.[83] These personnel changes were probably crucial to the outcome of the litigation in *Near* v. *Minnesota*, since the four conservatives dissented in that case. Had Taft and Sanford still been on the bench, the *Near* case would probably have been decided differently.

Stromberg v. *California*, however, was decided first by the Court on May 18, 1931, and in a majority opinion written by Chief Justice Hughes, the Court confirmed the assumption in the *Gitlow* case in explicit terms. Hughes accepted the argument by John Beardsley that it was impossible to determine whether Yetta Stromberg had been convicted by the jury for displaying a red flag as a symbol of "opposition to organized government," or as an "invitation or stimulus to anarchistic action," or as an "aid to propaganda that is of a seditious character"—or, indeed, for displaying a red flag for all three of these purposes. "The verdict against [Yetta Stromberg] was a general one," Chief Justice Hughes said. "It did not specify the ground upon which it rested. . . . It follows that instead of its being permissible to hold, with the state court, that the verdict could be sustained if any one of the clauses of the statute were found to be valid, the necessary conclusion from the manner in which the case was sent to the jury is that, if any of the clauses in question is invalid under the Federal Constitution, the conviction cannot be upheld."[84]

And, Hughes continued, Yetta Stromberg's conviction had to be reversed because the provision of the Red flag law prohibiting the displaying of a red flag as a symbol of "opposition to organized government" violated the freedom of speech protected by the Due Process Clause of the Fourteenth Amendment. "It has been determined," Hughes said, "that the conception of liberty under the due process clause of the 14th Amendment embraces the right of free speech." The first clause of the Red flag law, he concluded, was an invalid restriction of freedom of speech because it could be construed to prohibit legitimate, lawful opposition to the government, while the "maintenance of the opportunity for free political discussion to the end that government may be responsive to the will of the people and that changes may be obtained by lawful means, an opportunity essential to the security of the Republic, is a fundamental principle of our constitutional system."[85]

Two weeks after the decision in the *Stromberg* case, the Court decided *Near* v. *Minnesota*, and with Chief Justice Hughes again writing for the Court, it repeated its validation of the *Gitlow* assumption in declaring the Minnesota gag law unconstitutional. "It is no longer open to doubt," Hughes said, "that the liberty of the press and of speech is within the liberty safeguarded by the due process clause of the 14th Amendment. It was found impossible to conclude that this essential personal liberty of the citizen was left unprotected by the general guaranty of fundamental rights of person and property."[86]

Tracing the evolution of the right of freedom of the press in England and in America, Hughes pointed out that it had been "generally, if not universally, considered that it is the chief purpose of the guaranty to prevent previous restraints upon publication." Blackstone, he noted, had thus said that the "liberty of the press is indeed essential to the nature of a free state; but this consists in laying no *previous* restraints upon publications, and not in freedom from censure for criminal matter when published." And the "fact that for approximately one hundred and fifty years," Hughes said, "there has been almost an entire absence of attempts to impose previous restraints upon publications relating to the malfeasance of public officers is significant of the deep-seated conviction that such restraints would violate constitutional right."[87]

The injunctions authorized by the Minnesota gag law, Hughes held, constituted prior restraints upon the press, and in light of the historic purposes of freedom of the press, the law was unconstitutional. "The recognition of authority to impose previous restraint upon publications in order to protect the community against the circulation of charges of misconduct, and especially of official misconduct," Hughes concluded, "necessarily would carry with it the admission of the authority of the censor against which the constitutional barrier was erected."[88]

Justices McReynolds and Butler dissented in the *Stromberg* case, and Butler also explicitly acknowledged the important step the Court was taking in validating the *Gitlow* assumption. The Court, he said, had held that the first clause of the Red flag law "denied the right of free speech, and the court holds that right to be included in the concept of 'liberty' safeguarded against state action by the due process clause of the 14th Amendment." On the basis of the record in the *Stromberg* case, Butler argued, "the court is not called on to decide whether the mere display of a flag as the emblem of a purpose, whatever its sort, is speech within the meaning of the constitutional protection of speech and press or to decide whether such freedom is a part of the liberty protected by the 14th Amendment. . . ."[89]

Justice Butler, joined by Justices Van Devanter, Sutherland, and McReynolds, again dissented in the *Near* case and again noted the significance of the step the Court was taking. The federal Constitution did not protect freedom of speech or of the press against state action prior to the adoption of the Fourteenth Amendment, he noted, and the Court "was not called on until 1925 to decide whether the 'liberty' protected by the 14th Amendment includes the right of free speech or press." That question, Butler pointed out, "has now been finally answered in the affirmative." But even assuming the Court was correct in its ruling on this point, he argued that scandalous, defamatory, or malicious publications such as the *Saturday Press* could not legitimately claim protection under a proper construction of the freedom of the press.[90]

"The girl Red," as Yetta Stromberg had been dubbed by the press, drifted back into obscurity after the decision of her case by the Court. And John Beardsley must have been amused when the International Labor Defense announced that the *Stromberg* case was a major ILD victory in its defense of "class-war prisoners." "The most recent victory of the working class through the ILD," it proclaimed, "is the decision of the United States Supreme Court, which freed Yetta Stromberg. . . . " The protest and anger of "the workers in the whole country against the California 'Red Flag' law was so strong," the ILD asserted, "that it forced the Supreme Court to reverse the decisions of the lower courts."[91]

Howard Guilford and J. M. Near resumed their careers as publishers in Minneapolis after the gag law was invalidated in the *Near* case. On September 6, 1934, however, Guilford was again ambushed as he drove home. Another car pulled alongside him, and Guilford was hit in the head by a shotgun blast that killed him instantly. Near charged that Guilford had been assassinated by Communists. "Undoubtedly Howard was killed by hired assassins," he said, "and I think the killers were hired by Communists. Of course, Guilford had plenty of personal enemies, but I'm positive they had nothing to do with his murder." Near himself escaped such a violent death. He died of natural causes on April 18, 1936, at the age of sixty-two.[92]

The legal difficulties of Yetta Stromberg, Howard Guilford, and J. M. Near had led to decisions by the Court in which freedom of speech and freedom of the press were finally explicitly acknowledged as guarantees of the Due Process Clause of the Fourteenth Amendment. In retrospect, it seems somewhat startling that this development was not the subject of more vigorous argument before the Court than was the case. After Walter Pollak persuaded the Court to state its assumption in the *Gitlow* case, appellants in the subsequent cases simply took that assumption for granted and devoted little time to questioning the validity of that assumption. Aside from two or three anemic attacks on the *Gitlow* assumption, counsel for the states did not really contest the issue. Freedom of speech and freedom of the press were read into the Due Process Clause, therefore, with little real debate over the significance of the step the Court was taking.

This lack of debate by litigants before the Court was apparently also matched by a lack of debate inside the Court. Professor Klaus Heberle has examined the papers of the justices on the Court during the period in question and has discovered little evidence of any full consideration of the step the Court was taking. The process of reading freedom of speech and freedom of the press into the Due Process Clause, he concluded, was apparently a process of "absent-minded incrementalism."[93]

This lack of any thorough debate—either on or off the Court—on the issue of nationalizing freedom of speech and freedom of the press may explain the lack of agreement on the part of close observers of the Court,[94] as well as among the justices themselves, as to when freedom of speech and freedom of the press were in fact made applicable to the states. Justice Stone, writing to Justice Frankfurter, later asserted that "free speech was held to be guaranteed by the 14th Amendment in *Fiske* v. *Kansas* by a unanimous Court, Sanford writing in 1926."[95] Not only was Stone's date wrong, but others who had participated in the *Gitlow-Fiske-Stromberg-Near* line of cases disagreed with his assessment of the *Fiske* case. Chief Justice Hughes left a memorandum in his autobiographical notes referring to the *Stromberg* and *Near* cases and stating that it "fell to my lot as Chief Justice in 1930 to write the opinions of the Court . . . holding that freedom of speech and of the press was embraced by the Fourteenth Amendment."[96]

Hughes's date, like Stone's, was incorrect, but his position is buttressed by the dissents in the *Stromberg* and *Near* cases. Justices Butler, McReynolds, Sutherland, and Van Devanter had also participated in the *Gitlow-Fiske-Stromberg-Near* line of cases, and Butler, speaking for the four in the *Near* case, clearly indicated that the Court was taking a step it had not taken previously. The Court had not been called upon to answer the question of whether freedom of speech or freedom of the press were guaranteed by the Due Process Clause until 1925, Butler said, but that "question has now been finally answered in the affirmative." It seems apparent that Butler and the other conservatives did not believe that the *Fiske* case had supplied such an affirmative answer.[97]

It would appear, therefore, that some justices—Stone, and perhaps Brandeis and Holmes—accepted the *Gitlow* assumption as an immediate reality that was soon confirmed by the *Fiske* case, even though the Court did not mention freedom of speech in that case. Other justices—notably Butler, McReynolds, Sutherland, and Van Devanter—apparently felt that the *Gitlow* assumption left the question of nationalizing freedom of speech and freedom of the press undecided, and the issue was not decided for them until the *Stromberg* and *Near* cases. It is probably most accurate, therefore, when speaking of the nationalization of freedom of speech and of the press, to say that the process occurred in the minds of different justices at different times during the *Gitlow-Fiske-Stromberg-Near* line of cases, but that a majority of the Court did not explicitly acknowledge what had happened until the *Stromberg* and *Near* cases in 1931. Perhaps the most accurate summation of what had occurred is Justice Sutherland's statement in 1936 that freedom of speech and freedom of the press had been held to be guarantees of the Due Process Clause in "a series of decisions of this court, beginning with *Gitlow* v. *New York* . . . and ending with *Near* v. *Minnesota.* . . ."[98]

Despite the lack of agreement on the question of when freedom of speech and freedom of the press were nationalized, the Court quickly closed ranks on the question of whether those freedoms were guarantees of the Due Process Clause. The unity of the Court on this point was symbolized in 1936 by its unanimous decision in *Grosjean* v. *American Press Company*, invalidating a Louisiana tax on newspapers that was measured by circulation. The tax violated the freedom of the press, Justice Sutherland declared for the Court, and "the states are precluded from abridging freedom of speech or of the press by force of the due process clause of the Fourteenth Amendment."[99] And this momentum in favor of the nationalization of First Amendment freedoms continued on into 1937, when the Court, again unanimously, held in *DeJonge* v. *Oregon* that the First Amendment's guarantee of freedom of assembly and petition was also embraced by the Due Process Clause.[100]

Criminal Syndicalism in Oregon: The *DeJonge* Case

As in many other states during the post–World War I Red Scare, the Oregon legislature had passed a criminal syndicalism act in 1919. In addition to prohibiting the advocacy of force, violence, or sabotage as a means of political or industrial change, a 1933 amendment to the Oregon act provided that "any person who shall orally or in writing or by printed matter call together or who shall distribute or circulate written or printed matter calling together or who shall preside at or conduct or assist in conducting any assemblage of persons, or any organization, or any society, or any group which teaches or advocates the doctrine of criminal syndicalism or sabotage is guilty of a felony. . . ."[101]

In 1934, forty-three year old Dirk DeJonge was a leader of the Communist party in Oregon and had been the Communist candidate for mayor of Portland. He was heavily engaged in organizing unemployed councils under Communist auspices when a maritime strike closed Portland to shipping in the spring of 1934. DeJonge later said that the maritime employers "had boasted that, should the maritime workers walk out, thousands of unemployed would be clamoring at the docks for jobs—that Portland's jobless army would break the strike." The employers "got a rude jolt," DeJonge said, since the "unemployed of Portland did not scab."[102]

On July 11, however, some maritime companies attempted to move cargo over the opposition of picketing strikers, and in the melee that followed the Portland police shot four of the pickets. At approximately the same time, the "Red Squad" of the Portland Police Department conducted a series of raids on the Communist party's Workers' Book Store, the headquarters of the party and of the International Labor Defense, making arrests and seizing files and literature.

In response to these events, the Communist party called for a mass protest meeting to be held at the Unemployed Unity Center at 68 Southwest Alder Street on Friday, July 27. The meeting was advertised by mimeographed handbills issued by the party, denouncing the raids and the shooting of the longshoremen. A crowd of between 150 and 300 persons, only 10 to 15 percent of whom were Communists, gathered at the center and were addressed by several speakers. The meeting was clearly being held under the auspices of the Communist party, and Edward R. Denny, a party member, served as chairman.

Among those addressing the meeting was Dirk DeJonge. He protested conditions in the county jail and denounced the police raids and the shooting of the longshoremen. The police raids, DeJonge charged, constituted a "stepping stone on the part of the steamship companies and stevedoring companies to break the maritime longshoremen's and seamen's strike by pitting the maritime longshoremen and seamen against the Communist movement." DeJonge urged the crowd to join the Communist party and to attend a Communist street rally at Fourth and Alder Streets the next evening.[103]

While the meeting was in progress, it was raided by the Portland police, and DeJonge and fellow Communists Edward Denny, Don Cluster, and Earl Stewart were arrested. They were charged with violating the criminal syndicalism act and were remanded to the county jail in lieu of bail. On September 29, the Multnomah County grand jury indicted DeJonge, Cluster, Stewart, and Denny, charging that they had violated the criminal syndicalism act by unlawfully presiding at, conducting, and assisting in conducting a meeting of the Communist party at which the doctrine of criminal syndicalism had been advocated. Bail was finally reduced to $500 for each of the accused, and they were released on bail on October 2, after spending seventy days in jail.[104]

There was a branch of the American Civil Liberties Union as well as the

International Labor Defense in Portland, but while the ILD appealed to the Portland CLU for help in defending DeJonge, some members of the Portland CLU had strong objections to associating themselves with the Communist-controlled ILD, since, as one of them said, "cooperation with the ILD has brought [the ACLU] only grief. . . ." The result was that De-Jonge's defense at his trial was undertaken by the ILD without the Portland CLU's aid.[105]

DeJonge's trial began on October 30, 1934, in the Circuit Court of Multnomah County before Judge Jacob Kanzler and a jury. DeJonge was defended by ILD attorneys Irwin Goodman, Harry Gross, Dan Hartley, and Clifford O'Brien. Although the district attorney's office nominally represented the state, a special prosecutor, Stanley M. "Larry" Doyle, was the principal prosecutor. Doyle was a former leader of the American Legion–affiliated Forty et Eight organization, and his services were volunteered in the *DeJonge* case by the American Legion and other veteran's groups in Portland.[106]

Members of the Communist party attended the trial, wearing red badges and banners reading "Workers' Jury" on their coats. Special prosecutor Doyle also charged that he had received threats demanding the "unconditional release" of DeJonge and the others charged under the criminal syndicalism act. The threats had also demanded that Doyle "stop Fascist attacks on Portland workers and free class war prisoners."[107]

The state put on evidence at the trial demonstrating that the Communist party advocated the violent overthrow of the government and that the party had organized the meeting at the Unity Center. It was an offense under the criminal syndicalism act, the state contended, if a meeting was held under the auspices of an organization advocating violent overthrow of the government, even if no advocacy of violent overthrow or advocacy of other unlawful action occurred at the meeting. DeJonge, the state said, had unlawfully presided at, conducted, or assisted in conducting a meeting under the auspices of the Communist party, and he was therefore guilty of violating the criminal syndicalism act.

Counsel for DeJonge argued, on the other hand, that under the criminal syndicalism act, and under the indictment returned by the grand jury, not only was the state required to prove that the meeting at the Unity Center had been held under the auspices of the Communist party, it also had to prove that violent overthrow or other unlawful action had been advocated at the meeting. And the defense produced several witnesses who had attended the meeting and who testified that there had been no advocacy of any illegal acts at the meeting.

During DeJonge's trial, special prosecutor Doyle engaged in serious misconduct. At one point, Doyle approached a retired military officer, who had testified in DeJonge's behalf, with an offer of a job and restored military retirement pay if he would change his testimony.[108] Doyle also suggested to the jury in his closing argument that DeJonge was lucky not to have been subjected to mob justice. "I will tell you the type of man this DeJonge is," Doyle told the jury. "And I will tell you further than that, each and every one of this jury, if these were war times, there wouldn't be a trial here at all; I wouldn't be able to hold down the sentiment that has accumulated as a result of this man's dangerous activities."[109] The prosecution also charged that DeJonge's Communist comrades had packed the courtroom during the trial and had left Communist literature in the rest rooms of the courthouse, where the jurors would find it. Two hundred Communists had lined the corridors outside the courtroom, the prosecution also alleged, forcing the jury to pass by them when it retired.[110]

DeJonge was allowed to address the jury at the end of the trial, and during a forty-five minute statement, he argued that "Communists do not advocate force and violence. It is the capitalist class, not the workers, that uses force and violence." Commenting on DeJonge's address to the jury in an editorial entitled "Their Song of Hate," the Portland *Oregon Journal* labeled DeJonge's denial that Communists advocated violence a "farce of farces." DeJonge's statement had been "absurd," the *Journal* said, since force "and violence are what Communism exists for." Under Oregon law, a jury in a noncapital criminal case could convict a defendant by a less than unanimous vote of ten to two, and on November 20, 1934, the jury in the *DeJonge* case returned a verdict of guilty by a ten to two vote, but recommended leniency.[111]

Although the Portland branch of the American Civil Liberties Union had not participated in DeJonge's defense, one of the Union's attorneys, Gus Solomon, followed the trial closely and reported to the national ACLU office on the proceedings. The trial had been "bitterly fought," Solomon reported, "and we believe the Court permitted a great number of things in evidence that were clearly erroneous and which constitute reversible error." The jury had recommended leniency, he continued, but "Judge Kanzler, the trial judge, is a big American Legion man and he is very amenable to pressure from the so-called respectable groups. It seems to me that the probabilities are that Dirk DeJonge will be sent to the penitentiary for a long term. . . . " Solomon suggested that it might help DeJonge if lawyers affiliated with the national ACLU office, who were graduates of Columbia Law School, sent letters to Judge Kanzler urging him to be lenient in sentencing DeJonge, since the judge was also a Columbia Law School graduate. The letters should emphasize that their authors were Columbia graduates, Solomon stressed, and "[n]othing should be left to the Judge's imagination because he has none."[112]

Before his sentencing, DeJonge addressed Judge Kanzler and stated that he did not ask for "clemency." The judge asked DeJonge if "you want me to understand that you do not want me to follow the recommendation of leniency made by the jury?" "No, not that," DeJonge responded, "but I am not asking for clemency." Judge Kanzler concluded that "you do not want me to follow the recommendation [of the jury]." The judge had reportedly received many letters and telegrams urging him to spare De-Jonge, and supporters of DeJonge packed the courtroom at his sentencing. Judge Kanzler assured his audience that he knew what "it is to earn bread by the sweat of my brow" and that his "utmost sympathies are with the working class." He had done everything in his power to assure De-Jonge a fair trial, he said, but a "jury composed of good American citizens returned the verdict of guilty." Judge Kanzler then sentenced DeJonge to seven years in the Oregon state prison.[113]

Although the ILD again requested the aid of the Portland CLU in appealing the *DeJonge* case to the Oregon Supreme Court, members of the Portland CLU continued to object to any association with the ILD, arguing that such cooperation with the ILD was against ACLU policy. Roger Baldwin wrote to Gus Solomon explaining that in general the ACLU did not "take cases jointly with [the ILD] when the responsibility is divided. Our policies are different and it simply does not work out." "But on appeals," Baldwin continued, "where the question of law alone is involved and there is no chance to use a proceeding for propaganda, we often do go in either by filing a brief *amicus curiae*, associating one of our lawyers on the appeal, or by raising money." Nevertheless, the Portland CLU did not aid in the appeal of the *DeJonge* case to the Oregon Supreme Court by the ILD.[114]

On November 26, 1935, the Oregon Supreme Court upheld the criminal syndicalism act as it had been applied in DeJonge's case, and held that it was not necessary for illegal advocacy to occur in a meeting held under the auspices of the Communist party in order for a violation of that act to occur. It was sufficient to establish a violation of the act, the court continued, for the state to prove that a meeting had been held under the auspices of the Communist party and that DeJonge had aided in the conduct of, or had presided at, such a meeting. And since the evidence clearly proved that the Communist party engaged in illegal advocacy, that the meeting at the Unity Center had been held under the party's auspices, and that De-Jonge had assisted in conducting the meeting, the court affirmed his conviction under the act.[115]

The Oregon Supreme Court also affirmed the conviction of DeJonge's colleague Edward Denny, who had also been convicted under the criminal syndicalism act for his participation in the meeting at the Unity Center, and both were confined to prison to begin serving their sentences. The International Labor Defense denounced the court's rulings and declared DeJonge and Denny to be the newest "recruits in the ranks of labor's prisoners, just begun to serve your vicious sentences in Oregon's dungeons, victims of Oregon's criminal syndicalism law—the workers of the Northwest, steeled in struggle, and strengthened by the solidarity of the workers throughout the land will get you free." DeJonge also denounced the decision of the Oregon Supreme Court. "That the ruling class courts intend making an example of me is clear," he declared, "and their attacks upon the working class will not end there."[116]

After the Oregon Supreme Court's decision, the American Civil Liberties Union for the first time actively intervened in the *DeJonge* case. The court's decision, Gus Solomon pointed out to the ACLU national office, allowed prosecutions of individuals participating in entirely peaceful meetings held under the auspices of the Communist party, and the decision in that respect was "particularly vicious." The ILD attorneys were preparing a petition for a rehearing in the case, Solomon said, and he sought and received permission to file an *amicus curiae* brief on behalf of the American Civil Liberties Union supporting the petition for a rehearing. The ACLU staff attorney with whom Solomon was corresponding agreed that the *DeJonge* decision was "as rotten a bit of opinion writing as one will find any place. . . ."[117] The Oregon Supreme Court, however, denied the petition for a rehearing.

After the court had refused to rehear the case, Gus Solomon said later, it appeared that "the ILD was going to drop the matter there, and after talking it over with [one of the ILD attorneys] and some members of the ILD and the District Organizer of the Communist Party, I suggested that this would be a proper case for the ACLU to handle"; it was agreed that the ACLU would undertake an appeal to the United States Supreme Court. On January 25, 1936, Solomon therefore wrote the ACLU national office, requesting that it "have some of your lawyers in New York look into the problem [of the *DeJonge* case], and let me know whether they think that there is a possibility of getting the United States Supreme Court to reverse the case. If so, will you kindly send us the forms? The reason why we are asking you for them is that we have had no experience appealing a case from the State Supreme Court to the United States Supreme Court. . . ." "We can write the brief in Portland, but of course would appreciate any suggestions and help which may be given to us by men who appeared in the previous cases which have been appealed to the Supreme Court of the U.S.," Solomon continued. "If the Supreme Court accepts jurisdiction, it will be pretty difficult for one of us to go back to Washington, D.C., to argue [the case]. No doubt you could get somebody to do that who lives on the east coast."[118]

The national board of the ACLU approved an appeal in the *DeJonge* case on January 27, and the national office reported to Solomon that "Osmond Fraenkel, a member of the board, has agreed to advise you re-

garding procedure." The attorneys on the board, the national office continued, believed that "it is time to raise the issue [of the validity of criminal-
syndicalism laws] again in the U.S. Supreme Court and . . . it is important
to keep these issues to the front in the Supreme Court whenever possible.
If the need arises we are sure we can find an attorney at Washington or
New York to argue the case." "This ought to be a good case for the Portland [ACLU] Committee to rally support," the national office concluded,
"and we hope, if you appeal to the Supreme Court, that you will make it
the basis of a local financial appeal."[119] The ACLU and the ILD also
posted $2000 bail for Dirk DeJonge, and he was released from prison
pending the outcome of the appeal to the Supreme Court on October 3,
1936, after having served eight months of his sentence.[120]

Under Osmond Fraenkel's tutelage, Gus Solomon filed the appeal in the
DeJonge case with the Supreme Court, and after the Court granted the
appeal, Fraenkel and Solomon collaborated on the brief on behalf of De-
Jonge.[121] Solomon was understandably shaken, therefore, when Anna
Damon of the national ILD office called upon him and "expressed her
gratitude for the assistance which the ACLU was giving to the ILD in the
appeal of the [*DeJonge*] case," but asserted that the "ILD originally handled the case and they are handling it now, and that the ACLU is merely
rendering assistance, but they have control of the case." Ms. Damon also
indicated to Solomon that the brief in the case would have to be cleared
with Joseph Brodsky, counsel for the ILD's national office.[122]

Solomon reported this to the ACLU national office and pointed out that
after the Oregon Supreme Court's decision, the ILD had appeared to be
preparing to abandon the *DeJonge* case and that during the preparation of
the appeal to the Supreme Court, he had had "no contact with the ILD at
all. . . ." Although he personally did not object to cooperating with the
ILD, Solomon said, "it is my understanding that the ACLU does not col-
laborate with the ILD in the prosecution or the appeal of any case." Also,
Solomon reported, Ms. Damon had indicated that the ILD was preparing
to organize committees for DeJonge, which would raise money and distribute leaflets on the case. The local Portland CLU was undergoing re-
organization, Solomon pointed out, and "we are attempting to get a representative group of people interested in our local committee," using the
DeJonge case as a cause around which the new members could rally.
"However, as you know," he continued, "some of the members of the
present ACLU, and no doubt most of the members of the new ACLU are
hesitant about working with the ILD, and if this is going to be an ILD
case, I doubt very much whether we can get very much enthusiasm out of
our members. . . . I am just wondering what effect this is going to have on
our local committee."[123]

Harry Poth, Legal Secretary of the ACLU national office, shared Solomon's concern, although he indicated that the ACLU had no objection to having "Mr. Brodsky look over the papers when they are finished, nor will Mr. Fraenkel, as he is a close friend of Mr. Brodsky." The ILD should also be free to make any suggestions it liked, Poth said. "Beyond this, however, we feel that we should have a free hand in directing the appeal." "In consequence I will communicate with the local office of the ILD and torpedo the idea of their setting up money-raising committees in Oregon," Poth concluded. "This I hope will be sufficient to prevent a loss of enthusiasm in present and potential ACLU members in Portland."[124]

Although a jurisdictional battle between the ILD and ACLU over the control of the *DeJonge* case thus appeared to be brewing, the battle did not materialize. Solomon spoke to "Dirk DeJonge and explained we haven't any time to start discussing the matter with the ILD, and that Mr. Fraenkel is going to be the sole arbiter of the contents and form of the brief. To this statement he had no objection." Harry Poth, on the other hand, reported to Solomon that Fraenkel had discussed the *DeJonge* brief with ILD attorneys, and they "are perfectly satisfied with this arrangement and consequently the jurisdictional question no longer exists." The ILD had also assured Poth that it merely wanted to point out that the issue of criminal syndicalism was not dead in Oregon and that the ILD "in no way intend[s] to interfere with our handling of the appeal." "I think if you point out this distinction to our present and potential members," Poth told Solomon, "the contemplated activity of the International Labor Defense should not militate against our work in Portland."[125]

With these organizational squabbles settled, the brief on behalf of De-Jonge was filed in the Supreme Court. The Oregon Criminal Syndicalism Act as applied in the *DeJonge* case, the brief said, violated the right to assemble peaceably and to petition for redress of grievances. The right of assembly and petition, it was argued, must be protected by the Due Process Clause against impairment by the states, since it was as fundamental a personal liberty as the freedom of speech and the freedom of the press that had been read into the Due Process Clause in the *Gitlow-Fiske-Stromberg-Near* line of cases.[126]

As applied in the *DeJonge* case, the argument continued, the Oregon Criminal Syndicalism Act was a gross and absurd invasion of the right of assembly, since it branded as a criminal anyone participating in a meeting held under the auspices of the Communist party, no matter how peaceful the meeting or how lawful the discussions that occurred. This was an attempt "to make criminal the mere association in even a casual way with any persons accused of any wrongdoing at all—a doctrine wholly repugnant to the American system of justice."[127]

The Communist party, it was noted, had been on the ballot in Oregon in 1932, but if the state's interpretation of the criminal-syndicalism law was valid, then "anyone who took part in any of the meetings which were called to discuss the issues of [the 1932] campaign, must have been guilty under the law. That, of course, is an absurdity. If a State permits a party to have a place on its ballot, how can it be heard to say that the mere association with that party can constitute a crime?"[128]

The Oregon law was clearly unconstitutional, the brief on behalf of De-Jonge concluded, because it was a violation of the freedom of peaceable assembly protected by the Due Process Clause. DeJonge's acts "from no point of view can reasonably be said themselves to produce danger to the State. The acts as such were harmless. No situation existed from which an inference could possibly be drawn that danger to the State might result merely because the meeting had been called by the Communist Party."[129]

Counsel for Oregon did not dispute the proposition that freedom of assembly and petition was protected by the Due Process Clause, but rather argued that the criminal syndicalism act embodied the reasonable judgment of the Oregon legislature that clear and present dangers of unlawful action would result if meetings under the auspices of the Communist party were permitted. The criminal syndicalism law, Oregon counsel said, "is founded on the principle that the moron, especially if he is class conscious, and [believes] that men in high places got there through imposition upon the toilers, [is] likely to translate into action the words of [his] voluble leaders. The will of the schemer is often carried out by the acts of the un-thinking. . . ."[130]

By prohibiting meetings held under the auspices of organizations that engaged in illegal advocacy, Oregon counsel said, the legislature had attempted to put a stop to activities that led to "crimes against persons and property" and at the same time to deny to organizations like the Communist party opportunities to disseminate their propaganda and solicit members. It could therefore not be said, Oregon counsel concluded, that the legislature had acted unreasonably "when in the exercise of its judgment as to the measures necessary to protect the public peace and safety, it makes it a crime for any one to preside at, conduct or assist in conducting a meeting of an organization which has as its objective the advocacy, teaching or affirmative suggestion of criminal syndicalism and sabotage."[131]

The ILD paid Osmond Fraenkel's travel expenses to Washington to argue the *DeJonge* case on December 9, 1936,[132] and Fraenkel sensed victory after the argument. Counsel for Oregon was subjected to hostile questions from even the most conservative members of the Court, and in "answer to a direct question by Mr. Justice Sutherland, [Oregon counsel] admitted that the [criminal syndicalism] statute purported to denounce mere meetings." His own argument, Fraenkel reported to the ACLU, had, on the other hand, "proceeded more favorably than I had anticipated. Generally speaking, the Justices did not question my principal contention, namely, that a statute was void if it permitted the punishment of a person for participating at a lawful meeting merely because the meeting was called by an organization which elsewhere advocated the overthrow of the Government by force and violence." "While it is always difficult to draw inferences from the attitude of the Court during argument," Fraenkel said, "I have great hopes for a reversal." "Apparently you did a masterly job and stirred up the old boys at a point where they vastly needed stirring," Roger Baldwin wrote Fraenkel. "We share your hopes."[133]

Fraenkel's evaluation of the oral argument proved to be correct when on January 4, 1937, the Court unanimously decided *DeJonge* v. *Oregon* by invalidating the Oregon Criminal Syndicalism Act as applied to Dirk De-Jonge and reversing his conviction. Writing for the Court as he had in the *Stromberg* and *Near* cases, Chief Justice Hughes noted that the Court had held that freedom of speech and freedom of the press were guarantees of the Due Process Clause of the Fourteenth Amendment, and he held that the "right of peaceable assembly is a right cognate to those of free speech and free press and is equally fundamental." While acknowledging that the First Amendment protected freedom of assembly from impairment by Congress, Hughes held that "explicit mention there does not argue exclusion elsewhere. For the right is one that cannot be denied without violating those fundamental principles of liberty and justice which lie at the base of all civil and political institutions—principles which the Fourteenth Amendment embodies in the general terms of its due process clause."[134]

Hughes noted that under the interpretation of the criminal syndicalism act by the Oregon courts, anyone actively assisting in the conduct of a meeting held under the auspices of the Communist party was guilty of a felony, no matter what the purpose of the meeting or what was advocated at the meeting. While the states could prohibit incitement to violent overthrow of the government, he said, it was also necessary to "preserve inviolate the constitutional rights of free speech, free press and free assembly in order to maintain the opportunity for free political discussion, to the end that government may be responsive to the will of the people and that changes, if desired, may be obtained by peaceful means. Therein lies the security of the Republic, the very foundation of constitutional government."[135]

It followed, therefore, that "consistently with the federal Constitution, peaceable assembly for lawful discussion cannot be made a crime." If persons participating in meetings were guilty of committing offenses elsewhere, Hughes continued, they could, of course, be prosecuted for those offenses, but the state could not seize "upon mere participation in a peaceable assembly and a lawful public discussion as the basis for a criminal charge." Although Dirk DeJonge was a member of the Communist party, Hughes concluded, he "still enjoyed his personal right of free speech and to take part in a peaceable assembly having a lawful purpose, although called by the Party," and he was "entitled to discuss the public issues of the day and thus in a lawful manner, without incitement to violence or crime, to seek redress of alleged grievances. That was of the essence of his guaranteed personal liberty."[136]

Dirk DeJonge was therefore a free man once again. Never "before in all the history of Oregon jurisprudence," he said, "has there been such a bald faced acknowledgment of class interests as those displayed in the case of 'Oregon State v. Dirk DeJonge.'" The special prosecutor in the case, Stanley M. Doyle, was denounced by DeJonge as a "200% patriot who made his last appeal to the jury in a drunken stupor," and Judge Kanzler was charged with being a member of the Nazi group "Friends of New Germany." Even if the Supreme Court had upheld his conviction, DeJonge said, "I would do the same thing over again because I believe in the rights of freedom of speech, press and assemblage." The criminal syndicalism prosecution against him, he declared, had been an attempt to "imprison with me Free Speech, Democratic Tradition, and the inalienable rights set forth in the Declaration of Independence."[137]

Dirk DeJonge remained adamant in asserting his rights as he conceived them to be. In 1956, at the age of sixty-five, he was summoned before the Committee on Un-American Activities of the United States House of Representatives and was questioned as to whether he was a Communist and whether he was a member of the American Committee for Protection of the Foreign Born, a Communist-front group. True to form, DeJonge refused to answer the questions, asserting his right to be free from compulsory self-incrimination under the Fifth Amendment.[138]

In addition to freeing Dirk DeJonge and reading freedom of assembly and petition into the Due Process Clause, the *DeJonge* case had an impact also on the attitude toward the criminal syndicalism act in Oregon. Two months after the Supreme Court's decision, the Oregon legislature repealed the criminal syndicalism act and replaced it with a general criminal-conspiracy statute.[139] One of the ILD attorneys who had defended De-Jonge at his trial hailed the legislature's action, declaring that with the repeal of the criminal syndicalism act, "which blotted the statute books of our state eighteen years, we who believe in the preservation of democracy have occasion to rejoice."[140]

One month after the Court's decision in the *DeJonge* case, President Franklin Roosevelt announced his court-packing plan, through which he hoped to add six new members to the Court and thus overcome the Court's resistance to the New Deal, and some of the reactions to the *DeJonge* decision were colored by the larger conflict over the court-packing plan. "To my mind this decision [in the *DeJonge* case] is another argument for the maintenance of the Court unsullied and unharrowed by the temporary, vindictive and uncontrolled temper of one man," one lawyer wrote to

Roger Baldwin. But another of Baldwin's correspondents refused to respond favorably to the *DeJonge* decision, since "I hope very much that the Roosevelt legislation goes through and anything I said in favor of the Supreme Court at this time might not help that program."[141]

It is thus one of the ironies of American constitutional development that the assumption of the *Gitlow* case was translated into the reality that the freedoms of speech, of the press, and of assembly and petition were guaranteed under the Due Process Clause by a Supreme Court that was being castigated as a group of "nine old men" who were erecting reactionary roadblocks to the implementation of the liberal programs of the New Deal. As a consequence, the beginning of the nationalization of First Amendment freedoms during the 1930s was overshadowed by the controversy surrounding the Court's resistance to New Deal reform measures, the debate over the court-packing plan, and the Court's subsequent dramatic reversal of its opposition to New Deal measures.[142]

More than any other justice, Chief Justice Hughes was the symbol of the Court during the turbulence of the 1930s and of the Court's confrontation with the New Deal. Upon his appointment in 1930 and during the constitutional crisis of the New Deal period, Hughes was denounced as a reactionary and a tool of corporate interests. Momentarily overlooked during this period, however, was Hughes's defense of Socialist legislators who were denied admission to the New York legislature during the Red Scare. On that occasion, Hughes had said that the government could legitimately protect itself against violent overthrow, but "let it also be known, as our surest protection, that with calmness and sanity we propose to maintain the guarantees of free speech, free assembly and the right of representation, and that no one, however poor, friendless or accused, shall be deprived of liberty without due process of law."[143] However much he was responsible for the constitutional crisis of the New Deal period—and his responsibility was substantial—in his opinions in the *Stromberg, Near*, and *DeJonge* cases, Hughes had translated the ideals expressed in his defense of the New York Socialists into the law of the Due Process Clause of the Fourteenth Amendment.

5

The Nationalization of the Religion Clauses

The *Cantwell* and *Everson* Cases

The membership of the Supreme Court underwent rapid change after 1937, and by 1940 only Chief Justice Hughes and Justices Roberts and McReynolds remained from the 1930s Court that had begun the nationalization of First Amendment rights. With the replacement of Hughes and McReynolds in 1941, all but one of the members of the Court had been appointed by President Roosevelt. The "Roosevelt Court" reinforced and made permanent the Court's 1937 withdrawal as censor of the nation's economic policy, but the nationalization of First Amendment rights begun by the Hughes Court was not repudiated. The Roosevelt Court rather extended the nationalization process, and by 1947 it had read the religion clauses of the First Amendment into the Due Process Clause, as restrictions on state power.

With the Court's decision in the *DeJonge* case, freedom of religion and the prohibition of an establishment of religion remained the only First Amendment rights that had not been imposed as restrictions upon the states under the Due Process Clause. It was, of course, difficult to perceive how freedom of religion could be considered a less-fundamental right than the freedoms of speech, of the press, and of assembly, and indeed, in the Court's decisions, there had been strong dicta that freedom of religion was a guarantee of the Due Process Clause. In *Meyer* v. *Nebraska*, decided in 1923, for example, the Court had held that the Due Process Clause of the Fourteenth Amendment included the right "to worship God according to the dictates of [one's] own conscience. . . ." And in *Hamilton* v. *Board of Regents*, decided in 1934, the Court had upheld compulsory ROTC at the University of California against a claim that requiring conscientious objectors to enroll in the program violated their religious liberty. Speaking for the Court, Justice Butler nonetheless held that the liberty protected by the Due Process Clause undoubtedly "does include the right to entertain the beliefs, to adhere to the principles and to teach the doctrines on which these students base their objections to the order prescribing military training." Concurring in the judgment of the Court, Justice Cardozo also stated that he assumed "for present purposes that the religious liberty protected by the First Amendment against invasion by the nation is protected by the Fourteenth Amendment against invasion by the states."[1] That Cardozo's assumption was correct was confirmed by the Court when it decided *Cantwell* v. *Connecticut* in 1940 and held the Free Exercise Clause to be applicable to the states.[2]

Jehovah's Witnesses in New Haven: The *Cantwell* Case

The *Cantwell* case involved members of the Jehovah's Witnesses, a remarkable group that originated as a religious sect in Philadelphia during the 1870s. The sect began as a small Bible class led by Charles Taze Russell, who continued to lead the group until 1916. Originally known as International Bible Students, or "Russellites," the sect adopted the name *Jehovah's Witnesses* in 1931.[3]

Russell taught that there were a few individuals who were among the "elect" at birth, and that these individuals would survive the battle of Armageddon between God's children and the forces of evil and would ascend to heaven. Russell's successor, "Judge" Joseph F. Rutherford, amended Russell's teachings, however, to include not only the elect but those who embraced the Witness theology among the survivors of Armageddon. The possibility of a large group of people in addition to the elect who could be saved thus justified extensive proselytizing by the Witnesses and also opened up the possibility of substantial increases in their numbers. Under Judge Rutherford, therefore, the number of Witnesses in the United States grew to over 70,000 by 1943.

Under the doctrines of the Witnesses, every convert to the faith was considered to be a minister of religion, whose duty was to spread the word of salvation. The Witnesses also believed that all worldly institutions, including all governments, were instruments of the Devil. They therefore condemned—sometimes in rather vitriolic terms—all established religions as servants, not of God, but of the Devil. The Roman Catholic Church was especially singled out for denunciation. Much of the literature peddled by the Witnesses in carrying on their ministries was violently anti-Catholic, having been written by C. W. Woodworth, a leader of the sect who condemned the Catholic Church in the strongest possible terms. Judge Rutherford also began radio broadcasts during the 1930s that were anti-Catholic in much of their content; a Catholic boycott forced an end to the broadcasts in 1937.

Their condemnation of all other religions and their, at times, overly aggressive proselytizing activities led to a great deal of hostility to the Witnesses. They were often harassed, officially and unofficially, in many communities throughout the country, and they were prosecuted sporadically for distributing leaflets in violation of local ordinances. Public hostility toward the Witnesses intensified during the late 1930s, when they adopted the position that their children could not pledge allegiance to the flag in the public schools.

The legal harassment to which the Witnesses were subjected led Judge Rutherford to revive their legal department in 1937. Olin R. Moyle, a Witness and a lawyer from Wisconsin, was recruited as legal counsel. As early as 1933, the Witnesses had adopted the practice of appealing all adverse decisions against them in the lower courts, and with the revival of their legal department in 1937, the Witnesses became frequent litigants in the United States Supreme Court. The ultimate result was a notable series of victories in the Court, through which the First Amendment's guarantees of freedom of speech, press, and religion were significantly expanded.

One of the key cases for the Witnesses involved the activities of sixty-year-old Newton Cantwell and his two sons, sixteen-year-old Jesse and eighteen-year-old Russell, who were Witnesses residing in Woodbridge, Connecticut, a suburb of New Haven. On April 26, 1938, Mr. and Mrs. Cantwell and their two sons drove from their home in Woodbridge to New Haven for the purpose of proselytizing for their faith. They carried a large volume of Witness materials, including pamphlets of the Watchtower Bible and Tract Society and books imparting the Witness message entitled *Enemies, Riches, Preservation,* etc. In addition, the Cantwells each had a portable phonograph, upon which they could play records describing the books they hoped to distribute.

With what appears to have been singular inappropriateness, the Cantwells selected the neighborhood around Cassius Street in New Haven as the target area for their proselytizing activities. The population of the Cassius Street neighborhood was approximately 90 percent Catholic. Nevertheless, while Mrs. Cantwell waited in their automobile, Newton, Russell, and Jesse Cantwell began to canvass the neighborhood. Their routine included knocking on doors, asking the residents if they would like to hear a record explaining the books they were peddling, and then, if given permission, playing the records. Afterward, the residents would be offered the various books and informed that a small contribution would be appreciated, although the books could be obtained free upon the promise that they would be read.

Since much of the literature the Cantwells were distributing was virulently anti-Catholic—especially the book *Enemies* and the record that introduced it—the Cantwells were not warmly received by the residents of the Cassius Street neighborhood. When Russell Cantwell called upon Mrs. Anna Rigby, a Catholic resident at 10 Cassius Street, she angrily turned him away and called the police. By late afternoon of April 26, all of the Cantwells had been taken into custody by officers of the New Haven police department.[4]

Newton, Russell, and Jesse Cantwell were ultimately charged with five offenses. They were charged with publicly exhibiting or advertising "certain offensive, indecent or abusive matter"; with ridiculing individuals and holding them up to contempt because of "creed, religion, color, denomination, nationality or race"; with soliciting "money, services, subscriptions or other valuable things for an alleged religious, charitable or philanthropic cause without having obtained a permit from the Public Welfare Council"; with possessing with intent to sell, lend, give, offer, or show "certain books, pamphlets, paper or other things containing obscene, indecent or impure language"; and, finally, with disturbing "the public tranquility by certain acts or conduct inciting to violence or tending to provoke or incite others" to a breach of the peace. The Cantwells were tried on these charges in the City Court of New Haven and were found guilty.[5]

Under Connecticut procedure, however, the convictions of the Cantwells in the city court could be appealed to the Court of Common Pleas of New Haven County, where a trial *de novo* of the charges could be obtained. The Cantwells took an appeal to the court of common pleas, criminal side, in conformity with the Witness policy of appealing all convictions. Olin R. Moyle, the chief legal counsel for the Jehovah's Witnesses, and Otto H. LaMacchia represented the Cantwells in the court of common pleas.

Moyle and LaMacchia challenged the validity of the charges against the Cantwells, and on September 8, the court of common pleas sustained their objections to most of the charges. The court ruled, however, that the Cantwells could be tried for failing to secure a permit from the Public Welfare Council to solicit door-to-door for a religious purpose and for inciting a breach of the peace. The Cantwells had clearly failed to secure a permit from the Public Welfare Council, the court ruled, and on the breach-of-the-peace issue, it held that while there was "little danger to either government or any substantial religion resulting from stupid, bigoted or fanatical attack," it was possible the Witness materials when "forced upon the unwilling attention of persons whose sensibilities are thereby offended may arouse relations of such character as to endanger the public peace and thereby fall within the common law conception of unlawful conduct."[6]

The statute requiring a license from the Public Welfare Council in order to solicit for a religious purpose had been passed by the Connecticut legislature in 1917. In 1938, it was section 6294 of the Connecticut General Statutes, and provided that no person could solicit money, services, subscriptions, or any valuable thing for any "alleged religious, charitable, or philanthropic cause" unless "such cause shall have been approved by the secretary of the public welfare council." Before issuing a license, the secretary of the Public Welfare Council was required by the statute to "determine whether such cause is a religious one or is a bona fide object of charity or philanthropy and conforms to reasonable standards of efficiency and integrity." Failure to secure a license was made punishable by a fine not exceeding $100 or imprisonment for not more than thirty days or both.

Newton, Russell, and Jesse Cantwell were tried in the Court of Common Pleas, Criminal Side, in September of 1938. Although LaMacchia and Moyle contended that the requirement of a license as a condition of religious solicitation violated the Connecticut Constitution and the Fourteenth Amendment, there was no denial at the trial that the Cantwells had not secured such a license. The testimony at the trial therefore primarily revolved around whether or not the Cantwells had incited a breach of the peace. The prosecution called as witnesses the police officers who had arrested the Cantwells, and they testified regarding the numerous complaints against the Cantwells by the residents of the Cassius Street neighborhood.

The prosecution also introduced as evidence the materials the Cantwells had been distributing, including the book *Enemies* and the phonograph record that described the book. *Enemies* used very strong language in condemning all organized religions, especially the Catholic Church. The names *Babylon* and *harlot*, the book said, "specifically apply to the leading religious organization, the Roman Catholic church, which claims to be the mother of the so-called Christian religion." The objective of the Roman Catholic hierarchy, *Enemies* charged, was "to set up a Fascist government controlling the nations of the earth, that the Hierarchy may arbitrarily rule the nations in a dictatorial manner." The Church has "fraudulently posed as the representative of God," while "in truth and in fact she is the representative of the Devil." Fascism and nazism, the book continued, were the instruments of the Catholic Church, and the Church was the "greatest and worst public enemy," which for centuries "scornfully and arrogantly has ridden upon the backs of the peoples and nations and robbed the people of their just earnings."[7]

The prosecution, however, did not produce any evidence that Newton Cantwell's activities had incited anyone to commit a breach of the peace; instead, the prosecution's witnesses at the trial related exclusively to the reactions of the residents of the Cassius Street neighborhood to the activities of Russell and Jesse Cantwell. Mrs. Anna Rigby testified that when Russell called at her residence, she felt "like getting them out of there, as I said, and I really was mad enough, I suppose, to hit him if he wouldn't get away." On cross-examination, however, Mrs. Rigby admitted that instead of inflicting punishment on Russell, she had called the police, because she "thought it was the proper thing to do."[8]

The fullest testimony on the breach-of-the-peace issue was produced in regard to Jesse Cantwell's activities. About four o'clock on the afternoon of April 26, Jesse had approached John J. Ganley, John Cafferty, and Mentor Canelli, who were standing outside a residence at 13 Cassius Street. Although they were aware of the arrests of Newton and Russell Cantwell, the group agreed to listen to the *Enemies* record when Jesse approached them.

John Ganley testified that after hearing Jesse's record, "we felt like hitting this young lad and told him that he had better take his bag and victrola and be on his way." Ganley admitted that when he and his companions told Jesse "to go, why, he went," but if Jesse had "stayed there, why, we might have started something." John Cafferty also testified that he had thought Jesse's record was "a pretty rotten attack on the religion" and that he had felt like throwing Jesse off the street. "I told him," Cafferty said, "he had better get off the street before something happened to him," and Jesse then "picked up his books and walked up the street." On cross-examination, however, Cafferty admitted he knew that Jesse's record was an attack on the Catholic religion, yet he had consented to hear it because he "wanted to find out for myself."[9]

The defense did not call any witnesses, and Newton, Russell, and Jesse were convicted on both of the counts against them. Newton was fined $65.80, and Russell and Jesse were fined $40.07 each. Despite these nominal fines, the *Cantwell* case was appealed to the Connecticut Supreme Court of Errors in accordance with the general policy of the Jehovah's Witnesses of appealing all adverse decisions.[10]

On June 26, 1939, however, the supreme court of errors upheld the validity of the statute requiring a license of those engaging in solicitation for religious, charitable, or philanthropic purposes. Rejecting arguments that the statute violated the rights of free speech and free exercise of religion, the court held that the Cantwells had been engaged in both the sale and dissemination of religious literature and solicitation of money for a religious cause. While freedom of speech and freedom of religion protected their right to disseminate and sell religious literature, the court said, the Cantwells could be validly required to secure a license to engage in the solicitation of money. Since the Cantwells had not secured a license as required by section 6294 of the Connecticut statutes, the court sustained their convictions for violating that statute.

On the count of inciting a breach of the peace, the supreme court of errors held that to sustain such a charge it was unnecessary for the prosecution to show that the Cantwells had actually provoked others to the point of violence against them. It was only necessary for the prosecution to prove that an individual had performed acts or had used language under circumstances that the individual should know were likely to provoke another person to react violently. It was apparent from the record in the *Cantwell* case, the court said, "that the playing for audition by loyal Catholics of a record violently attacking their religion and church could well be found to constitute [incitement to a breach of the peace]." Since there was no evidence that either Newton or Russell had played the record in such circumstances, the court reversed their convictions on the breach-of-the-peace count. On the other hand, the court found that Jesse had played the record in circumstances likely to provoke a breach of the peace, and his conviction on that count was affirmed.[11]

Although the Witnesses had obtained a partial victory in the supreme court of errors, the *Cantwell* case was nonetheless appealed to the United States Supreme Court on December 15, 1939. During this period, Olin R. Moyle, who had been cocounsel at the trial and appeal of the *Cantwell* case in the Connecticut courts, was dismissed as chief counsel for the Jehovah's Witnesses by Judge Rutherford. Rutherford himself assumed control of Witness litigation, along with a young Texas lawyer and Witness, Hayden Covington. It was under this new legal direction that the *Cantwell* case was appealed to the Supreme Court, which agreed to hear the case on February 26, 1940.[12]

Invoking the religious doctrines of the Witnesses, Rutherford and Covington argued before the Court that the Cantwells were ordained ministers "of Jehovah God" and were commissioned "to preach the gospel of God's kingdom." Relying heavily on the Court's decision in *Hamilton* v. *Board of Regents*, they contended that the "freedom to worship ALMIGHTY GOD, Jehovah, in accordance with God-given commands recorded in Holy Writ and with the dictates of one's own conscience is definitely and clearly included within the liberties and rights secured under the 'due process' clause of the Fourteenth Amendment against state invasion." The Cantwells, Rutherford and Covington continued, were exercising their religious freedom by canvassing the neighborhood on Cassius Street. They were acting "as duly ordained ministers of Almighty God preaching the gospel of His Kingdom under Christ Jesus, and were thus exclusively worshipping and serving Almighty God, JEHOVAH, in spirit and in truth according to the God-given commands recorded in Holy Writ and in accordance with the dictates of their conscience."[13]

Section 6294 of the Connecticut statutes, by requiring a license for religious solicitation, Rutherford and Covington argued, was "totalitarian in spirit and in principle" because it authorized a prior restraint upon religious freedom. The secretary of the Public Welfare Council could refuse a license under the terms of the statute for completely arbitrary reasons, and this was "purely prior restraint and absolutely amputates the right of a true follower of Jesus Christ to worship and serve ALMIGHTY GOD as commanded by him." If Jesus Christ were on earth, they said, "and went from house to house in the State of Connecticut as He did in ancient Palestine, He would be liable to be incarcerated because of this statute."[14]

In regard to Jesse Cantwell's conviction for inciting a breach of the peace, Rutherford and Covington argued that there was no evidence produced at the trial indicating that Jesse had engaged in such conduct. Jesse had behaved in an entirely peaceful manner, they contended, and had moved on when requested to do so, having done "no harm to anyone." Since there was no evidence justifying Jesse's conviction for inciting a breach of the peace, and since the licensing statute imposed a prior restraint on religious freedom, the Court was urged to reverse the Cantwells' convictions on all counts.[15]

The Connecticut attorney general argued, on the other hand, that section 6294 was a valid and reasonable exercise of the police power of the state to protect the public from fraudulent solicitation of money. The Cantwells were free under the statute, he said, to disseminate religious views and literature, but they had been convicted for the unlawful solicitation of money without a license. In issuing licenses, the attorney general continued, the secretary of the Public Welfare Council did not impose any limitations regarding religious beliefs, and if he abused his discretion in this regard, judicial review of his actions was available in the Connecticut courts.[16]

The attorney general also argued that Jesse Cantwell had been validly convicted for inciting a breach of the peace. A reasonable person should have known, he said, that the playing of the *Enemies* record to a Catholic audience would be likely to provoke a violent reaction. Jesse's actions had therefore justified his conviction in the Connecticut courts, the attorney general concluded, and his conviction should be affirmed by the Court.[17]

Cantwell v. *Connecticut* was decided by the Court on May 20, 1940, with an opinion by Justice Roberts squarely holding that the free exercise of religion was guaranteed by the Due Process Clause of the Fourteenth Amendment. "The fundamental concept of liberty embodied" in the Fourteenth Amendment, Roberts said, "embraces the liberties guaranteed by the First Amendment. The First Amendment declares that Congress shall make no law respecting an establishment of religion or prohibiting the free exercise thereof. The Fourteenth Amendment has rendered the legislatures of the states as incompetent as Congress to enact such laws."[18] Not only did Roberts hold that freedom of religion was guaranteed by the Due Process Clause, but he therefore rather unnecessarily declared that all of the First Amendment rights, including the prohibition of an establishment of religion, were so guaranteed.

Section 6294 of the Connecticut statutes was invalid, Roberts held, because it delegated to the secretary of the Public Welfare Council the discretionary power to determine what was and was not a truly religious cause prior to issuing a license for religious solicitation. "Such a censoring of religion," he said, "as the means of determining its right to survive is a denial of liberty protected by the First Amendment and included in the liberty which is within the protection of the Fourteenth." To condition "the solicitation of aid for the perpetuation of religious views or systems upon a license, the grant of which rests in the exercise of a determination by state authority as to what is a religious cause," he said, "is to lay a forbidden burden upon the exercise of liberty protected by the Constitution."[19]

Turning to the conviction of Jesse Cantwell for inciting a breach of the peace, Roberts held that Jesse had engaged in "no assault or threatening or bodily harm, no truculent bearing, no intentional discourtesy, no personal abuse. On the contrary, we find only an effort to persuade a willing listener to buy a book or to contribute money in the interest of what Cantwell, however misguided others may think him, conceived to be true religion." Strong views, including exaggeration and vilification, characterized political and religious beliefs, Roberts continued, but "the people of this nation have ordained in the light of history, that, in spite of the probability of excesses and abuses, these liberties are, in the long view, essential to enlightened opinion and right conduct on the part of citizens of a democracy." Jesse had not created such a "clear and present menace to public peace and order as to render him liable to conviction of the common law offense in question," and his conviction was reversed by the Court.[20]

With the reversal of the Cantwells' convictions by the Court, the Jehovah's Witnesses had succeeded in firmly establishing freedom of religion within the Due Process Clause of the Fourteenth Amendment. Shortly after the *Cantwell* case, however, the Witnesses lost the first Flag Salute case when the Court refused to invalidate compulsory flag-salute requirements in the public schools as violative of the religious consciences of Witness children. But in 1943, in a remarkable reversal, the Court upheld the Witnesses' arguments and invalidated the compulsory flag salute in *West Virginia Board of Education* v. *Barnette*.[21]

The ultimate victories of the Witnesses in the Flag Salute cases and in *Cantwell* v. *Connecticut* formed only a part of a notable record of victory by the Witnesses in litigation. During the 1930s and 1940s, the Witnesses won 150 state supreme court appeals and almost all of their 40 appeals to the United States Supreme Court, through which the freedoms of speech, press, and religion were significantly expanded.[22] "In American history," Milton Konvitz has said, "this will be reckoned as no mean contribution made to the Republic, paradoxically by a sect that is, on religious grounds, opposed to all states, governments, and laws."[23]

Hayden Covington, counsel for the Witnesses, argued, on the other hand, that despite the Witnesses' opposition to government, there was biblical precedent for their litigation activities, since the Apostle Paul had twice "appealed his own case to Caesar" and had said that he was "'defending and legally establishing' the reality and virtue of the good news." That, Covington said, was what the Witnesses had done in *Cantwell* and in similar cases. At the time of the *Cantwell* case, he continued, the maze of local and state laws and ordinances "virtually nullified the Bill of Rights and wallowed the Constitution in an undemocratic sea." The litigation by the Witnesses, he concluded, "served like a sieve to strain out insidious bylaws that were cluttering up freedom of worship, speech, and press. Not only for them. But for everybody alike—whether it was realized or not."[24]

In the *Cantwell* case, not only had the Witnesses persuaded the Court to read freedom of religion into the Due Process Clause, but Justice Roberts had held in addition that the entire First Amendment was applicable to the states. This statement was repeated by the Court in numerous cases after the *Cantwell* case, to the extent that Chief Justice Stone could accurately say in 1943 that the Court had "repeatedly held that the Fourteenth Amendment has made applicable to the states the guarantees of the First."[25]

Without having had a case specifically requiring such a holding, after the *Cantwell* case in 1940 it was clear that the Court was proceeding on the assumption that all of the provisions in the First Amendment were applicable to the states—including the Establishment Clause, with its prohibition of an establishment of religion. In contrast with the slow, incremental manner in which the other First Amendment rights had been nationalized, the Establishment Clause had been applied to the states, at least in the language of the Court, suddenly and without any argument on the question. All that remained after the *Cantwell* case was for a state case raising Establishment Clause issues to be appealed to the Court, giving it an opportunity for a formalization of what was already assumed. This opportunity came to the Court in 1947 in the New Jersey Bus case.[26]

The New Jersey Bus Case and the Junior Order of Mechanics

The Court was finally confronted with an Establishment Clause issue arising under the Due Process Clause in regard to the question of whether public funds could be used for the transportation of students to parochial schools. By the middle 1940s, sixteen states and the District of Columbia in one way or another provided for the transportation of students to both public and nonpublic schools. These provisions had been the subject of considerable litigation in the state courts, and a majority of the state supreme courts passing on the provisions had declared them invalid.

The state courts invalidating such provisions generally relied on state constitutional guarantees prohibiting establishments of religion or prohibiting the expenditure of public funds for the support of other than public schools. The theory utilized to uphold public support for transportation of non-public school students, on the other hand, was generally known as the child-benefit theory. This theory supported the view that public aid expended in behalf of the health, safety, or welfare of children constituted a valid public expenditure. Under the child-benefit theory, public support for the transportation of all students attending either public or parochial schools contributed to the safety and welfare of all children and was a valid public policy, even though religious bodies maintaining parochial schools might be indirectly benefited thereby.[27]

The leading case rejecting the child-benefit theory on the free-school-transportation question was *Judd* v. *Board of Education*, decided by the New York Court of Appeals in 1938. "Any contribution," the court held, "directly or indirectly made in aid of the maintenance and support of any private or sectarian school out of public funds would be a violation of the concept of separation of Church and State in civil affairs and of the spirit and mandate of our fundamental law." The use of the child-benefit theory to justify free transportation of parochial school children, the court continued, was "utterly without substance," since the "purpose of the transportation is to promote the interests of the private school or religious or sectarian institution that controls and directs it."[28]

Nevertheless, the *Judd* case was soon reversed by a vote of the people of New York. Revisions of the state's constitution in 1938 included a provision allowing the legislature to provide transportation of students to any school, whether public or private, at public expense. Msgr. J. Francis McIntyre urged Catholics to back the proposal, while such groups as the American Civil Liberties Union opposed it with the editorial support of the *New York Times*. The proposal was adopted on November 8, 1938, by a majority vote of the electorate.[29]

In the neighboring state of New Jersey, the legislature took similar action in 1941. Since 1903 the legislature had provided by statute that in any school districts in which children lived "remote from the schoolhouse, the board of education of the district may make rules and contracts for the transportation of such children to and from school." This statute was amended in 1941 to provide that school districts could contract to provide transportation for children living remote from "any schoolhouse" including "the transportation of school children to and from school other than a public school, except such school as is operated for profit in whole or in part."[30]

The New Jersey bus law had been supported by approximately 500,000 citizens who had signed petitions urging its passage by the legislature, but the law had also been opposed by such organizations as the New Jersey Taxpayers Association, the League of Women Voters, the American Association of University Women, the state education association and the Federation of District Boards of Education, the state council of churches, the

Seventh Day Adventists, and the New Jersey chapter of the ACLU.

The bus law was also opposed by the Junior Order of United American Mechanics (JOUAM) of New Jersey, the Daughters of America, the Sons and Daughters of Liberty Patriotic Order, the Sons of America, and the Patriotic Order of Americans. These fraternal and patriotic groups were represented in the hearings on the bus bill in the New Jersey legislature by the counsel for the Junior Order of United American Mechanics, Albert C. McCay.[31] McCay had grown up in rural Mansfield Township and had received his law degree from Temple University. He served as a Republican assemblyman and subsequently as senator from Burlington County during the mid-1940s, but he also became the key figure in the attack upon the validity of the New Jersey bus law in the courts in his capacity as counsel for the JOUAM.

The JOUAM was a fraternal patriotic order that had been incorporated in New Jersey in 1875. The order had approximately 20,000 members in New Jersey during the 1940s. According to its constitution, one of its principal objects was to foster the public school system, and the order actively lobbied the legislature in support of the public schools. The order's constitution also pledged its dedication to the principle of separation of church and state.[32]

Shortly after the bus law had been passed by the legislature, Albert McCay began mapping strategy for challenging its validity in the New Jersey courts, but it was not until the fall of 1942 that a firm commitment was agreed to between McCay's law firm and the Junior Order of Mechanics regarding a challenge of the bus law's validity. On September 4, 1942, Roscoe C. Walker, State Council Secretary of the Junior Order of Mechanics, communicated to McCay and his law firm that the JOUAM State Council Legislative Committee had authorized him "to direct you to proceed with the case [challenging the validity of the bus law], with the understanding that the fees mentioned shall cover the total cost of the case, [b]elieving you will leave no stone unturned to bring about a successful conclusion to this very important litigation. . . ."[33]

In order to launch an attack upon the validity of the bus law, of course, an individual had to be found who would be willing to serve as plaintiff in a test case. On December 15, 1942, JOUAM State Council Secretary Walker informed McCay that "in further reference to the testing of the constitutionality of New Jersey's Bus Transportation Bill . . . , Mr. A. R. Everson, 508 Maple Ave., Trenton, Ewing Township, N.J., has agreed to act as the taxpayer and property owner in the bringing of the action referred to." Arch R. Everson had long been active in New Jersey public affairs and was executive vice-president of the state taxpayers association as well as a member of the Junior Order of Mechanics, but the litigation to which he lent his name would make him nationally known.[34]

The township of Ewing in Mercer County is a suburb of Trenton. The Ewing Township Board of Education operated public schools only through the eighth grade, and students of the township customarily attended the public junior and senior high schools either in Trenton or in neighboring Pennington. Tuition for these students was paid by the township to the Trenton and Pennington public schools. The Ewing Township Board of Education also reimbursed the parents of students attending the Trenton and Pennington public schools for their costs in paying the bus fares of their children.

After the 1941 passage of the New Jersey bus law, the Ewing Township Board of Education was authorized also to reimburse the transportation costs of the parents of children attending the Trenton Catholic parochial schools, a policy the board of education adopted in a resolution of September 21, 1942. In administering this policy, the clerk of the board of education, Charles G. Latham, would check the attendance records of each child attending the Trenton or Pennington public schools or the Trenton Catholic parochial schools. On the basis of these attendance records, the parents of each child would be reimbursed for the cost of transportation at the end of the fall and spring semesters of school. For the first half of the school year beginning in September 1942, the transportation costs reimbursed totaled $8,034.95. This amount included $357.74 reimbursed to the parents of twenty-one children from Ewing Township who attended Catholic parochial schools in Trenton.

The reimbursement for transportation costs to the Catholic parents for the second half of the 1942–43 school year did not occur, however. The payments were suspended by the clerk of the board of education when the attorney for the board, William Abbotts, advised the board that the payments for the transportation costs of parochial school students were subject to legal challenge. This advice was given to the board by Abbotts in light of the fact that Albert McCay had filed a suit on behalf of Arch Everson challenging the New Jersey bus law in July of 1943.[35]

Very early in the history of the state, the New Jersey courts had construed the availability of the common law writ of certiorari very liberally, and certiorari thus became an almost all-purpose method by which the New Jersey courts could "do justice between the private citizen and the public official."[36] Albert McCay therefore filed a petition for a writ of certiorari in the New Jersey Supreme Court, and the court granted the writ on July 31, directing the clerk of the Ewing Township Board of Education to deliver to the court the records of the board authorizing the payment of transportation costs of Catholic parochial school students.[37]

On August 23, a hearing was held before Supreme Court Commissioner William N. Cooper sitting in Trenton. The principal testimony at the hearing was given by Charles Latham, the school-board clerk, who described the system by which students in Ewing Township were reimbursed for their transportation costs. Latham testified as to the amount of money expended on the transportation costs for parochial school students and detailed the $357.74 spent for that purpose in the first half of the 1942–43 school year. The superintendent of the Catholic schools in Trenton, Father John J. Endebrock, also testified that religion was a part of the curriculum of all the Trenton Catholic schools and that the parochial schools were not operated for profit—that indeed, all of the parochial schools operated at a loss.[38]

In attacking the bus law in the New Jersey Supreme Court, Albert McCay was aware of the 1930 decision of the United States Supreme Court in *Cochran* v. *Board of Education*, in which the Court had sustained the validity of a Louisiana statute furnishing textbooks at state expense to students attending public, private, and parochial schools. In the *Cochran* case, the Louisiana free-textbook law had been challenged on the ground that state expenditures of taxpayers' money for textbooks for private and parochial school students was a use of public funds for a private purpose in violation of the Due Process Clause of the Fourteenth Amendment. The Louisiana Supreme Court nevertheless upheld the free-textbook law on the basis of the child-benefit theory, holding that the expenditure of public funds for textbooks for children attending all schools in the state—private, parochial, and public—constituted an expenditure of money for the welfare of the children and not of the schools they happened to attend. And since the free-textbook law involved the expenditure of funds for the welfare of children, the Louisiana Supreme Court held, the funds thus expended were for a public purpose and not a private purpose.

Accepting this construction of the free-textbook law, the United States Supreme Court unanimously upheld the law. "Viewing the statute as having the effect thus attributed to it, we can not doubt that the taxing power of the state is exerted for a public purpose," Chief Justice Hughes said. "The legislation does not segregate private schools or their pupils, as its beneficiaries, or attempt to interfere with any matters of exclusively private concern. Its interest is education, broadly; its method, comprehensive. Individual interests are aided only as the common interest is safeguarded."[39]

In light of the *Cochran* decision, McCay assumed it would be useless to base any attack on the New Jersey bus law on an argument that the law constituted a use of public funds for a private purpose in violation of the Due Process Clause of the Fourteenth Amendment. As he said later, "in view of *Cochran* v. *Louisiana State Board of Education*, I had concluded that we could not successfully urge that the New Jersey statute violates the Constitution of the United States."[40] At the outset of the *Everson* case, therefore, McCay's strategy was to attack the bus law on the grounds that it involved violations of the New Jersey Constitution, which prohibited the expenditure of public funds for private purposes, the expenditure of public school funds for any purpose other than the maintenance of the public schools, and the establishment of a religion. The idea that the First Amendment, including the Establishment Clause, applied to the states was therefore not considered by McCay in his attack on the bus law in the New Jersey courts. Indeed, the only mention by McCay of the federal Constitution in that attack was a general allegation that the bus law violated "the provisions of the Fourteenth Amendment of the Constitution of the United States."[41]

While it was pending before the New Jersey Supreme Court, the *Everson* case attracted the attention of the American Civil Liberties Union. The ACLU had of course opposed the adoption of the provision of the New York Constitution providing for the transportation of students to parochial schools at public expense in 1938, and it had also opposed through its New Jersey affiliate the bus law of 1941. The ACLU Board of Directors authorized a filing of an *amicus curiae* brief urging the invalidation of the New Jersey bus law in July of 1943, and upon the recommendation of Albert McCay, it retained Joseph Beck Tyler of Camden to write and file an *amicus* brief on the ACLU's behalf.[42] The ACLU also established close contact with Albert McCay through Clifford Forster, one of the ACLU's staff attorneys in New York, and the Union would continue its *amicus* role in opposition to the bus law throughout the litigation in the *Everson* case.

Albert McCay, the Junior Order of Mechanics, and the ACLU were heartened by the decision of the New Jersey Supreme Court in September of 1943 invalidating the bus law. The court rested its decision primarily on article 4, section 7, of the New Jersey Constitution, which prohibited the legislature from borrowing, appropriating, or using the public school fund for any purpose other than the support of the public schools. The court noted that the courts of six states had held invalid the public financing of transportation of parochial school students, while some state courts supported the theory that such expenditures of public money did not aid the schools or the religion running the schools, but, rather, were for the welfare and safety of the students. This child-benefit theory, the court held, could not justify such a policy in New Jersey, since prior decisions of the state's courts had ruled out any public aid for sectarian schools. The court therefore concluded that the 1941 statute was invalid because it authorized expenditures of school funds for a purpose other than the support and maintenance of public schools in violation of article 4 of the state constitution.[43]

The Junior Order of Mechanics lauded Albert McCay and his law firm for the victory in the New Jersey Supreme Court, noting that the JOUAM had "opposed State aid for bus transportation for children attending private schools since the question was first raised in the New Jersey legislature" and extending the JOUAM's congratulations to McCay and his firm "for their successful victory in this very controversial question." The victory in the New Jersey Supreme Court proved to be short-lived, however, since the New Jersey Court of Errors and Appeals reversed the decision of the New Jersey Supreme Court in the *Everson* case in October of 1945.[44]

Under state law, the court of errors and appeals said, parents were required to send their children to school under threat of criminal penalties for failure to do so. State provision of free transportation to the school of the parents' choice aided in the enforcement of the compulsory-school-attendance law and expenditures of public money for such a purpose did not constitute "the expenditure of public moneys for private purposes." There was nothing on the face of the bus law or the Ewing Township Board of Education's resolution implementing it, the court held, "showing that either the statute or the resolution thereunder is unconstitutional or does violence to the [New Jersey] Constitution for any of the reasons urged."[45]

After the decision of the court of errors and appeals, the management of the *Everson* case on behalf of the board of education changed hands. William Abbotts, as attorney for the board of education, had defended the bus law in the New Jersey Supreme court and in the court of errors and appeals, but in the latter court he had been joined by William H. Speer of Newark. And after the decision of the court of errors and appeals, Speer became the principal attorney for the school board.[46] It would appear that Speer was retained by Catholic interests, which of course had an important stake in the defense of the bus law.[47]

The decision of the court of errors and appeals was of course deeply discouraging to the Junior Order of Mechanics, Albert McCay, and the ACLU. Clifford Forster, on behalf of the ACLU, corresponded with McCay and expressed his feeling that it "was not with great surprise, but I can assure you with much regret, that I learned . . . of the reversal by the court of errors and appeals of the *Everson* case." "I think," Forster continued, "it would be worth the effort [to appeal to the United States Supreme Court], although I do not have much hope that the Court would agree to review."[48]

Given the fact that he had not raised an Establishment Clause issue under the First Amendment in the New Jersey courts, and, indeed, had only raised a Fourteenth Amendment issue in the most general terms, Albert McCay was constrained to agree with Forster's bleak assessment of any appeal to the Supreme Court. "At the present time," McCay replied to Forster, "I do not feel at all hopeful that we could obtain a favorable decision in the Supreme Court of the United States, in view of the opinion of former Chief Justice Hughes in the case of *Cochran* v. *Louisiana State*

Board of Education . . . , which sustained the decision of the Louisiana Court in a free textbook case."[49]

Forster and the ACLU were soon attempting, however, to divert Mc-Cay's attention from his fixation with the use of public funds for a private purpose as the only possible issue upon which an appeal to the Supreme Court might be based. "There is, as we have tried to point out in our *amicus* brief [in the court of errors and appeals] a question of religious freedom," Forster wrote McCay, "and I believe that some argument can be made that violation of the doctrine of separation of church and state abridges the freedom of religion protected against state encroachment by the Fourteenth Amendment." "Much water has flowed [over] the dam since the *Cochran* case . . . ," Forster continued, again suggesting "an appeal to the Supreme Court so that we can get some indication of what it thinks about all these transportation statutes."[50]

Albert McCay was soon educating himself regarding the nationalization of the First Amendment via the Due Process Clause of the Fourteenth Amendment, and he discovered that since 1940 the Supreme Court had on numerous occasions declared that all of the First Amendment, including the Establishment Clause, applied to the states via the Fourteenth Amendment. McCay's attitude toward an appeal to the Supreme Court rapidly changed from one of hopelessness to one of optimism. By December of 1945 he was writing Roscoe Walker of the Junior Order of Mechanics that he now would "strongly recommend that the *Everson* decision be appealed to the Supreme Court of the United States. . . . Such an appeal is the only means by which we can ever hope to have the New Jersey statute declared unconstitutional." "I also believe," McCay continued, "that the statute and resolution [of the board of education implementing the statute] violate the First Amendment to the Constitution of the United States, which provides for freedom of religion, in view of the cases . . . which hold that the Fourteenth Amendment makes applicable to the states the guarantees of the First Amendment."[51]

Despite his enthusiasm for an appeal to the Supreme Court, Albert Mc-Cay did not feel qualified to handle such an appeal without assistance, since he was not a member of the Supreme Court bar and was unfamiliar with Supreme Court procedure. He therefore soon began contacting attorneys who had had experience in Supreme Court litigation, seeking the assistance he needed in the appeal of the *Everson* case. McCay noticed that the principal attorney in the attack upon the validity of the Louisiana textbook law in *Cochran* v. *Board of Education* had been Challen B. Ellis of Washington, D.C., and in early December of 1945, McCay sought the advice of Ellis regarding an appeal in the *Everson* case.

After noting Ellis's participation in the *Cochran* case, McCay informed

Ellis that "[w]e are considering the advisability of taking an appeal to the United States Supreme Court in the *Everson* case and we are wondering whether you would be willing to handle the matter for us." The New Jersey bus law, McCay said, could be attacked on the grounds that it constituted a use of public money for private purposes in violation of the Due Process Clause and because it constituted an aid to religion in violation of the Establishment Clause. "It seems clear to us that a statute and resolution which authorizes the use of tax moneys for transportation of children to sectarian schools violates the principle of separation of church and state and is a 'law respecting an establishment of religion, or prohibiting the free exercise thereof,' within the meaning of the First Amendment," McCay continued. "A law that compels a citizen to pay taxes for the purpose of transporting children to such schools clearly interferes with the free exercise of religion." He would appreciate, McCay closed, "any comments you care to make at this time with respect to our chances of success in the event an appeal is taken to the United States Supreme Court."[52]

In his reply to McCay's letter, Challen Ellis was hardly encouraging. He could see, Ellis informed McCay, "serious difficulties in getting an allowance of appeal to the Supreme Court in this particular case," primarily because a substantial federal question did not appear to have been adequately raised in the litigation in the New Jersey courts. Indeed, Ellis pointed out, in the decision of the court of errors and appeals "the majority of the Court did not pass upon the Federal constitutional question at all but ignored it as though not involved in the case." Without completely closing the door to his participation in any appeal of the *Everson* case, Ellis plainly indicated to McCay that it was his opinion that the chances of the Supreme Court's even accepting jurisdiction in the case were poor.[53]

McCay refused to be discouraged, however, and again pressed Ellis to aid in the appeal with arguments based upon his newly acquired knowledge regarding the nationalization of the First Amendment. Thus, in January of 1946 McCay again wrote Ellis that "I am hopeful that you will reach the conclusion that the United States Supreme Court might hold that the [New Jersey bus] statute and resolution [of the board of education implementing the statute] authorize an unconstitutional taking of private property for a private purpose in violation of the Fourteenth Amendment and that the statute and resolution violate the First Amendment to the Constitution of the United States, which provides for freedom of religion, in view of the cases . . . which hold that the Fourteenth Amendment makes applicable to the states guarantees of the First Amendment." Congress was barred by the First Amendment from "enacting legislation for the support of any religious tenets," McCay argued, "and that prohibition is now applicable by reason of the Fourteenth Amendment to the states and their political sub-divisions."[54]

Ellis continued to be doubtful regarding the potential for success of any appeal in the *Everson* case, however, and he replied to McCay that he had "gone over the matters you call attention to in your letter and I am still not sure that [an] appeal will stick. . . ." He was too busy "to take care of the details connected with the preparation of the papers for appeal," Ellis continued, although he offered to "advise with you after the appeal is filed, and when you come to the preparation of [a] brief or argument, if you so desire."[55]

McCay still persisted in trying to secure Ellis's experience in Supreme Court litigation for the appeal of the *Everson* case, and finally Ellis gave in. Accompanied by JOUAM State Council Secretary Roscoe Walker, McCay visited Ellis in Washington in late January of 1946, and Ellis finally agreed at this meeting to conduct the appeal of the *Everson* case, with the JOUAM paying his fee. Walker reported to the JOUAM Board of Managers and State Council Legislative Committee that Ellis's law firm "was interested in the case [as a] matter of principle and advised if they took the case the question would be orally argued by former [United States] Senator [Edward R.] Burke of Nebraska."[56] Challen Ellis filed the appeal in *Everson* v. *Board of Education*, and the Supreme Court, contrary to Ellis's initial prediction to McCay, noted probable jurisdiction in the case on May 6, 1947.[57]

While Ellis handled the proceedings in the Supreme Court, Albert McCay began a drive to secure the filing of as many favorable *amicus curiae* briefs in the *Everson* case as possible. Challen Ellis, McCay wrote Clifford Forster, considered an *amicus* brief by the ACLU as "exceedingly important," and the ACLU assured McCay that its *amicus* participation in the case would continue.[58] McCay also contacted the American Jewish Congress (AJC) and solicited an *amicus* brief,[59] but the AJC ultimately failed to participate in the *Everson* case as *amicus curiae*. McCay himself wrote an *amicus* brief on behalf of the Junior Order of Mechanics and arranged its submission to the Court by another attorney, Milton T. Lasher of Hackensack.[60] *Amicus* briefs attacking the validity of the bus law were also filed by the General Conference of the Seventh-Day Adventists and the Joint Baptist Conference Committee on Public Relations. *Amicus* briefs supporting the bus law were filed, however, by the attorneys general of Illinois, Indiana, Louisiana, Massachusetts, Michigan, and New York, defending similar laws in those states, and by the National Councils of Catholic Men and Women.

In his brief and argument in the *Everson* case, Challen Ellis attacked the validity of the school bus law on the ground that it involved the use of public funds for a private purpose in violation of the Due Process Clause, and on the ground that the law aided religion in violation of the Establishment Clause of the First Amendment as applied to the states. On the first point, Ellis relied heavily on *Loan Association* v. *Topeka*, decided by the Court in 1875, in which it was held that the appropriation of public funds for private purposes involved the taking of property without due process of law.[61] The New Jersey bus law thus violated the Due Process Clause, he argued, because it involved the appropriation of New Jersey taxpayers' money for the benefit of a private organization, the Catholic Church and its parochial schools.

William H. Speer, who had taken over the defense of the bus law on behalf of the Catholic interest, was aided in the Supreme Court by Porter R. Chandler, a well-known legal adviser to Cardinal Spellman of New York, who had been retained by the Archdiocese of New York to aid in the defense of the law before the Court.[62] Speer and Chandler met Ellis's use of the public-money-for-a-private-purpose argument by citing *Cochran* v. *Board of Education*. In sustaining Louisiana's policy of supplying free textbooks to both public and parochial school students in the *Cochran* case, Speer argued, the Court had rejected an argument that the policy involved the expenditure of public funds for private purposes. And, Speer continued, the furnishing of "free textbooks to a pupil attending a denominational school is certainly more obnoxious, on [Ellis's] theory, than giving that pupil a free bus ticket to enable him to reach the same school."[63]

Given the Court's oft-repeated statements since the *Cantwell* case in 1940 that all of the First Amendment applied to the states, neither side in the *Everson* case spent much time arguing the question of whether the Establishment Clause applied to the states via the Due Process Clause. As Challen Ellis said, with ample citations of the Court's decisions, "the principles enunciated in the First Amendment—including the prohibition against any law respecting an establishment of religion or forbidding the free exercise thereof—constitute a chart by which due process of law may be measured, and . . . a violation of the First Amendment to the Constitution is a violation also of the Fourteenth Amendment."[64]

Unless the Court called a halt to even minor violations of the principle of separation of church and state, Ellis said, there could be no logical stopping place as far as state aid to parochial schools was concerned. If free transportation for parochial school students were upheld, it would "follow logically from this that if the facilities of the private parochial schools were inadequate for reasons other than transportation such schools might be helped financially, thus supposedly promoting education in the state and only incidentally affecting or relating to an establishment of religion."[65]

William Speer replied that the bus law no more constituted an establishment of religion than did supplying free textbooks to parochial school children, or hot lunches for both public and private school students, or grants to denominational colleges by the federal government under the just-enacted G.I. bill of rights. No income was added to the parochial schools under the bus law, Speer noted, although perhaps students attended such schools more regularly with the aid of the bus law and were better fitted for instruction when they arrived. "The conclusion," he continued, "nevertheless remains the same—that private or religious interests are advanced by this legislation only to the extent that they coincide with, and are part of, the public interest." The New Jersey bus law, Speer concluded, was a valid exercise of the police power of the state because it promoted the safety and welfare of all children and aided parochial schools only incidentally, if at all.[66]

Everson v. *Board of Education* was argued orally before the Court on November 20, 1946, and in the conference of the Court following the argument, Chief Justice Vinson and Justices Burton, Reed, Jackson, Black, and Douglas voted to uphold the bus law. Justice Murphy was uncertain and passed, while only Justices Frankfurter and Rutledge voted to invalidate the bus law as a violation of the Establishment Clause. "First it has been books, now buses, next churches and teachers," Rutledge said. "Every religious institution in [the] country will be reaching into [the] hopper for help if you sustain this. We ought to stop this thing right at [the] threshold of [the] public school." Because the Court had never before authoritatively construed the Establishment Clause, the preliminary conference votes were uncertain and, as sometimes happens, changes took place in the votes of the justices. Justices Jackson and Burton ultimately changed their votes, while Justice Murphy, who had initially passed, finally decided to vote to uphold the bus law. The final vote was therefore five to four, rather than the initial vote of six to two with one pass, to affirm the decision of the New Jersey Court of Errors and Appeals upholding the bus law.[67] Despite the division on the Court regarding the validity of the bus law, however, the Court was unanimous in holding that the Establishment Clause applied to the states via the Due Process Clause.

Justice Black's opinion for the majority was a rather schizoid affair, since most of his opinion embraced principles that seemed to point to the invalidation of the bus law under the Establishment Clause, while in the concluding pages of the opinion the bus law was upheld. According to Black's opinion, the Establishment Clause meant at least that neither "a state nor the Federal Government can set up a church. Neither can pass laws which aid one religion, aid all religions, or prefer one religion over another." Neither the states nor the federal government, he said, could compel any person to attend or not attend any church or could punish beliefs or disbeliefs or church attendance or nonattendance. "No tax in any amount, large or small," Black continued, "can be levied to support any religious activities or institutions, whatever they may be called, or whatever form they may adopt to teach or practice religion. Neither a state nor the Federal Government can, openly or secretly, participate in the affairs of any religious organizations or groups and vice versa. In the words of Jefferson, the clause against establishment of religion by law was intended to erect 'a wall of separation between Church and State.'"[68]

Given this very strict interpretation of the Establishment Clause, one would have concluded before reading further in the opinion that the bus law was doomed, but this, however, was not to be the case. The bus law, Black concluded, was a public-welfare measure aimed at protecting the safety and welfare of all children, regardless of the school they attended, and did not involve an aid to the parochial schools as such. The bus law, Black said, "does no more than provide a general program to help parents get their children, regardless of their religion, safely and expeditiously to and from accredited schools." The First Amendment, Black held, had "erected a wall between church and state. That wall must be kept high and impregnable. We could not approve the slightest breach. New Jersey has not breached it here."[69]

Black's opinion, Justice Jackson said in dissent, was most supported by the precedent of "Julia who, according to Byron's reports, 'whispering, I will ne'er consent,'—consented."[70] And in a powerful dissenting opinion, Justice Rutledge accused the majority of the Court of ignoring the historical principles embodied in the Establishment Clause.

The Establishment Clause, Rutledge noted, was the direct product of the struggle of Jefferson and Madison against the establishment of religion in Virginia, a struggle that Madison finally won with the approval of the Bill for Establishing Religious Freedom in 1786. The lessons and principles learned in the Virginia struggle, Rutledge said, had subsequently been translated by Madison into the Establishment Clause, the principles of which meant that in the United States "we have staked the very existence of our country on the faith that complete separation between the state and religion is best for the state and best for religion."[71]

In Rutledge's opinion, the New Jersey bus law clearly aided the parochial schools, and by upholding such a breach of the principle of separation of church and state the Court was encouraging future sectarian conflicts over and competition for more and more governmental aid. "Two great drives are constantly in motion to abridge, in the name of education, the complete division of religion and civil authority which our forefathers made," Rutledge concluded. "One is to introduce religious education and observances into the public schools. The other, to obtain public funds for aid and support of various private religious schools. . . . In my opinion both avenues are closed by the Constitution. The matter is not one of quantity, to be measured by the amount of money expended. Now as in Madison's day it is one of principle, to keep separate the separate spheres of the First Amendment, to prevent the first experiment upon our liberties; to keep the question from becoming entangled in corrosive precedents. We should not be less strict to keep strong and untarnished the one side of the shield of religious freedom than we have been of the other."[72]

By upholding the New Jersey bus law, the Court, of course, was not saying that the states were required to furnish free transportation to students attending parochial schools, but rather that the states were free to do so without violating the Establishment Clause as applied to the states via the Fourteenth Amendment. In addition, the state courts remained free to consider the validity of free-transportation laws for parochial school students under provisions of their own state constitutions similar to the Establishment Clause, and despite the Court's decision in the *Everson* case, most state courts, interpreting state constitutional provisions similar to the Establishment Clause, have invalidated bus laws like that at issue in the *Everson* case.[73]

The subsequent refusal of most state courts to follow the reasoning in the *Everson* case is consistent with the generally negative initial reaction to the Court's decision in the case. Justice Rutledge's eloquent dissent brought him overwhelmingly favorable mail, and a sample of the leading newspapers from all sections of the country indicated a negative editorial response to the majority opinion.[74] The Baptist Joint Conference Committee on Public Relations also denounced the decision in the *Everson* case, charging that the Court had turned "back the hands of the clock as far as religious liberty and the separation of Church and State are concerned in these United States." As Baptists, the committee continued, "we are resolved that the struggle for religious liberty, in terms of the separation of Church and State, must be continued. Having lost a battle, we have not lost the war."[75]

The executive committee of the General Conference of Seventh-Day Adventists also passed a resolution pledging not to accept any public funds for bus transportation of students attending over nine-hundred Adventist day schools.[76] And the *Everson* decision spurred the formation of Protestants and Other Americans United for Separation of Church and State (POAU). The POAU pledged to fight to maintain a high wall of separation between church and state.[77]

While critical of the strict interpretation of the Establishment Clause in the first part of Justice Black's opinion for the Court, spokesmen for the Catholic Church were, of course, pleased that the New Jersey bus law had been upheld. Cardinal Spellman condemned the "bigotry" that was again "eating its way into the vital organs of the greatest nation on the face of the earth." The Supreme Court, Spellman continued, "has settled the question which never should have been raised. To me, an American citizen, it is embarrassing that this issue was raised in our nation which prides itself before the whole world as an example of fair play and tolerance."[78]

Msgr. William F. Lawlor, superintendent of the schools in the Newark,

New Jersey, archdiocese, praised the *Everson* decision and noted that the bus law had been passed in 1941 only after five years of debate and after petitions signed by 500,000 people had been presented to the legislature. Because of the litigation in the *Everson* case, only three township boards of education in New Jersey had continued to provide free transportation for parochial school students, but Father John Endebrock, secretary of education for the Trenton diocese, indicated that he would ask the school boards in Ewing Township and elsewhere in the diocese to resume free transportation to the parochial schools.[79]

For Albert McCay, Challen Ellis, and the Junior Order of Mechanics, the Court's decision was, of course, an extreme disappointment. "I am, of course, keenly disappointed by the decision," McCay wrote Ellis, "but feel that we did everything possible to win the case. Your brief and Senator Burke's argument were both excellent." And Challen Ellis wrote the JOUAM that he still felt "we are right in our stand and that the views of the Court, both majority and minority, on the First Amendment will be very helpful when another case comes up as is almost a certainty."[80] After a careful reading of the Court's opinion, however, McCay was not prepared to quit. In a letter to Ellis, McCay said that "I thoroughly agree with your statement that the first 13 pages of the Court's 15¼ page opinion lays down principles which would have fully justified a decision in our favor. The last 2¼ pages are devoted to grounds upon which the decision against us is based. It is difficult to follow the reasoning contained in those 2¼ pages." "The Court's opinion is so obviously unsound," McCay continued, "that I have reached the conclusion we should make application for rehearing." Ellis accordingly petitioned the Court for a rehearing, but the Court denied the petition on March 10, 1947.[81] The litigation in the *Everson* case thus came to an end.

The Supreme Court's decision in the *Everson* case, however, did not still the controversy over free transportation for parochial school students in New Jersey, since a new constitution was proposed for the state in 1947, and it contained a provision authorizing the legislature to provide free transportation for all students attending either private or public schools. Meeting at its seventy-eighth annual convention in Atlantic City on October 9, 1947, the Junior Order of Mechanics adopted a resolution opposing the new constitution because of the free-transportation provision and stated that the JOUAM had "as one of its cardinal principles the complete separation of church and state and has stood firm in the conviction that furnishing free bus transportation as provided in the new constitution is a direct violation of the First Amendment . . . of the Bill of Rights, establishing this complete separation."[82]

Unfortunately for the Junior Order of Mechanics, few other groups in New Jersey supported its position in regard to the new constitution. Most of the state's Protestant churches supported the constitution, although some recorded a specific objection to the school-bus provision. In addition to the JOUAM, the constitution was opposed by the Rev. Carl McIntyre's Bible Presbyterian Church in Collingswood and by the Taxpayers Association for Separation of Church and State.[83]

The new constitution was nevertheless adopted in November of 1947 by an overwhelming majority of the voters of New Jersey,[84] and the state legislature subsequently exercised the power to provide free bus transportation for both private and public school students in the state. The Junior Order of Mechanics, therefore, had not only lost the *Everson* case in the Supreme Court but had also seen the policy they had attacked in that case written into the New Jersey Constitution.[85]

With the *Everson* case having joined the *Gitlow-Fiske-Stromberg-Near* line of cases and the *DeJonge* and *Cantwell* cases, the nationalization of the rights in the First Amendment of the Bill of Rights had been completed. It was clear that the Court had reached a consensus that the rights of the First Amendment were so fundamental to a free society that they had to be included in the Due Process Clause of the Fourteenth Amendment as guarantees against state action. The most important guarantees in the Bill of Rights that had not been nationalized by the Court were the criminal-procedure provisions, and at the end of the 1930s, the Court appeared to have reached a consensus also that these provisions should not be applied to the states, at least in the same manner as they applied to the federal government. In the 1940s, however, the issue of the applicability of the criminal-procedure provisions of the Bill of Rights to the states produced serious differences on the Court, and these differences exploded publicly in the same year that the *Everson* case was decided. The result was that the theoretical problems associated with the nationalization of the Bill of Rights were treated more publicly and explicitly by the Court than ever before, revealing serious divisions over the prospect of nationalizing the Bill of Rights beyond the rights of the First Amendment.

6

From the
Palko Case to the *Adamson* Case
The Theoretical Conflict

During the course of applying the First Amendment rights to the states, the Supreme Court engaged in almost no theoretical discussion regarding the nationalization process. In contrast with its application of the First Amendment rights to the states, the Court refused to hold that the criminal-procedure provisions of the Bill of Rights applied to the states in the same fashion as they applied in federal proceedings, and it was therefore necessary for the Court to articulate in its criminal-procedure decisions during the 1930s and 1940s the principles that were guiding the nationalization process. Consequently, the fullest discussion of nationalization theory occurred in cases raising the question of whether various criminal-procedure provisions of the Bill of Rights applied to the states. A consensus on the theory of nationalization appeared to have been achieved by the end of the 1930s, but by 1947 this consensus had been shattered, and the Court was revealed to be badly divided over the theory of the nationalization process.

The fullest discussion by the Court of the theory of nationalization after the initial breakthrough of the *Gitlow-Fiske-Stromberg-Near* line of cases occurred in *Powell* v. *Alabama* in 1932. In the *Powell* case, the Court held that the Due Process Clause required the appointment of counsel for indigent defendants in state criminal proceedings involving capital crimes. Since the Sixth Amendment guaranteed the right to counsel in federal cases, the Court again sought to clarify the relationship between the Bill of Rights and the Due Process Clause.[1]

In what was perhaps his finest opinion for the Court, Justice Sutherland conceded in *Powell* that under the doctrine of nonsuperfluousness enunciated in *Hurtado* v. *California*, "it would be difficult to justify the conclusion that the right to counsel, being thus specifically granted by the Sixth Amendment, was also within the intendment of the due process of law clause." But the *Hurtado* case, Sutherland added, did "not stand alone." He pointed out that the *Chicago, Burlington & Quincy Railroad* case had undermined the doctrine of nonsuperfluousness and had been reinforced by the *Gitlow-Fiske-Stromberg-Near* line of cases. "These later cases," he said, "establish that notwithstanding the sweeping character of the language in the *Hurtado* Case, the rule laid down is not without exceptions. The rule is an aid to construction, and in some instances may be conclusive; but it must yield to more compelling considerations whenever such considerations exist."[2]

The Court was justified in not following the doctrine of nonsuperfluousness, Sutherland said, in those cases dealing with rights under the Due Process Clause that constituted the "fundamental principles of liberty and justice which lie at the base of all our civil and political institutions." In the *Chicago, Burlington & Quincy Railroad* case and in the *Gitlow-Fiske-Stromberg-Near* line of cases, he said, the Court had "regarded the rights there under consideration as of this fundamental character. That some such distinction must be observed is foreshadowed in *Twining* v. *New Jersey.* . . . " Sutherland then quoted the passage from *Twining* in which the Court acknowledged that rights similar to those in the Bill of Rights might be embraced by the Due Process Clause, not because they were listed in the Bill of Rights, but because a denial of them would also deny due process of law.[3]

Sutherland's opinion in the *Powell* case was the fullest discussion of the nationalization process the Court had yet offered. What had been implicit in the Court's decisions since *Twining* v. *New Jersey* was now made explicit. The doctrine of nonsuperfluousness was subject to major qualifications, and those qualifications would be made by the Court when a right listed in the Bill of Rights was asserted under the Due Process Clause, and when the Court determined that the right was fundamental. By citing and quoting the *Twining* opinion, on the other hand, the Court appeared to be holding that the rights protected by the Due Process Clause were not identical in scope and meaning to their namesakes in the Bill of Rights, but rather had as their sources, not the Bill of Rights, but the words *liberty* and *property* and the phrase *due process of law* in the Due Process Clause.

Although in *Powell* v. *Alabama* the Court dealt with and qualified the result in the *Hurtado* case, it did not adequately deal there with the logic behind the *Hurtado* doctrine of nonsuperfluousness—just as it had not in the *Twining* case. Since the logic of the doctrine of nonsuperfluousness was irreconcilable with a holding that any right either similar or identical to one of those in the Bill of Rights was also a guarantee of the Due Process Clause, the doctrine of nonsuperfluousness could not be, as Sutherland said in the *Powell* case, "an aid to construction" which "in some instances may be conclusive. . . . " The nationalization process was well under way when the *Powell* case was decided, and that process necessarily involved an abandonment by the Court of the doctrine of nonsuperfluousness, but, as in the *Twining* case, that abandonment continued to be unacknowledged.

The Court had also held in the *Powell* case that the Due Process Clause guaranteed a right to counsel for indigent defendants in state criminal proceedings, although in the past—in cases like *Hurtado* v. *California*, *Maxwell* v. *Dow*, and *Twining* v. *New Jersey*—it had consistently rejected arguments that some of the criminal-procedure provisions of the Bill of Rights were guaranteed by the Due Process Clause. But the Court had not adequately articulated the guiding principles by which it was distinguishing the right to counsel from the right against self-incrimination, the right to trial by jury, and the right to a grand jury indictment. And as the nationalization of the First Amendment rights proceeded apace, the Court gave little indication of why First Amendment rights were more fundamental than other rights in the Bill of Rights. Such questions were addressed by the Court, however, in a restatement of the theory of the nationalization process in *Palko* v. *Connecticut*, decided in 1937.

A Theoretical Restatement: The *Palko* Case

Shortly after midnight on September 30, 1935, the display window of Gilman's Music Store in Bridgeport, Connecticut, was smashed by two young men, who grabbed two radios and ran. Bridgeport police officers Wilfred Walker and Thomas P. Kearney observed Frank Jacob Palko (Palka) carrying a cheap radio, but when confronted by the officers, Palko shot and killed both of them. Detective Sergeant John Geraghty and Detective Peter McCarran arrived at the shooting scene and exchanged shots with Palko, but he made good his escape.[4]

Frank Palko was arrested by the police in Buffalo, New York, on October 29, 1935, a month after the killings. He had in his possession a revolver, a blackjack, and a large sum of money that he had apparently obtained through another robbery, and under questioning by the Buffalo police, he admitted the Bridgeport killings. The Bridgeport police, in the meantime, discovered revolver grips that had apparently broken when the window of Gilman's Music Store had been smashed. These broken grips were identified as belonging to a revolver stolen from a Bridgeport tavern, a crime Palko was also suspected of having committed.

Palko was indicted by the Fairfield County (Bridgeport) grand jury on the charge of first-degree murder, and he was brought to trial in the Superior Court of Fairfield County during January of 1936. On January 24, a jury found Palko guilty of second-degree murder, but the prosecution charged that several rulings of the trial judge had prejudiced its case before the jury.[5]

Palko had testified in his own behalf at the trial, and on cross-examination, the prosecution had attempted to show that he had acquired the revolver used to smash the music-store window in an earlier tavern robbery. The prosecution had also attempted to demonstrate that the money he had had in his possession when arrested was the fruit of a robbery. The trial judge, however, had refused to permit this kind of cross-examination and had also ruled that Palko's confession of the killings to the Buffalo police was inadmissible as evidence.

The trial judge's charge to the jury on the issue of premeditation as an element of first-degree murder, however, was, in the eyes of the prosecution, his most serious error. The judge had instructed the jury that first-degree murder must involve premeditation, and in order for there to be premeditation, an interval of time had to elapse between a decision to kill and the actual killing. When a person "suddenly makes up his mind to kill another and instantly shoots or otherwise fatally injures him," the judge told the jury, "there is no opportunity for such consideration of what he is doing to enable him to comprehend the nature of his act or the result of it to the object of his attack. In such a case there can be no premeditation since intent to kill and the performance of the act of killing coincide and practically take place at the same instant."[6]

The state objected to this charge to the jury because the judge had emphasized the time between the instant Palko saw the police officers and his shooting them. The judge should also have told the jury that Palko had left his apartment armed with a revolver to commit a robbery, the prosecution argued, and this action indicated a resolution on his part to kill rather than be captured. Although Palko had been convicted of second-degree murder, the prosecution felt that with a different charge on the issue of premeditation, the jury might have convicted him of murder in the first degree.

Palko was sentenced on January 28 to life imprisonment at hard labor, with a recommendation that he never be paroled. Under title 60, section 6494, of the General Statutes of Connecticut, however, the prosecution could appeal the outcome of a criminal trial if errors prejudicial to the state had occurred and if the trial judge granted his permission. The judge in the *Palko* case granted his permission, and the prosecution appealed the case to the Connecticut Supreme Court of Errors.

On July 30, 1936, the supreme court of errors upheld the state's arguments and reversed Palko's second-degree-murder conviction on the ground that the trial judge had indeed committed errors prejudicial to the prosecution at the trial. The trial judge, the court held, should not have excluded the confession Palko had made to the Buffalo police, since it appeared from the record to have been voluntary. But the principal error the trial judge had made, the court said, was in his instructions to the jury on the issue of premeditation. In confining the attention of the jury to the brief interval of time between Palko's confrontation by the police officers and his shooting them, the court held, "and giving no instructions as to the significance of the conduct of the accused in setting out armed under the circumstances as claimed by the State," the trial judge had committed reversible error, and the second-degree-murder conviction of Palko had to be reversed.[7]

Frank Palko was therefore once again placed on trial on the charge of first-degree murder. His court-appointed attorney, David Goldstein, objected to a retrial, however, on the ground that "this action would place [Palko] twice in jeopardy for the same offense, in violation of the Constitution of the State of Connecticut and the Constitution of the United States since [Palko] had already been convicted of murder in the second degree in a former trial for the same offense." The trial judge nonetheless overruled this objection, and Palko was tried again for first-degree murder during October of 1936. On October 15, the jury returned a verdict finding him guilty of murder in the first degree, and Judge Arthur F. Ellis sentenced him to be electrocuted at the state prison in February of 1937.[8]

David Goldstein secured a reprieve to allow an appeal of Palko's conviction to the Connecticut Supreme Court of Errors, and in his arguments before the court, Goldstein again objected that the retrial of Palko had constituted double jeopardy. The conviction of Palko for second-degree murder at the first trial, Goldstein argued, had involved an implicit acquittal on the first-degree-murder charge, and his retrial on that charge was equivalent to the retrial of a person who had been acquitted of the same offense. Palko's right not to be subjected to double jeopardy as guaranteed by both the Connecticut Constitution and the federal Constitution, Goldstein said, had therefore been violated by the state of Connecticut.

On April 7, 1937, however, the supreme court of errors rejected Goldstein's arguments and upheld Palko's first-degree-murder conviction. It had consistently held that the statute permitting the state to appeal a criminal case did not violate the right against double jeopardy, the court said, on the basis of the reasoning that "there is but one jeopardy and one trial; that where material error is committed on a trial and a new trial is ordered by the appellate court upon the State's appeal, the second trial is not a new case but is a legal disposal of the same original case in the first instance." Palko "had the benefit of a fair and impartial trial in accordance with the settled course of judicial proceedings prevailing in this State," the supreme court of errors concluded. "Our statute, which permits the State to appeal with the permission of the trial court, was first adopted in 1886 and has been in force for more than fifty years." And the statute did "not subject the accused to double jeopardy or abridge his privileges and immunities as a citizen of the United States, or deprive him of his life or liberty without 'due process of law.' There is no error."[9]

Despite this setback, Goldstein pursued his argument that Palko's retrial constituted double jeopardy on appeal to the United States Supreme Court. Indeed, in his argument to the Court, Goldstein contended that the

Privileges and Immunities Clause, or, alternatively, the Due Process Clause, of the Fourteenth Amendment had been intended to apply all of the Bill of Rights to the states, including the Fifth Amendment's Double Jeopardy Clause. In support of this contention, Goldstein relied heavily on Horace E. Flack's *The Adoption of the Fourteenth Amendment*, which had been published in 1908.

Flack had reviewed the congressional debates on the Fourteenth Amendment and the subsequent interpretation of the amendment by Congress, and he concluded that one of the purposes of the first section of the Fourteenth Amendment had been to "make the Bill of Rights (the first eight Amendments) binding upon, or applicable to, the States." In light of the intentions of Congress in proposing the amendment, Flack concluded, he had "little hesitancy in saying" that the application of the Bill of Rights to the states "was unquestionably one of the leading motives for the inclusion of [the first] section in the Fourteenth Amendment."[10]

Goldstein called Flack's book "a scholarly document which, to counsel's knowledge, has not hitherto been called to the court's attention," and he argued that Flack's research fully justified a decision by the Court holding that the Double Jeopardy Clause of the Fifth Amendment, along with the rest of the Bill of Rights, was applicable to the states. The right against double jeopardy, Goldstein also said, was just as fundamental a personal right as the right to counsel—which the Court had applied to the states in the *Powell* case—since the right against double jeopardy was "a fundamental and immutable principle of law necessary to the protection of the life and liberty of every citizen and not to be abridged by any state."[11] For a state to appeal a criminal case, and to retry a person for an offense of which he had been implicitly acquitted, Goldstein concluded, was a clear violation of the right against double jeopardy and justified a reversal of Palko's conviction.

Connecticut counsel, on the other hand, denied that the Fourteenth Amendment protected a right against double jeopardy in state criminal cases. The Court had refused to apply the Fifth Amendment's Grand Jury Clause and Self-Incrimination Clause to the states in the *Hurtado* and *Twining* cases, they noted, and for the same reasons the Double Jeopardy Clause should not apply in state proceedings.

Counsel for Connecticut also denied that the statute allowing the prosecution to appeal a criminal case violated double jeopardy. There was only one continuing jeopardy in a criminal case, beginning at the trial and continuing through any appeals, they contended, and if errors were committed at the trial, whether favorable to the accused or to the prosecution, either could appeal the result of the trial without violating the prohibition against double jeopardy. If the appellate court reversed the decision of the trial court, a new trial could be held and would be only an element of the continuing jeopardy to which the defendant was subjected. The retrial of Palko after the defective first trial, Connecticut counsel said, had not, therefore, violated his right against double jeopardy—even assuming that right was guaranteed by the federal Constitution in a state proceeding. The contemporary problem in criminal law, they concluded, was "how better to secure decent, law abiding citizens against the growing threat of daring and defiant crime. We respectfully submit that the statute condemned by this accused is an intelligent effort toward a solution of that problem."[12]

Like the *Twining* case almost thirty years earlier, *Palko* v. *Connecticut* once again offered the Court the opportunity to pass upon the question of whether the Fourteenth Amendment applied all of the Bill of Rights to the states. Given the nationalization that had begun in regard to First Amendment rights, the *Palko* case also offered the Court the opportunity to comment more fully on the principles governing its decisions relative to the nationalization process. When the Court affirmed Palko's conviction on December 6, 1937, Justice Cardozo's opinion for the Court consequently came to be considered one of the most influential in the history of the Court.

Cardozo began by once again rejecting out of hand the argument that all of the Bill of Rights applied to the states via the Fourteenth Amendment. "There is," he said, "no such general rule." He noted that the Fifth Amendment guarantee of the right to an indictment by a grand jury had been held in the *Hurtado* case not to apply to the states, and that the Fifth Amendment right against self-incrimination in state proceedings "will fail if the state elects to end it." The jury-trial guarantees for criminal and civil cases in the Sixth and Seventh Amendments, he also pointed out, did not apply to the states, since "trial by jury may be modified by a state or abolished altogether."[13]

On the other hand, Cardozo conceded that such rights as freedom of speech and of the press and the right to counsel had been held applicable to the states via the Due Process Clause. In these cases, he said, "immunities that were valid as against the federal government by force of specific pledges of particular amendments have been found to be implicit in the concept of ordered liberty, and thus, through the Fourteenth Amendment, become valid as against the states."[14]

The "rationalizing principle" that separated those rights in the Bill of Rights that were and those that were not protected by the Due Process Clause, Cardozo continued, was whether the particular right involved was "of the very essence of a scheme of ordered liberty." The right against compulsory self-incrimination, the right to grand jury indictment, or the right to jury trials could be abolished, he said, "and justice still be done." The Court's exclusion of these rights from protection by the Due Process

Clause had not "been arbitrary or casual. It has been dictated by a study and appreciation of the meaning, the essential implications, of liberty itself."[15]

A "different plane of social and moral values" was reached, Cardozo said, "when we pass to the privileges and immunities that have been taken over from the earlier articles of the federal bill of rights and brought within the Fourteenth Amendment by a process of absorption. These in their origins were effective against the Federal government alone. If the Fourteenth Amendment has absorbed them, the process of absorption has had its source in the belief that neither liberty nor justice would exist if they were sacrificed." Freedom of thought and speech, he continued, was a right of this nature, and indeed it was the "matrix, the indispensable condition, for nearly every other form of freedom." Fundamental also was "the thought that condemnation shall be rendered only after trial," a trial that provided a real hearing that might entail the appointment of counsel for indigent defendants. The decision in *Powell* v. *Alabama*, Cardozo said, did not turn upon "the fact that the benefit of counsel would have been guaranteed to defendants by the provisions of the Sixth Amendment if they had been prosecuted in a federal court. The decision turned upon the fact that in the particular situation laid before us in the evidence the benefit of counsel was essential to the substance of a hearing."[16]

The question in the *Palko* case, therefore, Cardozo said, was whether the "kind of double jeopardy to which the statute has subjected [Palko] is a hardship so shocking that our polity will not endure it? Does it violate those 'fundamental principles of liberty and justice which lie at the base of all our civil and political institutions?'" The answer, he continued, "surely must be 'no.'" Connecticut was only insisting that Palko be subjected to a trial free of error. If errors had been made prejudicial to Palko, he could have appealed and won a retrial, and a "reciprocal privilege, subject at all times to the discretion of the trial judge . . . , has now been granted to the state." Such a procedure was "no seismic innovation," Cardozo concluded. "The edifice of justice stands, in its symmetry, to many, greater than before."[17]

Cardozo's discussion of the theory of nationalization in his opinion was not entirely satisfactory, although some matters were made clear. The Fourteenth Amendment did not guarantee all of the rights in the Bill of Rights against impairment by the states. And those rights that were protected by the Due Process Clause had to be considered by the Court to be "implicit in the scheme of ordered liberty," or "of the very essence of a scheme of ordered liberty," or the denial of such rights must impose hardships "so shocking that our polity will not endure it" or violate the "fundamental principles of liberty and justice which lie at the base of all our civil and political institutions." These vague formulations did not supply any more understandable criteria as far as the nationalizing process was concerned than had been supplied in the *Twining* case almost thirty years before, and Justice Sutherland's opinion in *Powell* v. *Alabama* had been at least as clear on that point.

Nevertheless, Cardozo did list those rights that clearly were not embraced by the Due Process Clause. The right against self-incrimination, the right to grand jury indictment, the right to jury trials in criminal and civil cases, and the right against double jeopardy were not considered to be "implicit in the scheme of ordered liberty." In contrast, Cardozo had said, were the freedom of speech and of the press, freedom of religion, the right of assembly, and the "right of one accused of crime to the benefit of counsel," all of which were guaranteed by the Due Process Clause.

These rights, he said, had been "absorbed" by the Fourteenth Amendment, but the term "absorbed" could, and would, be read in different ways. It could be interpreted as meaning that once a right in the Bill of Rights was considered by the Court to be "implicit in the scheme of ordered liberty" and was "absorbed" by the Due Process Clause, such a right was identical in scope and meaning, when applied to the states, or when applied to the federal government directly from the Bill of Rights. On the other hand, "absorption" of a right by the Due Process Clause could also be read to mean that such a right was guaranteed because it was considered a fundamental right, and not because it was listed in the Bill of Rights. This interpretation of "absorption" would leave open the possibility that rights in the Due Process Clause similar to those in the Bill of Rights might be interpreted to have a different scope and meaning than their counterparts in the Bill of Rights.

Certainly Cardozo felt that the right to counsel guaranteed by the Due Process Clause was not necessarily identical with the Sixth Amendment's guarantee of counsel in federal proceedings. The *Powell* case, he had noted, did not turn on the fact that the defendants therein would have been guaranteed the right to counsel by the Sixth Amendment if tried in a federal court. The fundamental right guaranteed by the Due Process Clause was the right to a fair trial or hearing, and counsel was guaranteed by the Due Process Clause in those circumstances where such a guarantee was "essential to the substance of a hearing." The clear implication of Cardozo's opinion was that if a fair hearing in a state court were afforded a defendant unrepresented by counsel, the Due Process Clause would not require counsel in those circumstances. This was of course the rationale the Court pursued in state right-to-counsel cases until 1963.[18] But if the right to counsel guaranteed by the Due Process Clause was not identical to the provision in the Sixth Amendment, the question remained after the *Palko* case whether the other rights listed as being absorbed in the Due Process Clause were also not identical to their Bill of Rights' counterparts.

Cardozo also did not repeat Sutherland's statement in the *Powell* case that the *Hurtado* doctrine of nonsuperfluousness was "an aid to construction" of the Due Process Clause that "in some instances may be conclusive. . . ." The *Hurtado* doctrine simply ceased being discussed by the Court at this point in the nationalization of the Bill of Rights. Chief Justice Hughes reflected what was obviously the Court's current position on the relationship between the Bill of Rights and the Due Process Clause when he rather cryptically remarked in the *DeJonge* case that "explicit mention [of a right in the Bill of Rights] does not argue exclusion elsewhere."[19] Nonetheless, the *Hurtado* doctrine was subsequently revived by Justice Frankfurter and was utilized in his rather puzzling approach to the meaning of the Due Process Clause.

Despite its vague aspects, Cardozo's opinion in the *Palko* case apparently reflected the consensus of the Court in regard to the nationalization process, since only Justice Butler dissented from the judgment of the Court. And although there was a rapid turnover of justices with the coming of the Roosevelt Court after 1937, Cardozo's discussion of the fundamental nature of First Amendment freedoms in the *Palko* case inspired one of the most influential judicial doctrines during the 1940s, the doctrine of preferred freedoms.

Freedom of speech and freedom of thought, Cardozo had said, were at a "different plane of social and moral values," and formed the "matrix, the indispensable condition for nearly every other form of freedom."[20] These expressions inspired Justice Stone to propose the doctrine of preferred freedoms in his famous footnote number four in the *Carolene Products* case in 1938. Stone suggested in the footnote that the presumption of constitutionality might have "narrower scope for operation" when the Court was faced with policies which fell "within a specific prohibition of the Constitution, such as those of the first ten amendments, which are deemed equally specific when held to be embraced within the Fourteenth." Also, he suggested, the Court might subject to "more exacting judicial scrutiny" statutes restricting the political processes upon which the correction of undesirable policies was dependent, as well as statutes subjecting "discrete and insular minorities" to discrimination in the political process, which could ordinarily be counted upon to protect minorities from such discrimination.[21]

Stone's footnote suggested, therefore, that those constitutional provisions —especially First Amendment rights—that were essential to the maintenance of an open, democratic system should be considered "preferred freedoms." And the Court's principal role should be that of policing the openness of the democratic process to insure that unwise policies in other fields would be fully subject to the democratic check. With its emphasis upon First Amendment freedoms, the doctrine of preferred freedoms undoubtedly hastened the completion of the nationalization of First Amendment rights during the 1940s.

The doctrine of preferred freedoms may also have contributed to the Court's abandonment, in regard to First Amendment freedoms, of the *Twining* theory that rights protected by the Due Process Clause were only similar, and not identical, to their counterparts in the Bill of Rights. The Court began to express the view during the early 1940s that much of the vagueness of the Due Process Clause would be removed if its meaning was determined by the application of the rights in the Bill of Rights to the states in the identical way in which they applied to the federal government. The pre-1937 Court's perversion of the Due Process Clause to frustrate economic reform, it was argued, could be avoided in the future if the meaning of due process was defined by the specific rights in the First Amendment.

This idea was clearly expressed by Justice Jackson in his opinion for the Court in *West Virginia Board of Education* v. *Barnette* in 1943. "In weighing arguments of the parties," Jackson said, "it is important to distinguish between the due process clause of the Fourteenth Amendment as an instrument for transmitting the principles of the First Amendment and those cases in which it is applied for its own sake. The test of legislation which collides with the Fourteenth Amendment, because it also collides with the principles of the First, is much more definite than the test when only the Fourteenth is involved. Much of the vagueness of the due process clause disappears when the specific prohibitions of the First become its standard."[22]

Reflecting the influence of the doctrine of preferred freedoms, Jackson noted that economic regulations challenged under the Due Process Clause standing alone could be sustained if they were reasonably designed to promote a legitimate legislative purpose. But the First Amendment freedoms of "speech and of press, of assembly, and of worship may not be infringed on such slender grounds. They are susceptible of restriction only to prevent grave and immediate danger to interests which the state may lawfully protect. It is important to note that while it is the Fourteenth Amendment which bears directly upon the States it is the more specific limiting principles of the First Amendment that finally govern this case."[23]

That the Court now considered the First Amendment to apply to the states with the same meaning as it had when applied to the federal government was also indicated in the *Cantwell* and *Everson* decisions, nationalizing freedom of religion and the guarantee of separation of church and state. Justice Roberts said in the *Cantwell* case that the Court now regarded the Fourteenth Amendment as rendering "the legislatures of the states as incompetent as Congress" to enact laws violating First Amendment rights,[24] and the debate within the Court in the *Everson* case did not involve the question of whether the concept of separation of church and state applied with less vigor to the states than it did to the federal government.

Whether the rights of free speech, press, assembly, and religion and the guarantee of separation of church and state were still considered to have as their source the Due Process Clause alone, or whether the First Amendment was considered to be applicable directly to the states via the Due Process Clause, was left largely unexplained by the Court. Such questions were in any case theoretical distinctions without much difference, since the Court clearly felt that it was dealing with identical rights in relation to the First Amendment in both state and federal cases, whatever their sources might be.[25]

This full application of the First Amendment to the states, however, created more important theoretical problems on other fronts. If the First Amendment applied to the states in the identical fashion in which it applied to the federal government, the question arose as to how the Court could continue to justify its insistence that the right to counsel guaranteed by the Due Process Clause in state proceedings was, or had to be, different in scope and meaning from its counterpart in the Sixth Amendment. And if, as Justice Jackson suggested in the *Barnette* case, the nationalization of First Amendment freedoms supplied more definite content to the Due Process Clause—thus obviating the old problems of interpretation—it seemed reasonable to ask whether parts or all of the rest of the Bill of Rights might not also define even more specifically the word *liberty* and the phrase *due process of law* in the Due Process Clause.

Despite its abandonment of the *Twining* approach in First Amendment cases, however, the Court continued to deal with state criminal-procedure cases under the *Twining* theory. In *Powell* v. *Alabama*, the Court had held that the Due Process Clause required the appointment of counsel for indigent defendants in state capital cases, and four years later, in 1936, it held in *Brown* v. *Mississippi* that the Due Process Clause required the exclusion of coerced confessions in state criminal trials.[26] In neither the *Powell* nor the *Brown* case, however, did the Court hold that the Sixth Amendment's guarantee of the right to counsel or the Fifth Amendment's Self-Incrimination Clause were applicable to the states. The Due Process Clause, the Court held instead, required that the states accord to criminal defendants a fair hearing, and the admission of a coerced confession against a defendant, or the denial of counsel, at least in a capital case, would result in an unfair hearing. The appointment of counsel or the exclusion of coerced confessions were required in state criminal proceedings not by the commands of the Fifth and Sixth Amendments applying to the states via the Due Process Clause, but rather because they were essential elements of a fair hearing required by the Due Process Clause standing alone.

Thus, Chief Justice Hughes said in *Brown* v. *Mississippi* that the question of whether the state could abolish "the privilege against self-incrimination is not here involved. . . . Compulsion by torture to extort a confession is a different matter." The admission of a coerced confession extorted by torture in a state criminal trial was constitutionally offensive, Hughes said, not because it violated the Self-Incrimination Clause as applied to the states, but because it was "a wrong so fundamental that it made the whole proceeding a mere pretense of a trial and rendered the conviction and sentence wholly void."[27]

Similarly, in *Betts* v. *Brady*, decided in 1942, the Court refused to hold that the Sixth Amendment's Assistance of Counsel Clause applied to the states via the Due Process Clause. In 1938 the Assistance of Counsel Clause had been interpreted by the Court to require the appointment of counsel for indigent defendants in all federal criminal trials involving serious offenses, whether capital or noncapital. But in *Betts* v. *Brady*, the Court ruled that the states were required to appoint counsel for indigent defendants in capital cases only, whereas appointed counsel was required in noncapital state cases only when the absence of counsel would deprive the defendant of a fair hearing. Whether or not a fair hearing were accorded a state defendant who lacked counsel, the Court said, would depend upon such factors as the conduct of the prosecutor and the judge and the age and mental capacity of the defendant.[28]

While it had recognized a form of protection against self-incrimination in the *Brown* case and a limited right to counsel in the *Powell* and *Betts* cases, the Court's interpretation of those rights under the Due Process Clause clearly indicated that they were only similar to the rights protected by the Self-Incrimination Clause of the Fifth Amendment and the Assistance of Counsel Clause of the Sixth Amendment. And this treatment of due process rights arising in state criminal cases contrasted sharply with the Court's treatment of First Amendment rights that, it now said, applied to the states in the identical way in which they applied to the federal government. The *Twining* approach had been abandoned by the Court during the 1940s in First Amendment cases, but paradoxically, it continued to be followed in state criminal-procedure cases.

The Court's approach to state criminal-procedure issues under the Due Process Clause required a case-by-case evaluation of whether or not a fair hearing had been accorded criminal defendants. As the leading exponent of this approach to the application of the Due Process Clause, Justice Frankfurter said that when "a conviction in a state court is properly here for review, under a claim that a right protected by the Fourteenth Amendment has been denied, the question is not whether the record can be found to disclose an infraction of one of the specific provisions of the first eight amendments." The Due Process Clause, Frankfurter continued, "inescapably imposes upon this Court an exercise of judgment upon the whole course of the proceedings in order to ascertain whether they offend those canons of decency and fairness which express the notions of justice of English-speaking peoples even toward those charged with the most heinous offenses." Such standards were nowhere formulated, he said, "as though they were prescriptions in a pharmacopoeia," yet the discretion of the justices in interpreting the Due Process Clause was still confined "within the limits of accepted notions of justice and is not to be based upon the idiosyncracies of a merely personal judgment. The fact that judges among themselves may differ whether in a particular case a trial offends accepted notions of justice is not disproof that general rather than idiosyncratic standards are applied."[29]

To some of the justices, and especially to Justice Black, however, the Court's "fair trial" approach on a case-by-case basis did allow too much judicial discretion in determining what was or was not "fair" under the Due Process Clause, despite Frankfurter's eloquent defense of the approach. To Black and those who agreed with him, such an approach was similar to the "natural law" approach utilized by the pre-1937 Court to read its own economic predilections into the Due Process Clause, thus creating roadblocks to economic reform. Such an approach to the Due Process Clause in state criminal cases seemed to Black and others not only to involve the repetition of the sins of the past but to involve also the substitution of pale and faded replicas for the procedural guarantees of the Bill of Rights in state criminal cases.

Although Black had voted with the majority in *Palko* v. *Connecticut,* in which the Court held that the Double Jeopardy Clause of the Fifth Amendment as well as other procedural rights in the Bill of Rights did not apply to the states, J. Woodford Howard has indicated that as early as 1939 Black had begun to argue within the Court that all or some of the procedural guarantees of the Bill of Rights were applicable to the states via the Due Process Clause. And by 1943, Frankfurter was writing to Black, asking him "quite humbly to lead me to the materials that show that the Fourteenth Amendment incorporated by reference the provisions —any or all—of the earlier nine Amendments."[30]

Black did publicly hint at his evolving position that the Fourteenth Amendment had made all of the Bill of Rights applicable to the states in his opinion for the Court in *Chambers* v. *Florida* in 1940. In a footnote, Black cited "a current of opinion—which this Court has declined to adopt in many previous cases—that the Fourteenth Amendment was intended to make secure against State invasion all the rights, privileges and immunities protected from Federal violation by the Bill of Rights (Amendments 1 to 8). . . ."[31] And in *Betts* v. *Brady* two years later, Black, joined by Justices Murphy and Douglas, dissented from the Court's refusal to apply the Assistance of Counsel Clause of the Sixth Amendment to the states. "I believe," he said, "that the Fourteenth Amendment made the Sixth applicable to the states. But this view, although often urged in dissents, has never been accepted by a majority of this Court and is not accepted today. A statement of the grounds supporting it is, therefore, unnecessary at this time."[32]

Black indicated in a footnote, however, that David Goldstein's argument in the *Palko* case, based on Horace Flack's *The Adoption of the Fourteenth Amendment*, may have impressed him more than his vote had indicated. "Discussion of the Fourteenth Amendment by its sponsors in the Senate and House," Black said, "shows their purpose to make secure against invasion by the states the fundamental liberties and safeguards set out in the Bill of Rights. The legislative history and subsequent course of the amendment to its final adoption have been discussed in Flack, 'The Adoption of the Fourteenth Amendment.'" Black acknowledged, however, that the application of the Bill of Rights to the states via the Fourteenth Amendment had been considered and rejected by the Court on several occasions.[33]

While Black was postponing his full statement justifying the total incorporation of the Bill of Rights into the Fourteenth Amendment, Justice Frankfurter took the offensive and began to attack publicly the total-incorporation position. Frankfurter struck in *Malinski* v. *New York*, a coerced-confession case decided in 1945, and pounded the total-incorporation theory hip and thigh. "The suggestion that 'due process of law,' as guaranteed by the Fourteenth Amendment," Frankfurter declared, "is a compendious expression of the original federal Bill of Rights (Amendments First to Eight) has been rejected by this Court again and again and after impressive consideration." In language reminiscent of the *Hurtado* doctrine of nonsuperfluousness, Frankfurter argued that the Due Process Clause of the Fifth Amendment was obviously not a "shorthand statement" of the other clauses in the same amendment, including the Double Jeopardy Clause and the Self-Incrimination Clause. Such a contention, he said, would be to charge the framers of the Bill of Rights with "meretricious redundancy by indifference to a phrase—'due process of law'—which was one of the great instruments in the very arsenal of constitutional freedom which the Bill of Rights was to protect and strengthen." Of course, he continued, "the Due Process Clause of the Fourteenth Amendment has the same meaning [as that of the Fifth Amendment]. To suppose that 'due process of law' meant one thing in the Fifth Amendment and another in the Fourteenth is too frivolous to require elaborate rejection."[34]

During the consideration of the *Malinski* case by the Court, Justice Black apparently circulated within the Court a memorandum stating that he would one day write an opinion refuting Frankfurter's "natural law" approach to the Due Process Clause.[35] Yet despite Frankfurter's open challenge in the *Malinski* case and subsequently,[36] Black still held back from stating fully and publicly his argument for the total incorporation of the Bill of Rights by the Fourteenth Amendment until 1947. But Admiral Dewey Adamson's trouble with the law in California provided the opportunity for Black to fully state his total-incorporation theory, and in the ensuing debate, the Court was revealed to be fundamentally divided over the underlying theory by which the nationalization of the Bill of Rights had proceeded.

The Incorporation Debate: The *Adamson* Case

Mrs. Stella Blauvelt was a sixty-four-year-old widow who lived alone in an apartment at 744 Catalina Street in Los Angeles. Her late husband had been a Chicago insurance executive, and as a moderately wealthy widow, Mrs. Blauvelt had led an apparently uneventful life in Los Angeles for twenty years.[37] That uneventful existence ended for her one day in July of 1944. Mrs. Blauvelt had become active in the Red Cross during World War II, and on Tuesdays she usually accompanied one of her neighbors in the apartment building to the Red Cross center. On the evening of the twenty-fifth of July, the neighbor went to Mrs. Blauvelt's apartment but received no answer after knocking on the door. The neighbor then consulted the manager of the apartment building, and the two of them returned to the Blauvelt apartment. Using a passkey, the manager opened the door and discovered Mrs. Blauvelt lying dead on the living-room floor.[38]

The police were immediately summoned, and after a brief inspection of the body, they determined that Mrs. Blauvelt had been murdered. Two bloodstained pillows were lying on her face and head, and a coat covered the lower portion of her body. An electric-lamp cord had been wound around Mrs. Blauvelt's throat. A subsequent medical examination determined that Mrs. Blauvelt had been severely beaten, but that the cause of her death had been strangulation. The time of death was determined to have been on Monday, July 24.[39]

Further investigation of the Blauvelt apartment revealed that the motive for the murder had been burglary. Diamond rings that Mrs. Blauvelt had been known to wear on her left hand were missing, and her purse had also been rifled. The burglar had apparently gained entrance to the apartment through a garbage compartment in the kitchen. This compartment was connected with the apartment by a door through which garbage cans could be inserted, and another door connected the garbage compartment with the hallway, so that garbage from the compartment could be collected from the hallway. The burglar had apparently entered the garbage compartment from the hallway door. The inside door to the compartment had been latched, but the burglar had simply forced the inside door off its hinges and entered the apartment. The inner door was found by the police leaning against the kitchen sink.

This inner door of the garbage compartment provided the police with their first solid clues to the murderer of Mrs. Blauvelt. On the door a police fingerprint expert discovered several latent fingerprints that did not belong to Mrs. Blauvelt. Further investigation of the murder apartment also turned up some interesting facts about the murderer. Although Mrs. Blauvelt had not been sexually assaulted, under her body the police discovered one of her stockings with the top missing. The other stocking was not in the apartment. The police deduced that they were looking for a burglar who had a fixation in regard to women's stockings, particularly women's stocking tops.[40]

A month after the murder, on August 24, the Los Angeles police arrested Admiral Dewey Adamson, a forty-three-year-old black man, and charged him with first-degree murder and burglary in the Blauvelt case. Adamson had a prior criminal record, although it dated from twenty years earlier. He had been convicted in Missouri of burglary in 1920 and of robbery in 1927, and he had served time for these offenses in the Missouri state prison. Adamson was booked in at the University Police Station on the charge of murder and burglary in the early morning hours of August 24, but from the beginning he maintained his innocence and told the police that he had an alibi for the day of the murder.[41]

At his preliminary hearing, Dewey Adamson entered a plea of not guilty, but he was bound over for trial on charges of murder and burglary in the Superior Court for Los Angeles County. His trial began on November 14, 1944, before a jury of eleven women and one man. Judge Charles W. Fricke presided at the trial; Deputy District Attorney S. Ernest Roll represented the state; and Dewey Adamson was represented by Milton B. Safier.

The most important evidence introduced against Adamson at the trial was fingerprint evidence from the unhinged inner door of the garbage compartment in the Blauvelt apartment. A police expert testified that the fingerprints were definitely those of Adamson, and this testimony was supported by a court-appointed fingerprint expert.[42]

Only two other items of evidence were introduced by the prosecution that tended to link Dewey Adamson directly to the murder of Mrs. Blauvelt. Frances Jean Turner, a black woman who patronized the Colony Club bar, testified that she had overheard Adamson offer to sell a diamond ring to another customer in the bar. Also, Officer William H. Brennan of the homicide detail of the Wilshire Detective Bureau, along with his partner, had located the apartment where Dewey Adamson lived, and during a search of the apartment, they had discovered women's stocking tops in a bureau drawer in the bedroom. Over the objections of defense counsel, these stocking tops were admitted into evidence by Judge Fricke, although they were not those of Mrs. Blauvelt.[43]

No witnesses were called in Adamson's behalf, and he himself did not testify because of his prior criminal record. If he had testified in his own behalf, the prosecution could have revealed his prior record to the jury for the purpose of impeaching his credibility as a witness. Under article I, section 13, of the California Constitution, on the other hand, the prosecution could comment on Dewey Adamson's failure to testify in his own behalf, and Deputy District Attorney Roll took full advantage of this opportunity in his closing argument to the jury.[44]

Roll pointed out that the jury had not "heard from the lips of the defendant or a single witness called by the defendant where he was other than in that apartment." As far as Adamson was concerned, he said, "he does not have to take the stand. But it would take about twenty or fifty horses to keep someone off the stand if he was not *afraid*. He does not tell you. No." Adamson had had the presumption of innocence at the outset of the trial, Roll continued, but as the state's case developed, he had been stripped "of that presumption of innocence, and finally, at the conclusion of the People's case, when he did not take the stand or did not put any witnesses on the stand, he stood here with that presumption removed, based on the evidence in this case." Adamson could have explained a lot of things, Roll declared. "If he wasn't [in the Blauvelt apartment], where was he? Where was he? . . . He could explain how his prints got on there." Adamson had the right to testify in his own behalf, Roll continued, "and he did not do it. You can consider that with all the testimony in this case, and I ask you to consider it." In conclusion, Roll said, "I am going to make this one statement to you: Counsel asked you to find this defendant not guilty. But does the Defendant get on the stand and say, under oath, 'I am not guilty'? Not one word from him, and not one word from a single witness. I leave the case in your hands."[45]

On November 22, 1944, the jury returned verdicts of guilty on both the murder and burglary counts against Dewey Adamson. And on November 27, Adamson was sentenced by Judge Fricke to death in the gas chamber in the state prison at San Quentin. Adamson was also adjudged an habitual criminal because of his prior criminal record, and he was sentenced to life imprisonment on the burglary count. The execution of Adamson's sentence was stayed, however, pending the outcome of an appeal of his case to the California Supreme Court.[46]

The California Supreme Court nonetheless unanimously affirmed Adamson's conviction on January 4, 1946. Relying on *Twining* v. *New Jersey*, the court held that California's comment practice did not violate the federal Constitution. "Although there has been much discussion as to the wisdom of allowing comment upon and consideration of a defendant's failure to deny or explain incriminating evidence . . . ," it said, "the freedom from federal constitutional limitations of state provisions allowing such comment and consideration was settled in *Twining* v. *New Jersey.* . . ."[47]

Counsel for Adamson had also argued that he had been denied a fair trial by the introduction of the women's stocking tops as evidence against him. The introduction of the stocking tops by the prosecution had been solely for the purpose of inflaming an all-white jury against a black defendant accused of murdering a white woman, Adamson's counsel argued, and the effect had been so prejudicial that Adamson had been denied a fair trial. But the California Supreme Court ruled that the stocking tops were evidence that Adamson "had some use for women's stocking tops. This interest in women's stocking tops is a circumstance that tends to identify defendant as the person who removed the stockings from the victim and took away the top of one and the whole of another." The stocking tops therefore constituted "a logical link in the chain of evidence," the court said, and "demonstrative evidence that tends to prove a material issue or clarify the circumstances of the crime is admissible despite its prejudicial tendency."[48] Neither the comment by the prosecution on his failure to testify nor the admission of the stocking tops as evidence against him, had denied Adamson a fair trial, the court held, and his convictions were affirmed.

After the decision of the California Supreme Court, the fight to save Dewey Adamson's life was carried to the United States Supreme Court. Since Adamson was incarcerated and without funds, the appeal to the Supreme Court had to proceed *in forma pauperis*, and Milton B. Safier's law partner, Morris Lavine, conducted the appeal on behalf of Adamson without fee.

Morris Lavine urged the Court to reverse *Twining* v. *New Jersey* and to hold that the Self-Incrimination Clause of the Fifth Amendment was applicable in state proceedings via the Due Process Clause. If the Self-Incrimination Clause applied to the states, he argued, California's comment practice was clearly unconstitutional, since it penalized a defendant's exercise of the right against self-incrimination, which included the right not to testify at one's trial. The nearly forty years that had passed since the *Twining* decision, he said, "have given us a new concept of ordered liberty, a concept based upon a clear examination of those things which should be included and excluded in a living world under a Constitution that was meant to protect all the human rights for which this republic stands." And under this new concept of ordered liberty, Lavine argued, "Justice Harlan's able and analytical dissenting opinion in *Twining* v. *New Jersey* should be the standard of due process today."[49]

Even if it is assumed that the Self-Incrimination Clause does not apply to the states, however, Lavine argued, Dewey Adamson's convictions should still be reversed on the ground that he had been denied a fair trial as guaranteed by the Due Process Clause. Both the introduction of the stocking tops as evidence and the prosecution's comments to the jury on his failure to testify, Lavine said, constituted violations of due process. The comment practice denied the right to a fair trial in much the same manner as the admission into evidence of a coerced confession, Lavine contended, since the comment practice put "statutory heat" on a defendant to incriminate himself, replacing the "club, the fist, the bludgeon, and the rubber hose." If Adamson had testified, the prosecution could have brought out his prior criminal record, Lavine noted, and by not testifying the prosecutor could infer his guilt to the jury. The California comment practice, he concluded, required that "you get on the witness stand and subject yourself to the questioning of a clever prosecutor who is prepared to shrivel you to pieces, very much like the star chamber methods which were disapproved in England and the earlier ecclesiastical courts. The statute says, in effect, if you don't do so there is a presumption or inference of guilt which the jury has a right to consider from the mere fact of silence in the courtroom." The result, Lavine declared, was that "you are damned if you do and you are damned if you don't."[50]

California counsel, on the other hand, denied that the comment practice violated the federal Constitution. The Due Process Clause did not protect a right against self-incrimination, they argued, and the "case of *Twining* v. *New Jersey* . . . would seem to be, and generally is considered by courts and text writers, as determinative of this question." Adamson had been accorded a fair trial, California counsel said, and the record disclosed that "if there were procedural errors they were not prejudicial and not of a character nor importance to warrant this court in taking cognizance of them." There was nothing in the record, they concluded, "that can be said to 'shock the conscience' or that is 'abhorrent to the sense of justice' or that offends any principle of justice so rooted in the conscience as to be ranked as fundamental."[51]

Adamson v. *California* was argued before the Court on January 15 and 16, 1947, and was considered in the conference of the Court on January 18. According to Justice Rutledge's conference notes, Justice Burton voted to affirm the California Supreme Court's decision upholding Adamson's convictions. Rutledge, who voted next, voted to reverse, as did Justices Murphy and Douglas. Justices Jackson, Frankfurter, and Reed voted to affirm, with Reed arguing that even if the Self-Incrimination Clause applied to the states, there had been no violation of the right in the *Adamson* case. Justice Black passed, saying that although he believed the Self-Incrimination Clause applied to the states, he was unsure as to whether comment upon the failure of a defendant to testify violated the clause. Voting last, Chief Justice Vinson voted to affirm, and the vote was thus five votes to affirm and three to reverse, with Black passing.

Justice Reed was ultimately assigned the task of writing the majority opinion, but while the opinions were being written, Justice Black resolved his doubts and began writing a dissenting opinion in which he fully elaborated upon his theory that all of the Bill of Rights applied to the states via the Fourteenth Amendment. Black was supported by Douglas, Murphy, and Rutledge, with the result that in the *Adamson* case more votes were cast in favor of the total-incorporation theory than ever before or since. As the leading opponent of Black's theory, Justice Frankfurter felt that the *Adamson* case should be affirmed exclusively on the basis of the "cloudless" decision in *Twining* v. *New Jersey*, and he therefore wrote a concurring opinion sharply attacking the total-incorporation position.[52]

When the Court's decision was announced on June 23, 1947, Justice Reed's opinion affirming Adamson's convictions largely on the basis of the *Twining* case was overshadowed by his colleagues' battling over the theory of the nationalization process. Relying on the *Twining* case, Reed again reaffirmed that the Fourteenth Amendment did not guarantee a right of self-incrimination in state proceedings. The Due Process Clause, he said, guaranteed a state criminal defendant a fair trial, but it did not protect "by virtue of its mere existence the accused's freedom from giving testimony by compulsion that is secured to him against federal interference by the Fifth Amendment."[53]

As far as comment upon the failure of a defendant to testify was concerned, Reed held that a "state may control such a situation in accordance with its own ideas of the most efficient administration of criminal justice. The purpose of due process is not to protect an accused against a proper conviction but against an unfair conviction. When evidence is before a jury that threatens conviction, it does not seem unfair to require him to choose between leaving the adverse evidence unexplained and subjecting himself to impeachment through disclosure of former crimes." And finally, Reed said, the introduction of the stocking tops had not denied Adamson a fair trial. "We do not think," he concluded, "the introduction of the evidence violated any federal constitutional right."[54]

In his dissent, Justice Black attacked the *Twining* case and "the 'natural law' theory of the Constitution upon which it relies" because it degraded "the constitutional safeguards of the Bill of Rights and simultaneously appropriates for this court a broad power which we are not authorized by the Constitution to exercise." Prior to the adoption of the Fourteenth Amendment, he acknowledged, the Bill of Rights did not apply to the states under the ruling of the Court in *Barron* v. *Baltimore* in 1833. But his study of the history of the adoption of the Fourteenth Amendment had persuaded him, Black continued, "that one of the chief objects that the provisions of the Amendment's first section, separately, and as a whole, were intended to accomplish was to make the Bill of Rights, applicable to the states." The framers and backers of the Fourteenth Amendment had proclaimed that its purpose was to reverse the *Barron* decision, Black contended, but this "historical purpose has never received full consideration or exposition in any opinion of this court interpreting the Amendment." To make up for this deficiency, Black included an appendix to his opinion containing extensive quotes from the congressional debates involving the Fourteenth Amendment, especially the comments of Senator Howard and Congressman Bingham, who had been the amendment's chief sponsors.[55]

Black also justified the application of the Bill of Rights to the states on a ground other than his interpretation of the intentions of the framers of the Fourteenth Amendment. The natural law approach to the Due Process Clause that allowed the Court from time to time to determine what fundamental rights were protected under its provisions, Black argued, had been the basis for the Court's perversion of due process to limit legitimate state economic policies according to the Court's economic predilections. In Black's view, therefore, the natural law formula symbolized by the *Twining* case had been utilized to give the Court unwarranted discretionary power over state policies, and it had become an "incongruous excrescence on our Constitution. I believe that it subtly conveys to courts, at the expense of legislatures, ultimate power over policies in fields where no specific provision of the Constitution limits legislative power."[56]

To Black, therefore, the use of the Bill of Rights to define the meaning of the Due Process Clause would bridle an unrestricted and unwarranted judicial discretion in interpreting due process. He acknowledged that the natural law approach had been utilized to make applicable to the states some of the rights in the Bill of Rights, and he conceded that if "the choice must be between the selective process of the *Palko* decision applying some of the Bill of Rights to the States, or the *Twining* rule applying none of them, I would choose the *Palko* selective process." But rather than follow either the *Twining* or the *Palko* case, he concluded, "I would follow what I believe was the original purpose of the Fourteenth Amendment—to extend to all the people the complete protection of the Bill of Rights. To hold that this Court can determine what, if any, provisions of the Bill of Rights will be enforced, and if so to what degree, is to frustrate the great design of a written Constitution."[57]

Although Justices Douglas, Murphy, and Rutledge joined Black's dissent, Murphy and Rutledge added a caveat to their adherence to the total-incorporation theory. He agreed, Murphy said, that the "Bill of Rights should be carried over intact into the first section of the Fourteenth Amendment. But I am not prepared to say that the latter is entirely and necessarily limited by the Bill of Rights." Occasions might arise, Murphy continued, "where a proceeding falls so far short of conforming to fundamental standards of procedure as to warrant constitutional condemnation in terms of a lack of due process despite the absence of a specific provision in the Bill of Rights."[58]

Murphy and Rutledge therefore endorsed what was to be called the total-incorporation-plus theory. While they agreed that all of the Bill of Rights should apply to the states, they were unwilling to say that practices not specifically condemned by the Bill of Rights could not also still be invalidated under the Due Process Clause standing alone. This position, of course, was at odds with at least part of Justice Black's reasoning justifying the application of the Bill of Rights to the states—that is, the argument that total incorporation would supply specificity to the Due Process Clause and bridle judicial discretion in its interpretation. Rutledge and Murphy were unwilling to confine the meaning of the Due Process Clause exclusively to the terms of the Bill of Rights, but would have left the door open to future applications of due process beyond the Bill of Rights. On this point, their position was ultimately vindicated, over the strong objections of Justice Black.[59]

In his concurring opinion in the *Adamson* case, Justice Frankfurter continued the attack he had begun on the total-incorporation position in the *Malinski* case. Among the justices who had sat on the Court since the adoption of the Fourteenth Amendment, he said, only Justice Harlan, "who may respectfully be called an eccentric exception," had been of the view that the Fourteenth Amendment "was a shorthand summary of the first eight Amendments theretofore limiting only the Federal Government, and that due process incorporated those eight Amendments as restrictions upon the powers of the States."[60]

If the framers of the Fourteenth Amendment had intended the Due Process Clause to include the Bill of Rights within its terms, Frankfurter continued, they had selected a "strange way of saying it." The notion that the Fourteenth Amendment "was a covert way of imposing upon the States all the rules which it seemed important to Eighteenth Century statesmen to write into the Federal Amendments," he said, "was rejected by judges who were themselves witnesses of the process by which the Fourteenth Amendment became part of the Constitution."[61]

Frankfurter defended the natural law or fair trial approach to the meaning of the Due Process Clause in state criminal cases, and again argued that for one to assume that the Due Process Clauses of the Fifth and Fourteenth Amendments were not identical in meaning would be to attribute to the framers of the Bill of Rights an "ignorance of, or indifference to, a historic conception which was one of the great instruments in the arsenal of constitutional freedoms which the Bill of Rights was to protect and strengthen." And again Frankfurter argued that in applying the Due Process Clause in state criminal cases, the Court's function was not to apply the specific safeguards of the Bill of Rights but rather to determine if the state proceedings conformed to "those canons of decency and fairness which express the notions of justice of English-speaking peoples even toward those charged with the most heinous offenses."[62]

Despite the strong conflict between Justices Black and Frankfurter, there was perhaps a certain degree of agreement between them on the problem of interpreting the Due Process Clause. Both were cognizant of the lessons to be learned from the pre-1937 Court's use of due process to read its own economic views into the Constitution and thereby to frustrate progressive reforms. The lessons to be learned from the pre-1937 history of the Due Process Clause, however, were perceived differently by Black and by Frankfurter.

From Black's viewpoint, the perversion of due process prior to 1937 had resulted from the Court's assumption of the power to declare which fundamental rights were protected by the Due Process Clause and which were not. And for Black, the unbridled discretionary power that the Court had so acquired could only be checked by defining the meaning of the Due Process Clause to include the Bill of Rights and nothing more.

In Frankfurter's eyes, however, the pre-1937 Court's mistake had been its willingness to impose its views of what it thought was wise policy upon the states, rather than recognizing that in a democratic society policy must be almost completely the responsibility of the democratic process and not of the judicial process. The pre-1937 Court had demonstrated a rigidity in the application of due process and a lack of respect for variation and experiment within the several states. To impose upon the states all of the procedural requirements of the Bill of Rights, including such requirements as indictment by grand jury or jury trials in all civil cases involving more than twenty dollars, Frankfurter felt, would be to again rigidify federal due process standards and to deprive the states of the flexibility needed in a changing and progressive society. As he said in his *Adamson* concurrence, the Due Process Clause "neither comprehends the specific provisions by which the founders deemed it appropriate to restrict the federal government nor is it confined to them. The Due Process Clause of the Fourteenth Amendment has an independent potency."[63] In the field of criminal procedure, Frankfurter therefore argued, the Fourteenth Amendment did not impose the uniform requirements of the Bill of Rights on the states, but rather imposed standards of decency that derived from the Due Process Clause standing alone and without reference to the Bill of Rights.

Because Black had relied on his historical research regarding the intentions of the framers of the Fourteenth Amendment to support his total-incorporation position, his position was vulnerable to attack by other researchers, who would dispute the validity of his findings. Such an attack soon appeared with the publication of an article by Professor Charles Fairman in 1949. After inspecting the records of the Congress and the state legislatures in adopting the Fourteenth Amendment, Fairman concluded that as far as Black's "contention that Section I [of the Fourteenth Amendment] was intended and understood to impose Amendments I to VIII upon the states, the record of history is overwhelmingly against him."[64] On the other hand, Black's position has subsequently been supported by other researchers in an ongoing debate.[65]

It would appear, however, that Black's position never recovered from Fairman's initial and rather devastating attack. And Black never posed the more relevant question of whether the Bill of Rights ought to apply to the states as a matter of judicial policy. Because of his rather primitive judicial philosophy, Black believed that judicial policymaking could be removed from Due Process Clause decisions by making the Bill of Rights applicable to the states, and he also believed that his role was that of an essentially nondiscretionary transmitter of the "true" meaning of the Constitution as a whole. An historical approach to this true meaning of the Constitution was therefore essential to Black's conception of his role as the conduit for a Constitution of which the meaning was fixed and unchanging.[66]

The question of whether the Bill of Rights should be applied to the states was therefore irrelevant under such a philosophy, and the only consideration was whether the Fourteenth Amendment could be determined to have been intended to apply the Bill of Rights to the states. Historical analysis, however faulty, of the true meaning of the Constitution was the only relevant consideration to Black, and the total-incorporation position was therefore left vulnerable to rebuttal historical analyses, such as Fairman's, while valid arguments justifying the application of all or parts of the Bill of Rights to the states were left largely unstated. And given the weaknesses in the position opposed to Black's position, this was to leave an important part of the battle unfought.

Although his total-incorporation theory was never accepted by the Court, Black lived to see almost all of the Bill of Rights applied to the states by a process of selective incorporation. And in 1968, Black declared that he believed "as strongly as ever that the Fourteenth Amendment was intended to make the Bill of Rights applicable to the States," while he rejoiced that the selective-incorporation process had made "most of the Bill of Rights protections applicable to the States." It is more than ironic that this leader of the most significant change in American constitutional doctrine since the Civil War denied to the end that he was an innovator at all.[67]

Justice Frankfurter was the immediate victor, however, in the due process battle in the *Adamson* case, and his defense of the fair-trial approach to the Due Process Clause in state criminal cases would be followed by the

Court until the 1960s. Taken together, Frankfurter's enunciations of due process theory in the *Malinski* and *Adamson* cases were nevertheless seriously deficient. In both cases, Frankfurter relied upon reasoning similar to the *Hurtado* doctrine of nonsuperfluousness to assert that the Due Process Clauses in the Fifth and Fourteenth Amendments were identical, and therefore it was illogical to say that the Due Process Clause of the Fourteenth Amendment embraced the procedural protections listed in the Bill of Rights.

It would have been defensible if Frankfurter had argued in opposition to the total-incorporation position that it was historically unsupportable and also that the Due Process Clause did not apply to the states the criminal-procedure provisions of the Bill of Rights because they were not regarded as fundamental rights like the rights in the First Amendment. And Frankfurter did make the defensible argument that the Self-Incrimination Clause should not apply to the states because the states had historically been primarily responsible for the administration of criminal justice and that the extension of the criminal-procedure provisions of the Bill of Rights to the states would be an illegitimate intrusion of federal power into the domain of the states.

Frankfurter went even further in the *Malinski* and *Adamson* cases, however, and asserted that the Due Process Clauses in the Fifth and Fourteenth Amendments were identical in meaning, and—reviving the doctrine of nonsuperfluousness—he argued that therefore the Due Process Clause of the Fourteenth Amendment did not apply the Self-Incrimination Clause to the states. Yet by 1947, the Court had held in many cases in which Frankfurter had joined that the Due Process Clause applied the First Amendment to the states. And Frankfurter did not disavow these decisions in his *Adamson* opinion or later. To paraphrase his own language, it was pretty late in the day for him to revive the *Hurtado* doctrine of nonsuperfluousness and to argue that because the Due Process Clauses of the Fifth and Fourteenth Amendments were identical, the criminal procedure provisions of the Bill of Rights did not apply to the states. If—as the Court had decided time and time again with Frankfurter's apparent support—the First Amendment was applicable to the states, then it simply was not correct to say that the Due Process Clauses in the Constitution were identical.[68]

The question in the *Adamson* case was properly why—if the First Amendment applied to the states—some or all of the procedural guarantees of the Bill of Rights were not also applicable to the states. Although his denunciation of the total-incorporation position was typically eloquent, Frankfurter simply did not meet this question in the *Adamson* case. Instead, he resorted to a form of the discredited doctrine of nonsuperfluousness, which resulted in a kind of rhetorical overkill that supported a position neither logical nor consistent with his apparent position or the Court's position on the applicability of the First Amendment to the states via the Due Process Clause. However deficient the justification for Black's total-incorporation theory was, either historically or otherwise, it was at least understandable; Frankfurter's position in the *Adamson* case was not.[69]

Since he eschewed the Bill of Rights as defining due process standards to be applied in state criminal cases, it was also important for Frankfurter to indicate with acceptable precision the standards the Court should apply under the Due Process Clause. Neither in his *Adamson* opinion nor in subsequent cases was he able to do this. According to his *Adamson* opinion, due process standards were to be based upon those "canons of decency and fairness which express the notions of justice of English-speaking peoples even toward those charged with the most heinous offenses." The standards of due process, he said in later opinions, involved "a psychological judgment that reflects deep, even if inarticulate, feelings of our society" and "those permanent and pervasive feelings of our society as to which there is compelling evidence of the kind relevant to judgments on our social institutions." State criminal procedure must not involve, he said, "methods that offend civilized standards of decency and fairness" or involve conduct that "shocks the conscience."[70]

As the late Carl Swisher said, Frankfurter's due process position thus "remained hauntingly if intriguingly unclear." He seemed to be asking the justices to perform "a herculean task. They must not only divest themselves of personal prepossessions of which they might not be aware, but they must also peer into society for still deeper, and in some sense universal, prepossessions about which particular individuals were ignorant as far as their conscious minds were concerned, or at any rate were likely to be inarticulate."[71]

Adhering to the fair trial approach to the Due Process Clause, the Court followed a meandering and ofttimes puzzling course in state criminal cases during the 1950s. And, despite Frankfurter's admonitions to defer to the policy judgments of the states, the Court's performance under the Due Process Clause was such as to involve it in unpredictable intrusions into the state criminal process on the basis of standards nowhere satisfactorily articulated—with the result that serious federal-state strains developed.

The theoretical debates that their cases had produced were, of course, of little consequence to Frank Jacob Palko and Admiral Dewey Adamson. After the Court had denied a stay of execution in his case, Frank Palko was put to death by electrocution on April 12, 1938, as the trial court had directed, "before the hour of sunrise, and within an enclosure within the prison walls so constructed as to exclude the public view, and prepared for that purpose, under the direction of the Warden of the State Prison, and the Board of Directors thereof, and in accordance with law."[72]

After losing Dewey Adamson's case in the Court, Morris Lavine promptly filed a petition for a rehearing; when this was denied,[73] he filed a petition for a writ of habeas corpus with the California Supreme Court, but was again rebuffed. Lavine then filed an appeal of this decision in the United States Supreme Court, but the Court denied review.[74] Lavine then petitioned the United States District Court for the Northern District of California for a writ of habeas corpus, and when that court denied the writ, he appealed its decision to the United States Court of Appeals for the Ninth Circuit. The court of appeals, however, upheld the district court in May of 1948, and the Supreme Court refused to review the court of appeals's decision.[75] This was the end of the appellate road for Lavine and Adamson. Dewey Adamson was executed in the gas chamber at San Quentin on December 9, 1949.[76]

In the 1960s, the Court began to apply some of the procedural guarantees of the Bill of Rights to the states through a process of selective incorporation, and in 1964, the Court reversed the *Twining* case and held the Self-Incrimination Clause to be applicable to the states.[77] In 1965, the Court also reversed the *Adamson* case, holding in *Griffin* v. *California* that the California comment practice violated the right against self-incrimination. Griffin's counsel before the Court, again serving without fee, was Morris Lavine.[78]

7

The Nationalization Process under the Fair Trial Rule

Justice Black lost the battle to win acceptance of his total-incorporation position in the *Adamson* case, and only he and Justice Douglas remained as supporters of total incorporation after the deaths of Justices Murphy and Rutledge in 1949. The fair trial interpretation of the Due Process Clause was consequently the dominant approach by the Court in state criminal cases during the late 1940s and the 1950s, but even under the fair trial rule two significant advances in the nationalization process occurred. One such advance involved *In re Oliver*, decided by the Court in 1948.[1]

The Michigan One-Man Grand Jury Case

The Michigan Constitution of 1850 abolished the right to be indicted by a grand jury, and by 1859, grand juries had been abandoned in the state as the principal means of investigating and indicting criminal offenses. The Michigan Bar Association recommended in 1915, however, that state judges be given the power to serve as one-man grand juries in order to ferret out criminal activities more effectively, and the bar association's recommendations were enacted into law by the Michigan legislature in 1917.

Under the 1917 law, Michigan judges, usually judges of the circuit courts, could constitute themselves as one-man grand juries, subpoena witnesses and examine them in secret, and issue indictments. The judge–grand juror could hire his own investigators and special prosecutors without the consent of the local prosecutor, and he could maintain secret accommodations where witnesses could be summoned and interrogated without counsel and without being advised of their right to remain silent. Recalcitrant witnesses could be granted immunity from prosecution or, alternatively, could be sentenced for contempt of court.

The most famous use of the one-man grand jury procedure was by Wayne County Circuit Judge Homer Ferguson during the period 1939–42. Judge Ferguson, acting as a one-man grand jury, hired a large staff of investigators, accountants, and attorneys and conducted a wide-ranging probe of corruption in Detroit related to the Purple Gang and other racke-teering and corruption involving public officials. Ferguson maintained se-cret hideouts on the nineteenth floor of the National Bank Building and two other locations, where more than five thousand witnesses were sum-moned, sometimes in the middle of the night, and were held incommuni-cado for days. Ferguson was charged with sometimes using third-degree methods, such as dangling a recalcitrant witness by his heels from a seventeenth-floor window; nonetheless, he ultimately issued 360 indict-ments charging, among others, a former mayor of Detroit, the Wayne County prosecutor, and the county sheriff with corruption in office. The investigation attracted wide publicity, and Ferguson was subsequently elected United States Senator.[2]

Supporters of the one-man grand jury system emphasized its effective-ness in ferreting out crime in contrast to the traditional grand jury system. Critics, on the other hand, argued that civil liberties were being sacrificed to efficiency and charged that the one-man grand jury system resulted in a dangerous combination of the powers of judge, inquisitor, and prosecutor in the hands of a person who was properly only a judge.[3]

Just as J. W. N. Whitecotton had been a persistent critic of Utah's jury system in the litigation of *Maxwell* v. *Dow* over forty years earlier, Wil-liam Henry Gallagher, a Detroit attorney, was a persistent opponent of Michigan's one-man grand jury system. "Any one who has any regard for civil rights," Gallagher said, "cannot but be disturbed by the reports com-monly current as to the practices . . . of some of those who have partici-pated in inquisitions under this [one-man grand jury] statute." In the mid-1940s, Gallagher attacked the system on behalf of a client, Francis P. Slattery, who had been held in contempt by a one-man grand jury; he ap-pealed this ruling to the Michigan Supreme Court and twice to the United States Supreme Court in a losing battle.[4]

Despite this setback, Gallagher gained support for his attack on the one-man grand jury system when the American Civil Liberties Union sup-ported his appeal to the U.S. Supreme Court in the *Slattery* case by filing an *amicus curiae* brief. When the Court denied review, the ACLU assured Gallagher that it was "interested in the problem, and should you have an-other opportunity to bring the matter before the Supreme Court, we shall be glad to give you what assistance we can." The Michigan one-man grand jury system, the ACLU said, permitted individuals to be jailed "without notice of a hearing or trial, and where one man is not only prose-cutor, judge, and jury, but the only witness as well. This is a practice which strikes at the very heart of the due process of law guaranteed by the Constitution."[5]

The Detroit chapter of the National Lawyers' Guild supplied additional support for Gallagher's cause when it urged that the one-man grand jury system be abolished and called upon the Michigan State Bar to support abolition at its convention in 1946. The *Detroit Free Press*, however, editorially attacked the Guild's proposal, charging that the "Left-wing Lawyers Guild is not acting in the public interest." While the one-man grand jury system "admittedly has flaws," the *Free Press* said, "and while it is subject to all of the weaknesses of the human element, it still remains the only proven agency that the people of this State have to combat graft and corruption in official circles."[6]

At the 1946 Michigan State Bar convention, a compromise resolution was unanimously adopted creating a fifteen-member committee to investigate the one-man grand jury and to propose any necessary changes in the system. William Henry Gallagher was appointed a member of the committee, which was chaired by former-governor Wilber M. Brucker, and a feud began between Brucker and Gallagher that they would eventually carry to the United States Supreme Court.[7]

Twelve members of the committee reported in 1947 that the one-man grand jury system should be retained with only minor changes, and they endorsed the view that there were "cogent and compelling reasons in favor of this modern, efficient and thorough method for the investigation of crime and criminals, and that it would be a backward step to repeal or substantially alter the One-Man Grand Jury Law."[8]

The committee minority report strongly opposed the majority report and charged that the effectiveness of the one-man grand jury system "appears to depend upon the extent to which the grand juror disregards constitutional rights." Efficiency was not the true measure of any law enforcement technique in a constitutional republic, the minority declared, since otherwise "we should adopt the medieval inquisition or the German gestapo system." The use of the contempt power by judge–grand jurors was particularly subject to abuse, the minority said, since it denied "the constitutional right to a trial on any charge of contempt not committed in the presence of a court."[9]

The Michigan State Bar nonetheless rejected the minority report and overwhelmingly adopted the majority report at its 1947 convention. While the bar was debating the merits of the one-man grand jury system, however, Judge George B. Hartrick of the Oakland County (Pontiac) Circuit Court was conducting a one-man grand jury investigation that would give William Henry Gallagher another chance to challenge the system.

Judge Hartrick was investigating an apparent gambling-protection racket in Oakland County, involving C. A. Mitchell and his operation of the Midwest Bonding Company. Mitchell sold "bonds" to owners of pinball machines in the county, and those buying the bonds could place a sticker on each of their machines identifying them as being bonded by the Midwest Bonding Company. Mitchell's sale of bonds to pinball machine owners was apparently a scheme to pay police and other officials to protect gambling on the machines, and the stickers on the machines identified their owners as participants in the scheme.[10]

William D. Oliver was the owner of the Pontiac Amusement Company, who leased fifty pinball machines in Oakland County, and in September of 1944, he had purchased bonds from Mitchell and the Midwest Bonding Company for his machines. In September of 1946, he was subpoenaed to appear before Judge Hartrick, acting as a one-man grand jury, and was interrogated in regard to the purpose of the bonds he had purchased.[11]

Oliver testified that he had purchased the bonds because Mitchell had assured him that the bonds would recompense the county for any costs involved if Oliver's pinball machines were being used for gambling purposes and the county instituted proceedings. Oliver was asked by Judge Hartrick what had become of the bonds he had purchased, but he said he could not remember. Since they had expired in 1945, Oliver said, he assumed that he had "just got rid of them. I imagine I threw them into the waste paper basket. That is what I usually do. I get lots of circulations, papers, things that I have no use whatever for, [and I throw] them in the waste paper basket." Judge Hartrick then asked Oliver what kind of protection he expected to receive from the bonds, and Oliver said that he was aware that people sometimes gambled on pinball machines, and he "figured it would show our good faith, we were trying to run them legitimately." But he admitted that he had not consulted the county prosecutor or any other official as to whether the bonds actually were intended to reimburse the county for expenses incurred in proceeding against gambling on his machines.[12]

When Oliver completed his testimony, Judge Hartrick informed him that his story, "if you want it put in language you understand, doesn't jell. . . ." The two other circuit judges of Oakland County were sitting as advisers to Judge Hartrick, and they agreed with Hartrick's statement that "I don't think any one could believe this story." Hartrick then transformed himself from a grand juror to a judge and sentenced Oliver to sixty days in jail for contempt of court for his "evasive" and "false" answers.[13]

Oliver had not been given notice of the charges against him or time to prepare a defense on advice of counsel, nor was he afforded a trial in open court on the contempt charge, where he could have confronted the evidence against him and produced witnesses in his behalf. He was instead taken into custody by the sheriff of Oakland County, without even a formal order indicating the offense he had committed. And when his attorney, William F. Dohany, requested permission to consult with him in the county jail, Dohany's request was denied by both the sheriff and the circuit judges.[14]

Dohany promptly filed a petition for a writ of habeas corpus in the

Michigan Supreme Court, arguing that Oliver was being held illegally in the Oakland County jail. Judge Hartrick responded that Oliver had been validly held in contempt for giving false and evasive answers to his questions and urged the court to uphold the contempt citation.[15] The supreme court divided evenly on the legality of Oliver's confinement, however, with the result that his contempt sentence was upheld.

Four of the eight judges of the supreme court held that in light of Oliver's "vague and uncertain" answers to the one-man grand jury's questions, the "grand juror and his associates were fully justified in concluding that Oliver was intentionally evasive. He offered no plausible reason whatsoever for the payments made by him to Mitchell. . . ." Oliver's "evasive replies clearly tended to obstruct the investigation," the judges said, "and were contemptuous in character."[16]

The four dissenting judges attacked the result of the court's action in the *Oliver* case. "Can it be said that a witness who is unable to testify definitely as to how he disposed of, for example, an automobile policy that had expired a year previously is thereby shown to be evasive in his testimony or that he is giving false testimony?" the dissenting judges asked. "If so, many an honest person would hazard being headed for jail whenever summoned as a witness." Judge Hartrick had also not specified which of Oliver's answers were false, the dissenters argued, with the result that both Oliver and the court had to guess as to the reasons for the contempt citation. Both Oliver and the court, they said, "are entitled to be specifically informed of the claimed falsity, so that issue may be accurately reviewed by this Court and so [Oliver] may purge himself of the contempt, if he finds occasion so to do."[17]

Following the decision of the Michigan Supreme Court, William F. Dohany dropped out of the litigation as counsel for Oliver and was replaced by the arch foe of the one-man grand jury system, William Henry Gallagher, who was joined by two other Detroit attorneys. The American Civil Liberties Union also entered the case, and Osmond K. Fraenkel joined the Detroit lawyers in the case on behalf of the ACLU. The *Oliver* case was therefore appealed to the United States Supreme Court under new management.[18]

In addition to briefs on behalf of William Oliver and the State of Michigan, *amicus curiae* briefs were filed in the *Oliver* case by the Michigan State Bar, defending the one-man grand jury system, and by the Detroit chapter of the National Lawyers' Guild, attacking the system. The arguments in the case largely centered on the validity of combining the powers of a grand jury and those of a judge, and focused in particular on the contempt powers of the Michigan one-man grand juries. The abuse of this power was obvious in Oliver's case, William Henry Gallagher told the Court, since he had been tried and sentenced in secret, and a system "which permits the head of a secret tribunal to clap a citizen into jail whenever he does not like his testimony and deny the citizen a trial on the charge laid against him suggests a forgetfulness of those pernicious practices, the necessity of abolishing which has given rise to the enumeration of many of our basic principles of civil rights."[19]

In a continuation of the Gallagher-Brucker feud, the *amicus* brief for the State Bar of Michigan was written by Wilber Brucker, who charged that counsel for Oliver were "badly mistaken in their sweeping assertions of wholesale abuses" by the one-man grand jury system. "They are likewise illogical," he said, "in uging that the one-man grand jury law should be condemned and . . . Oliver should go unpunished simply because in some other case some other official has transgressed the rules."[20]

Oliver's contempt conviction was also supported by the Michigan attorney general, who denied that it was a violation of due process "to convict one of contempt of court summarily when the alleged misconduct is committed in the immediate presence of a Michigan circuit judge who, in a judicial capacity and pursuant to a valid law of that State, is acting as a one-man grand jury in the conduct of an investigation of suspected criminal offenses."[21] But the Detroit chapter of the Lawyers' Guild replied in its *amicus* brief that Oliver had been summarily jailed because he lacked both "fanatic curiosity and mnemonic concern for the techniques of waste paper disposal." The requirement that criminal charges should be sufficiently specific to be informative, the Guild said, "has an almost perfunctory significance until, in a situation worthy of Kafka, a man is sent to jail for two months for speaking 'falsely' on a matter which is never identified, and for being 'evasive' on a detail which, if lingeringly remembered, would suggest psychiatric rather than penal interest."[22]

The arguments before the Supreme Court in the *Oliver* case generally were either attacks on or defenses of the Michigan one-man grand jury system, indicating that the attack on that system spearheaded by William Henry Gallagher and the Detroit Lawyers' Guild had been carried to the Court. In light of the meaning retrospectively attributed to the *Oliver* case, it is worthy of note that neither the principal parties nor the *amici* argued that the Sixth Amendment's guarantees of notice or the right to a public trial should be applied to the states via the Due Process Clause. Rather, the arguments in the case centered on the scope of the contempt power, if any, of the one-man grand juries and the general guarantees of procedural fairness protected by the Due Process Clause, without reference to the procedural guarantees in the Sixth Amendment or the rest of the Bill of Rights.

When the Court decided *In re Oliver* on March 8, 1948, Justice Black's opinion for the majority also did not mention the application of any of the provisions of the Bill of Rights to the states. The requirement that trials be conducted in public, Justice Black pointed out, was a part of our common-law heritage and was a reaction to abuses of judicial power in secret proceedings such as those of the Star Chamber in England. The importance attached to public trials in the United States, Black noted, was indicated by the guarantees of public trials in the Sixth Amendment of the Bill of Rights and by similar provisions in the constitutions of almost all of the states. "Whatever other benefits the guarantee to an accused that his trial be conducted in public may confer upon our society," he continued, "the guarantee has always been recognized as a safeguard against any attempt to employ our courts as instruments of persecution. The knowledge that every criminal trial is subject to contemporaneous review in the forum of public opinion is an effective restraint on possible abuse of judicial power."[23]

Oliver, Black said, had been interrogated, tried, and sentenced in secrecy, and he had been led away to prison "still without any break in the secrecy." In view of the nation's "historic distrust of secret proceedings, their inherent dangers to freedom, and the universal requirement of our federal and state governments that criminal trials be public," he held, "the Fourteenth Amendment's guarantee that no one shall be deprived of his liberty without due process of law means at least that an accused cannot be thus sentenced to prison."[24]

Black further held that Oliver's due process rights had been violated because he had been denied the opportunity to defend himself against the contempt charge. "A person's right to reasonable notice of a charge against him, and an opportunity to be heard in his defense—a right to his day in court—are basic to our system of jurisprudence; and these rights include, as a minimum, a right to examine the witnesses against him, to offer testimony, and to be represented by counsel."[25]

Black also rejected the state of Michigan's argument that Oliver's contempt conviction was valid because he had given false and evasive answers that had constituted contemptuous conduct before the judge's very eyes, justifying summary treatment. Summary convictions for contempt were justified, Black said, only when the contemptuous conduct occurred before the eyes of the judge and summary action was necessary in order to prevent "demoralization of the court's authority" before the public. No "demoralization of the court's authority," he continued, would have occurred if Oliver had been given a "reasonable opportunity to appear and offer a defense in open court to a charge of contempt." The Due Process Clause, Black concluded, required that "no man's life, liberty or property be forfeited as a punishment until there has been a charge fairly made and fairly tried in a public tribunal. . . . [Oliver] was convicted without that kind of trial."[26]

Justices Frankfurter and Jackson dissented on the ground that the

Court had decided the case on issues insufficiently raised in the Michigan courts, and Justice Rutledge took the opportunity to once again emphasize his adherence to the total-incorporation position. The *Oliver* case demonstrated, Rutledge said, "how far this Court departed from our constitutional plan when, after the Fourteenth Amendment's adoption, it permitted selective departure by the states from the scheme of ordered personal liberty established by the Bill of Rights." The abuses revealed in the *Oliver* case, he asserted, were the "immediate offspring" of the *Hurtado* case and its progeny, in which the Court had allowed the states to experiment with departures from traditional liberties. The entire Bill of Rights should apply to the states, Rutledge concluded. "It was good enough for our fathers. I think it should be good enough for this Court and for the states."[27]

Dean Henry M. Bates of the University of Michigan Law School praised Rutledge's opinion and agreed that the one-man grand jury in Michigan "has been dangerous."[28] Reactions to the Court's decision in the *Oliver* case were otherwise mixed. The Court had not, of course, invalidated the one-man grand jury system, but rather had held that contempt cases arising before one-man grand juries in the future must be tried in open court with adequate notice to the defendants. Michigan officials therefore generally expressed acceptance of the Court's decision. Although he had catapulted to fame as a one-man grand jury, United States Senator Homer Ferguson commented that he did not feel that the Court's decision would "hurt the one-man grand jury too much." And Michigan Governor Sigler indicated that the system might be even more effective than before the Court's decision. "I don't think the effectiveness of the law," he said, "was greatly endangered by the Court's finding." Wilber Brucker also "scoffed at the suggestion that the law had been nullified" and noted that the "Court did not pass on the merits of the one-man grand jury law at all."[29]

Judge George Hartrick, who had sentenced Oliver for contempt, on the other hand, thought that the *Oliver* decision would have a more serious effect on the system and would "deprive grand juries of one of the most effective weapons at hand in getting the truth from witnesses." Hartrick suggested that perjury prosecutions be substituted for contempt proceedings, and he insisted that Oliver had been lying in his responses to the questions asked him. "No one in sound mind," he said, "would believe the testimony Oliver gave to be truthful."[30]

Basking in the light of victory, William Henry Gallagher praised the Court's decision and indicated that it would have beneficial effects on the one-man grand jury system. "It now appears," he commented, "that the United States Supreme Court has recognized the distinction between acting as an inquisitor and as a judge."[31] Although the *Detroit Free Press* had been a defender of the system, it editorially agreed with Gallagher.

"Thoughtful citizens of this State," it said, "can not do otherwise than to applaud the decision of the United States Supreme Court relative to Michigan's one-man grand jury system." The Court had upheld, the *Free Press* said, "a fundamental principle of American justice."[32]

After evaluating the *Oliver* decision, the majority of the Michigan State Bar committee on the one-man grand jury system reported that the Court had "clearly settled the scope of the contempt power under the One-Man Grand Jury Law, and had handed down the rule to be followed in contempt cases arising under the law in the future." This involved merely a procedural change in the operations of one-man grand juries, the committee concluded, and it would not be necessary to amend the law establishing the system in any way. William Henry Gallagher, however, again filed a minority report urging the Bar to recommend to the legislature that the system be abolished.[33]

Although the Michigan State Bar accepted the recommendations of a majority of the committee, rather drastic amendments to the grand jury law were passed in the 1949 session of the Michigan legislature. The amendments required that grand juries henceforth be composed of three judges, prohibited the granting of immunity from prosecution to witnesses, provided that grand juries must meet in public places, and required that judge–grand jurors must attest that witnesses had some knowledge of matters under investigation before such witnesses could be summoned. Reflecting an apparent feeling among legislators that one-man grand juries like Homer Ferguson had used their positions to further their political ambitions, the 1949 amendments also prohibited judges, prosecutors, and attorneys general from seeking elective or appointive office for two years after they had served in such positions. Finally, the amendments also limited the pay of special prosecutors retained by one-man grand juries.[34]

The majority of the Michigan State Bar committee on the one-man grand jury system denounced the 1949 amendments, declaring that the legislature had "completely emasculated the one-man grand jury law" and had rendered it "ineffective, unworkable, impotent, and lifeless." A minority of the committee, however, argued that the 1949 amendments were an "unmistakable demonstration that the People of the State have been vehemently dissatisfied with the one-man grand jury system despite 'results accomplished' and the zeal of its defenders." For almost a quarter of a century, the minority declared, "the Michigan Judiciary uniformly infringed upon the constitutional rights of witnesses, and neither the number nor the prominence of those who participated makes the practice the less blameworthy." In the battle over the one-man grand jury system, it was therefore clear in 1949 that William Henry Gallagher had won at least a temporary victory.[35]

The *Oliver* case was clearly decided on the basis of traditional due process principles, particularly those that required that criminal defendants be given notice of the charges against them and be afforded a fair hearing in open court. In the 1960s, however, when the Court embarked upon a course of selective incorporation of parts of the Bill of Rights into the Due Process Clause, the *Oliver* case was retrospectively interpreted as having applied the Sixth Amendment's Public Trial Clause to the states.[36] It is, of course, true that the Court condemned the proceedings in the *Oliver* case for the secrecy involved and for the lack of a public trial on the contempt charge, but the Court also condemned the proceedings under the Due Process Clause because of the lack of notice of the nature of the accusation involved and, as Black said, because of the failure of the state of Michigan to afford Oliver the "right to examine witnesses against him, to offer testimony, and to be represented by counsel." Viewed in relation to the specifics of the Bill of Rights, therefore, the *Oliver* case could be said to have involved not only the Public Trial Clause, but also the Notice, Confrontation, Compulsory Process, and Assistance to Counsel Clauses of the Sixth Amendment. The *Oliver* case was nonetheless decided on the basis of traditional procedural due process principles, regardless of the interpretation retrospectively given to it.

In addition to the *Oliver* case, the majority consensus on the Court during the 1940s and 1950s in favor of the fair trial approach to issues of state criminal procedure produced another important decision in relation to the nationalization of the Bill of Rights in 1949. This time the Court considered whether the Fourth Amendment's prohibition of unreasonable searches and seizures was applicable to the states via the Due Process Clause and, if so, whether it was enforceable in the state courts in the same manner as in the federal courts.

The Case of the Denver Abortionist: *Wolf* v. *Colorado*

On April 25, 1944, the chief investigator for the Denver County District Attorney's office, Ray Humphreys, received an anonymous telephone call that a woman was in room 602 of the Cosmopolitan Hotel, seriously ill from the effects of an illegal abortion. Humphreys and another investigator with the district attorney's office went to the hotel and found Gertrude Martin, whom they immediately sent to the Denver General Hospital.

Under questioning, Ms. Martin admitted that she had had an abortion and revealed that her abortion had been induced by Dr. A. H. Montgomery, while Dr. Julius A. Wolf had cooperated in the abortion by examining her both before and after she had aborted. Both Montgomery and Wolf were arrested by the district attorney's office on the charge of conspiracy to perform a criminal abortion. Dr. Wolf practiced medicine at his office in the Republic Building in Denver and lived at the Cosmopolitan Hotel.

A graduate of the University of Denver and the University of Colorado Medical School, he had been a resident of Denver for forty-three years and specialized in the treatment of women's diseases and obstetrics. Andrew Harrison Montgomery, on the other hand, was a chiropractor and druggist and had lived in Colorado for fifteen years.

When Julius Wolf was arrested on April 17, officials of the district attorney's office searched Wolf's office and seized a book on the table in the reception room and another book in a bookcase. These books were Dr. Wolf's daybooks for 1943 and 1944, in which he had listed his patients' names and the dates on which he had seen them. The officials who arrested Wolf had neither a warrant for his arrest nor a warrant to search his office.[37]

Ray Humphreys reported to the press that the investigation was "going ahead full blast, with new angles being developed on the basis of information gleaned from an examination of records seized in the raids."[38] The investigation consisted of contacting Wolf's female patients and questioning them regarding their visits to Wolf's office. By this process, six women admitted to the authorities that Wolf had aided them in securing abortions and that Charles H. and Betty Fulton had also been involved in the process, along with Wolf and Montgomery. The Fultons were also subsequently arrested on the charge of conspiracy to perform illegal abortions.[39]

Julius Wolf was tried twice for conspiracy to perform criminal abortions during the spring and summer of 1944. His codefendant at the first trial was Andrew Montgomery, while Charles and Betty Fulton were his codefendants at the second trial. Wolf was convicted by juries at both trials and was sentenced to not less than one year nor more than eighteen months in the Colorado state prison on his first conviction and to not less than fifteen months nor more than five years on the second conviction. Andrew Montgomery and the Fultons also were convicted and received prison sentences.[40]

At both his trials, the principal evidence against Julius Wolf were his daybooks and the testimony of women patients whom he had aided in securing abortions. Wolf's attorney, Philip Hornbein, strenuously objected to the introduction of this evidence on the ground that it was the product of an unlawful search and seizure of Wolf's office. The district attorney, Hornbein therefore argued, "was absolutely without right to go into this doctor's private office without any warrant, without any order of court, and engage in a general raid, and take his private books, and then with those books, open them up and find out the names of the patients; this information which is privileged under the law, and go out and contact the patients to see whether any law had been violated." The defense was arguing, Hornbein said, "the straight proposition, the constitutional proposition, that here there was an unlawful seizure and violation of the . . . Constitution." The prosecution, he declared, had searched Wolf's office without a warrant "and got that book from a doctor's office, a private doctor, looked at the book and found the patients, and went and checked those patients up to see what they had been suffering from. I say to this Court, in all seriousness, that is a proposition I do not believe will stand."[41]

The District Court for the City and County of Denver, however, overruled Hornbein's objections, and allowed Wolf's daybooks and the testimony to which they had led to be admitted as evidence. On the appeal of Wolf's convictions to the Colorado Supreme Court, Hornbein nonetheless renewed his argument that the search of Wolf's office had been illegal and that the evidence secured in that search should have been excluded at his trial. The Colorado Supreme Court, however, affirmed Wolf's convictions on November 24, 1947.

In *Weeks* v. *United States*, decided in 1914, the United States Supreme Court had held that evidence seized in searches by federal officers in violation of the Fourth Amendment's prohibition of unreasonable searches and seizures had to be excluded in federal criminal trials.[42] The *Weeks* exclusionary rule, as well as the Fourth Amendment, however, did not apply to the states, and the Colorado Supreme Court had ruled in 1925 that evidence secured through searches and seizures in violation of the Colorado Constitution was still admissible in the state's courts. The only test of the admissibility of evidence, the court had held, was whether it was relevant, material, and competent, and not whether it was the product of an unlawful search and seizure.[43]

The court therefore held in the *Wolf* case that even if the search of Wolf's office had been illegal, the evidence seized in that search was still admissible at his trial under the law of Colorado. If a case were ever to come before it that indicated its 1925 ruling upholding the admissibility of illegally seized evidence had produced an injustice, the court continued, "it will be time enough to consider alteration or modification of that rule. Certainly [Wolf is] in no position to contend that the law of Colorado which has stood for twenty years and been affirmed and reaffirmed by this tribunal and the decisions of sister states, should now be overturned or so modified that [he] may escape the toils in which [his] own felonious conduct has involved [him]."[44]

The Colorado Supreme Court's decision in the *Wolf* case left unclear whether the search of Wolf's office had been an illegal search and seizure. Since the evidence seized in that search was admissible in Colorado courts whether the search was legal or illegal, this question was irrelevant as far as the court's ruling was concerned. Philip Hornbein had also argued on behalf of Wolf that the search of his office had violated his rights under the Fourth and Fifth Amendments of the federal Constitution, but the Colorado Supreme Court did not address this question either. Hornbein nevertheless appealed the *Wolf* case to the United States Supreme Court on the basis that the Fourth Amendment applied to the states via the Due Process Clause, and the Court agreed to hear the case on April 26, 1948.[45]

Philip Hornbein argued before the Court that the Fourth Amendment's prohibition of unreasonable searches and seizures applied to the states via the Due Process Clause. If this was so, he continued, state courts were required to exclude evidence seized in violation of the Fourth and Fourteenth Amendments, just as such evidence was excluded in the federal courts under the doctrine of *Weeks* v. *United States*. The right of a "citizen to be free from wrongful search and seizure by the federal government," Hornbein said, "is of little value if he may be subjected to arbitrary raids by the officials of the forty-eight states." Unless the Court held that the Due Process Clause prohibited illegal searches by state officers, he argued, "their only guide is their free and unfettered will. They may search for such books as their unbridled zeal directs, and they may seize as many as they feel will answer their purpose." A government of laws "means that the citizen will not violate the laws of his government, but it also means that government will not violate the *rights of its citizens*. When police officers flout the laws of their government, it is anarchy and anarchy always ends in despotism."[46]

The seizure of Wolf's books had violated the Fourth and Fourteenth Amendments, Hornbein contended, and the books should have been excluded as evidence at his trial, since the exclusionary rule as well as the prohibition against unreasonable searches and seizures applied to the states. "The Fourth Amendment protects the citizen against the Federal Government," he concluded. "It is equally important that the citizen be protected against the tyranny and oppression of state governments. It matters little whether the invasion of a man's freedom is directed by federal officers or state officers: therefore the Fourteenth Amendment with its guarantee of due process was inevitable. The Fourteenth Amendment is the complement of the Bill of Rights, and together they constitute the American Magna Charta of human rights."[47]

The attorney general of Colorado, on the other hand, denied that the prohibition of unreasonable searches and seizures was implicit in the concept of ordered liberty as defined in the *Palko* case. The right against unreasonable searches and seizures, he said, was no more fundamental than the right against self-incrimination, which the Court had held in the *Twining* case was not guaranteed in state proceedings by the Due Process Clause. "We respectfully submit," the attorney general said, "that if the court subjects the privileges set forth in the Fourth Amendment to the same test to which it put the privilege referred to in the Fifth Amendment [in the *Twining* case], it is inevitable that here, as there, the court will determine that freedom from unreasonable search and seizure is not an inalienable possession of every citizen. . . ."[48]

Even assuming that a prohibition of unreasonable searches and seizures applied to the states, the attorney general argued, the seizure of Wolf's books from his office had been legal. Upon receipt of the information that Wolf was performing illegal abortions, the Denver officials had probable cause to arrest Wolf for a felony. And as an incident of the lawful arrest of Wolf in his office, the officers had the legal right to seize the evidence that was in plain sight and under the immediate control of Wolf at the time of his arrest. When a medical doctor "so far forgets the oath of his profession that he capitalizes on his knowledge of medicine," the attorney general said, "and openly and brazenly violates the law, all because of his insatiable greed for gold, we submit that his records are no more inviolate than those of any other law breaker." The *Wolf* case therefore involved, he argued, "a lawful arrest, even though made without a warrant, and, incident thereto, the seizure of evidence in plain sight, and in the possession and control of defendant at the time of the arrest. Hence there are no facts to sustain [Wolf's] contention of *unreasonable* search and *unreasonable* seizure. The evidence thus procured by the officers was, we submit, competent and admissible against [Wolf] in any court, state or federal. . . ."[49]

Finally, the attorney general argued, even if a prohibition against unreasonable searches and seizures applied to the states via the Due Process Clause, and even if the search of Wolf's office was held to violate such a prohibition, the Court should not hold that illegally seized evidence was inadmissible in state courts. Colorado, and many other states, the attorney general pointed out, had rejected the doctrine of the *Weeks* case as applied in the federal courts, and the Court should respect such determinations by the state courts.[50]

The Colorado attorney general's argument on this latter point was challenged in an *amicus curiae* brief filed in the *Wolf* case by the New York County Criminal Courts Bar Association. The association urged the Court to hold that the Fourth Amendment applied to the states, and, it argued, the prohibition of unreasonable searches and seizures could not be effectively vindicated except through an exclusionary rule prohibiting the admission of illegally seized evidence in state criminal trials. The association therefore joined with Philip Hornbein in urging the Court to impose both the Fourth Amendment and the *Weeks* exclusionary rule upon the states, and to reverse Wolf's convictions.[51]

The Court decided *Wolf* v. *Colorado* on June 27, 1949, and in an opinion by Justice Frankfurter, affirmed Wolf's convictions. At the outset, Frankfurter took the occasion to reiterate that the Court continued its adherence to the fair trial approach to the Due Process Clause. "The notion that the 'due process of law' guaranteed by the Fourteenth Amendment is shorthand for the first eight amendments of the Constitution and thereby incorporates them," he said, "has been rejected by this Court again and again, after impressive consideration." The Court was still guided, he said, by holding in the *Palko* case that the Due Process Clause did not apply all of the Bill of Rights to the states, but rather guaranteed those rights "implicit in the concept of ordered liberty."[52]

Turning to the issues in the *Wolf* case, Frankfurter held that the "security of one's privacy against arbitrary intrusion by the police—which is at the core of the Fourth Amendment—is basic to a free society. It is therefore implicit in 'the concept of ordered liberty' and as such enforceable against the States through the Due Process Clause." The knock at the door, "whether by day or by night, as a prelude to a search, without authority of law but solely on the authority of the police," he added, "did not need the commentary of recent history to be condemned as inconsistent with the conception of human rights enshrined in the history and the basic constitutional documents of English-speaking peoples."[53]

While he therefore held that the "core" of the Fourth Amendment was applicable to the states via the Due Process Clause, Frankfurter nonetheless concluded that the *Weeks* exclusionary rule did not apply to the states. He noted that the overwhelming majority of the states did not exclude illegally seized evidence in their criminal trials. Violations of the prohibition against unreasonable searches and seizures, he also suggested, could be deterred through civil damage suits filed by those subjected to such searches as well as through the internal discipline of local police departments. Frankfurter additionally indicated that the federal exclusionary rule might not be a command of the Fourth Amendment, but rather was a judicially created rule that Congress might have the power to repeal. "We hold, therefore," he concluded, "that in a prosecution in a State court for a State crime the Fourteenth Amendment does not forbid the admission of evidence obtained by an unreasonable search and seizure."[54]

In a concurring opinion, Justice Black reaffirmed his adherence to the total-incorporation position that he had advanced in the *Adamson* case, but noted the "plain implication of the Court's opinion that the federal exclusionary rule is not a command of the Fourth Amendment but is a judicially created rule of evidence which Congress might negate." While he believed that the Fourth Amendment applied fully to the states, Black nevertheless voted to affirm Wolf's convictions, since in his view the *Weeks* rule was not a command of the Fourth Amendment and therefore was not applicable to the states along with that amendment.[55]

Justices Douglas, Murphy, and Rutledge dissented from the judgment of the Court, with Murphy declaring that it was "disheartening to find so much that is right in an opinion which seems to me so fundamentally wrong." The alternatives facing the Court, he said, were to enforce the Fourth Amendment in the state courts via an exclusionary rule or to depend upon civil suits for damages or criminal prosecutions against officers who violated the amendment. The effectiveness of suits for damages and criminal prosecutions to enforce the Fourth Amendment, he continued, was largely illusory. Most states severely limited the damages collectable for unreasonable searches, and it was unlikely that prosecutors were willing to prosecute themselves and the police for violations of the Fourth Amendment. The only viable alternative for enforcing the prohibition of unreasonable searches and seizures, Murphy felt, was the exclusionary rule. "Today's decision," Murphy concluded, "will do inestimable harm to the cause of fair police methods in our cities and states. Even more important, perhaps, it must have tragic effect upon public respect for our judiciary. For the Court now allows what is indeed shabby business: lawlessness by officers of the law."[56]

Justice Rutledge, joined by Murphy, also dissented and assailed the Court's holding that the exclusionary rule did not apply to the states along with the whole Fourth Amendment. The "version of the Fourth Amendment today held applicable to the states," Rutledge said, "hardly rises to the dignity of a form of words; at best it is a pale and frayed carbon copy of the original, bearing little resemblance to the Amendment the fulfillment of whose command I had heretofore thought to be 'an indispensable need for a democratic society.'" The entire Fourth Amendment and the exclusionary rule should apply to the states, Rutledge declared. "Compliance with the Bill of Rights betokens more than lip service."[57]

Julius Wolf and Philip Hornbein had therefore won the battle but lost the war. The majority of the Court had held that at least the core of the Fourth Amendment applied to the states via the Due Process Clause, but had also held that the states were still free to devise their own methods to prevent illegal searches and seizures, since the *Weeks* exclusionary rule did not apply in state proceedings. While the Due Process Clause would henceforth be considered to prohibit unreasonable searches and seizures, the effect of the Court's ruling in the *Wolf* case was that the states remained free to admit in their criminal trials evidence seized in violation both of state constitutional prohibitions of unreasonable searches and seizures and of the prohibition embodied in the Due Process Clause.

It is one of the peculiarities of the *Wolf* case that the issue of whether the seizure of Wolf's books had in fact been illegal was never discussed either in the Colorado Supreme Court or the United States Supreme Court. Under the then-prevailing standards governing the scope of searches incidental to lawful arrests, it was certainly arguable that the seizure in the *Wolf* case had been legal. But as Justice Rutledge said, the Court had simply made "the illegality of this search and seizure its inarticulate premise of decision" without actually passing on the issue. Since the Court held that illegally seized evidence need not be excluded in state courts under the Due Process Clause, the issue of the legality of the search became irrelevant.[58]

It is important to note that the *Wolf* case did not incorporate the Fourth Amendment into the Due Process Clause. Rather—as Frankfurter's opinion for the majority emphasized—only a right similar to that contained in the Fourth Amendment, embracing the core of the prohibition against unreasonable searches and seizures, was embodied in the Due Process Clause. The Court therefore continued in the *Wolf* case the fair-trial approach to state criminal cases. The *Wolf* case was a reaffirmation by a majority of the Court of the position that none of the procedural safeguards in the Bill of Rights applied per se to the states, although rights similar to those in the Bill of Rights might be guaranteed by the Due Process Clause.

All of this was, of course, small comfort to Julius Wolf, whose convictions had been affirmed by the Court despite the fact that the core of the Fourth Amendment was held to apply to the states. Wolf, however, was not required to serve his prison term, since after the Court's decision in his case, he applied for and was granted probation by the Denver District Court. Indeed, he retained his medical license and continued to practice medicine until his death.[59]

The *Oliver* and *Wolf* cases were the only significant advances in the nationalization of the Bill of Rights during the regime of the fair-trial approach to the interpretation of the Due Process Clause. A majority of the Court had proven willing to apply all of the rights in the First Amendment to the states via the Due Process Clause, with the same scope and meaning as they applied to the federal government. In the field of criminal procedure, however, the Court proved unwilling to follow the course it had pursued in regard to the First Amendment, but continued instead to follow the theory of the *Twining* case. The Court's adherence to the fair-trial rule was nevertheless subjected to heavy strains during the 1950s because of the rather nebulous standards the Court was imposing on state criminal proceedings under the Due Process Clause. And nowhere, perhaps, were these strains more evident than in the area of searches and seizures under the regime of the *Wolf* case.

Under the fair-trial rule, the Court did on occasion hold that evidence secured by methods violating standards of civilized conduct and decency had to be excluded in state criminal trials, despite the holding in the *Wolf* case that evidence seized in an unreasonable search and seizure need not be excluded by state courts. The Court had rejected in the *Wolf* case the general proposition that an exclusionary rule should be imposed upon the states requiring the exclusion of the fruits of illegal searches and seizures. Nonetheless, the Due Process Clause did impose exclusionary rules in state criminal trials when the totality of the circumstances surrounding the eliciting of a confession indicated coercion or when methods by which evidence against a defendant was secured fell below civilized standards of conduct—although the teaching of the *Wolf* case was that an illegal search and seizure was not regarded per se as sufficiently indecent to require an exclusion of evidence thus acquired.

In *Rochin* v. *California*, decided in 1952, the Court condemned methods of gathering evidence that "shocked the conscience." Three deputies of the Los Angeles County Sheriff's office had broken into Antonio Richard Rochin's bedroom without warrants either for his arrest or for a search, and when Rochin seized two capsules from a nightstand and swallowed them, the deputies grabbed his throat and poked their fingers into his mouth in an attempt to retrieve the capsules. When these efforts were unavailing, the deputies rushed Rochin to a hospital, where, at the request of deputies, a doctor administered an emetic solution via a tube forced down Rochin's throat. Rochin vomited into a pail, and a deputy recovered two capsules floating in the contents of the pail. The capsules contained morphine, and Rochin was subsequently charged with violating the California Health and Safety Code, which prohibited the possession of narcotics.[60]

Under *People* v. *Mayen*, which had been decided by the California Supreme Court in 1922, illegally seized evidence was admissible in California courts, and the capsules were therefore admitted as evidence at Rochin's trial. The trial judge also found Rochin guilty, but he encouraged Rochin's counsel to appeal the conviction and force a reconsideration of the *Mayen* case by the California appellate courts.[61]

The California District Court of Appeal held that the deputies' conduct had constituted "unlawfully breaking and entering" Rochin's room, that they were guilty of "unlawfully assaulting and battering" Rochin, and that the deputies and doctor who had pumped Rochin's stomach were guilty of "unlawfully assaulting, battering, torturing and falsely imprisoning" him. Nevertheless, the court affirmed Rochin's conviction, since under the *Mayen* case, evidence obtained through unlawful methods was admissible in the California courts.[62]

The *Rochin* case was then appealed to the Supreme Court of California, but that court denied a hearing in January of 1951. In dissent, Justices Carter and Schauer decried the conduct of the officers in the case. "Could any one imagine [the right of privacy] being any more ruthlessly violated under a totalitarian regime than it was in the case at bar?" Justice Carter asked. "It makes little difference whether the minion of the law who perpetrates such outrages has the official title of commisar, gestapo, sheriff, policeman, constable, game warden, or what-not, the violation of one's right to privacy is just as deplorable." The police would commit such acts "again and again," Carter declared, "if the courts continue to hold that the evidence they obtain by such unlawful means may be used in criminal prosecutions."[63]

The United States Supreme Court reversed the California courts in *Rochin* v. *California* in January of 1952. Writing for the Court, Justice

Frankfurter again defended the fair trial approach to the Due Process Clause. The Due Process Clause required "a continuing process of application," he said, during which the Court could "not draw on our merely personal and private notions and disregard the limits that bind judges in their judicial function. Even though the concept of due process of law is not final and fixed, these limits are derived from considerations that are fused in the whole nature of the judicial process." Again using the occasion to attack Black's total-incorporation position, Frankfurter said that to believe that the responsibility of the Court in divining the meaning of the Due Process Clause "could be avoided by freezing 'due process of law' at some fixed stage of time or thought is to suggest that the most important aspect of constitutional adjudication is a function for inanimate machines and not for judges. . . ."[64]

The interpretation of the Due Process Clause, Frankfurter continued, demanded of judges "the habit of self-discipline and self-criticism, incertitude that one's own views are incontestable and alert tolerance toward views not shared." These traits were to be brought to bear in each case, where the Court would make an "evaluation based on disinterested inquiry pursued in the spirit of science, on a balanced order of facts exactly and fairly stated, on the detached consideration of conflicting claims, . . . on a judgment not ad hoc and episodic but duly mindful of reconciling the needs both of continuity and of change in a progressive society."[65]

Applying these "general considerations" to the facts in the *Rochin* case, Frankfurter held that the proceedings in the case "do more than offend some fastidious squeamishness or private sentimentalism about combatting crime too energetically." The actions of the deputies in the *Rochin* case, he said, was "conduct that shocks the conscience" and was "bound to offend even hardened sensibilities. They are methods too close to the rack and the screw to permit of constitutional differentiation." In administering their criminal laws, he continued, the states must "respect certain decencies of civilized conduct. Due process of law, as a historic and generative principle, precludes defining, and thereby confining, these standards of conduct more precisely than to say that convictions cannot be brought about by methods that offend 'a sense of justice.'" Since the methods by which the Los Angeles deputies had secured evidence against Rochin offended "a sense of justice," the Court therefore reversed his conviction and held that the trial court should have excluded the evidence obtained by such methods.[66]

Justice Black concurred in the judgment of the Court, but he renewed his attack on Frankfurter's due process position. Faithful adherence to the "specific guarantees of the Bill of Rights," he argued, "insured a more permanent protection of individual liberty than that which can be afforded by the nebulous standards stated by the majority." The "accordion-like qualities" of the majority's due process position, Black concluded, "must inevitably imperil all the individual liberty safeguards specifically enumerated in the Bill of Rights." And Justice Douglas also charged in a concurring opinion that the majority's approach to the Due Process Clause "is part of the process of erosion of civil rights of the citizen in recent years."[67]

The Court did not discuss the *Wolf* case in its opinion in the *Rochin* case, since it still adhered to the position that an unreasonable search and seizure was not per se sufficiently offensive to "a sense of justice" to require state courts to exclude evidence obtained by such means. The *Rochin* case did stand for the proposition, on the other hand, that if evidence was obtained by sufficiently shocking or indecent methods by state officers, the Due Process Clause required the exclusion of such evidence in the state courts.

Despite Justice Frankfurter's assurance that the decision in the *Rochin* case was not based on a judgment that was "ad hoc and episodic," the "shocking to the conscience" test of that case proved to be exceedingly difficult for the Court to apply to varying factual situations. In *Irvine* v. *California*, decided in 1954, the Court was confronted with a case involving police conduct that appeared to be as shocking as the conduct condemned in the *Rochin* case. In *Irvine*, the police had had a key to Irvine's house made by a locksmith, and they had entered the house four times to install microphones in various places, including the bedroom. The conversations thus obtained were admitted in evidence against Irvine when he was subsequently tried on a bookmaking charge.[68]

Faced with these facts, the Court could not agree on a majority opinion. Justice Jackson, joined by Chief Justice Warren and Justices Reed and Minton, admitted that the conduct of the police had constituted trespass and probably burglary, and conceded that the fact that "officers of the law would break and enter a home, secrete such a device, even in a bedroom, and listen to the conversation of the occupants for over a month would be almost incredible if it were not admitted. Few police measures have come to our attention that more flagrantly, deliberately, and persistently violated the fundamental principle declared by the Fourth Amendment. . . ."[69]

Jackson, Warren, Reed, and Minton, however, adhered to the ruling in *Wolf* v. *Colorado* that evidence seized in an unreasonable search and seizure was admissible in state courts. The police conduct in the *Irvine* case, they also held, was insufficiently "shocking" to bring it under the rule of the *Rochin* case, since no physical assault, brutality, or coercion were involved. "However obnoxious are the facts in the case before us," Jackson said, "they do not involve coercion, violence or brutality to the person, but rather trespass to property, plus eavesdropping." Jackson and his colleagues therefore refused "to make inroads upon *Wolf* by holding that it applies only to searches and seizures which produce on our minds a mild shock, while if the shock is more serious, the states must exclude the evidence or we will reverse the convictions."[70]

Justice Clark concurred in the decision to affirm Irvine's conviction, although he noted that if he had been on the Court in 1949 when the *Wolf* case had been decided, he would have voted to apply the *Weeks* exclusionary rule to the states. "In light of the 'incredible' activity of the police here, it is with great reluctance that I follow *Wolf*," he said. "Perhaps strict adherence to the tenor of that decision may produce needed converts for its extinction."[71]

Although Justice Frankfurter had been the author of both the *Wolf* and the *Rochin* opinions for the Court, he was constrained to dissent in the *Irvine* case, and was joined by Justice Burton. Frankfurter again defended the fair-trial approach to the Due Process Clause that had produced the *Rochin* rule, but he argued that under that rule Irvine's conviction should have been reversed. Under the Due Process Clause, he said, a state "cannot resort to methods that offend civilized standards of decency and fairness." Under the *Wolf* case, he conceded, the admission in a state court of evidence obtained in an unreasonable search and seizure did not call for the reversal of a conviction under the Due Process Clause, but if there were "additional aggravating conduct which the Court finds repulsive," reversal was required by due process. And in the *Irvine* case, Frankfurter concluded, there had been such aggravating, repulsive conduct by the police, which justified the reversal of Irvine's conviction under the Due Process Clause.[72]

The Court's difficulties in applying the *Rochin* rule continued with its decision in *Breithaupt* v. *Abram* in 1957. In the *Breithaupt* case, the Court upheld the use as evidence of a blood sample obtained from the unconscious body of an automobile-accident victim. The blood sample had revealed a high alcohol content, and was admitted as evidence in a manslaughter prosecution in the New Mexico courts. In addition to reaffirming that the Self-Incrimination Clause and the *Weeks* exclusionary rule did not apply to the states and thus bar the use of such evidence, the Court held relative to the *Rochin* rule that there was "nothing 'brutal' or 'offensive' in the taking of a sample of blood when done, as in this case, under the protective eye of a physician."[73]

Chief Justice Warren, joined by Justices Black and Douglas, however, dissented in the *Breithaupt* case and argued that there was no essential difference between the use of stomach pumping in the *Rochin* case and the nonconsenting withdrawal of blood from Breithaupt. "Only personal reaction to the stomach pump and the blood test can distinguish them," Warren said. "To base the restriction which the Due Process Clause imposes on state criminal procedures upon such reactions is to build on shifting sands."[74]

Chief Justice Warren's dissent in the *Briethaupt* case signified an increasing disillusionment on his part with the case-by-case, fair trial approach to the interpretation of the Due Process Clause. Warren therefore began to join more frequently with the incorporationists, Black and Douglas, in their attacks on the dominant approach to the Due Process Clause. The ranks of these dissenters were also swelled by the appointment of Justice William Brennan in 1956, since he too was soon protesting the prevailing fair trial approach to the Due Process Clause. By the late 1950s, therefore, Warren, Black, Douglas, and Brennan were only one vote away from scuttling the fair trial approach.[75]

The fair trial approach nevertheless remained in the saddle throughout the 1950s, and was, if anything, strengthened by the appointments of Justices John Marshall Harlan in 1955 and Charles Evans Whittaker in 1957, both of whom supported the dominant approach. Harlan was the grandson of the first John Marshall Harlan—who had been the first total incorporationist—but as the second Justice Harlan he became the most powerful and persuasive opponent of the incorporationist position, surpassing in this regard his former professor at Harvard, Justice Frankfurter.[76]

In the skirmishing between the two groups during the late 1950s, it became evident that the history of the nationalization of the Bill of Rights was interpreted quite differently by each side. Warren, Black, Douglas, and Brennan clearly felt that in imposing such rights as the freedom from unreasonable searches and seizures upon the states, the Court was applying to the states the Fourth Amendment in the same way and with the same force as it applied to the federal government. When the Court held that a right in the Bill of Rights was protected by the Due Process Clause, they argued, that right had the identical scope and meaning in its application in state proceedings as it had in federal proceedings.

Joined by Warren, Black, and Douglas, Justice Brennan thus stated in 1960 that the question of the applicability of the Bill of Rights to the states via the Due Process Clause did not "involve the theory that the matter is one for the judges to solve on an ad hoc basis, according to their over-all reaction to particular cases." Brennan noted that Black and Douglas supported the total incorporation of the Bill of Rights into the Fourteenth Amendment, but indicated that he and Chief Justice Warren "have neither accepted nor rejected that view. . . ." Whether or not total incorporation was accepted, he continued, it was clear that Justice Cardozo's declaration in the *Palko* case—that certain rights in the Bill of Rights were carried over into the Due Process Clause "by a process of absorption"—had meant that the rights so absorbed applied to the states in the identical way that they applied to the federal government. The *Palko* case, Brennan concluded, had not been "a license to the judiciary to administer a watered-down subjective version of the individual guarantees of the Bill of Rights when state cases come before us."[77]

Such views were of course fundamentally at war with the fair trial approach to the Due Process Clause as expounded by the leading defenders of that approach, Justices Frankfurter and Harlan. Just because the Court had held that the Due Process Clause protected a right to counsel or a freedom from unreasonable searches and seizures, Frankfurter argued time and again, did not mean that the Court was applying the Assistance of Counsel Clause of the Sixth Amendment and the Fourth Amendment to the states in the identical form in which those provisions applied in federal proceedings. The right to counsel and the prohibition against unreasonable searches and seizures secured by the Due Process Clause emanated from the concept of due process itself, Frankfurter argued, without reference to the Bill of Rights. Such rights were therefore not necessarily identical in scope and meaning to their namesakes in the Bill of Rights.

As his opinion in the *Adamson* case revealed, a major problem with Frankfurter's approach to the Due Process Clause was the acceptance by the Court, in many cases in which he had joined, of the proposition that the First Amendment freedoms applied fully and in identical form to the states and to the federal government. And, it appears, Frankfurter was concerned with this point up to his death.[78] For Justice Harlan, however, the First Amendment point was not a problem, since his starting point was that the Court's decision in *Barron* v. *Baltimore* holding that the Bill of Rights applied exclusively to the federal government had never been reversed. For Harlan, therefore, it was axiomatic that no right in the Bill of Rights applied to the states. He also accepted, however, the Court's indication in the *Twining* case that if the Due Process Clause protected rights that were comparable to some of those in the Bill of Rights, such rights were only similar to their counterparts, and not identical. In Harlan's view, therefore, the freedoms of speech, press, religion, and assembly and petition—as well as the separation of church and state, the right to counsel, and the prohibition of unreasonable searches and seizures—that the Court had held to be protected by the Due Process Clause did not have as their origins the First, Fourth, and Sixth Amendments (except perhaps as inspiration), nor were they the same as the similar rights protected by those amendments.[79]

Both Frankfurter and Harlan shared the belief that the fair trial approach to the Due Process Clause was also justified by the federal nature of the constitutional system. And both took as their inspirational text the philosophy expressed by Justice Brandeis in 1932 that for the Court to "stay experimentation in things social and economic is a grave responsibility. Denial of the right to experiment may be fraught with serious consequences to the Nation." It was one of the "happy incidents of the federal system," Brandeis had continued, "that a single courageous State may, if its citizens choose, serve as a laboratory; and try novel social and economic experiments without risk to the rest of the country."[80]

Although Brandeis was speaking in dissent to a decision of the Court invalidating a state economic regulation under the Due Process Clause, the received understanding of his philosophy according to Frankfurter and Harlan was that the states should not be straitjacketed by the Due Process Clause in terms of implementing novel experiments, whether they involved economic policy or criminal procedure. The incorporationist position—that some or all of the specific procedural provisions of the Bill of Rights should be held to be binding on the states via the Due Process Clause—was therefore anathema to the Frankfurter-Harlan position. Such a result, they felt, would stifle experimentation by the states and would violate a basic principle of the federal system that allowed the states to serve as insulated laboratories, free of all but the most fundamental interests secured by the federal Constitution.

In opposition to this position, the incorporationists argued that some, if not all, of the rights listed in the Bill of Rights constituted basic elements of American freedom that should not be subject to state experimentation. The fair trial approach advocated by Harlan and Frankfurter, they argued, allowed the Court to substitute the personal predilections of the justices as to what were fundamental rights for the specifics of the Bill of Rights. And, as the *Rochin-Irvine-Breithaupt* line of cases indicated, the fair-trial approach also resulted in the articulation of nebulous standards on a case-by-case basis that served as vehicles for unpredictable federal interventions in state criminal proceedings. The consequence, the incorporationists argued, was to aggravate federal-state frictions rather than to serve the interests of the federal system.

Justice Brennan delivered one of the James Madison Lectures at the New York University School of Law in February of 1961, and he took the opportunity to attack the fair trial approach and to defend the incorporationist position. He attacked the view that considerations of federalism justified the fair trial approach to due process in state proceedings. "Federalism makes its own contribution to the preservation of our freedoms," he said. "The specifics of the Bill of Rights so far absorbed in due process have enhanced, not diminished, that contribution. The absorption of more can only further increase respect for federalism."[81]

Would Madison, Brennan asked, have considered the rights against double jeopardy, against compulsory self-incrimination, to a speedy and public trial by jury, to be informed of the nature and cause of the accusation and to confront witnesses, to have compulsory process for obtaining witnesses, and to have the right to counsel "as unnecessary to 'the very essence of a scheme of ordered liberty,' or that any was not among 'the fundamental principles of liberty and justice which lie at the base of all our civil and political institutions,' or not among the personal immunities which are 'so rooted in the traditions and conscience of our people as to be ranked as fundamental?'" What the Due Process Clause had meant "to the wisdom of other days," Brennan continued, "cannot be its measure to the vision of our time. The importance of keeping aglow the fires of freedom was never greater." Excessive emphasis on "states' rights," Brennan declared, "must not make the process of absorption 'a license to the judiciary to administer a watered-down subjective version of the individual guarantees of the Bill of Rights when state cases come before' the Court."[82]

Brennan spoke on the eve of a major breakthrough for the incorporationists, since four months after his James Madison Lecture, the Court decided *Mapp* v. *Ohio*, reversing *Wolf* v. *Colorado* and applying the full Fourth Amendment and the exclusionary rule to the states. And before the decade of the 1960s had run its course, all of the rights Brennan had mentioned in his lecture would be incorporated by the Court into the Due Process Clause.

8

The Incorporation Breakthrough
From *Mapp* to *Gideon*

The Supreme Court's consistent refusal to apply the criminal procedure provisions of the Bill of Rights to the states ended abruptly in the early 1960s. In *Mapp* v. *Ohio*, decided in 1961, a bare majority of the Court applied the full Fourth Amendment and the *Weeks* exclusionary rule to the states.[1] By 1963, however, when the Court applied the full Assistance of Counsel Clause of the Sixth Amendment to the states in *Gideon* v. *Wainwright*, the dominance of the fair trial approach in state criminal cases had clearly been broken, and selective incorporation of most of the rest of the Bill of Rights into the Due Process Clause had obviously become the wave of the future.[2]

The fair-trial approach to search-and-seizure issues was substantially undermined by the Court's decision in *Elkins* v. *United States* in 1960. Prior to the *Elkins* case, the Court had upheld the admission in the federal courts of evidence illegally seized by state officers, on the premise that the Fourth Amendment applied only to federal officers, and not to state officers. Under this so-called silver-platter doctrine, state officers could seize evidence illegally, and because the Fourth Amendment was inapplicable to them, could present the illegally seized evidence to federal officers on a silver platter for use in federal prosecutions.[3]

Joined by Chief Justice Warren and Justices Black, Douglas, and Brennan, Justice Potter Stewart held in the *Elkins* case that the silver-platter doctrine had been undermined by *Wolf* v. *Colorado*, in which, Stewart asserted, it had been "unequivocally determined by a unanimous Court that the Federal Constitution, by virtue of the Fourteenth Amendment, prohibits unreasonable searches and seizures by state officers." The foundation "upon which the admissibility of state-seized evidence in a federal trial originally rested—that unreasonable state searches did not violate the Federal Constitution—thus disappeared in 1949." Exercising its power to supervise the administration of justice in the lower federal courts, the Court therefore held that "evidence obtained by state officers during a search which, if conducted by federal officers, would have violated the defendant's immunity from unreasonable searches and seizures under the Fourth Amendment is inadmissible over the defendant's timely objection in a federal criminal trial."[4]

To justify the imposition of this new exclusionary rule in the federal courts, Stewart stated that the purpose of such a rule was "to prevent, not repair. Its purpose is to deter—to compel respect for the constitutional guaranty in the only effectively available way—by removing the incentive to disregard it." He also noted that prior to the decision in *Wolf* v. *Colorado*, only eighteen states excluded illegally seized evidence, but by 1960, twenty-six states excluded such evidence, while twenty-four states continued to admit illegally seized evidence. "The movement towards the rule of exclusion," Stewart concluded, "has been halting but seemingly inexorable."[5]

Stewart also pointed to the most dramatic reversal by a state court on the issue of the exclusionary rule—that of the California Supreme Court— to justify the *Elkins* ruling. Although the California Supreme Court had consistently adhered to the position that illegally seized evidence was admissible in California, in *People* v. *Cahan*, decided in 1955, it adopted the exclusionary rule. The court concluded that "other remedies have completely failed to secure compliance with the constitutional provisions on the part of police officers with the attendant result that the courts under the old rule have been constantly required to participate in, and in effect condone, the lawless activities of law enforcement officers." Neither "administrative, criminal nor civil remedies," the California court concluded, "are effective in suppressing lawless searches and seizures."[6]

The implication in the majority opinion in the *Elkins* case that the full Fourth Amendment applied to the states produced an impassioned dissenting opinion by Justice Frankfurter, who was joined by Justices Harlan, Clark, and Whittaker. The *Wolf* case, Frankfurter argued, had held that only the "core of the Fourth Amendment, not the Amendment itself, is enforceable against the States," since the *Wolf* decision had been based on "the Due Process Clause of the Fourteenth Amendment, and not . . . the specific guarantees of the Fourth Amendment."[7]

Restating the fair trial approach once again, Frankfurter said that "some of the principles underlying the specific safeguards of the first eight Amendments are implied limitations upon the States drawn out of the Due Process Clause of the Fourteenth Amendment, and to that extent, but no more, afford federal protection to individuals against state power." But it was basic to "the structure and functioning of our federal system," he maintained, "to distinguish between the specifics of the Bill of Rights of the first eight Amendments and the generalities of the Due Process Clause translated into concreteness case by case. . . ."[8]

The *Wolf* case, Frankfurter continued, had not held that the Fourth

Amendment per se applied to the states via the Due Process Clause, but had held only that the Due Process Clause prohibited arbitrary searches by state officers measured by general due process standards. "The identity of the protection of the Due Process Clause against arbitrary searches with the scope of protection of the Fourth Amendment," he declared, "is something the Court assumes for the first time today. It assumes this without explication in reason or in reliance upon authority, and entirely without regard for the essential difference, which has always been recognized by this Court, between the particularities of the first eight Amendments and the fundamental nature of what constitutes due process."[9]

If Frankfurter was correct in charging that the majority of the Court was now applying the full Fourth Amendment to the states, the question left unanswered by the *Elkins* case was whether the *Weeks* exclusionary rule was not also applicable to the states. Justice Stewart had said in the *Elkins* case that the exclusionary rule was necessary to compel respect for the Fourth Amendment "in the only effectively available way—by removing the incentive to disregard it." If the Fourth Amendment was now considered to apply to the states, and if a majority of the Court felt the exclusionary rule was the only effective way to enforce it, then a reversal of *Wolf* v. *Colorado* on this point was clearly in the wind. A decision holding that the full Fourth Amendment, along with the exclusionary rule, applied to the states would, of course, entail breaking with the fair trial approach, which had prevented the incorporation of any of the Bill of Rights beyond the First Amendment. The barrier that the fair trial approach imposed in regard to the nationalization process was breached, however, and the breach came in *Mapp* v. *Ohio* in 1961.

Dolly Mapp's Case

Officers of the Cleveland, Ohio, police department received an anonymous tip on May 23, 1957, that a fugitive wanted in a recent bombing was hiding at 14705 Milverton Road. The tipster also said that paraphernalia relating to the numbers racket was hidden at that address. Acting upon this information, several officers converged on the residence.

The residence was a two-story brick dwelling divided into first- and second-floor apartments. The second-floor apartment was occupied by Mrs. Dollree (Dolly) Mapp, a twenty-nine-year-old black woman who lived in the apartment with Barbara Bivins, her daughter by a former marriage to Jimmy Bivins, a heavyweight prizefighter. Dolly Mapp had subsequently been the girl friend of light-heavyweight champion Archie Moore, and the Cleveland press described her as being a "confidante of numbers racketeers."[10]

When the police officers rang the bell on the side entrance to the Milverton Road residence, Mrs. Mapp appeared at an upstairs window and asked what the officers wanted. They requested permission to enter the house, but Mrs. Mapp said that she would first call her attorney for his advice. Her attorney advised her that she should not allow the police into the residence unless they produced a search warrant and allowed her to read it. Dolly Mapp therefore informed the waiting officers that she would allow them to enter the residence only if they had a search warrant.

The police had arrived at the Mapp residence shortly after 1:00 P.M., but it was not until after 4:00 P.M. that a police lieutenant arrived with what was purported to be a search warrant. Dolly Mapp still refused to admit the officers, and the door of the house was forced by the police. Mrs. Mapp met the officers on the stairs leading to her apartment and demanded to see the search warrant. An officer waved a piece of paper in the air, and Dolly Mapp seized it and shoved it down her blouse. A struggle ensued in which the officers retrieved the paper and handcuffed Dolly Mapp.

During the subsequent search of the Mapp apartment and the basement of the building, the officers discovered four obscene pamphlets, some obscene photographs, and a hand-drawn picture. A trunk containing numbers-racket paraphernalia was also discovered in the basement. All of these items were seized as evidence to be used against Dolly Mapp in subsequent proceedings.[11]

A misdemeanor prosecution against Mrs. Mapp based on the numbers-racket paraphernalia was initiated in the Cleveland Police Court, but she was acquitted. Section 2905.34 of the Ohio Statutes, however, prohibited any person from having under his control or in his possession any obscene, lewd, or lascivious materials. Dolly Mapp was indicted and tried under this statute in September of 1958. Her attorney, A. L. Kearns, objected to the admission as evidence of the obscene items on the ground that the search of Dolly Mapp's residence had been illegal. The Ohio Supreme Court had held in State v. Lindway in 1936 that illegally seized evidence was admissible in the Ohio courts, and relying on the Lindway case, the trial judge overruled Kearns's objection and admitted the obscene items as evidence against Mrs. Mapp. She was convicted of possession of obscene materials by a jury in the Cuyahoga County Court of Common Pleas and was subsequently sentenced to an indeterminate term in the Ohio State Women's Reformatory. Under Ohio law, this sentence meant a minimum of one year and a maximum of seven years in the reformatory.[12]

The Mapp case was appealed to the Court of Appeals of Cuyahoga County; on March 28, 1959, however, the court held that upon a "review of the entire case, we find no error prejudicial to the rights of the defendant."[13] An appeal was then pursued to the Ohio Supreme Court, where A. L. Kearns argued that the statute under which Dolly Mapp had been convicted violated the freedom of expression guaranteed by the First and

Fourteenth Amendments, and that the seizure of the obscene items from her residence had been illegal under both the Ohio Constitution and the federal Constitution.

On March 23, 1960, however, the Ohio Supreme Court affirmed Mrs. Mapp's conviction. The court admitted that there was "considerable doubt as to whether there ever was any warrant for the search of defendant's home," but held that the absence of a warrant was irrelevant, since under the *Lindway* case illegally seized evidence was admissible in the Ohio courts. And, the court noted, under *Wolf* v. *Colorado*, state courts were also not required to exclude illegally seized evidence.[14]

The court also considered whether the obscene materials had been obtained by the police through methods that "shocked the conscience" under the doctrine of *Rochin* v. *California*, but concluded that the evidence had not been secured by "use of brutal or offensive physical force against defendant." The Due Process Clause of the Fourteenth Amendment had not been violated, the court held, "although [Mrs. Mapp's] conviction was based primarily upon the introduction in evidence of books and pictures unlawfully seized during an unlawful search of defendant's home."[15]

Finally, four of the seven judges on the Ohio Supreme Court agreed that the possession-of-obscenity statute violated the First and Fourteenth Amendments because it was likely to "discourage law abiding people from even looking at books and pictures." The Ohio Constitution required a vote of at least six of the judges for the court to invalidate a statute, however, except in cases in which the court of appeals had also invalidated the statute. Since the court of appeals had not so ruled in the *Mapp* case, and only four of the seven judges of the supreme court agreed that the possession-of-obscenity statute was invalid, the conviction was affirmed by the court.[16]

Mapp v. *Ohio* was appealed to the United States Supreme Court in July of 1960, but in the briefs filed by all parties in the case, the search-and-seizure issue was largely ignored. Both the American Civil Liberties Union and its Ohio affiliate intervened in the case as *amici curiae*, but they focused their arguments on the free-expression issue. The search-and-seizure issue was addressed only in a short concluding paragraph of the ACLU brief, where the Court's decision in *Wolf* v. *Colorado* was noted, and the Court was urged to "re-examine this issue and conclude that the ordered liberty concept guaranteed to persons by the Due Process Clause of the Fourteenth Amendment necessarily requires that evidence illegally obtained in violation thereof, should not be admissible in state criminal proceedings."[17]

Counsel for the state of Ohio also primarily addressed the issue of the possession-of-obscenity statute's validity under the First and Fourteenth Amendments, but did admit that a search warrant had not been obtained by the police before they entered Dolly Mapp's house. Under the *Wolf* and

Lindway cases, Ohio counsel pointed out, the absence of a warrant was irrelevant, since illegally seized evidence was admissible in the Ohio courts.[18] In his arguments on behalf of Dolly Mapp, on the other hand, A. L. Kearns did not even cite *Wolf* v. *Colorado* in his brief and did not ask the Court to apply the exclusionary rule to the states. Kearns instead argued that the conduct of the police in the *Mapp* case had been "shocking to the conscience" under the doctrine of *Rochin* v. *California*, and the obscene items should have been excluded as evidence on that ground.[19]

Although *Mapp* v. *Ohio* would prove to be a major breakthrough for the incorporationists on the Court as well as one of the Warren Court's most important criminal-procedure decisions, the oral argument of the case before the Court was disappointingly poor, and the performance of counsel on both sides ranged from mediocre to verging on incompetence.[20] The lack of a thorough discussion of the search-and-seizure issue in the briefs was therefore not remedied during the oral argument.

Opening on behalf of Dolly Mapp, A. L. Kearns began with what was essentially a jury argument, disputing evidentiary matters, attacking the trial judge's charge to the jury, and detailing the lack of a search warrant in the case. Never long on patience, Justice Frankfurter finally interrupted Kearns and asked what he "deemed to be the questions open before the Court," pointing out that questions of evidence or the charge to the jury were not before the Court under the decision of the Ohio Supreme Court. Kearns replied that he was "asking the Court to decide the question that eight and a half million citizens of the State of Ohio" were being denied their right against unreasonable searches and seizures under the Ohio Supreme Court's decision in the *Lindway* case. "Are you asking us to overrule the *Wolf* case in this Court?" Frankfurter asked. "I notice it isn't even cited in your brief." Kearns dodged the question, but under persistent questioning by Frankfurter he stated that the *Mapp* case involved two questions: the validity of the possession-of-obscenity statute and the search-and-seizure question. "Well, that means you're asking us to overrule *Wolf* against *Colorado*," a justice responded, but Kearns said, "No, I don't believe we are. All we're asking is, that we have this *Lindway* case . . . that is controlling the entire State of Ohio." But the *Lindway* case "holds that although evidence is illegally procured it is admissible," Frankfurter exasperatedly told Kearns. "That's the familiar doctrine in so many states of this Union and which we dealt with in the *Wolf* case, and yet you do not even refer to it in your brief." Dodging again, Kearns replied, "Well, we went through the *Wolf* case but we don't refer to it here. I think maybe the state does. But the fact of the matter is that we are, as citizens of Ohio, deprived of our constitutional rights against unlawful search and seizure."

It was clear from his exchanges with Frankfurter that Kearns did not know of the *Wolf* case nor what it had held, yet he persisted in emphasizing that the Cleveland police had lacked a search warrant and that the *Lindway* case was the source of all of Dolly Mapp's troubles.[21] Again, however, Frankfurter interrupted to ask, "Mr. Kearns, does the state contend that there was a valid search warrant here?" Kearns replied that he didn't believe that was the state's contention, and then Frankfurter asked with irritation, "Do you have to argue anything when the [Ohio Supreme] Court itself tells you it decided upon the basis of an unlawful search? Is there anything to be argued about? I'm not saying they are correct in sustaining it, but is the question of was there an unlawful search in controversy in this case?" Kearns finally admitted, "No there isn't. There was an unlawful search." Chief Justice Warren then asked if a motion to suppress the illegally seized evidence had been filed in the trial court, and Kearns said that such a motion had been filed but had been overruled on the basis of the *Lindway* case. "And," Frankfurter again pointed out with irritation, "the *Lindway* case says—conceded that there was an unlawful search—the fruits of it may nevertheless if relevant be admitted in the trials in your state."

Having drawn withering fire from Frankfurter because of his ignorance of the *Wolf* case, Kearns turned briefly to an attack on the validity of the Ohio possession-of-obscenity statute. But in his rebuttal remarks, he again raised the search-and-seizure issue and inexplicably began reading the Ohio Constitution's provisions on searches and seizures. Again he was interrupted, this time by Justice Black, who inquired what relevance the Ohio Constitution had to the case and "what do you do with the *Wolf* case" that had held that illegally seized evidence was admissible in state courts. "Well, we feel that in the *Wolf* case," Kearns replied, "this Court did not intend to make it a *general* matter or proposition of that sort." Having again inadequately responded to questions regarding the *Wolf* case, Kearns closed by revealing that he was also largely unaware of the facts in the *Rochin* case, which his brief argued justified a holding by the Court that police conduct in the *Mapp* case had "shocked the conscience." At the close of Kearns's argument, Chief Justice Warren asked, "What particular acts bring [the *Mapp* case] within the *Rochin* case?" And Kearns replied, "I can't say definitely, Your Honor. I'm very sorry, I don't have all the facts in the case, only the conclusion that I reached—came to."

Although Kearns appeared to be familiar with neither the *Wolf* case nor the *Rochin* case, he did allot some of his oral-argument time to Bernard A. Berkman, representing the American Civil Liberties Union and its Ohio affiliate. And in his opening remarks, Berkman said that "before I get into the area that was allotted to me, I would like to say that the American Civil Liberties Union and its Ohio affiliate, the Ohio Civil Liberties Union, is very clear in response to a question that was directed to counsel for the appellant, that we are asking this Court to reconsider *Wolf* v. *Colorado* and to find that evidence which is unlawfully and illegally obtained should not be permitted into a state proceeding and that its production is a violation of the federal Constitution, the Fourth Amendment, and Fourteenth Amendment. We have no hesitancy about asking the Court to reconsider it, because we think it is a necessary part of due process." Was Berkman asking the Court "to reexamine *Wolf*, or are you relying on *Rochin* against *California*?" Justice Brennan asked. "We are asking the Court to reexamine *Wolf* . . . ," Berkman replied. Berkman then turned to the question of the validity of the possession-of-obscenity statute under the First and Fourteenth Amendments, which was the focus of the remainder of his argument.

Counsel for the state of Ohio was Mrs. Gertrude Bauer Mahon, the assistant prosecuting attorney who had prosecuted the *Mapp* case in the trial court, and Mrs. Mahon also focused her argument on the question of the validity of the obscenity statute. Mrs. Mahon was almost immediately caught in a cross fire from the justices because of her insistence that the Ohio Supreme Court had misinterpreted the statute as prohibiting mere knowing possession of obscene items.[22] As a consequence, the search-and-seizure issue was dealt with only briefly by Mrs. Mahon.

She did note, however, that the *Lindway* case in Ohio was in conformity with the *Wolf* case, and that "Ohio does not follow the exclusionary rule." The Ohio Constitution guaranteed the criminally accused a fair trial, she said, but "neither the laws of Ohio" nor "the Ohio courts are solicitous of aiding" criminal defendants in concealing their guilt. Protection of the rights of the accused, she continued, "does not extend to the rejection of competent evidence, because of the method by which it was procured," and the lack of a search warrant in the *Mapp* case had "no bearing whatsoever" on the admissibility of the evidence seized at Dolly Mapp's home. Toward the conclusion of Mrs. Mahon's argument, Chief Justice Warren asked, "Is the search warrant in existence?" and Mrs. Mahon replied, "Insofar as the record is concerned, it doesn't show any." Warren persisted, however, asking, "Is there any record of it in the records?" and Mrs. Mahon conceded, "There is no record there was a search warrant. . . ."

Although the briefs and oral argument in the *Mapp* case dealt inadequately with the search-and-seizure issue, on June 19, 1961, the Court announced its decision in *Mapp* v. *Ohio* and by a five-to-four vote held that the full Fourth Amendment and the *Weeks* exclusionary rule applied to the states. Justice Clark wrote the prevailing opinion and was joined by Chief Justice Warren and Justices Douglas and Brennan. Justice Black concurred in the result, while Justices Harlan, Frankfurter, and Whittaker dissented. Justice Stewart filed a separate memorandum agreeing that Dolly Mapp's conviction should be reversed but avoiding the search-and-seizure issue.

"Today we once again examine [*Wolf* v. *Colorado's*] constitutional documentation of the right of privacy free from unreasonable state intrusion," Clark declared in the prevailing opinion, "and, after its dozen years on our books, are led by it to close the only courtroom door remaining open to evidence secured by official lawlessness in flagrant abuse of that basic right, reserved to all persons as a specific guarantee against that very same unlawful conduct." The Court held, he continued, "that all evidence obtained by searches and seizures in violation of the Constitution is, by that same authority, inadmissible in a state court." Since the Fourth Amendment had been held to be applicable to the states via the Due Process Clause, "it is enforceable against them by the same sanction of exclusion as is used against the Federal Government."[23]

The *Wolf* case had recognized that the Fourth Amendment applied to the states, Clark asserted, and for the Court to continue to refuse to enforce its terms via the exclusionary rule would be "to grant the right but in reality to withhold its privilege and enjoyment." As the *Elkins* case had indicated, he said, the purpose of the exclusionary rule was to deter violations of the Fourth Amendment "in the only effectively available way—by removing the incentive to disregard it." The Court had not hesitated, Clark continued, to "enforce as strictly against the States as it does against the Federal Government the rights of free speech and of a free press, the rights to notice and to a fair, public trial, including, as it does, the right not to be convicted by use of a coerced confession, however logically relevant it may be, and without regard to its reliability." Since coerced confessions were excluded by the Court from state criminal proceedings, he argued, why "should not the same rule apply to what is tantamount to coerced testimony by way of unconstitutional seizure of goods, papers, effects, documents, etc.?" The Due Process Clause's prohibition of coerced confessions and unreasonable searches and seizures were "complementary to, although not dependent upon, that of the other in its sphere of influence— the very least that together they assure in either sphere is that no man is to be convicted on unconstitutional evidence."[24]

Finally, Clark argued that the Court's holding that the exclusionary rule was part and parcel of the Fourth and Fourteenth Amendments made "very good sense" in relation to the federal system. To allow state officers to illegally seize evidence and state courts to admit such evidence would not promote a healthy federalism, he argued, but rather federal-state co-operation in "the solution of crime will be promoted, if only by recognition of their new mutual obligation to respect the same fundamental criteria in their approaches." The ignoble "shortcut to conviction left open to the State," he said, "tends to destroy the entire system of constitutional restraints on which the liberties of the people rest. Having once recognized that the right to privacy embodied in the Fourth Amendment is enforceable against the States, and that the right to be secure against rude invasions of privacy by state officers is, therefore, constitutional in origin, we can no longer permit that right to remain an empty promise." The Fourth Amendment was enforceable against the states "in the same manner and to like effect as other basic rights secured by the Due Process Clause," Clark concluded, and the Court would no longer permit it to be "revocable at the whim of any police officer who, in the name of law enforcement itself, chooses to suspend its enjoyment." And since the evidence in the *Mapp* case had been seized in a search violative of the Fourth and Fourteenth Amendments, the Court held that the Ohio courts should have excluded it at Dolly Mapp's trial, and on that ground the Court reversed her conviction.[25]

Justice Black had agreed in *Wolf* v. *Colorado* that the exclusionary rule was a judicially created rule and not a command of the Fourth Amendment, but he nonetheless concurred in the Court's reversal of Dolly Mapp's conviction on the ground that the Fifth Amendment's Self-Incrimination Clause taken together with the Fourth Amendment did compel the exclusion of illegally seized evidence in the state courts.[26] Justice Stewart also concurred in the reversal in the *Mapp* case, but argued that the search-and-seizure issue was not properly before the Court. The reversal was justified, he argued, only on the basis that the Ohio possession-of-obscenity statute violated the freedom of expression protected by the Due Process Clause.[27]

Given the repudiation of the fair trial approach that the *Mapp* decision represented, it is not surprising that Justice Harlan, joined by Justices Frankfurter and Whittaker, charged in dissent that the Court had unnecessarily "reached out" to overrule *Wolf* v. *Colorado*. Since only the core of the Fourth Amendment applied to the states, Harlan argued, the exclusionary rule did not apply to the states even it if were considered a command of the full Fourth Amendment. "I do not see how it can be said that a trial becomes unfair," he continued, "simply because a State determines that evidence may be considered by the trier of fact, regardless of how it was obtained, if it is relevant to the one issue with which the trial is concerned, the guilt or innocence of the accused." And again indicating that the Court had reached the search-and-seizure issue unnecessarily, Harlan declared, "I regret that I find so unwise in principle and so inexpedient in policy a decision motivated by the high purpose of increasing respect for Constitutional rights. But in the last analysis I think this Court can increase respect for the Constitution only if it rigidly respects the limitations which the Constitution places upon it, and respects as well the principles inherent in its own processes. In the present case I think we exceed both, and that our voice becomes only a voice of power, not reason."[28]

Suddenly, and in a case in which the search-and-seizure issue had not been adequately argued, the incorporation breakthrough therefore occurred. The *Wolf* case had been reinterpreted to hold that the Fourth Amendment applied fully to the states, and the *Weeks* exclusionary rule was held in the *Mapp* case to be a constitutional command, either of the Fourth Amendment—or as Justice Black would have it, a command of the Fourth Amendment and the Self-Incrimination Clause taken together. The barrier that had existed since the 1940s against the imposition on the states of the procedural safeguards of the Bill of Rights had finally fallen.[29]

The immediate consequence of the *Mapp* decision was of course that the possession-of-obscenity conviction of Dolly Mapp was reversed, and she no longer faced a sentence of from one to seven years in the Ohio State Women's Reformatory. The reaction in Cleveland was otherwise minimal, with little recognition in the press of the important step the Court had taken in the *Mapp* case. Mrs. Gertrude Bauer Mahon admitted that "there was never any evidence that a search warrant was issued" in the case, and A. L. Kearns seemed to be uncomfortable, as well he should have been, in winning the *Mapp* case on a point he had not argued. He lamented the fact that the Court had not invalidated the Ohio possession-of-obscenity statute under the First and Fourteenth Amendments. Kearns would be vindicated on this issue eight years later, however, when the Court held that under the First and Fourteenth Amendments, the possession of obscene materials for private, personal use could not be validly prohibited.[30]

Although the reactions in Cleveland generally overlooked the significance of the incorporation breakthrough in the *Mapp* case, the *New York Times* quite properly referred to the decision as an "historic step." And Anthony Lewis, the *New York Times*'s perceptive reporter of Supreme Court activities, noted accurately that a significant corner had been turned in the relationship between the Bill of Rights and the states. If the Fourth Amendment and the exclusionary rule applied to the states, Lewis observed, it was open to question whether other procedural rights in the Bill of Rights might not also now be applied fully to the states. "Inevitably," he said, "observers are wondering whether other distinctions in the constitutional treatment of the states and the Federal Government may now be erased."[31]

The incorporation of the Fourth Amendment fully into the Due Process Clause in the *Mapp* case had of course been achieved by the narrowest of margins on the Court. The incorporationists, Chief Justice Warren and Justices Black, Douglas, and Brennan, had not yet achieved a solid majority, but rather were dependent on the votes of Justice Stewart, as in the *Elkins* case, or Justice Clark, as in the *Mapp* case. On April 5, 1962, however, Justice Frankfurter suffered a stroke, and he was subsequently constrained to announce the end of his long and distinguished career on the Court. On March 29, Justice Whittaker had also announced his retirement, ending a short career of five years on the Court.[32] Both Frankfurter and Whittaker had supported the fair trial approach to the interpretation of the Due Process Clause, and their retirements further reinforced the breakthrough achieved by the incorporationists in the *Mapp* case, since President Kennedy replaced them with two incorporationists, Arthur J. Goldberg and Byron R. White.[33]

The California Narcotics-Addiction Case

More mundane events were also occurring that would prove to extend the breakthrough of the incorporationists in the *Mapp* case. On February 4, 1960, for example, Officer Lawrence E. Brown of the Los Angeles Police Department stopped an automobile at Pico and Serrano streets. After observing fresh needle marks on the arms of one of the occupants of the automobile, a twenty-five-year-old black man named Walter Lawrence Robinson, Brown arrested him for violation of section 11721 of the Health and Safety Code, which made it a misdemeanor to be addicted to narcotics.[34]

Walter Lawrence Robinson was tried in the Municipal Court of the Los Angeles Judicial District in June of 1960 on the charge of being willfully under the influence of or addicted to narcotics. A major issue at the trial was the legality of the arrest and search of Robinson by Officer Brown and his partner, Officer Wapato. Brown testified that he and Wapato had stopped Robinson's automobile because it did not have a license-plate light and because it was moving very slowly through a neighborhood where a series of purse snatchings from automobiles had occurred. When the automobile containing Robinson had been stopped, Brown testified, the driver, Charles Banks, got out wearing a shirt with the sleeves rolled up, and because a fresh needle mark was visible on his arm, he was immediately arrested. Robinson and two women occupants of the car were then ordered out, and Brown testified that Robinson seemed nervous and admitted that he had used narcotics, while his "eyes were pinpointed and glassy." Robinson was ordered to take off his coat and roll up his shirt sleeves, and Brown testified that he "saw scar tissue and discoloration on the inside of his right arm, and I saw numerous fresh needle marks on the inside of his left arm and also a fresh scab."[35]

Although Robinson challenged Officer Brown's version of the arrest and search, and was supported by his girl friend, Ruth Fairlur, Judge Kenneth L. Holaday ruled that both the arrest and search of Robinson had been based on probable cause. A member of the Los Angeles Police Department's narcotics division then testified that he had examined Robinson after his arrest and had concluded that he was a narcotics user. Robinson, on the other hand, denied that he was an addict and testified that the marks on his arms were the result of an allergic reaction to vaccinations he had received in military service. On June 9, 1960, however, the municipal court jury found Robinson guilty of being a narcotics addict, and Judge Holaday subsequently sentenced him to ninety days in jail and two years probation. Robinson's attorney, Samuel C. McMorris, filed notice of an appeal, however, and Robinson was released on bond on June 22, pending the outcome of the appeal.[36]

On appeal to the appellate department of the Superior Court of Los Angeles County, Samuel McMorris argued that the statute making narcotics addiction an offense was unduly vague and invalid because it made a mere status a criminal offense, while the arrest and search of Robinson had also been unlawful. The appellate department, however, affirmed Robinson's conviction on March 31, 1961. The court nonetheless acknowledged that the California Supreme Court had held in 1960 that a statute making it an offense to be a common drunk was invalid for being unduly vague, and that this ruling might also be applicable to the narcotics-addiction statute. The appellate department therefore encouraged McMorris to test the validity of the narcotics-addiction statute by filing a petition for a writ of habeas corpus in the California Supreme Court.[37]

McMorris followed this advice and filed a petition for a writ of habeas corpus in the District Court of Appeal, but that court denied the writ on May 2, 1961. The Supreme Court of California also denied a hearing in the *Robinson* case on May 31, and McMorris then appealed the case *in forma pauperis* to the United States Supreme Court, which noted jurisdiction on November 20, 1961.[38]

In his brief in the *Robinson* case, Samuel McMorris pursued a shotgun approach in attacking the validity of the narcotics-addiction statute under the Due Process Clause. The statute, he argued, was void for vagueness and was invalid because it made a mere status a crime without requiring any overt criminal behavior on the part of the offender and because it subjected defendants to double jeopardy. In addition, McMorris argued, Robinson had been subjected to an arrest and search without adequate probable cause.[39]

In a short section of his brief, McMorris also charged that the narcotics-addiction statute inflicted cruel and unusual punishment because it punished an involuntary status, since there was "no condition known to man which, in itself, is more compulsive, hence less voluntary, than the status of addiction to drugs. . . . " Could the California legislature, McMorris asked, "punish as a crime a mental and physical illness?"[40] Citing medical and psychiatric studies of narcotics addiction, he also argued that the punishment of addiction at all, "and especially the application of the violent, unmedicated withdrawal, is a modern example of the burning of witches at the stake, the criminal prosecution of illness, and as such is inherently a case of cruel, unusual, inhumane, and unnatural punishment."[41]

At the oral argument of the *Robinson* case, there was again no thorough canvassing of the cruel-and-unusual-punishment issue, or of whether or not the Cruel and Unusual Punishment Clause of the Eighth Amendment applied to the states via the Due Process Clause. McMorris instead again pursued his shotgun approach in attacking the validity of the narcotics-addiction statute—raising issues involving equal protection, due process, double jeopardy, freedom of movement, and the ex post facto prohibition, as well as the issue of cruel and unusual punishment. He focused primarily on the point that a mere status could not be treated as a crime under the Due Process Clause, and he told the Court that he was willing to "abandon, waive or withdraw from" the search-and-seizure issue, the central constitutional issue raised in the trial court, in order to concentrate on that point.[42]

Imprisoning drug addicts, he told the Court, was analogous to imprisoning alcoholics or persons with venereal diseases. "However," McMorris continued, "I think it is clear that an addict no more intended to become an addict . . . than does an alcoholic intend to become an alcoholic because he may have liked to drink socially, or [that] a person intended to acquire venereal disease, because he may have voluntarily committed some other act contrary to . . . the laws of social morality. The point I'm getting at is, these three things are similar—a person intends to take a drink, intends perhaps to take a shot of heroin or smoke a marijuana cigarette or intends to have an illicit sex act. None of these intended to acquire a venereal disease or to become an alcoholic or to become an addict." No one, McMorris said, "intends to become an addict," and narcotics addiction was therefore a "mental and physical illness" that the state should not make criminally punishable.

In the second and final reference to cruel and unusual punishment during the oral argument of the *Robinson* case, McMorris denounced the "cold turkey" withdrawal from addiction imposed by California's penal treatment of addicts. This penal treatment of addiction, he said, involved "terrible, violent withdrawal which we feel is such [an] absence of the operation of what we know about medicine and psychiatry that it is in fact cruel and unusual punishment for the condition of addiction which a person is found in."

This cruel-and-unusual-punishment argument drew no questions from the Court, and again on rebuttal argument McMorris contended that hospitalization was the only proper treatment of addiction. Society, he argued, "can't treat them as criminals, and let them kick this thing cold turkey and die and suffer from it." Justice Brennan then asked what happened "to someone convicted under this [statute]? Does he get any treatment at all?" And McMorris replied, "Not at all. I've known many cases of kicking it cold turkey right there in the cell. . . . The ones who are enforcing the narcotics law in California are the police, not the doctors."

The state of California was represented by Deputy Los Angeles City Attorney William E. Doran, but neither in his brief nor in his oral argument did Doran dwell on the cruel-and-unusual-punishment issue. He argued instead that the statute under which Robinson had been convicted was not unconstitutionally vague, and he emphasized the necessity of a statute prohibiting addiction as a part of the state's comprehensive regulation of narcotics. Without mentioning the Cruel and Unusual Punishment Clause, Doran agreed that narcotics addiction was an illness, and he pointed out to the Court that California had recently adopted a comprehensive system of medical treatment of addicts. But criminal punishment of the status of addiction, he said, was nevertheless "absolutely indispensable" to the control of narcotics trafficking.

Just as the full Fourth Amendment and the exclusionary rule had been applied to the states in the *Mapp* case without adequate argument on the issue, when the Court decided *Robinson* v. *California* on June 25, 1962, the Cruel and Unusual Punishment Clause was applied to the states, although that issue had received only passing mention in the briefs and oral argument. Writing the majority opinion, Justice Stewart conceded that the states had full power to deal with the abuse of narcotics, but he noted that the California courts had construed the narcotics addiction statute to make criminal the status of narcotics addiction per se, without any showing that narcotics had actually been used in the state. "California has said that a person can be continuously guilty of this offense," he said, "whether or not he has ever used or possessed any narcotics within the State, and whether or not he has been guilty of any antisocial behavior there."[43]

It would be highly unlikely, Stewart continued, for any state to make "it a criminal offense for a person to be mentally ill, or a leper, or to be afflicted with a venereal disease." Certainly a state could constitutionally require that persons with such public-health problems must submit to appropriate treatment, but "in the light of contemporary human knowledge," he said, "a law which made a criminal offense of such a disease would doubtless be universally thought to be an infliction of cruel and unusual punishment in violation of the Eighth and Fourteenth Amendments."[44]

California's narcotics-addiction statute, Stewart said, was "of the same category." Narcotics addiction was an illness that could even be innocently or involuntarily acquired, he said, and a "state law which imprisons a person thus afflicted as a criminal, even though he has never touched any narcotic drug within the State or been guilty of any irregular behavior there, inflicts a cruel and unusual punishment in violation of the Fourteenth Amendment." While the Court recognized, Stewart concluded, that a sentence of ninety days in jail was in the abstract not cruel and unusual punishment, nevertheless even "one day in prison would be cruel and unusual punishment for the 'crime' of having a common cold."[45]

The vote on the Court to invalidate the California narcotics-addiction statute was six to two. Justice Frankfurter had suffered a stroke more than two months before and was no longer participating in the work of the Court. Justice Douglas wrote a concurring opinion detailing his reasons for believing that the criminal penalization of narcotics addiction was cruel and unusual punishment, and Justice Harlan also concurred in the judgment of the Court, although solely on the ground that the statute punished "the bare desire to commit a criminal act" and not on cruel-and-unusual-punishment grounds.[46] Alone in dissent were Justice Clark and Justice White, who had replaced the retiring Justice Whittaker in April.[47]

Walter Lawrence Robinson, the Court had therefore held, had been subjected to cruel and unusual punishment under the Eighth and Fourteenth Amendments by the state of California, since the illness of narcotics addiction per se could not be validly treated as a criminal offense. Robinson had of course been free on bond since June 22, 1960, and as it turned out, he had subjected himself to more cruel punishment than that contemplated by the state of California. Walter Robinson had died in August of 1961, even before the Supreme Court had accepted jurisdiction in his case. An autopsy was performed on his body by the Los Angeles County Coroner's Office, and the probable cause of death was listed as "drug intoxication, overdose of narcotic drug." The autopsy report also stated that there were needle marks on the body. Robinson died at the age of twenty-six and was buried in the Evergreen Cemetery.[48]

Counsel for the state of California filed a petition for a rehearing in the *Robinson* case, arguing that the Court had failed to adequately consider the non-penal-treatment aspects of the state's narcotics-addiction program and also pointing out that Robinson had died before the Court's decision. A petition for a rehearing is granted by the Court only when a member of the majority that has decided the case agrees to grant the petition, and a majority of the Court then concurs. In the *Robinson* case, Justice Stewart, who had written the majority opinion, voted to grant the petition for a rehearing, but he was joined by only Justices Clark and Harlan. The Court therefore denied the petition for a rehearing on November 13, 1962, leaving the decision in *Robinson* v. *California* undisturbed.[49]

The immediate reaction to the *Robinson* decision was otherwise minimal. A spokesman for the Los Angeles city attorney's office asserted that the Court had removed "an effective tool of law enforcement" and that the decision would "greatly handicap our effort to curb the use of narcotics," but Los Angeles Police Chief William Parker nonetheless immediately ordered that no more arrests were to be made under the invalidated statute. Public response elsewhere was muted, perhaps because of the relative obscurity of the Cruel and Unusual Punishment Clause and because the *Robinson* decision was announced on the same day as the decision in the New York Regents' Prayer case, in which the Court invalidated state support for prayer in the public schools under the Establishment Clause.[50]

With little public notice, therefore, the Cruel and Unusual Punishment Clause of the Eighth Amendment was applied to the states via the Due Process Clause. It was not fully clear from Justice Stewart's opinion in the *Robinson* case whether the Court was incorporating the Cruel and Unusual Punishment Clause into the Fourteenth Amendment, or whether it was only holding that the Due Process Clause prohibited cruel and unusual punishments in terms not necessarily identical to the terms of the Eighth Amendment. Stewart's language, however, did appear to be incorporationist in tone. A statute making a disease a criminal offense, he said, would be "universally thought to be an infliction of cruel and unusual punishment in violation of the Eighth and Fourteenth Amendments." But whatever may have been in the minds of the majority in the *Robinson* case, subsequent decisions of the Court made it clear that the Cruel and Unusual Punishment Clause was fully applicable to the states via the Due Process Clause.[51]

The application of the Fourth Amendment and the exclusionary rule to the states in the *Mapp* case had been achieved by a bare majority of the Court, and it was not clear even after the *Robinson* case that the dominance of the fair-trial approach to the interpretation of the Due Process Clause had been broken. In 1963, however, the Court decided *Gideon* v. *Wainwright* and repudiated the approach it had used in state right-to-counsel cases for over twenty years, while at the same time dealing a devastating blow to the fair-trial interpretation of the Due Process Clause.

Gideon's Case

Clarence Earl Gideon was arrested on June 19, 1961, for breaking and entering the Bay Harbor Poolroom in Panama City, Florida, with the intent to commit petty larceny. Gideon was a fifty-year-old drifter and part-time gambler with an eighth-grade education, and at the time of his arrest, he had served approximately seventeen years in various federal and state prisons on four felony convictions.[52]

Gideon was brought to trial in the Circuit Court for Bay County before Judge Robert L. McCrary, Jr., and a jury, but he insisted that "this Court appoint Counsel to represent me in this trial." Judge McCrary replied that under the law of Florida "the only time the Court can appoint Counsel to represent a Defendant is when that person is charged with a capital offense. I am sorry, but I will have to deny your request to appoint Counsel to defend you in this case." Although Gideon insisted that the "United States Supreme Court says I am entitled to be represented by Counsel," he was required to defend himself at his trial, and the jury returned a verdict of guilty. On August 25, 1961, Judge McCrary sentenced Gideon to five years in the Florida state prison.[53]

While in the Bay County jail awaiting transfer to prison, Gideon began the litigation activities that were to make him famous. He wrote a petition for a writ of habeas corpus directed to the United States District Court in Tallahassee, but, he later claimed, the sheriff refused to allow him to file the petition. Undaunted, Gideon filed a handwritten petition for a writ of habeas corpus in the Supreme Court of Florida on October 11, 1961, alleging that he "did not have a fair trial and was denied my constitutional rights that is guaranteed by the Constitution and the Bill of Rights by the United States Government." He had requested the appointment of counsel in the trial court, Gideon said in his petition, but the court had refused, even though "the United States Supreme Court of the United States of America had ruled that the State of Florida should see that everyone who is tried for a felony charge should have legal counsel." The Florida Supreme Court, however, denied Gideon's petition for a writ of habeas corpus on October 30, 1961.[54]

The Florida courts were, of course, following the United States Supreme Court's decision in *Betts* v. *Brady* in 1942 that counsel need not be appointed for indigent state criminal defendants in noncapital cases unless the lack of counsel would result in a denial of a fair trial. And in subsequent cases the Court had held that the "special circumstances" requiring the appointment of counsel in noncapital state cases included such factors as the relative maturity and mental capacity of the defendant, the complexity of the crime charged against the defendant, and the conduct of the judge and prosecutor at the trial. If such factors would result in an unfair trial for a defendant not represented by counsel, the Court had said, then the state courts were required to appoint counsel under the Due Process Clause.[55]

Gideon did not seem to fit any of the special circumstances that would have required the Florida courts to appoint counsel for him. He was a mature adult, was obviously literate, and had had prior experience in the criminal courts. The charge against him had not been unduly complicated, and Judge McCrary had obviously attempted to be fair in his conduct of the trial. The prosecutor had also not taken unfair advantage of Gideon because he was unrepresented by counsel at the trial. Contrary to *Betts* v. *Brady* and its progeny, however, Gideon thought he had a right to counsel and held on to that idea with bulldog determination.

Consequently, Gideon filed a handwritten petition for a writ of certiorari in the United States Supreme Court on January 8, 1962, arguing that his conviction should be reversed because the Florida courts had denied him counsel at his trial. "It makes no difference how old I am or what color I am or what church I belong to if any," he told the Court. "The question is I did not get a fair trial. The question is very simple. I requested the court to appoint me [an] attorney and the court refused. . . ."[56]

The Supreme Court granted Gideon's petition for a writ of certiorari and his motion to proceed *in forma pauperis* on June 4, and in addition appended the following notation to its grant of certiorari in the *Gideon* case: "In addition to other questions presented by this case, counsel are requested to discuss the following in their briefs and oral argument: Should this Court's holding in *Betts* v. *Brady*, 316 U.S. 455, be reconsidered?" Gideon also subsequently obtained his long-sought goal of being represented by counsel, since the Court appointed Abe Fortas, one of the most successful of Washington lawyers, to brief and argue Gideon's case.[57]

In his approach to the issues in the *Gideon* case, Fortas did not argue that the Assistance of Counsel Clause of the Sixth Amendment applied in state criminal trials via the Due Process Clause, but rather argued that indigent defendants could not receive a fair trial in serious state criminal cases unless they were represented by counsel. Even under the fair-trial approach to the Due Process Clause, Fortas therefore argued, *Betts* v. *Brady* should be overruled and the Fourteenth Amendment interpreted to require that "counsel be made available to the accused in every case of arrest and prosecution in the states for serious criminal offenses."[58]

Fortas also forthrightly admitted that Clarence Gideon did not meet any of the criteria under the special-circumstances rule that would have required the appointment of counsel at his trial. Gideon was not illiterate or mentally incompetent, nor had the judge or prosecutor taken advantage of his lack of representation by counsel at his trial. But Fortas noted that the Court had held in *Johnson* v. *Zerbst* in 1938 that the Sixth Amendment required the appointment of counsel in all serious federal criminal cases, and that all but five of the states had followed the same practice, indicating a well-nigh universal judgment that a defendant could not adequately defend himself without counsel in a criminal trial. Therefore, a reversal of *Betts* v. *Brady* would not introduce a seismic innovation, Fortas argued, but rather the Court would only be bringing "into line with the consensus of the states and professional opinion the few 'stragglers' who persist in denying fair treatment to the accused."[59]

Fortas also argued that the *Betts* rule was not justified by considerations of federalism, but rather that the special-circumstances rule had created needless friction between the state and federal courts. Under the Court's contradictory applications of the *Betts* rule, he said, whether counsel should be appointed in a state criminal case often could not be determined until after the trial had occurred, since prosecutorial or judicial misconduct in relation to an unrepresented defendant could not be evaluated until then. "The 'special circumstance' rule," Fortas told the Court, "involves federal supervision over state courts in a most obnoxious form: *ad hoc* and *post facto*." The reversal of *Betts* and the recognition of an absolute right to counsel in all serious state criminal cases, he continued, would supply a readily understood rule for the state courts to follow under the Due Process Clause and would reduce federal-state frictions. "Because of the intensely factual, subjective, and post-facto nature of its standards," Fortas concluded, a continuation of the *Betts* rule would mean "more federal intervention on a case by case basis, and in a much more exacerbating form."[60]

As the representative of the state of Florida in the *Gideon* case, Assistant Attorney General Bruce Jacob decided to invite the attorneys general of the other states to intervene as *amici curiae* in the case, hoping of course that they would support the continuation of the rule of *Betts* v. *Brady*. Jacob's plan backfired, however, and instead the attorneys general of twenty-three states, organized by Attorneys General Walter F. Mondale of Minnesota and Edward J. McCormack, Jr., of Massachusetts, filed an *amicus* brief with the Court, urging it to reverse *Betts* v. *Brady* and to hold instead that counsel must be appointed for indigent defendants in all serious state criminal cases. The position of Jacob and the state of Florida, on the other hand, was ultimately supported only by an *amicus* brief filed by the state of Alabama, joined by North Carolina.[61]

The intervention of the twenty-three states urging reversal of *Betts* v. *Brady* dramatically underlined Fortas's argument that the special-circumstances rule could not be supported on the basis of considerations of federalism. The right to counsel, the twenty-three attorneys general told the Court in their *amicus* brief, was essential to the idea of justice under law. "Somehow there is something doubly ignoble about subjecting an accused to the danger of conviction for lack of ability to hire counsel in the state court," they said, "where, perhaps across the street in a different courthouse, he would be entitled to this protection as a fundamental right under the Sixth Amendment."[62] The *Betts* case had been an "anachronism when handed down" and had "spawned twenty years of bad law," the attorneys general said, while demonstrating "how utterly has 'shocking to the universal sense of justice' failed as a beacon to guide trial judges." And the attorneys general therefore respectfully urged that Gideon's conviction be reversed, "that *Betts* v. *Brady* be reconsidered, and that this Court require that all persons tried for a felony in a state court shall have the right to counsel as a matter of due process of law and of equal protection of the laws."[63]

The reversal of Gideon's conviction was also urged upon the Court in an *amicus* brief on behalf of the American Civil Liberties Union. The brief was signed by J. Lee Rankin, a former United States solicitor general, and by Norman Dorsen of the New York University Law School, and it urged in incorporationist language that the Assistance of Counsel Clause be applied to the states via the Due Process Clause. The Court should hold, the ACLU brief said, that "the Fourteenth Amendment incorporated from the Sixth Amendment not only the abstract right to counsel, but also the rule applicable in federal courts under the Sixth Amendment that a lawyer must be appointed to assist a defendant unable to provide his own."[64]

The ACLU also provided the Court with a thorough review of all of the right-to-counsel cases decided by the appellate courts in those states that did not provide for the appointment of counsel in all felony cases since *Betts* v. *Brady* in 1942. The statistics demonstrated that the state courts had largely ignored the special-circumstances rule and had only provided counsel in capital cases, while denying counsel in noncapital cases involving indigent defendants. Of the 139 noncapital right-to-counsel cases since the *Betts* case, the ACLU reported, the state appellate courts had found special circumstances requiring the appointment of counsel in only 15.[65]

With the forces arrayed against the continuation of the rule of *Betts* v. *Brady* and the state of Florida in the *Gideon* case, Assistant Attorney General Bruce Jacob despaired of winning before the Supreme Court. His hopes were further diminished with the retirement of Justice Frankfurter in 1962, while the *Gideon* case was before the Court. Frankfurter had, of course, been the most articulate spokesman for the fair-trial approach to the Due Process Clause in state criminal cases, including the special-circumstances rule of the *Betts* case. "I had been developing some hope that the Court would draw back from this ultimate 'legislating'" in the *Gideon* case, Jacob said later, but when "Justice Frankfurter retired, I realized that we had very little chance."[66]

Jacob nonetheless defended the *Betts* rule and Gideon's conviction before the Court on the basis of the fair-trial approach. The Fourteenth Amendment, he argued, paraphrasing Frankfurter, did not "constitute a 'shorthand summary' of the Bill of Rights; and the specific procedural guarantees of the first eight Amendments are not included in the meaning of due process." Time and again, he noted, the court had refused to apply the specific procedural requirements of the Bill of Rights to the states and had held that in state right-to-counsel cases "the appointment of counsel is an element of due process only to the extent that a fair and just hearing would be prevented by the failure to appoint counsel and to that extent only."[67]

If the Court held that the Assistance of Counsel Clause applied to the states, Jacob warned, its ruling could not stop at imposing a requirement of appointed counsel in only serious criminal cases, but must apply to all criminal cases, no matter how trivial. And finally, Jacob warned that if the *Betts* case were reversed, "as many as 5,093 hardened criminals may be eligible to be released in one mass exodus in Florida alone, not to mention those in other states where automatic appointment of counsel in non-capital cases was not provided for at one time or another."[68]

In the oral argument of the *Gideon* case on January 15, 1963, Abe Fortas avoided any reference to the incorporation of the Sixth Amendment's Assistance of Counsel Clause into the Due Process Clause, but rather emphasized the point that a criminal defendant could not obtain a fair trial as guaranteed by the Due Process Clause if unrepresented by counsel. On the other hand, Fortas did not attempt to make the facts of the *Gideon* case fit any of the special circumstances justifying the appointment of counsel for indigent defendants under the regime of the *Betts* case. The right to a fair trial guaranteed by the Due Process Clause, he told the Court, required counsel for all defendants accused of serious crimes regardless of the presence or absence of special circumstances.

"I see no basis, or I do not see an adequate basis for an argument that special circumstances exist in this case," he told the Court. "If you will look at this transcript of record, perhaps you will share my feeling—which is a feeling of despondency—this record does not indicate that Clarence Earl Gideon is a man of inferior natural talents; this record does not indicate that Clarence Earl Gideon is a moron or a person of low intelligence; this record does not indicate that the judge of the trial court in the state of Florida or that the prosecuting attorney in the state of Florida was derelict in his duty. On the contrary, it indicates that they tried to help Gideon." But for him, Fortas continued, "if the Court please, this record indicates the basic difficulty with *Betts* against *Brady*. And the basic difficulty with *Betts* against *Brady* is that no man, certainly no layman, can conduct a trial in his own defense so that the trial is a fair trial."[69]

"I believe that this case dramatically illustrates the point that you cannot have a fair trial without counsel," he declared, but Justice Harlan interrupted to say that the question before the Court was not as "simple as that." The case had to be argued on "the basis of federalism," Harlan admonished Fortas. But Fortas replied that the *Betts* rule was actually detrimental to federal-state relations. "In some of this Court's decisions there has been a tendency from time to time, because of the pull of federalism," he said, "to forget . . . the realities of what happens downstairs, of what happens to these poor, miserable, indigent people when they are arrested" and are required to defend themselves against criminal charges. This "failure to remember what happens downstairs," Fortas continued, addressing Harlan directly, "has crept in, not because of an insensitivity of the judges, but because of the understandable pull of the sensitivity about the states' own jurisdiction. . . . I don't think that the argument of federalism here is either correct or soundly founded or stands the test of experience." Justice Harlan answered that "'understandable sensitivity' to describe a basic principle of our government does not seem to me to be a very happy expression." He also had regard for the principles of federalism, Fortas replied, but such principles were misapplied "when they are used for the purpose of negating a Fourteenth Amendment right to a fair trial."

The *Betts* special-circumstances rule also was subversive of the federal system, Fortas continued, since it required the Court to "exercise the kind of minute, detailed, ex post facto supervision over state court trials that you have been exercising for these past years and which in my opinion is the most corrosive possible way to administer our federal-state system. . . . I believe that *Betts* against *Brady* does not incorporate a proper regard for federalism," since it was unadministerable by the trial courts, and "it's wrong as a matter of federalism." Noting that almost all of the states provided for the appointment of counsel for indigent defendants, and citing the *amicus* brief of the twenty-three states supporting the reversal of *Betts* v. *Brady*, Fortas declared that "we may be comforted in this constitutional moment by the fact as it clearly is that what we are doing represents a deliberate change after twenty years of experience, and it represents a change that clearly has the overwhelming support of the bench, of the bar, and even of the states themselves."

Fortas's studious avoidance of any reference to the incorporation approach ultimately proved to be too much for Justice Black.

JUSTICE BLACK: Am I to understand . . . that the Constitution's guarantee of right to counsel has nothing to do with this [case, and that it is] solely due to due process? Am I to understand that you lay aside that federal guarantee of right to counsel?

MR. FORTAS: No, sir, I certainly do not lay it aside. As you will see in our brief— that we argue it—not, Mr. Justice Black, in terms of the argument that the Fourteenth Amendment incorporates with respect to the states the provisions of the Bill of Rights—

JUSTICE BLACK: Well, what then? How does the Fourteenth Amendment do it?

MR. FORTAS: . . . Mr. Justice Black, I like that argument that you have so eloquently made time and time again [laughter], but I can't make it to this Court as an advocate because this Court has turned it down so many times—I hope and pray that you will never cease contending for it.

JUSTICE BLACK: I'm inclined to think that the Court's accepted it in a number of cases. . .

MR. FORTAS: In a number of particulars . . . and frankly I think there are alternative forms of language that the Court can use, and I'm in favor of the Court's using the broadest possible language.

JUSTICE BLACK: I agree with that.

Justice Brennan then stepped in to say that Fortas seemed to be willing to accept the application of the right to counsel to the states whether the

Court used the words *absorbed* or *incorporated* or some other language. "You seem to know me well, Mr. Justice Brennan," Fortas replied.

The exchanges between Justice Harlan and Fortas on the fair trial-federalism issue and between Justice Black and Fortas on the incorporation approach to the issues in the *Gideon* case involved the only significant discussion of the nationalization process during the oral argument of the *Gideon* case. Although Justice Harlan admonished J. Lee Rankin, appearing on behalf of the ACLU as *amicus curiae*, that it did not "take this Court's decisions to reform everybody in the United States," even Harlan seemed to have difficulty defending the regime of *Betts* v. *Brady*. Assistant Florida Attorney General Bruce Jacob, assisted by Assistant Alabama Attorney General George Mentz, doggedly defended the *Betts* special-circumstances approach to the right to counsel, but the questions from the justices were almost uniformly hostile, and the demise of the regime of *Betts* v. *Brady* was clearly in the air. During Abe Fortas's brief rebuttal at the close of the oral argument, even Harlan acknowledged that "what one is left with is to get his hands on something that has happened between 1942 and 1963 that has made what the Court then regarded as constitutional suddenly become unconstitutional. . . ."

For Fortas, in summing up his position in rebuttal, it was clear that the answer to Harlan's rhetorical question was that *Betts* v. *Brady* had been wrong when decided. "The basic proposition that I believe that the Court has before it," he said, "is a problem of constitutional statesmanship perhaps, that this Court has recently traversed in *Mapp* against *Ohio*. *Mapp* against *Ohio* in my opinion presented a more difficult situation. . . . I believe, to paraphrase Mr. Justice Clark's notable opinion in *Mapp* against *Ohio*, that time has set its face against *Betts* v. *Brady*. . . ."

"On the side of principle," Fortas continued, "I respectfully submit from the depths of my heart and my understanding that there can be no two ways about it, that there can be no choice here, that there is no room for doubt. . . . I think that *Betts* against *Brady* was wrong when decided, and I think time has illuminated that fact." But perhaps time had also done a service, Fortas concluded, "because time has prepared the way so that the rule, the correct rule, the civilized rule, the rule of American constitutionalism, the rule of due process, may now be stated by this Court with minimum irritation and disruption in the states."

Justice Black was assigned the responsibility of writing the opinion of the Court in *Gideon* v. *Wainwright*, undoubtedly a recognition that his views in dissent in *Betts* v. *Brady* over twenty years before had finally become those of the Court. When the decision in the *Gideon* case was announced on March 18, 1963, the Court was unanimous in voting to reverse the *Betts* case and holding that the Due Process Clause required the appointment of counsel for indigent defendants charged with serious state criminal offenses.

In his opinion for the Court, Black eschewed the incorporationist position that the Assistance of Counsel Clause applied to the states and based the reversal of the *Betts* case instead on the grounds that unless represented by counsel, an indigent defendant faced with a serious state criminal offense could not possibly obtain a fair trial under the Due Process Clause. Comparing the facts in the *Betts* and *Gideon* cases, he acknowledged that Gideon did not fit within any of the special circumstances the Court had enunciated as conditioning the right to counsel in state cases under *Betts* v. *Brady* and its progeny. If the *Betts* case were reaffirmed by the Court, Black said, the Court would be required to "reject Gideon's claim that the Constitution guarantees to him the assistance of counsel. Upon full reconsideration we conclude that *Betts* v. *Brady* should be overruled."[70]

Black admitted that the Court had held in the *Betts* case that the Assistance of Counsel Clause of the Sixth Amendment did not apply to the states via the Due Process Clause, but he insisted that on the basis of the reasoning in *Powell* v. *Alabama* the Court more properly should have held in the *Betts* case that the right to counsel was essential to a fair trial. Reviewing the nationalization of the Bill of Rights, he concluded that the Court had held "that a provision of the Bill of Rights which is 'fundamental and essential to a fair trial' is made obligatory upon the States by the Fourteenth Amendment." The Court in the *Betts* case had been "wrong, however, in concluding that the Sixth Amendment's guarantee of counsel is not one of these fundamental rights."[71]

In deciding *Betts* v. *Brady*, Black continued, the Court had therefore "made an abrupt break with its own well-considered precedents." In the American system of adversary justice, he said, "any person haled into court, who is too poor to hire a lawyer, cannot be assured a fair trial unless counsel is provided for him. This seems to us to be an obvious truth." The Court in the *Betts* case had "departed from the sound wisdom upon which the Court's holding in *Powell* v. *Alabama* rested. Florida, supported by two other States, has asked that *Betts* v. *Brady* be left intact. Twenty-two States, as friends of the Court argue that *Betts* was 'an anachronism when handed down' and that it should now be overruled. We agree."[72]

Clarence Earl Gideon's belief that he had a right to counsel had therefore been finally vindicated by the Court. After the reversal of his conviction by the Court, he was retried by the state of Florida on the charge of breaking and entering the Bay Harbor Poolroom with the intent to commit petty larceny, but the state was careful the second time around to appoint counsel for him. Refusing counsel supplied by the Florida Civil Liberties Union, Gideon insisted upon and received the appointment of counsel of his choice. He was retried in July of 1963, but this time the jury returned a verdict of not guilty.[73]

Gideon, however, was not alone in gaining his freedom as a result of the

Supreme Court's decision in his case. In Florida alone, 976 prisoners were freed because they had not been represented by counsel at their trials, and 500 more prisoners petitioned the courts to review their convictions. Two months after the decision in the *Gideon* case, the Florida legislature adopted a public-defender system, and similar moves were soon under way in those states that had not provided counsel for indigent defendants in noncapital cases.[74]

Clarence Gideon himself became a nationally known figure with the publication of Anthony Lewis's classic study, *Gideon's Trumpet*, detailing the litigation in his case. Gideon had one further brush with the law when he was arrested for vagrancy in Jeffersonville, Kentucky, in 1965. After hearing who Gideon was, the trial judge offered to give him a sufficient sentence to allow Gideon to litigate the question of whether the *Gideon* case required the appointment of counsel for indigents in misdemeanor cases, a question the Court had left open. Gideon demurred, however, preferring to pay his fine and be on his way, but in June of 1972, the Supreme Court decided *Argersinger* v. *Hamlin* and held that a "serious" criminal offense requiring the appointment of counsel for indigent defendants was any offense that would lead to a loss of liberty upon conviction. The principle of the *Gideon* case was thus ultimately extended by the Court to apply to misdemeanor offenses that were punishable by a jail sentence of even one day. Gideon, unfortunately, did not live to see this extension of the principle of his case, since he died on January 18, 1972, in Fort Lauderdale, Florida, at the age of sixty-one.[75]

While the Court was unanimous in reversing Gideon's conviction, the incorporation versus fair-trial positions on the Due Process Clause were debated in concurring opinions in the *Gideon* case by Justices Douglas and Harlan. Douglas noted in his concurrence that the total-incorporation position had been supported by ten justices over the years, although the position had unfortunately not commanded a majority of the Court. Justice Harlan, he said, was "of the view that a guarantee of the Bill of Rights that is made applicable to the States by reason of the Fourteenth Amendment is a lesser version of that same guarantee as applied to the Federal Government." Harlan's view, Douglas said, "has not prevailed and rights protected against state invasion by the Due Process Clause of the Fourteenth Amendment are not watered-down versions of what the Bill of Rights guarantees."[76]

While he concurred in the reversal of *Betts* v. *Brady*, Justice Harlan stated in reply to both the opinion of the Court and Justice Douglas's opinion that he believed the *Betts* case was "entitled to a more respectful burial than has been accorded. . . ." The *Betts* case, Harlan noted, had not been "an abrupt break" with the Court's past precedents, as Black had said in the opinion of the Court. Rather the Court had held in *Powell* v. *Alabama* that special circumstances required the appointment of counsel in state cases, and it had subsequently fallen into a pattern of holding that special circumstances always existed in state capital cases. The *Betts* rule, Harlan acknowledged, had had "a troubled journey throughout the years that have followed," and he admitted that the *Betts* rule had continued to "exist in form while its substance has been steadily eroded." He therefore agreed with the Court that a serious criminal charge against an indigent defendant was sufficient to require the appointment of counsel under the Due Process Clause, and in the *Gideon* case the Court was only making explicit "something that has long since been foreshadowed in our decisions."[77]

Harlan reiterated his view, however, that while the right to counsel was guaranteed in all serious state criminal cases, the Court's ruling in the *Gideon* case did not mean that the Assistance of Counsel Clause of the Sixth Amendment applied to the states or that the right to counsel recognized by the Court in the *Gideon* case under the Due Process Clause was identical to the right guaranteed in the Sixth Amendment. "In what is done today I do not understand the Court to depart from the principles laid down" in *Palko* v. *Connecticut*, he concluded, "or to embrace the concept that the Fourteenth Amendment 'incorporates' the Sixth Amendment as such."[78]

Despite the sparring between Harlan and Douglas in their concurring opinions, the incorporationist and fair-trial approaches to the Due Process Clause had in fact converged on the right-to-counsel issue in the *Gideon* case. Black and his incorporationist colleagues undoubtedly felt that the Assistance of Counsel Clause of the Sixth Amendment applied to the states via the Due Process Clause. But it was unnecessary for Black to speak in incorporationist terms in his opinion for the Court, since whether the *Gideon* case was approached from the incorporationist or the fair-trial position, the result was the same. The Court had come to the unanimous conclusion that counsel was required to be appointed for indigent defendants in all serious state criminal cases. When Justice Black reported the Court's decision in the *Gideon* case to the retired Justice Frankfurter, he indicated to him that he had assured the other members of the Court that Frankfurter would also have voted to reverse *Betts* v. *Brady* under his stoutly defended fair-trial approach to the Due Process Clause. Frankfurter replied simply, "Of course I would."[79]

The *Gideon* case was nevertheless a significant defeat for the advocates of the fair-trial approach. Considerations of federalism, they had argued, required the Court to avoid the application of the specifics of the Bill of Rights to the states, and instead to impose due process standards upon state criminal procedure on a case-by-case basis. Yet after twenty years of experience with such an approach in state right-to-counsel cases, twenty-three states as *amici* in the *Gideon* case had requested the Court in an almost exasperated manner to impose a rigid rule requiring the appointment of counsel in all serious state criminal cases, a request that was tantamount to asking for the incorporation of the Assistance of Counsel Clause of the Sixth Amendment into the Due Process Clause. Federalism had not been served under the fair trial approach to the right to counsel, the state attorneys general had advised the Court, since such an approach had resulted in a "twenty years' accumulation of confusion and contradictions" that had utterly failed "as a beacon to guide trial judges."[80]

The attack by the twenty-three states on the fair trial approach undermined one of the principal bases upon which its advocates had defended it, while bolstering the arguments of the incorporationists that the fair-trial approach had resulted in unpredictable interventions by the Court in the field of state criminal procedure under nebulous standards that heightened frictions between the federal and state courts. Indeed, this precise argument had been considered by Abe Fortas as central to his argument against the regime of *Betts* v. *Brady*.[81] If the experience under the fair trial approach to right to counsel had been the failure the twenty-three states described it to be, the attack on the approach could easily be broadened to include other areas, such as that of coerced confessions, and the question could be asked whether in those areas also, the specifics of the Bill of Rights would not supply more readily ascertainable and more easily administerable standards in state criminal cases than those supplied by the fair trial approach to the Due Process Clause.

The fair trial approach to the Due Process Clause had therefore lost more than the brilliance and eloquence of Frankfurter and the support of Whittaker in the early 1960s, since the federalism premise upon which the approach was in part based had suffered a damaging blow in the *Gideon* case. And although the *Mapp*, *Robinson*, and *Gideon* cases had not been decided in explicit incorporationist terms, they were soon being treated as having incorporated the Fourth Amendment, the Cruel and Unusual Punishment Clause, and the Assistance of Counsel Clause into the Due Process Clause, thus supplying precedent for the further application of parts of the Bill of Rights to the states. Before the end of the decade, the result would be, as Archibald Cox has said, that never before was there "such a thorough-going reform of criminal procedure within so short a time."[82]

9

Incorporation Made Explicit
The *Malloy, Pointer,* and *Washington* Cases

The incorporation breakthrough of the early 1960s did not involve the use of explicit incorporationist language by the Court, but as the nationalization of the Bill of Rights proceeded apace after the *Gideon* decision in 1963, it soon became clear that the Court was dominated by a selective-incorporationist majority. The incorporationists—Chief Justice Warren and Justices Black, Douglas, and Brennan—had indicated as early as 1961 that they were prepared to reverse *Twining* v. *New Jersey* and apply the Self-Incrimination Clause to the states.[1] The opportunity to incorporate the Self-Incrimination Clause finally arose in proceedings involving William Malloy, a small-time gambler who operated in Hartford, Connecticut, and in Malloy's case, the incorporationist position on the nationalization of the Bill of Rights was explicitly stated.

The Reversal of *Twining*: William Malloy's Case

During September of 1959, William Malloy was arrested by the Hartford, Connecticut, police on a misdemeanor charge of pool selling (bookmaking). Malloy pleaded *nolo contendere* on the charge, and he was fined five hundred dollars and sentenced to one year in the county jail, the sentence to be suspended after ninety days with a condition of two years probation. During 1961, however, Malloy was summoned before a Connecticut one-man grand jury and was questioned by Hartford County States's Attorney John D. LaBelle. Malloy revealed in answer to questions that he lived at 418 Mattianuck Avenue in Windsor, but in answer to all other questions he refused to answer on the grounds his answers might incriminate him.

The one-man grand jury was Ernest A. Inglis, former chief justice of the Connecticut Supreme Court of Errors; Judge Inglis advised Malloy that he would be held in contempt for refusing to respond to the questions put to him and inquired if Malloy had consulted an attorney. Malloy replied that he had not spoken to an attorney, and he was advised by Inglis that he should do so.[2] As Malloy stepped out of the grand jury room, he chanced to meet Harold Strauch, a Hartford attorney, who had represented Malloy earlier in a civil matter. Recognizing Strauch, Malloy asked him if he had to answer questions put to him in the grand jury proceedings that might incriminate him, and as Strauch said later, he "gave him a rapid, curbstone opinion to the effect that he was not required to respond."[3]

Having secured this advice from Strauch, Malloy was again summoned before Judge Inglis on January 25, 1961, and State's Attorney LaBelle put to him essentially the same questions as before. Malloy, however, answered only to the extent of admitting that he had been arrested and convicted for pool selling in 1959 and of denying that either he or his family had received any pay from anyone while he had been in jail. But in response to questions regarding for whom he had been working in 1959, who paid his fine in the 1959 case, who selected his bondsman, who owned the apartment in which he had been arrested, and whether he knew John Bergoti, Malloy invoked the right against self-incrimination and refused to answer.[4]

On the following day, Malloy was tried for contempt before the Superior Court of Hartford County, was found guilty of refusing to answer proper questions put to him in the grand jury proceedings, and was committed to jail at his own expense until he agreed to answer the questions he had been asked. Two other colleagues of Malloy's, George Polashian and Eugene Picano, had also refused to answer Judge Inglis's questions, and they were also sentenced to jail for contempt of court. Harold Strauch was retained as attorney for all three men, and he announced to the press that he would "appeal the cases of Malloy, Polashian and Picano to the highest court in the land if they are sentenced for contempt"; with his clients resting in the county jail, his hand had clearly been called on this point.[5]

Strauch reacted to the contempt commitments of Malloy and the others by immediately filing a petition for a writ of habeas corpus in the Superior Court of Hartford County, alleging that Malloy and his colleagues were being illegally detained by the sheriff, Patrick J. Hogan. Strauch argued in the petition that Malloy, Polashian, and Picano had validly invoked their right against compulsory self-incrimination under both the Connecticut Constitution and the Self-Incrimination Clause of the Fifth Amendment of the federal Constitution.[6] The superior court, however, dismissed the petition for a writ of habeas corpus and held that neither Malloy nor his colleagues had validly invoked the right against self-incrimination.[7]

Fulfilling his pledge to fight the case as far as was necessary, Harold Strauch appealed the decision of the superior court to the Connecticut Supreme Court of Errors, but that court affirmed the decision of the superior court on January 23, 1963. In a very thorough opinion, the supreme court of errors analyzed Malloy's invocation of the right against self-incrimination not only from the standpoint of the Connecticut Constitution's self-incrimination provision but also in light of United States Supreme Court decisions interpreting the Self-Incrimination Clause of the Fifth Amendment. The court held that the question of whether the right against self-incrimination had been properly invoked could not be determined solely by the witness invoking it, but rather was a question that ultimately required judicial determination. A witness, the court said, could not be required to supply a "link in the chain" of evidence that might lead to a criminal prosecution, but, on the other hand, a witness invoking the right against self-incrimination must fear a "real and appreciable" danger of possible prosecution if he testified, and not invoke the right in relation to imaginary, remote, or improbable dangers of incrimination.[8]

Applying these considerations to Malloy's invocation of the right against self-incrimination, the supreme court of errors held that Malloy had not properly invoked the right in regard to the question of whether he knew John Bergoti, since Bergoti was nowhere described "or in any way identified, either as to his occupation, actual or reputed, or as to any criminal record he may have had" and Malloy had "made no attempt even to suggest to the court how an answer to the question whether he knew Bergoti could possibly incriminate him."[9]

Malloy had also refused to answer questions relating to the payment of his fine for the 1959 conviction, the selection of his bondsman, the ownership of the apartment where he was arrested, and for whom he had been working. The supreme court of errors admitted that Malloy's answers to these questions might have incriminated him in regard to another offense for pool selling that might have occurred at about the same time as his original arrest. The court noted, however, that there was a statute of limitations applicable to misdemeanor offenses like pool selling, and it was unlikely that Malloy had been engaged in felonious behavior. Since the statute of limitations would have barred any prosecution of Malloy in 1961 for a misdemeanor committed in 1959, the court held, he could not properly invoke the right against self-incrimination in response to questions relating to his 1959 arrest and conviction. There had been "nothing to indicate any danger to Malloy of a prosecution for a felony," the court said, and Strauch's argument to the contrary "confounds vague and improbable possibilities of prosecution with reasonably appreciable ones. Under claims like [Malloy's] it would always be possible to work out some finespun and improbable theory from which an outside chance of prosecution could be envisioned. Such claims are not enough to support a claim of privilege, at least where, as here, a witness suggests no rational explanation of his fears of incrimination, and the questions themselves, under all the circumstances, suggest none."[10]

Strauch had, of course, also argued that the Fifth Amendment's Self-Incrimination Clause applied to the states in the *Malloy* case, but the supreme court of errors noted that the United States Supreme Court had held in many decisions that this was not the case. The court nonetheless acknowledged that the Fourteenth Amendment, via the Due Process Clause, did "prohibit a state court from so ruling on a claim of privilege from self-incrimination as to violate the fundamental concepts of justice and a fair trial. . . ." Malloy did not, the court concluded, "in respect to any of the questions he refused to answer, bring himself within the settled rules defining the right to assert a privilege against self-incrimination. Thus there could be no violation of due process, and there was no error in Malloy's commitment for contempt."[11]

The supreme court of errors had not brushed aside Strauch's contention that the Self-Incrimination Clause applied to the states, but rather in a thoroughly professional opinion had rejected the argument on its merits, while at the same time citing and applying United States Supreme Court decisions interpreting the meaning of the Self-Incrimination Clause. Given *Twining* v. *New Jersey* and *Adamson* v. *California*, the Connecticut court not unnaturally rejected the idea that the Self-Incrimination Clause applied to the states, but it had further recognized that the Due Process Clause did impose limitations on the extent to which the state courts could erode the concept of self-incrimination.

From the beginning of the *Malloy* case, Harold Strauch had pledged to fight all the way to the Supreme Court, but the careful and thoughtful treatment of the case by the Connecticut Supreme Court of Errors made a successful appeal to the Court more difficult than an appeal from a less-competent treatment of the self-incrimination issue in the case would have been. Despite the difficult task ahead, however, Strauch filed a petition for a writ of certiorari in *Malloy* v. *Hogan* on April 19, and the Court granted the writ on June 3, 1963.[12]

In order to win a reversal of the decision of the supreme court of errors, Strauch had to convince the Court not only that the Self-Incrimination Clause applied to the states, but also that the Connecticut courts had not properly applied federal self-incrimination standards in Malloy's case. In the wake of *Mapp* v. *Ohio*, the Court had held in *Ker* v. *California* in 1963 that Fourth Amendment standards applicable in state courts were identical to those applicable in federal proceedings, and Strauch leaned heavily on the *Mapp* and *Ker* cases in his argument that the Self-Incrimination Clause applied to the states in the identical way it applied in federal proceedings.[13]

Assuming that the Self-Incrimination Clause applied to the states, Strauch then attacked the assumption of the Connecticut courts that, if he had answered the questions put to him, Malloy would have only implicated himself in misdemeanor offenses, and that under the one-year statute of limitations on misdemeanors, Malloy could not have feared being prosecuted on the basis of his answers. "To conclude," he said, "that a person, involved with many others in a field of criminal activity, necessarily limited himself to the commission of misdemeanors and had not, under any circumstances, committed or shared in a felony, is too naive to be given any standing. And the statute of limitations for felonies is five years." From the nature of the questions put to him, he continued, it was reasonable to assume that "the persons sought to be identified by [Malloy] could give testimony that might well involve him in a prosecution. Otherwise, there would be no sense to the questions posed to [Malloy]. And, at the very least, it is not amiss to assume that an experienced State's Attorney did not ask frivolous or harmless questions on this occasion."[14]

The Court had, Strauch concluded, "cleansed a smudge from the escutcheon of Justice" in the *Mapp* case by prohibiting the states from engaging in the "obnoxious practice" of unreasonable searches and seizures, and had made "one's home again the sanctuary that it was guaranteed to be by the Constitution." Another smudge could be removed, he said, "by a reversal of the decision of the State court in this case, which is as momentous as, and conceptually linked with, the *Mapp* case. The right to become untrammeled in this area of constitutional guarantees is of no less standing and validity than in *Mapp*."[15]

Defending the validity of Malloy's contempt conviction, Connecticut State's Attorney John LaBelle conceded that the states were not entirely free to deny a right against self-incrimination under the Due Process Clause. In its decisions involving coerced confessions, he said, the Court had "implicitly applied the core of the privilege against self-incrimination to the states," and he urged the Court to explicitly acknowledge that this was the case. "Frank recognition of the fact that the Due Process Clause prohibits the States from enforcing their laws by compelling the accused to confess," LaBelle said, "regardless of where such compulsion occurs, would not only clarify the principles involved in confession cases, but would assist the States significantly in their efforts to comply with the limitations placed upon them by the Fourteenth Amendment."[16]

LaBelle argued, however, that the right against self-incrimination guaranteed by the Due Process Clause was not identical in scope and meaning to the Fifth Amendment's Self-Incrimination Clause. Rather, he urged the Court to hold that only the core of the Self-Incrimination Clause applied to the states and that the states were allowed to devise their own flexible standards in dealing with self-incrimination free of the rigid standards developed under the Self-Incrimination Clause in federal proceedings.

Even if the Court rejected this argument and held that the Self-Incrimination Clause applied to the states in the identical way that it applied in federal proceedings, LaBelle argued, Malloy's conviction was still valid because the Connecticut courts had applied federal self-incrimination standards in evaluating his case. The Connecticut Supreme Court of Errors, he concluded, "*applied* federal standards and found the claim of privilege unwarranted. Thus, even if the Fourteenth Amendment is held to apply the full force of the Fifth Amendment's privilege against self-incrimination to the States, the decision of the Supreme Court of Errors of the State of Connecticut should be affirmed."[17]

LaBelle's argument in *Malloy* v. *Hogan* was both able and shrewd. Given the incorporationist decisions of the early 1960s—*Mapp, Gideon,* and *Robinson*—the continuing viability of the *Twining-Adamson* line of cases was subject to considerable doubt. LaBelle had forthrightly conceded that the states must recognize a self-incrimination limitation under the Due Process Clause, but had insisted that only the core of the Self-Incrimination Clause applied to the states, not the full Self-Incrimination Clause or all of the procedural refinements applicable in federal proceedings. He was therefore asking the Court to decide the *Malloy* case as it had decided *Wolf* v. *Colorado*, where the Court had held that the states were prohibited from engaging in unreasonable searches and seizures under the Due Process Clause but that they were not restricted by the full Fourth Amendment and the exclusionary rule. LaBelle's argument would probably prove eminently persuasive to a nonincorporationist Court, and, in order to overcome it, the incorporationists would have to muster a clear majority on the Court that was prepared to hold that the Self-Incrimination Clause applied fully to the states and that the Connecticut courts had improperly applied federal standards in the *Malloy* case.

The concessions made by LaBelle, however, prompted Attorney General Stanley Mosk of California to intervene as *amicus curiae* and to urge the Court to reaffirm the *Adamson* and *Twining* cases. The *Twining* and *Adamson* cases had clearly held that the Due Process Clause did not restrict the states in the area of self-incrimination, Mosk argued, and it would be "unthinkable" if those cases were "to be hastened into oblivion by any concession [by LaBelle] that they are tainted by time, that they are inconsistent with other decisions of this Court, or that they should no longer be law. In our view, the historical record does not require this Court to hold, and would not justify this Court in holding, that the Fifth Amendment privilege against self-incrimination was incorporated into the Fourteenth Amendment by virtue of the latter's adoption." He was aware, Mosk said, of the total-incorporation doctrine "argued with such eloquence and vigor by Mr. Justice Black," but, citing the scholarly refutations of Black's position, he submitted that the "historical evidence is to the contrary."[18]

Amicus curiae briefs were also filed in the *Malloy* case by the American Civil Liberties Union and the National District Attorneys' Association. These briefs dealt primarily with the validity of grants of immunity from prosecution at both the federal and state levels if the Self-Incrimination Clause were held to apply to the states in the *Malloy* case. These briefs, therefore, contributed little further to the principal issue in the *Malloy* case.[19]

Opening his argument before the Court on March 5, 1964, Harold Strauch rather humorously said that *Malloy* v. *Hogan*, "I believe is an uncomplicated case, which modestly requests of this Court a ruling that the Fifth Amendment applies to the individual states." After reciting the facts in the case, Strauch said that "a reasonable point to start this case is to go back to that famous case of *Barron* v. *Baltimore* where Chief Justice John Marshall held for the first time that the first eight Amendments applied to the federal courts only." With the adoption of the Fourteenth Amendment, he noted, the holding in *Barron* had been altered, with the result that many of the rights in the Bill of Rights had been held by the Court to be applicable to the states via the Due Process Clause. Justice Harlan interrupted at this point, and, contradicting Strauch's opening statement, insisted that he was "putting a very large question to the Court, obviously." The Connecticut Supreme Court of Errors, Harlan continued, appeared to have applied federal standards governing self-incrimination in the *Malloy* case, and he wondered "whether we have to reach this question [of the applicability of the Self-Incrimination Clause to the states] in this case." The question he was putting to Strauch, Harlan said, "is, assuming these broader premises that you're now arguing to this Court, assuming your premises, as a matter of federal law, would this be an invalid conviction under federal standards?"[20]

Strauch responded that Malloy might have incriminated himself in regard to a felony offense if he had answered the questions and that the Connecticut courts had failed to apply federal standards of self-incrimination, standards that were binding on the states just as the Fourth Amendment was fully binding on the states under the *Mapp* and *Ker* cases. "You are now suggesting that we overrule *Twining* v. *New Jersey, Adamson* . . . and a couple of dozen other cases," Harlan said. "Well," Strauch replied, "it isn't as if the Supreme Court has never reversed itself. Sometimes it does it at a slower pace, sometimes at a faster pace." Speaking for the incorporationists, Justice Brennan interrupted to say, "You start with four members of this Court who have already indicated that those cases should be overruled." And Strauch replied, "That's right. That's right."

Strauch noted that the court had held that the Due Process Clause of the Fourteenth Amendment guaranteed those "fundamental rights that lie at the base of all our civil and political institutions" and that were "of the very essence of a scheme of ordered liberty," and if "these formulas are valid, and I assume that they are, I have never been able to determine why the members of this Court, [who] have ruled that the Fifth Amendment does not apply to the states, have conceived that the right not to incriminate oneself is not as basic and as fundamental and as essential to a fair trial" as other rights that the Court had applied to the states. The Fourth Amendment and the Self-Incrimination Clause complemented one another, he argued, and if the Fourth Amendment were applicable to the states, "there's no valid, logical reason why the Fifth Amendment can't be equally applied."

After the Court had held that the First Amendment applied to the states, Strauch suggested, there was no logical reason why all the rest of the Bill of Rights did not also apply. This suggestion that total incorporation was appropriate brought an understandable response from Justice Black, who asked, "You want us to go that far in this case?" Strauch then backed away from advocating total incorporation, replying, "I want you to go as far as my particular case is concerned, and worry about the other cases in the future as they come up. I am unwilling to be a pioneer beyond reasonable grounds—distances."

Apparently sharing Justice Harlan's doubts, Justice Stewart interrupted Strauch's subsequent argument, noted that the Connecticut courts appeared to have cited more federal cases than state cases in evaluating Malloy's self-incrimination claim, and said, "I have difficulty in seeing that this big question you're addressing yourself to is before us at all." Strauch insisted, however, under questioning by Stewart and other justices that the Connecticut courts had failed to apply federal self-incrimination standards and had not recognized that by answering the questions put to him, Malloy might have exposed himself to a felony charge. It was the duty of the Court, he said, to evaluate the facts in the case and to determine for itself if federal standards had been properly applied. "We don't concede the questions were harmless," Strauch concluded, "[and] we don't have to explain why we don't have to testify."

Arguing on behalf of the state, John LaBelle pointed out that Malloy had been a "writer" who took bets phoned into the "office" where he worked, all of which constituted the misdemeanor offense of pool selling for which he had been convicted in 1959. Malloy was not a big-time criminal, LaBelle said, and other than the pool-selling conviction, he had been convicted only of traffic offenses and drunkenness. "To this day," he told the Court, "there has not been any indication of what fear" of incrimination Malloy had in the face of the questions asked him. And under the right against self-incrimination, a person invoking the right had to give at least some "inkling" of what his fear of incrimination was in order validly to invoke the right. There was nothing that indicated that Malloy was guilty of anything more than a misdemeanor in 1959, LaBelle said, and the statute of limitations on misdemeanors had run out. If the proceedings in the *Malloy* case had been federal proceedings, Justice Brennan asked, would a person invoking the Self-Incrimination Clause still be required to give some inkling of what incrimination he feared? "There isn't any court that has held yet, that I know of," LaBelle replied, "that says that he can simply say, 'I cannot answer because I fear self-incrimination,' and that's it." The person invoking the right must give a court some "scent" of what incrimination he fears in order to invoke the right validly, he continued, noting that Brennan had so held when he was a state judge. "Are you throwing the pillow back at me?" Brennan asked. "No," LaBelle replied, "the word is good, though. He must give the court some scent," but Brennan countered, "I was a state judge when I said that." The focus of the investigation in the *Malloy* case, LaBelle continued, had not been Malloy, but rather "we were trying to find out who ran this booking operation and who was the one behind this office. . . . Whom was he working for."

LaBelle denied that the Self-Incrimination Clause applied to the states in "all its sweep," but he conceded, as he had in his brief, that under the Due Process Clause "one of the things the states cannot do any longer, if they ever could, is compel the witness to criminate himself." In response to questions, he said, "I'm not saying the Fifth Amendment applies to the states," but rather that the Due Process Clause without reference to the Fifth Amendment did prohibit the states from compelling incrimination, as the Court had indicated in the coerced-confession cases. "I see no reason in this case . . . to have anything to do with the *Twining* and *Adamson* cases," LaBelle continued. "There is no reason to overrule any of those decisions."

In any event, LaBelle argued, the Connecticut Supreme Court of Errors had applied federal self-incrimination standards in the *Malloy* case, and under those standards a person invoking the right against self-incrimination could not just invoke the right without more. "He simply cannot remain silent and refuse to answer," he said, "it requires more than that. . . ." In Malloy's case, LaBelle concluded, "it appears from this record that this man was trying to protect third parties . . . ," and the right against self-incrimination was a shield only against personal incrimination and not against testimony that would incriminate third parties.

As with the argument in his brief, LaBelle's oral argument was designed to concede as much as possible short of the incorporation of the Self-Incrimination Clause and to attract a nonincorporationist majority on the Court. Justice Brennan's remark during the oral argument that Strauch's incorporationist position already was supported by four justices left in doubt only the question of whether the incorporationists could attract a fifth vote. That crucial fifth vote was supplied by Justice Goldberg, and on June 15, 1964, the Court, splitting five to four, announced its decision in *Malloy* v. *Hogan* and incorporated the Self-Incrimination Clause into the Due Process Clause of the Fourteenth Amendment.

Writing for the majority, Justice Brennan declared that the Court had not "hesitated to re-examine past decisions according the Fourteenth Amendment a less central role in the preservation of basic liberties than that which was contemplated by its Framers when they added the Amendment to our constitutional system," and the Court now held, he said, "that the Fifth Amendment's exception from compulsory self-incrimination is also protected by the Fourteenth Amendment against abridgment by the states." The Court's decisions in the coerced confession cases, Brennan maintained, had ultimately been based on a "recognition that the American system of criminal prosecution is accusatorial, not inquisitorial, and that the Fifth Amendment privilege is its essential mainstay," and both the federal and state governments are "constitutionally compelled to establish guilt by evidence independently and freely secured, and may not by coercion prove a charge against an accused out of his own mouth."[21]

The Court's holding that the Self-Incrimination Clause applied to the states, Brennan continued, was also supported by the application of the Fourth Amendment to the states in the *Mapp* case, since the right against unreasonable searches and seizures and the right against self-incrimination were complementary and intertwined rights. Rejecting LaBelle's argument that the concept of self-incrimination protected by the Due Process Clause was "to be determined by a less stringent standard than is applicable in a federal proceeding," Brennan argued that the Court had applied the First and Fourth Amendments and the Assistance of Counsel Clause of the Sixth Amendment to the states in the identical way in which they applied in federal proceedings, and had thereby rejected the idea that the Due Process Clause applied to the states only a "watered down, subjective version of the Bill of Rights. . . ." Reversing the holdings in *Twining* v. *New Jersey* and *Adamson* v. *California* that the Self-Incrimination Clause did not apply to the states, Brennan held that henceforth the states must recognize federal self-incrimination standards, since it would be "incongruous to have different standards determine the validity of a claim of privilege based on the same feared prosecution, depending on whether the claim was asserted in a state or federal court. Therefore, the same standards must determine whether an accused's silence in either a federal or state proceeding is justified."[22]

Having held that the Self-Incrimination Clause applied to state proceedings, Brennan also concluded that the Connecticut courts had failed to apply federal standards in evaluating Malloy's assertion of the federal right. The Connecticut courts, he said, had failed to consider adequately the setting in which the questions had been asked. Most of the questions put to Malloy had sought to identify his employer at the time of his 1959 arrest, Brennan noted, and Malloy could have properly feared that the revelation of his employer's name "might furnish a link in a chain of evidence sufficient to connect [him] with a more recent crime for which he might still be prosecuted." Malloy's refusal to say whether he knew John Bergoti had also been proper, Brennan concluded, since the state undoubtedly suspected Bergoti of involvement in criminal activities, and an answer to the question by Malloy might have connected him with Bergoti "or at least have operated as a waiver of his privilege with reference to his relationship with a possible criminal." Malloy had therefore properly invoked the Self-Incrimination Clause, and his conviction for contempt was reversed.[23]

An incorporationist majority had therefore applied the full Self-Incrimination Clause to the states in the identical way that it applied in federal proceedings. Brennan's opinion also began the process of what might be called retroactive incorporation that continued throughout the rest of the 1960s. During the course of the nationalization process, the Court had not, of course, always proceeded upon the basis of incorporationist principles. But Brennan was now characterizing the process of nationalization as always having involved the incorporation of rights in the Bill of Rights, with the result that all of the rights nationalized by the Court in the past were now considered to apply to the states in a form identical to their application to the federal government.

All of this tampering with the past was too much for Justice Harlan, who, in a dissent joined by Justice Clark, charged that the Court was following a premise that "the Due Process Clause of the Fourteenth Amendment is a short-hand directive to this Court to pick and choose among the provisions of the first eight Amendments and apply those chosen, freighted with their entire accompanying body of federal doctrine, to law enforcement in the States."[24] Retracing the nationalization process, Harlan argued that the Court had recognized in the *Twining* case that the Due Process Clause might protect some rights similar to those in the Bill of Rights, but that such due process rights would not apply to the states in the identical fashion as their counterparts in the Bill of Rights applied in federal proceedings.

Under the *Twining* theory of nationalization, Harlan continued, the Self-Incrimination Clause did not apply to the states via the Due Process Clause, since none of the rights in the Bill of Rights so applied. The Due Process Clause without reference to the Bill of Rights required of the states "fundamental fairness" in their criminal proceedings, and it was under this standard that Connecticut's treatment of Malloy should have been evaluated. And under this standard, Harlan argued, Malloy had been properly committed for contempt, since the Connecticut courts had even applied federal standards of self-incrimination in evaluating his case. "The Court's reference to a federal standard is, to put it bluntly, simply an excuse for the Court to substitute its own superficial assessment of the facts and state law for the careful and better informed conclusions of the state court," Harlan declared. "No one who scans the two opinions with an objective eye will, I think, reach any other conclusion."[25]

Justice White, joined by Justice Stewart, also dissented, but he did not challenge the Court's holding that the Self-Incrimination Clause applied to the states. White agreed with Harlan, however, that federal standards of self-incrimination had been properly applied by the Connecticut courts in the *Malloy* case. Under the Court's holding, White said, the right against self-incrimination "becomes a general one against answering distasteful questions."[26]

Although the Court's decision in the *Malloy* case was overshadowed by its decisions on the same day that state legislatures must be apportioned on the basis of population,[27] the *Malloy* decision had consequences far beyond the proceedings against William Malloy and his colleagues. As the California attorney general had feared, a year after the *Malloy* decision, the Court held that the California comment law penalized the right against self-incrimination and that the law was invalid under the Fifth and Fourteenth Amendments. Reflecting the new incorporationist order on the Court, Justice Douglas's opinion for the Court invalidating the comment law did not mention *Twining* v. *New Jersey*, and mentioned *Adamson* v. *California* only in a footnote.[28]

More importantly, however, the *Malloy* and *Gideon* cases formed the basis for the Court's 1966 decision in *Miranda* v. *Arizona* requiring the police to inform suspects of their right to remain silent and their right to counsel before interrogation. The Self-Incrimination Clause, the Court held, applied to custodial interrogations of suspects, and the right to counsel was required so that the right against self-incrimination could be effectively implemented in that setting. The *Malloy* case therefore led to one of the Warren Court's most controversial criminal-procedure decisions.[29]

The Court's decision in *Malloy* v. *Hogan* thus had important consequences for criminal procedure, but the decision was most immediately a personal victory for Harold Strauch. By a five-to-four vote of the Court, he had finally vindicated his "curbstone" advice to William Malloy in their chance meeting in the Hartford courthouse that he need not respond to the questions put to him before the one-man grand jury. As Strauch said later, he had taken on Malloy's case "feeling somewhat obliged to establish the soundness of my advice," and he had "become so interested in the case that I decided to follow it to the end." Although he knew the *Twining* case was against his contentions, Strauch added, "I was conscious of the fact that the Warren Court constituted the best forum in decades for a reversal." He had been proven correct, and after his victory in the Court, the proceedings were dropped against William Malloy and his colleagues, Polashian and Picano.[30]

With an incorporationist majority clearly in control of the Court, the nationalization process took on an inexorable quality after the decision in
Malloy v. *Hogan.* The Self-Incrimination Clause had long been one of the
most controversial provisions in the Bill of Rights, and with its application
to the states, the nationalization of other, less-controversial criminal-
procedure rights seemed certain to follow. The seeming inexorability of
the nationalization process is well-illustrated by the Court's decision in
Pointer v. *Texas* in 1965, applying the Confrontation Clause of the Sixth
Amendment to the states—although that was not the principal issue that
had been argued by counsel on either side in the case.[31]

The Texas Confrontation Case

The events that produced *Pointer* v. *Texas* began on June 16, 1962, as
Kenneth W. Phillips was finishing another day as manager of a 7-11 mar-
ket located at 1902 West 43rd Street in Houston, Texas. Phillips normally
closed the store at 11 P.M., but at 10:45 P.M. a young man entered the store
and went to the dairy case to get a six-pack of beer. Phillips had been robbed
on May 27, and he thought the young man looked familiar, but he nonetheless went to wait on him. At the counter the young man raised his shirt,
exposing a gun in his belt, and said, "This is just like last time, buddy."
Phillips handed over about three hundred and seventy-five dollars.

The robbery was witnessed by Phillips's sister, Juanita Lavon Phillips,
who was waiting in a car outside the store and saw the robber run down
the street and meet a white-haired man waiting next to what was apparently intended to be a getaway car. The car, however, had a flat tire, and
the two separated and continued their flight on foot. Using a police dog,
officers of the Houston police department soon apprehended the young
robber hiding behind a tree at 1803 Libbey Lane. The suspect was Bob
Granville Pointer, a twenty-four-year-old oil-field worker, who was free
on an appeal bond from a 1960 conviction and sentence of five years imprisonment for robbery by firearms. Pointer's white-haired accomplice,
Earl Dillard, was also taken into custody a short time later. Dillard was
fifty-four years old and had served five prison terms for forgery, robbery,
and burglary.[32]

The police found $146 on Pointer's person when he was arrested, and he
was booked on a charge of robbery "by assault, or violence, or by putting
in fear of life or bodily injury," a crime punishable in Texas by a sentence
of from five years to life imprisonment. Kenneth Phillips identified
Pointer in a police lineup as the person who had robbed him, and at an examining trial (preliminary hearing) on June 25, 1962, Phillips described
the robbery and again identified Pointer as the culprit. Pointer was not
represented by counsel at the examining trial and did not cross-examine

Phillips, although he did attempt to cross-examine some of the other witnesses for the state.[33]

Pointer was indicted by a grand jury on July 16, 1962, for robbery by assault or putting Kenneth Phillips in fear of his life or of bodily injury, and Pointer's trial on this charge was held in the criminal district court during November. At the trial, however, the prosecution discovered that Kenneth Phillips had moved to California and would not be available for the trial. In lieu of Phillips's testimony, the prosecution had Phillips's examining-trial testimony read to the jury. Counsel for Pointer objected to this procedure, arguing that it "is a denial of the confrontment of the witnesses against the defendant," but the trial judge overruled the objection. And, although Pointer testified in his own behalf and denied the robbery of the 7–11 store, the jury convicted him on November 7, 1962. Pointer was sentenced in January of 1963 to not less than five years or more than life imprisonment.[34]

Counsel for Pointer appealed his conviction to the Texas Court of Criminal Appeals, and argued that Pointer had been denied the effective assistance of counsel under the decision in *Gideon* v. *Wainwright* and the Sixth and Fourteenth Amendments. The only stage in the proceedings against him where Pointer could have confronted and cross-examined Kenneth Phillips, the principal witness against him, counsel for Pointer argued, had been at the examining trial, yet he had been unrepresented by counsel in that proceeding and therefore could not effectively exercise his right of cross-examination. The reading of Phillips's examining-trial testimony to the jury by the prosecution, counsel for Pointer argued, had therefore denied him the effective assistance of counsel at a critical stage of the proceedings against him.

The Texas Court of Criminal Appeals, however, affirmed Pointer's conviction on December 18, 1963. Under Texas procedure, the court said, the examining trial was not a critical stage in the proceedings against a defendant, requiring the appointment of counsel to defend him. The only purpose of the examining trial, the court continued, was to determine whether there was probable cause to bind an accused over for action by the grand jury. "There is no statutory provision in this state for the appointment of counsel for an accused prior to indictment," the court of criminal appeals concluded, and the state's failure to provide counsel at the examining trial did not violate Pointer's rights under the Due Process Clause of the Fourteenth Amendment.[35]

Pointer had exhausted his funds with the appeal to the Texas Court of Criminal Appeals, but at this point in the litigation, Orville A. Harlan of Houston took over the conduct of an appeal of Pointer's case to the United States Supreme Court. Harlan filed a petition for a writ of certiorari and a motion to proceed *in forma pauperis* in *Pointer* v. *Texas*, and the Supreme

Court granted both on October 12, 1964. On the appeal to the Court, however, Harlan also focused on the right-to-counsel issue, asking in his petition for a writ of certiorari whether "a preliminary hearing [was] a critical stage of a criminal proceeding requiring counsel under the Sixth and Fourteenth Amendments to the Constitution of the United States, if it is at such preliminary hearing that the sole opportunity for cross-examination of the complaining witness is made available by the state?"[36]

Orville Harlan's strategy of emphasizing the right-to-counsel issue was based on the Court's holding in *Powell* v. *Alabama* that a criminal defendant required "the guiding hand of counsel at every stage in the proceedings against him," a holding that had, of course, been supplemented in 1963 by the decision in *Gideon* v. *Wainwright*. Harlan also argued in behalf of Pointer that his right to counsel had been denied contrary to the Court's rulings in *Hamilton* v. *Alabama* and *White* v. *Maryland*, where the Court had held that in arraignments or preliminary hearings, representation by counsel was required when a defendant was required to assert certain vital defenses or to plead guilty or not guilty at that stage in the proceedings against him. Orville Harlan admitted in his argument to the Court that counsel was not required in every state criminal case during the proceedings prior to indictment, but he argued that counsel must be present, when, as in Pointer's case, substantial prejudice would result from the absence of counsel.[37]

When "the examining trial testimony, adduced at a time when the accused does not have counsel, is attempted to be reproduced at the trial on the merits," Harlan argued, "then . . . the accused should be forewarned of the plan of the state to introduce the testimony on the trial of the merits and give the accused an opportunity, prior to the examining trial, to secure counsel." Otherwise, Harlan argued, Pointer and other defendants would be denied the representation by counsel at the only stage in the proceedings against them where they could confront and cross-examine crucial witnesses against them.[38] Counsel for the state of Texas, on the other hand, denied that the examining trial was a critical stage in Texas criminal procedure, requiring that a defendant be represented by counsel. The only purpose of the examining trial, Texas counsel argued, was to determine probable cause to bind a defendant over for the grand jury, and the defendant was not required to plead guilty or not guilty or to proffer any particular defense to the charge against him at that stage in the proceedings. Lack of representation by counsel at the examining trial, it was therefore argued, did not deny a defendant counsel at a critical stage in the proceedings against him, in violation of the Assistance of Counsel Clause of the Sixth Amendment as applied to the states via the Due Process Clause.[39]

Although both Orville Harlan and counsel for Texas had argued the right-to-counsel issue in their briefs in *Pointer* v. *Texas*, during the oral argument of the case on March 15, 1965, the issue in the case was transformed—during the questioning by the justices—into one involving the right of confrontation. Arguing on behalf of Pointer, Orville Harlan reiterated the contention that Pointer had been denied the Sixth and Fourteenth Amendment right to counsel during a critical stage in the proceedings against him, since the examining trial was "the only opportunity that [Pointer] had for cross-examining the complaining witness, and we feel that the cross-examination of a complaining witness in a criminal proceeding is a critical stage . . . of a criminal prosecution." The fact of "the testimony of the major witness in the same case being adduced when [Pointer] did not have counsel," Harlan continued, "was tantamount to conducting a portion of the trial in which he was convicted without counsel."[40]

The testimony of Kenneth Phillips was crucial to Pointer's trial, Harlan argued, since the state could produce no other evidence that would prove the essential elements of the crime charged—that of robbery by assault or by putting the victim in fear of his life or of bodily injury. Only Phillips could have testified that he was in fear of his life or of bodily injury during the robbery, Harlan maintained, yet the only occasion at which Pointer had had the opportunity to confront and cross-examine Phillips's testimony was at the examining trial. The examining trial therefore became a critical stage in the proceedings against Pointer, requiring the presence of counsel to effectuate the right of confrontation and cross-examination, since the examining trial "was the only time that [Phillips] was confronted for cross-examination purposes and [Pointer] did not have counsel at that time."

Reversal of the *Pointer* case by the Court, Orville Harlan continued, would not "cause any stir in Texas. I don't think that it is necessary, as a general rule, to appoint counsel at an examining trial, because generally as a matter of policy it doesn't serve this type of purpose—it's only in a rare instance that the complainant or the necessary witness does not appear [at the trial]." But in Pointer's case, he argued, the examining trial had been a critical stage in the criminal process, just as the Court had held in *White* v. *Maryland* that a preliminary hearing at which a defendant must plead guilty or not guilty was a critical stage of the criminal process, requiring the presence of counsel for the defendant. "We feel . . . ," Harlan concluded, "that *White* v. *Maryland* certainly is the white horse case in this case."

Orville Harlan's argument before the Court therefore concentrated on the right-to-counsel issue, and neither he nor the justices in their questioning of him had come to focus on the confrontation issue as the principal issue in the case. But during Assistant Attorney General Gilbert J. Pena's argument on behalf of the state, questioning by the justices clearly shifted the issue in the *Pointer* case to the confrontation issue. Pena began by explaining to the Court that at the examining trial in Texas, a defendant did not have to offer a plea or do anything other than "just sit there and listen." Pointer had also been responsible for Phillips's unavailability as a witness at the trial, Pena suggested, since Pointer had delayed his trial for several months by claiming not to have found a suitable attorney. At this point, however, Justice Brennan interrupted Pena, and through his questions produced a decisive shift in the issue in the *Pointer* case.

JUSTICE BRENNAN: Mr. Pena, however that may be, the upshot of this was, because of the complaining witness's absence and permanent move to the State of California, the upshot of this was that the defendant was denied or at least prevented from any possibility of cross-examination of this essential witness at his criminal trial, isn't that correct?

MR. PENA: Yes, sir.

JUSTICE BRENNAN: There is a case in this Court, at least one, there are probably a good many others, implying that the right of cross-examination is an essential constitutional right. . . . So that, as I understand it, in the normal course of events, . . . this problem would not arise because the complaining witness presumably would be present at the criminal trial. Is that right?

MR. PENA: Yes, sir.

JUSTICE BRENNAN: So that normally there perhaps wouldn't be the necessity for counsel at the what you call the examining trial, . . . but when this problem does arise, doesn't what happened here result in Texas through its prosecuting attorney and judicial system by admitting this transcript of the complaining witness's prior testimony before the trial, doesn't Texas deprive the defendant of the right of cross-examination?

MR. PENA: I would have to answer that yes, Your Honor.

Pena argued, however, that the evidence against Pointer had been "overwhelming" and that "the state could have done without" Phillips's testimony. "But you don't suggest," Justice White asked, "that the state would have had a case without the testimony of the complaining witness, do you?" Pena agreed, but despite this response to Justice White, he reverted to the argument that Pointer's conviction was supported by overwhelming evidence even if one excluded Phillips's testimony. At that point, Chief Justice Warren engaged Pena in a discussion that continued to the conclusion of Pena's argument.

CHIEF JUSTICE WARREN: . . . Who but the complaining witness could have said that he gave up this money by reason of the force and the fear created in him on the part of this defendant? Who could have supplied that important element of the crime?

MR. PENA: Well it was attempted to be done by the sister who actually observed the robbery.

CHIEF JUSTICE WARREN: Could she tell what was in the mind of the complaining witness?

MR. PENA: No, but she saw the expression on her brother's face . . . and saw that he had turned pale white. And I realize that this is a very unusual position for the state to be in, but there was evidence beyond a reasonable doubt as to the man's guilt undoubtedly. There was the fruits of the crime, the dog who was certainly unbiased who followed him and caught him, there was—

CHIEF JUSTICE WARREN: But if a lawyer had cross-examined that complaining witness and had in some way or other discredited his testimony, would you still have had as good a case as you've got?

MR. PENA: No, sir, not if he had discredited his testimony.

CHIEF JUSTICE WARREN: All right, well now that's what cross-examination is afforded for, to give an opportunity to do that's all it's for.

Despite Warren's questions, Pena again began to insist that the evidence was sufficient, even without Phillips's testimony, to justify Pointer's conviction, and he again argued that the Court should not require the appointment of counsel for defendants in the examining trials in Texas. Again, Chief Justice Warren attempted to point out to Pena that the confrontation issue was the principal issue in the case.

CHIEF JUSTICE WARREN: Mr. Pena, if I understood [Orville Harlan] correctly, he said that if this testimony had not been introduced in the trial, or if the complaining witness had been questioned at the trial, that they would not claim error in this case. And he nods his head now, so that's all we're dealing with. Whether this man was entitled to confrontation at his trial, whether he got confrontation through this procedure that you have used, or whether that denied him a fair trial.

MR. PENA: As counsel has pointed out, Your Honor, we have no way in the world to appoint counsel at the examining trials, and even after the court appointed him a lawyer—

CHIEF JUSTICE WARREN: I know, but you can't unring a bell, Mr. Pena, and if this testimony was gotten from him at a time when he didn't have a lawyer and he didn't have a fair opportunity to cross-examine, and then you used it [at] the trial against him, that's the gravamen of the situation, not his conduct when he was at the trial. Isn't that true?

MR. PENA: Yes, that's true, Your Honor, that's true.

Again, however, Pena began to argue that the Court should not require the appointment of counsel for all defendants at examining trials in Texas, since the examining trial was not a critical stage in the criminal proceedings against defendants. But again Chief Justice Warren interrupted:

CHIEF JUSTICE WARREN: Well, I suppose, Mr. Pena, that whether the [examining trial] is a critical part of the procedure normally could be changed depending upon the use that was made of it, wouldn't it?

MR. PENA: Yes, sir, as a matter of fact—

CHIEF JUSTICE WARREN: That's what they complain of here. Not that . . . he didn't have a lawyer at that place but that the testimony that they took there was used at the trial where he had no real opportunity to cross-examine such as a man would have if he'd been advised of his right to have a lawyer and had had a lawyer. That's the critical thing, it seems to me.

MR. PENA: I believe that's right.

In his brief rebuttal remarks, Orville Harlan again urged the Court to reverse Pointer's conviction because he had been denied counsel at the only stage of the proceedings against him where he could have confronted and cross-examined the chief witness against him. Neither Pena nor Harlan, therefore, despite the Court's efforts, shifted from the right-to-counsel issue to the confrontation issue during the oral argument. *Pointer* v. *Texas* therefore became a case similar to *Mapp* v. *Ohio* and *Robinson* v. *California*, since when the Court decided the *Pointer* case on April 5, 1965, it held that the Confrontation Clause of the Sixth Amendment was applicable to the states via the Due Process Clause, a point not fully addressed by counsel for either party in the case.

Writing for the Court, Justice Black acknowledged that a right-to-counsel argument had been made in the *Pointer* case, but the Court held instead that "the Sixth Amendment right of an accused to confront the witnesses against him is . . . a fundamental right and is made obligatory on the States by the Fourteenth Amendment." There were few subjects on which the courts were more nearly unanimous, he said, "than in their expressions of belief that the right of confrontation and cross-examination is an essential and fundamental requirement for the kind of fair trial which is this country's constitutional goal." Black acknowledged also that the Court had held in *West* v. *Louisiana* in 1904 that the Sixth Amendment, including its Confrontation Clause, did not apply to the states, but in light of cases such as *Gideon* v. *Wainwright*, he said, "the statements made in *West* and similar cases generally declaring that the Sixth Amendment does not apply to the States can no longer be regarded as the law." The Court held, Black continued, that Pointer "was entitled to be tried in accordance with the protection of the confrontation guarantee of the Sixth Amendment, and that that guarantee, like the right against compelled self-incrimination, is 'to be enforced against the States under the Fourteenth Amendment according to the same standards that protect those personal rights against federal encroachment.' "[41]

Turning to the facts in the *Pointer* case, Black held that the use of the transcript of Phillips's examining-trial testimony against Pointer at his trial had denied him the right to confront and cross-examine a vital witness against him, and the use of such evidence "in a federal court in a criminal case against Pointer would have amounted to denial of the privilege of confrontation guaranteed by the Sixth Amendment." Since the

Court now held that "the right of an accused to be confronted with the witnesses against him must be determined by the same standards whether the right is denied in a federal or state proceeding," Black concluded, "it follows that use of the transcript to convict Pointer denied him a constitutional right, and that his conviction must be reversed."[42]

Although the Court was unanimous in reversing Pointer's conviction, Justices Stewart, Harlan, and Goldberg filed concurring opinions. Justice Stewart agreed that Pointer had been denied the right of confrontation, but would have based a reversal of his conviction on the Due Process Clause standing alone, without incorporating the Confrontation Clause of the Sixth Amendment.[43]

Justice Harlan agreed that Pointer had been denied the right of confrontation, but the right of confrontation that had been denied to Pointer, he argued, derived from the Due Process Clause standing alone and did not have as its source the Sixth Amendment, which applied only to the federal government. The majority opinion, Harlan declared, was "another step in the onward march of the long-since discredited 'incorporation' doctrine . . . , which for some reason I have not yet been able to fathom has come into the sunlight in recent years."[44]

Harlan again defended the *Twining* approach to the nationalization of the Bill of Rights—that the Due Process Clause guaranteed rights similar, but not identical, to some of those in the Bill of Rights. But the Court, he charged, was following instead a "selective incorporation" policy of applying parts of the Bill of Rights fully to the states in the identical way that they applied to the federal government. Such a course, he declared, was supported neither by history nor the concept of due process. "It is too often forgotten in these times that the American federal system is itself constitutionally ordained," Harlan concluded, "that it embodies values profoundly making for lasting liberties in this country, and that its legitimate requirements demand continuing solid recognition in all phases of the work of this Court. The 'incorporation' doctrine, whether full blown or selective, [is] both historically and constitutionally unsound and incompatible with the maintenance of our federal system on even course."[45]

Since he had not been on the Court "when the incorporation issue was joined" in the *Adamson* case, Justice Goldberg stated his position on the nationalization of the Bill of Rights in a concurring opinion, and at the same time offered a defense of selective incorporation. Reviewing the cases in which the Court had nationalized parts of the Bill of Rights, Goldberg disputed Harlan's contention that such rights did not apply to the states in the identical way in which they applied to the federal government. And he also rejected Harlan's argument that the principles of federalism required that rights applicable to the states via the Due Process Clause be only similar, and not identical to those in the Bill of Rights. Acknowledging that he accepted Brandeis's argument that the states should serve as experimental laboratories in socioeconomic policy, Goldberg nonetheless argued that he did not "believe that this includes the power to experiment with the fundamental liberties of citizens safeguarded by the Bill of Rights. My Brother Harlan's view would also require this Court to make the extremely subjective and excessively discretionary determination as to whether a practice, forbidden the Federal Government by a fundamental constitutional guarantee, is, as viewed in the factual circumstances surrounding each individual case, sufficiently repugnant to the notion of due process as to be forbidden the States." This fair-trial approach to the meaning of the Due Process Clause, Goldberg concluded, would not be considerate of the principles of federalism, but rather would subvert such principles, since it would require haphazard and unpredictable intrusions by the federal judiciary in state proceedings, as had been amply demonstrated by the experience under the rule of *Betts* v. *Brady* in the right-to-counsel field.[46]

The *Pointer* case revealed that the Court was dominated by a commanding incorporationist majority that accepted at a minimum the selective incorporation of some of the rights in the Bill of Rights into the Due Process Clause, making those rights apply to the states in the identical way they applied to the federal government. Chief Justice Warren and Justices Black, Douglas, Brennan, White, and Goldberg composed the incorporationist majority, while Justices Stewart and Clark appeared to be rather ambivalent on the incorporation issue. Justice Harlan, on the other hand, occupied an almost isolated position in support of a theory of the nationalization process that had as recently as 1960 received the support of a majority of the Court.

The Court had held that the Confrontation Clause applied to the states and that Bob Granville Pointer had been denied this right at the only stage of the proceedings against him where it could have been effectively exercised. The state of Texas, however, decided to retry Pointer after the Court reversed his conviction. Like Clarence Earl Gideon before him, Pointer proved to be somewhat recalcitrant on the issue of what attorney would represent him at the retrial. The Houston Criminal District Court appointed counsel to represent him, but Pointer objected to its selection and insisted upon the appointment of an attorney of his choice. The court acceded to this request, and Pointer was retried with counsel of his own choosing representing him, and his defense was also assisted by Orville Harlan, who had successfully appealed his case to the Supreme Court.

At the retrial, the state was, of course, careful to bring Kenneth Phillips back to Texas from California to testify as the principal witness against Pointer. Probably due to the passage of time, Phillips's testimony was less certain than previously in identifying Pointer, but it was nevertheless supportive of the prosecution's case. The jury was again convinced by the state's case, and Pointer was convicted and sentenced to from five years to life imprisonment. Unlike Clarence Gideon's experience, therefore, Pointer's involvement in the nationalization of the Bill of Rights turned out to be far from a happy one.[47]

The Texas Compulsory-Process Case

The state of Texas contributed another case in the nationalization process, however, two years after the decision of the *Pointer* case. The second Texas case began when at 2 A.M. on August 30, 1964, Herman Vassel was shot and killed by a shotgun blast on the front porch of a house in Dallas. Vassel had been visiting his girl friend, Jean Carter, who lived with her mother and grandmother in the house where Vassel's death occurred.

Soon after the shooting, the Dallas police arrested Jackie Washington and Charles Fuller and charged them with first-degree murder in the killing of Vassel. Fuller was tried first in the Criminal District Court of Dallas County, was convicted, and was sentenced to fifty years in the Texas state prison.

Jackie Washington, an eighteen-year-old black youth, was tried in March of 1965, and the prosecution's evidence indicated that Washington had once dated Jean Carter and that he had conspired to kill Herman Vassel out of jealousy. Washington had recruited a group of friends, the prosecution contended, who were instructed to throw bricks at the Carter house, and when Vassel came onto the front porch to investigate, Washington had shot him with a shotgun borrowed from his codefendant, Charles Fuller.

Jackie Washington testified in his own behalf, on the other hand, that he had not shot Vassel. According to his testimony, Charles Fuller had been drunk and while they were on their way to the Carter house, Fuller had taken the shotgun away from Washington. After the bricks were thrown, according to Washington, he tried to persuade Fuller to leave, but Fuller insisted that he was going to shoot someone. Washington testified that he had then run, but heard a shot and a woman scream.[48]

From the standpoint of Washington's defense, of course, it would have been valuable to have had Charles Fuller testify and corroborate Washington's account of the shooting. Fuller was willing to so testify, but when one of Washington's attorneys asked the court to call Fuller as a defense witness, Assistant District Attorney Jim Zimmermann objected to the calling of Fuller, "for the reason that Charles Fuller is currently under conviction for the crime of murder arising out of the same set of facts as Jackie Washington."[49]

Judge John Mead sustained Zimmermann's objection on the basis of article 711 of the Texas Code of Criminal Procedure and article 82 of the

Texas Penal Code, which prohibited codefendants from testifying on behalf of one another. Paradoxically, Texas criminal procedure did allow the prosecution to call a codefendant, and if Fuller had been willing to testify for the state, he could have been produced as a prosecution witness. But Texas procedure denied the defendant a similar right.[50]

The jury in Washington's case rendered a verdict of guilty, and Washington was sentenced to fifty years imprisonment. Counsel for Washington filed a motion for a new trial and argued that the Texas statutes prohibiting codefendant testimony had denied Washington his right to "compulsory process for obtaining witnesses in his favor in violation of the Sixth and Fourteenth Amendments to the Constitution of the United States." Judge Mead denied the motion for a new trial, but during the hearing on that motion he permitted Washington's counsel to enter into the record an affidavit detailing the testimony Charles Fuller would have given if he had been allowed to testify.[51]

In his affidavit, Fuller said that he had taken the shotgun from Washington as they approached the Carter house, but Washington had tried to get him to leave. "I wish to God I had left because all I really wanted to do was scare the people in Jean's house," Fuller said. Washington pulled at Fuller and tried again to get him to leave, but then had turned and run. "I continued on to the front of Jean's house," Fuller said, "and shot at the front porch. I don't know what got into me because I never really intended to hit anyone—just scare." Jackie Washington should not "have been convicted," Fuller concluded, "because if I had listened to him that night when he wanted us both to leave, I wouldn't have shot anyone."[52]

Counsel for Jackie Washington renewed the argument that the Texas statutes that had excluded this testimony by Charles Fuller at Washington's trial violated the federal Constitution on appeal to the Texas Court of Criminal Appeals. On January 5, 1966, however, the Texas Court of Criminal Appeals affirmed Washington's conviction. After reviewing the evidence produced at the trial in detail, the court held that it was sufficient to sustain the jury's verdict and rejected the claim that Washington had been denied compulsory process for obtaining witnesses in violation of the Sixth and Fourteenth Amendments. The prohibitions of codefendant testimony contained in the Texas statutes, the court held, "are procedural only and do not deprive the accused of any constitutional right. No cases declaring [articles] 711 and 82 . . . unconstitutional are cited and we are aware of none. The evidence is sufficient to support the conviction and no error appearing, the judgment is affirmed."[53]

Charles W. Tessmer, Washington's counsel, pursued the appeal of *Washington* v. *Texas* to the United States Supreme Court via a petition to proceed *in forma pauperis*. The Court agreed to hear the *Washington* case on October 10, 1966, but limited the question to be argued in the case to whether Washington's conviction was void because "he was denied his rights under the Sixth and Fourteenth Amendments to the Constitution of the United States to have compulsory process in obtaining an available witness in his favor, namely a Co-Defendant, charged and previously convicted under a separate indictment for the same transaction and which Co-Defendant, according to his Affidavit, could have exonerated [Washington] if such testimony were believed by the jury."[54]

At the oral argument on March 15, 1967, of *Washington v. Texas*, Charles Tessmer told the Court that the issue of the right of compulsory process involved in the case was a "simple one, but one of vital importance," and that the Texas prohibition of codefendant testimony on behalf of a defendant violated the Sixth and Fourteenth Amendments. The testimony of Charles Fuller that the Texas rule had denied to Washington, Tessmer said, had been vital to his defense. "The only other person in this world who could have exonerated . . . Washington was the co-defendant Fuller," he told the Court. "Fuller was available. Fuller would have testified that [Washington] was attempting to keep him from pulling the trigger, saying, 'Don't shoot, I'm going to leave, let's don't do it.' And Fuller would have testified that Jackie Washington left before he fired the fatal shot."[55]

For Texas to have denied Washington such vital testimony, Tessmer argued, was to deny the right to compulsory process for the securing of witnesses on behalf of a criminal defendant, a denial that was unconstitutional whether the case were approached on the basis of the theory of incorporation or on the basis of the Due Process Clause standing alone. Whether "we approach this case through the Sixth Amendment by way of the Fourteenth Amendment . . . ," Tessmer said, "or whether we approach it directly through the Fourteenth Amendment, the result should be the same—as the right to a witness in one's behalf, particularly a witness so vital as here, is implicit in the concept of ordered liberty as pointed out in *Palko v. Connecticut*."

Given the fact that the Court had held the Assistance of Counsel Clause and the Confrontation Clause of the Sixth Amendment to be applicable to the states via the Due Process Clause, Tessmer pointed out to the Court that some lower courts were beginning to hold that the Compulsory Process Clause of the Sixth Amendment must surely also be applicable to state proceedings. Such holdings, he said, were based on the proposition that in the "wake of *Gideon v. Wainwright*, of *Pointer v. Texas*, and all of those great decisions . . . that the result must be the same with reference to compulsory process, that it is implicit in any concept of ordered liberty and justice—whether we view it alone by virtue of the Fourteenth Amendment, or whether we view it that that provision of the Sixth Amendment is incorporated and obligatory on the states by virtue of the Fourteenth Amendment interacting with the Sixth, the result must be the same. . . ."

Arguing on behalf of the state of Texas, Assistant Attorney General Howard M. Fender contended that, even assuming that the Compulsory Process Clause applied to the states, the Texas rule prohibiting codefendant testimony was still the same as evidentiary rules that excluded the testimony of idiots, lunatics, and drunkards on the ground of incompetence. Second, Fender argued, the right to compulsory process only meant that a defendant had the right to secure the attendance in court of favorable witnesses, but it did not guarantee to the defendant the right to the testimony of such witnesses if their testimony were excluded by a valid rule of evidence.

He did not feel, Fender therefore told the Court, "that compulsory process has been violated at all. The witness that [Washington] wanted was available right there in the Dallas County jail and could have been used at any time. He did not issue a subpoena and the sheriff refuse to serve it. The man was there available. But he was prevented [from testifying] by an evidentiary rule. He was an incompetent witness in the same manner as an idiot, a lunatic, or a drunkard, because our state law says that he was an incompetent witness."

There was no difference between the exclusion of Fuller as a witness, Fender said, and a situation in which Washington might have "issued a subpoena and brought an idiot into the court and the state objected to the testimony of an idiot or a lunatic, and the court had quite properly under the statutes excluded such testimony." There would be no question of a denial of the right of compulsory process under the Sixth Amendment, he continued, "just because the court said that idiot cannot testify."

It was reasonable for the state to conclude, Fender contended, that just as the testimony of an idiot was incompetent and inadmissible in a criminal trial, "there was and still could be ample reason for saying that a codefendant has such an interest in the outcome or is so likely to lie, as to be unreliable and therefore they will not permit him to testify." At this point, Chief Justice Warren interrupted Fender's argument.

CHIEF JUSTICE WARREN: Can [a codefendant] testify for the government?

MR. FENDER: Yes, sir.

CHIEF JUSTICE WARREN: What!

MR. FENDER: Under our . . . new code of criminal procedure they can testify for anybody.[56]

CHIEF JUSTICE WARREN: Yes, but under the rule that we have here could he testify for the state? Do you customarily use codefendants to testify against others?

MR. FENDER: It's a matter of discretion on the part of the prosecutor—sometimes do and sometimes don't.

CHIEF JUSTICE WARREN: Well, you do it. In other words his reliability does not affect him in that case, but it does if he's to be used for the defendant?

MR. FENDER: Yes, sir, in much the same way that we can't call a man's wife to testify against him, but he can call his wife to testify for him.

CHIEF JUSTICE WARREN: If you block an idiot from testifying, he can't testify for either side, can he?

MR. FENDER: If he qualifies as an idiot, he can't testify for either side, that's correct.

CHIEF JUSTICE WARREN: Well, then there isn't any connection between the situation where you bar an idiot and where you bar a codefendant.

MR. FENDER: Only insofar as both of them fall within the rule that prohibits their testimony.

Fender subsequently argued that even if Fuller's testimony had been admitted and believed by the jury, the evidence proved that Jackie Washington was "the general that laid down the plan of action, and was therefore completely culpable for the death of the deceased in this case." But, although Fender and Tessmer disagreed on most other points in the case, they both agreed that the Compulsory Process Clause applied to the states, and Fender explicitly disavowed any argument to the contrary in an exchange with Justice Clark.

JUSTICE CLARK: You admit that the witness clause of the Sixth Amendment applies to the states?

MR. FENDER: Frankly, I would hope that it applied to the states, because the Fourteenth Amendment having brought in the rest [of the Sixth Amendment] . . . we might as well let the witness clause go with it—you mean the Compulsory Process [Clause]?

JUSTICE CLARK: Yes.

MR. FENDER: Yes, sir, I have no quarrel with the question as to whether the Compulsory Process Clause is applicable.

JUSTICE CLARK: I don't remember any case of the Court that said that—

MR. FENDER: Frankly, I couldn't find any, but I just assumed that since the hair goes with the hide that that section would go with the others in being applicable to the states.

JUSTICE BLACK: I hope your assumption is a sound one. [Laughter]

MR. FENDER: Sometimes the hair gets burned off, Mr. Justice Black.

JUSTICE CLARK: I'm afraid you won't get everyone on that.

MR. FENDER: I don't necessarily want everybody. I'm just not going to fight that point, sir. [Laughter]

Since there was no disagreement between the state and counsel for Washington on the question of the applicability of the Compulsory Process Clause to the states, the remainder of the argument in the *Washington* case centered on the extent to which rules of evidence excluding certain testimony, or rules extending a privilege not to testify to certain persons, were affected by the Compulsory Process Clause. Charles Tessmer was closely questioned on these points by Justices White and Stewart during his rebuttal argument, and he was constrained to admit that not all rules disqualifying witnesses from testifying on the grounds of competence, or excluding certain types of testimony, were invalid under the Compulsory Process Clause, if such rules were based on reasonable policy considerations. The question in the *Washington* case therefore came down to whether the Texas rule prohibiting codefendant testimony was a reasonable exception to the right to compel the attendance of witnesses in a criminal trial, especially in light of the fact that Texas had allowed such testimony on behalf of the state.

The Court unanimously reversed Jackie Washington's conviction on June 12, 1967, and held that the Compulsory Process Clause was applicable to the states. Writing for the Court, Chief Justice Warren said that prior decisions of the Court that had held the Sixth Amendment to be inapplicable to the states had been undermined by decisions such as the *Gideon* and *Pointer* cases that had held parts of the Sixth Amendment to be guarantees also of the Due Process Clause. Like the Assistance of Counsel Clause and the Confrontation Clause, he said, the Compulsory Process Clause was considered by the Court to be "so fundamental and essential to a fair trial" that it was incorporated into the Due Process Clause.

"The right to offer the testimony of witnesses, and to compel their attendance, if necessary, is in plain terms the right to present a defense, the right to present the defendant's version of the facts as well as the prosecution's to the jury so it may decide where the truth lies," Warren declared. "Just as an accused has the right to confront the prosecution's witnesses for the purpose of challenging their testimony, he has the right to present his own witnesses to establish a defense. This right is a fundamental element of due process of law."[57]

The exclusion of codefendant testimony by Texas, Warren said, could not be justified on the grounds that such testimony was untrustworthy, since the state allowed such testimony in support of the prosecution. "To think that criminals will lie to save their fellows but not to obtain favors from the prosecution for themselves," he said, "is indeed to clothe the criminal class with more nobility than one might expect to find in the public at large." Washington's conviction was therefore reversed because Texas had "arbitrarily denied him the right to put on the stand a witness who was physically and mentally capable of testifying to events that he had personally observed, and whose testimony was relevant and material to the defense." The framers of the Constitution, Warren concluded, "did not intend to commit the futile act of giving to a defendant the right to secure the attendance of witnesses whose testimony he had no right to use."[58]

If Justice Harlan had inherited anything from his grandfather, the first

Justice Harlan, it was a willingness to stand alone. As his grandfather had stood alone in support of the application of the Bill of Rights to the states, Harlan stood alone in the *Washington* case against the proposition that the Compulsory Process Clause of the Sixth Amendment was incorporated in the Due Process Clause. He agreed, he said in a concurring opinion, that Washington's conviction should be reversed, but only on the ground that Texas had violated general due process standards and not because the Compulsory Process Clause applied to the states.[59]

Harlan's isolated position in the *Washington* case symbolized the remarkable conversion to an incorporationist position the Court had undergone within a few short years. After the initial breakthrough in the *Mapp* case in 1961 in a closely divided decision, the incorporationists had steadily gained ground. Each succeeding year after 1961, with the exception of 1966, had witnessed a decision by the Court holding that a right also listed in the Bill of Rights was protected by the Due Process Clause against state action. Although by the mid-1960s a majority of the Court continued to be unwilling to embrace Justice Black's total-incorporation position, the majority was clearly willing to apply parts of the Bill of Rights to the states selectively. And this selective-incorporationist majority accepted an essential element of the Black position—that once a part of the Bill of Rights was deemed to be incorporated in the Due Process Clause, it applied to the states in the identical way that it applied to the federal government.

The incorporationist majority also reinterpreted the history of the nationalization process as having always involved the incorporation of rights into the Due Process Clause. That the Court had in the past approached the nationalization process in other ways, especially via the fair trial approach, was therefore downplayed during the 1960s.[60] Through a process of retroactive incorporation, the Court began to characterize decisions that had not been decided in incorporationist terms as involving the incorporation of parts of the Bill of Rights into the Due Process Clause. The *Gideon* and *Robinson* cases, for example, were characterized as having incorporated the Assistance of Counsel Clause and the Cruel and Unusual Punishment Clause into the Due Process Clause, although the language of the Court when it decided those cases had been far from explicit in that regard. And the *Oliver* case was held to have incorporated the Public Trial Clause of the Sixth Amendment, even though at the time of its decision in 1948, it had clearly been decided under the fair trial, and not the incorporationist, approach to the nationalization process.[61] To the incorporationists of the Warren Court, however, it was clear that the nationalization of the Bill of Rights had always involved the incorporation of rights in the Bill of Rights and the application of those rights to the states in a form identical to that in which they applied to the federal government.

The incorporationist majority on the Court had, of course, proved to be a godsend for Jackie Washington. The Court had not only held that the Compulsory Process Clause applied to the states but also held that Texas had violated the clause by refusing to allow Charles Fuller to testify in Washington's behalf at his trial. Given the fact that Fuller's testimony would have, if believed by a jury, exonerated Washington on the charge of first-degree murder, the state elected not to retry Washington after the Supreme Court reversed his conviction. Jackie Washington therefore avoided the fifty years of imprisonment that had been imposed upon him.[62]

10

The Civil Rights Struggle and the Nationalization Process

The *Klopfer* and *Duncan* Cases

The invalidation of racial segregation in the public schools by the Supreme Court in 1954 ultimately activated opposing forces on the issue of racial equality throughout the nation.[1] During the 1950s and 1960s, the struggle between the opposing forces was particularly intense in the South. Like similar sociopolitical struggles in the past, the conflict over racial equality generated new issues of constitutional policy, some of which did not directly concern the central issue of constitutional equalitarianism. The desegregation struggle, for example, produced important extensions of the concept of freedom of expression and association,[2] and the process of nationalization of the Bill of Rights was also affected. The result was two cases, *Klopfer* v. *North Carolina* and *Duncan* v. *Louisiana*, decided by the Supreme Court in 1967[3] and 1968, that extended the application of the Bill of Rights to the states.

Sitting-in in North Carolina: Peter Klopfer's Case

One of the most significant aspects of the struggle for racial equality in the South began with the sit-in movement in the early 1960s. Promoted by such groups as the Southern Christian Leadership Conference headed by Martin Luther King, Jr., the Congress for Racial Equality, and the Student Non-Violent Coordinating Committee, groups of blacks or integrated groups of blacks and whites sat in at segregated restaurants, lunch counters, and other facilities of public accommodation and refused to leave when they were denied service. Those participating in the sit-ins were commonly charged with criminal trespass.

In 1963 and 1964, the sit-in movement began in Chapel Hill, North Carolina, home of the prestigous University of North Carolina. Although Chapel Hill was commonly regarded as a comparatively liberal community, a survey of local facilities of public accommodation indicated that about one-third of the restaurants and three out of five motels refused to serve blacks. Altogether, 25 percent of the facilities of public accommodation in Chapel Hill were found to operate on a segregated basis. Attempts to desegregate these facilities via sit-in tactics met with a hostile reception in Chapel Hill and resulted in large numbers of arrests for criminal trespass.[4]

Although the Chapel Hill sit-ins were conducted mostly by students, on January 3, 1964, five professors from Duke University at nearby Durham and two University of North Carolina professors volunteered to participate in a sit-in. The Duke professors included Peter Klopfer, a zoologist, David Smith, a mathematician, and Frederick Herzog, Robert Osborn, and Harmon Smith, who were ministers and members of the Department of Religion at Duke. The UNC professors were William Wynn and Albert Amon, both psychologists.[5]

The professors were joined by several young demonstrators, and the decision was made that the integrated group should proceed to Watts Motel and Restaurant, which was operated by its owners, Mr. and Mrs. Austin Watts, on a segregated basis. What happened at the Watts's establishment was later a subject of disputed testimony. According to the sit-in group, Albert Amon approached the door of the restaurant and was confronted by Mrs. Watts and a waitress in the foyer between the outer and inner doors of the restaurant. When Amon asked if he could come in, he was pulled into the restaurant by Austin Watts, and Watts and a companion proceeded to hit and kick Amon, opening up a $3\frac{1}{2}$-inch cut on the back of his head. Two other demonstrators entered the premises and threw themselves on Amon to protect him from further blows. Spectators were meanwhile shouting, "Kill them, get the professors."

The remainder of the demonstrators never entered the restaurant, but rather sat down outside. Mrs. Watts pounded the demonstrators with a broom, while others turned on a garden hose and sprayed the group with water. Since it was a cold January night, the group of demonstrators was, needless to say, acutely uncomfortable. After the group had been abused for fifteen or twenty minutes, sheriff's deputies and officers from the Chapel Hill police department arrived and arrested the demonstrators on criminal-trespass charges.

Austin Watts, the 6 foot, 1 inch, 280-pound owner of the Watts Motel and Restaurant, later denied the accuracy of this description of the events. He subsequently testified that ten or eleven of the demonstrators had pushed his wife against the wall of the restaurant and had lain down in front of the cash register. "They were all laying down," he said, "like a bunch of hogs." When the group refused to leave, Watts said, he called the police, but he denied that he or anyone else had assaulted anyone in the group.[6]

Along with a host of other demonstrators arrested during the Chapel Hill sit-ins, the group that had participated at the Watts Motel and Restaurant sit-in was indicted by an Orange County grand jury for criminal trespass and was tried in the Superior Court of Orange County at Hillsboro during the March 1964 session of that court. The presiding judge during the trials of most of the demonstrators was Raymond B. Mallard, while the cases were prosecuted by District Solicitor Thomas D. Cooper. A young attorney, Wade H. Penny, Jr., was defense counsel for many of the demonstrators.[7]

Judge Mallard proved to be a martinet in the courtroom, and his hostility toward the demonstrators during the trials was ill-concealed. In a speech he gave during the trials, Mallard charged that outsiders were selling North Carolina's youth a "bill of goods" and that "Yankee money" was being used in the state to "enlighten the sinful South." The leaders of the sit-in movement, he continued, were using religion as a justification for violating the law and were destroying the minds of the state's young people. "We must not let anyone come along and destroy our minds and sell us a bill of goods that it is all right to violate the law," he declared.[8]

Although most of the demonstrators were convicted of criminal trespass in Judge Mallard's court, the jury that heard the case of Peter Klopfer, the Duke zoologist, could not agree on a verdict, and Judge Mallard was constrained to declare a mistrial in Klopfer's case. The case was then scheduled for retrial during the spring of 1965, at the next session of the court.[9]

Several weeks before the scheduled retrial of Klopfer's case, however, District Solicitor Cooper indicated to Wade Penny, Klopfer's counsel, that he was contemplating entering a *nolle prosequi* with leave in the case. The North Carolina trial courts customarily accepted such actions by the prosecution, and the entry of a *nol-pros* with leave in the *Klopfer* case would mean that the prosecution did not want to retry the case, but that at any time in the future the prosecution on its own motion could revive the charge and put Klopfer on trial on the criminal-trespass charge. The effect of a *nol-pros* with leave would therefore be to place Klopfer on a kind of probation that could be revoked at any time by the prosecutor's opting for a retrial of the trespass charge.

Wade Penny strenuously objected to the entry of a *nol-pros* in Klopfer's case, primarily because cases decided by the United States Supreme Court in 1964 made it highly unlikely that Klopfer could be validly prosecuted on the trespass charge. The Civil Rights Act of 1964 had been passed during the summer of 1964, and among other provisions, it outlawed racial discrimination in a wide variety of facilities of public accommodation, including cafes and restaurants. The public-accommodation sections of the act were subjected to almost immediate challenge on constitutional grounds, but the Supreme Court had upheld the provisions in December of 1964.[10]

On the same day that the Court upheld the validity of the public-accommodation sections of the Civil Rights Act, it also decided *Hamm* v. *Rock Hill* and *Lupper* v. *Arkansas*. Both the *Hamm* and *Lupper* cases involved sit-ins and prosecutions of demonstrators for refusing to leave facilities of public accommodation. The Court reversed the convictions in both cases on the ground that the public-accommodation provisions of the Civil Rights Act made the alleged offenses in both cases no longer punishable. "The Civil Rights Act of 1964," the Court said, "forbids discrimination in places of public accommodation and removes peaceful attempts to be served on an equal basis from the category of punishable activities. Although the conduct in the present cases occurred prior to enactment of the Act, the still-pending convictions were abated by its passage."[11]

After the Supreme Court's decision of the *Hamm* and *Lupper* cases, therefore, it was unlikely that Peter Klopfer could have been successfully prosecuted by District Solicitor Cooper on the criminal-trespass charge. Under the doctrine enunciated in those cases, the Civil Rights Act barred any convictions for peaceful sit-ins aimed at obtaining nondiscriminatory service in facilities of public accommodation covered by the act, even if the sit-ins had occurred prior to the passage of the act. When District Solicitor Cooper moved to enter a *nol-pros* with leave in the *Klopfer* case during the April 1965 criminal session of the Superior Court of Orange County, Wade Penny therefore strongly opposed the move. The *Hamm* and *Lupper* cases, he argued, made it impossible for the prosecution to succeed in a retrial of Klopfer on the trespass charge. But Cooper advised the court that he did not after all want to enter a *nol-pros* at that time and requested instead that the case be continued—a request that the court granted.[12]

When the trial calendar for the August 1965 criminal session of the superior court was announced, however, Klopfer's case was not listed as one of the cases to be tried. Still acting as Klopfer's counsel, Wade Penny filed a motion with the court on August 7, 1965, requesting the court to determine the status of the *Klopfer* case. Penny noted the long delay in the case and pointed out that the unliquidated trespass charge against Klopfer was interferring with Klopfer's professional activities, such as scheduling lecture and conference trips outside the state and research trips outside the country. Penny argued that the trespass charge should be "permanently concluded in accordance with the applicable laws of the State of North Carolina and the United States as soon as is reasonably possible."[13]

In response to this motion, the status of Klopfer's case was considered by the superior court on August 9, 1965. At that time, Solicitor Cooper requested the entry of a *nolle prosequi* with leave, and, over the objections of Wade Penny, the judge granted Cooper's request. The result was that after over a year's delay, the trial of the trespass charge against Klopfer was indefinitely postponed, subject, however, to an unlimited discretion in Solicitor Cooper to revive the charge and put Klopfer to trial at any future date. Klopfer was therefore placed in limbo, having been denied a trial at which he could have been either convicted or acquitted. Instead, he apparently was to have a criminal charge perpetually hanging over his head.[14]

Arguing that this use of the *nol-pros* with leave denied Klopfer the right to a speedy trial as guaranteed by the Due Process Clause of the Fourteenth Amendment, Wade Penny appealed the *Klopfer* case to the North Carolina Supreme Court. On January 14, 1966, however, the court upheld the use of the *nol-pros* procedure in Klopfer's case. Klopfer had a right to a speedy trial, the court said, only if there was to be a trial, but he did not have the right to compel the state to prosecute him. "In this case," the court continued, "one jury seems to have been unable to agree. The solicitor may have concluded that another go at it would not be worth the time and expense of another effort." Solicitor Cooper and the superior court, the supreme court concluded, "in entering the *nolle prosequi* with leave followed the customary procedure in such cases. Their discretion is not reviewable under the facts disclosed by this record."[15]

Refusing to accept this rejection of his speedy-trial argument, Wade Penny appealed *Klopfer* v. *North Carolina* via a petition for a writ of certiorari to the United States Supreme Court on April 14, 1966. The American Civil Liberties Union and its North Carolina affiliate supported the certiorari petition with an *amicus curiae* brief, and the Court granted the petition on May 31.[16]

In his brief in the *Klopfer* case, Wade Penny argued that it did not matter whether the Court approached the issue in the case from the fair-trial or the incorporationist position, since either would lead it to the conclusion that a speedy trial was guaranteed by the Due Process Clause. Relying on the Court's decision in *In re Oliver*, Penny argued that the logic of that case indicated that "the imperative of protecting an accused from judicial harassment, intimidation, and persecution which makes the right to a public trial an essential of due process of law, justifies with equal force and validity the conclusion that the right to a speedy trial is likewise an essential of due process of law."[17]

Under the doctrine enunciated by the Court in the *Hamm* and *Lupper* cases, Penny continued, the prosecution in the *Klopfer* case faced almost certain defeat if the case had been brought to trial. By taking a *nol-pros* with leave, Solicitor Cooper had avoided being defeated at trial, while leaving Peter Klopfer with the trespass charge hanging over his head indefinitely. The result was that Klopfer was kept in continuing anxiety regarding the possible future revival of the charge against him and was subjected to inconvenience regarding his professional activities. The *nol-pros* procedure, Penny said, had, on the other hand, given the state the leverage by which it could "attempt to stifle, penalize, and discourage the exercise of First Amendment rights such as free speech and assembly whenever the accused has challenged the prevailing opinion of the community, as did Klopfer."[18]

The *amicus curiae* brief filed by the American Civil Liberties Union and its North Carolina affiliate reemphasized the argument that the right to a speedy trial was a basic right in criminal proceedings protected by the Due Process Clause. The ACLU also argued that the effect of the *nol-pros* procedure in Klopfer's case was to inhibit the exercise of First Amendment rights. To the extent that this procedure was being used to prevent Klopfer "from again engaging in racial protest," the ACLU said, "this procedure does not pass constitutional muster." If Klopfer "is ever again to feel free to express an unpopular belief in North Carolina, the indictment pending against him must be dismissed."[19]

The arguments on behalf of the state of North Carolina in support of the *nol-pros* procedure used in the *Klopfer* case were notably halfhearted. In the state's seven-page brief, it was noted that the *nol-pros* with leave procedure was a customary one in the state and that it had been uniformly approved by the state's courts. The procedure, it was argued, "does, for all practical purposes, terminate the proceedings once and for all and in no way jeopardizes a defendant's standing."[20]

Although state counsel pointed out that the Court had never "held expressly that the Sixth Amendment right to a speedy trial is made mandatory in state proceedings," it was conceded that the Court had held that "most of the other Sixth Amendment rights are in fact binding on the states through the Fourteenth Amendment." Counsel for the state nevertheless concluded that Klopfer had no "right to compel the State to prosecute," and his right to a speedy trial could be asserted as a shield if the state decided to prosecute, but it could not be used as "a sword, compelling the State to go to the expense of a trial when obviously the Solicitor feels that 'another go at it would not be worth the time and expense of another effort.'"[21]

In his oral argument before the Court, Wade Penny charged that in Klopfer's case the state of North Carolina had taken the "unprecedented view" that the "state may permanently and completely deprive a defendant of his day in court, and in doing so repudiates the basic principles of our system of law that every man accused of crime, regardless of his station in life, is nevertheless unequivocally entitled to his day in court to establish his innocence with the opportunity to secure his exoneration." Penny again pointed out to the Court that under its decisions in the *Hamm* and *Lupper* cases, applying the Civil Rights Act of 1964 retroactively to abate sit-in prosecutions, Peter Klopfer could not have been successfully prosecuted by the state. But because of the use of the *nol-pros* with leave procedure, Klopfer had not had, and presumably never would have, an opportunity to vindicate himself. Rather, he had a criminal indictment permanently hanging over his head. Justice Brennan asked Penny what specific relief he was seeking from the Court, and Penny replied that "the action of the state here was so arbitrary and capricious as to justify this Court in finding that the right to speedy trial applies, that it has been unpardonably violated here, and that further prosecution is barred in this case because of the constitutional right."[22]

Assistant North Carolina Attorney General Andrew A. Vanore, Jr., argued the *Klopfer* case on behalf of the state, and it is probable that few attorneys have received as rough treatment as Vanore received from the Court. The crux of the case, he told the Court, was "whether [Klopfer] can compel the state to prosecute." The state's position, he said, was that a defendant had the right to a speedy trial only if there was to be a trial, and in practical terms, the *nol-pros* with leave in North Carolina constituted a dismissal of a case. "But it isn't a dismissal," Justice Stewart said. "This thing is actually hanging over this petitioner's head for the rest of his life." Theoretically, Vanore replied, "I must agree with you. In ten years from now this case could be brought against the petitioner." Klopfer would "probably have a very good defense . . . , forgetting about *Hamm* and *Lupper*, in terms of his right to a speedy trial," Stewart said, "but nonetheless this is hanging over his head, isn't it?"

Subsequently, Chief Justice Warren observed that under the *nol-pros* with leave procedure, the state could elect to try Klopfer at any time in the indefinite future. "That is correct," Vanore said, "but of course, Mr. Chief Justice, the state contends that the defendant would certainly have a good defense. In fact, there is no doubt that he would have been denied a speedy trial. . . ." As far as the state's position was concerned, he continued, "the defendant is entitled to a speedy trial, if there is to be a trial," but the *nol-pros* with leave procedure was "in effect a dismissal."

Justice Black then interrupted to begin an extensive and hostile interrogation of Vanore:

JUSTICE BLACK: I'd like to ask you a question, whether I understood you correctly or not. Did I understand you correctly to say that if [the] solicitor were to decide now to prosecute this very man, that this very man could then offer a defense which the state would accept, because of the delay in prosecuting him?

MR. VANORE: Well, I'm not sure whether or not the state would accept it, but I would certainly think that in light of the decisions of the North Carolina Supreme Court and the decisions of this Court, that that would certainly be a good defense—that he was denied his right to a speedy trial.

JUSTICE BLACK: Then all you're . . . contending here is, as I gather it, [the] state's right to keep something pending against him that the state knows he couldn't be convicted of?

MR. VANORE: I think that is the crux of the matter, yes.

JUSTICE BLACK: Well, why does the state do that?

MR. VANORE: I cannot give any reason for why the state does that, I simply say. . . .

JUSTICE BLACK: What you are saying is, that here is a man charged with an offense, for which he has a good defense which would be recognized and he'd be turned loose, that he is denied any right to raise it in the State of North Carolina.

MR. VANORE: He is denied the right due to the fact that—

JUSTICE BLACK: Well, whatever it is, he is denied the right to raise it. He can't do it.

MR. VANORE: That is correct, yes.

JUSTICE BLACK: He's under the thumb of the prosecuting attorney for the rest of his life. Is that right?

MR. VANORE: That is correct. I would like to point this out—

JUSTICE BLACK: Well, why does not the State of North Carolina . . . confess error?

MR. VANORE: I was just going to suggest one thing, if Your Honor pleases, as Mr. Penny mentioned to the Court, it would seem that where a *nol-pros* with leave is requested by the solicitor and there is no objection by the defendant that that certainly would be proper. As in this case, when the defendant has objected, quite candidly, perhaps this Court should allow some redress to that. . . .

Having been forced by Justice Black's questions into confessing error, Vanore was asked by Justice Brennan what action the Court should take. "Well," he replied, "I might suggest that the Court remand to the Supreme Court of North Carolina with directions that the state either try this man within a reasonable time or that the [state] supreme court itself quash the indictment." Justice White asked, however, on what constitutional provision the Court could base such a decision. "On what ground do we take this action," he asked. "Do we say speedy trial?" Vanore replied that the Speedy Trial Clause had never been applied to the states and refused to say that it should be applied in the *Klopfer* case. Justice Harlan then bailed him out temporarily by suggesting that the case could be decided on general due process grounds.

This gave Vanore only a brief respite, however, since again he was subjected to hostile questioning by both Chief Justice Warren and Justice Black.

CHIEF JUSTICE WARREN: I wonder why in both your answer to the petition for certiorari and also in your brief on the merits, that no such concession as you now make was made there. In both those documents you asked the Court to deny this petitioner any relief. Now why do you . . . come to us in that posture?

MR. VANORE: I preferred quite frankly not to put it in the brief, Mr. Chief Justice, and that if any admission of error was made that it be made orally, because I was not sure at that particular time in my own mind [that] it was error.

JUSTICE BLACK: Well, why are you not confessing the plain, open, flagrant violation of the Sixth Amendment as it applies to the states this provision, "in all criminal prosecutions, the accused shall enjoy the right to a speedy, public trial by an impartial jury," and so forth.

MR. VANORE: If there is to be a trial, Mr. Justice Black.

JUSTICE BLACK: Well, there is to be a trial if this Amendment applies to the states, isn't [there]?

MR. VANORE: Well, I don't believe that any of the—all the cases that have come up to this Court on the question of speedy trial have arisen—

JUSTICE BLACK: I don't care how they have come up before, what we have here . . . as the record shows and you admit, . . . the man is being denied a speedy, public trial when he's charged with an offense. Now, if the Sixth Amendment applies to the states, why isn't that a violation of it? He's not enjoying—

MR. VANORE: Well, the state has not elected to prosecute him—

JUSTICE BLACK: But they have charged him, they have an offense pending against him, and they will not give him the benefit of a speedy trial. And you admit it.

MR. VANORE: They haven't given him the benefit of any trial.

JUSTICE BLACK: That's right. Why doesn't that violate the Sixth Amendment?

MR. VANORE: That is correct. Well, as far as—all of the cases that come up under the Sixth Amendment right arise where the state has elected to prosecute and the defense is raised of speedy trial.

JUSTICE BLACK: Why certainly they raise it that way, but why do they have to raise it in any one particular manner? If a man is charged with an offense in a state, and they will not give him a trial, why doesn't that violate the Sixth Amendment, if it applies to the states?

MR. VANORE: It's a question of whether or not the state must try him or whether this *nol-pros* with leave suffices.

JUSTICE BLACK: No. Is he not directly, unequivocally entitled to a speedy trial if the Sixth Amendment applies to the states?

At this point, Justice Douglas intervened and diverted the questioning to another subject. He had understood Vanore to say, Douglas helpfully said, that Vanore agreed with Justice Harlan that the case involved only a question of "procedural due process." A relieved Vanore agreed, and Justice Harlan also intervened to calm the atmosphere. "I would like to ask you one thing," Harlan said, "are you authorized to confess error for the state?" Vanore replied that he took "it that I would be, Mr. Justice Harlan, yes." He then indicated that he was willing to admit that the Court should invalidate the *nol-pros* with leave procedure where the defendant objected to the entry of such a motion, but that he hoped the Court would not invalidate the procedure altogether. "The reason I asked the question," Harlan said, "if the Court accepts your suggestion of confession of error, [we are] not putting you in the position where you are subject to criticism by your superiors for having confessed error on behalf of the state?" Vanore replied, "No definitely not, I have already discussed that point with my superiors." And with that, an undoubtedly relieved Vanore concluded his argument in the *Klopfer* case.

For anyone who had heard the oral argument, the result in *Klopfer* v. *North Carolina* was entirely predictable; the Court announced on March 13, 1967, a unanimous decision invalidating the North Carolina *nolle prosequi* with leave procedure as employed in Klopfer's case. Writing for the Court, Chief Justice Warren held that the "consequence of this extraordinary criminal procedure is made apparent by the case before the Court. A defendant indicted for a misdemeanor may be denied an opportunity to exonerate himself in the discretion of the solicitor and held subject to trial, over his objection, throughout the unlimited period in which the solicitor may restore the case to the calendar." During this unlimited period, Warren continued, the defendant had no means by which he could obtain either a trial or a dismissal of the charges. "In spite of this result," he said, "both the [North Carolina] Supreme Court and the Attorney General state as a fact, and rely upon it for affirmance in this case, that this procedure as applied to the petitioner placed no limitations upon him, and was in no way violative of his rights." With this, Warren declared, "we cannot agree."[23]

Warren noted that the state's proposition in the *Klopfer* case—that the right to a speedy trial did not afford protection against an unjustified postponement of a trial for an accused discharged from custody—"has been explicitly rejected by every other state court which has considered the question." The Court held, he continued, that Klopfer had a right to a speedy trial "guaranteed to him by the Sixth Amendment of the Constitution of the United States" and that "the right to a speedy trial is as fundamental as any of the rights secured by the Sixth Amendment. That right has its roots at the very foundation of our English law heritage." North Carolina's use of the *nol-pros* with leave procedure in Klopfer's case, Warren therefore concluded, was violative of the Sixth and Fourteenth Amendments' guarantee of the right to a speedy trial.[24]

Justice Stewart concurred in the invalidation of the judgment of the Court without opinion, and Justice Harlan also concurred in a brief opinion. "While I entirely agree with the result reached by the Court," he said, "I am unable to subscribe to the constitutional premises upon which that result is based—quite evidently the viewpoint that the Fourteenth Amendment 'incorporates' or 'absorbs' *as such* all or some of the specific provisions of the Bill of Rights. I do not believe that this is sound constitutional doctrine." He would rest the decision in the *Klopfer* case, Harlan continued, "not on the 'speedy trial' provision of the Sixth Amendment, but on the ground that this unusual North Carolina procedure, which in effect allows state prosecuting officials to put a person under the cloud of an unliquidated criminal charge for an indeterminate period, violates the requirement of fundamental fairness assured by the Due Process Clause of the Fourteenth Amendment."[25]

The passage of the public-accommodation sections of the Civil Rights Act of 1964 had of course largely vindicated the cause for which Peter Klopfer and his colleagues had been arrested and prosecuted. Within days after President Johnson had signed the Civil Rights Act into law, the civil-rights forces in Chapel Hill began to test the willingness of the owners of previously segregated facilities to comply with the law. When an integrated group went to the Watts Motel and Restaurant, they were told to leave. "You aren't going to comply with the law?" one of the group asked. "If you want to get served here," the group was told, "you've got to get that small-assed President of yours to serve you." When a member of the group persisted in asking if the law was going to be obeyed, Austin Watts hit him hard on the jaw, knocking him to the floor. As the group prepared to leave, a woman stuck a butcher knife through the window of their automobile and said, "I'm going to kill all you niggers and nigger lovers." The following day, however, an integrated group again entered the Watts's establishment and was served. Indeed, shortly after the passage of the Civil Rights Act, almost all of the facilities of public accommodation in Chapel Hill, including Watts Motel and Restaurant, were reported to be operating on a nondiscriminatory basis.[26]

Bolstered by the Supreme Court's decision invalidating the *nol-pros* procedure employed in his case, Peter Klopfer and his attorney, Wade Penny, sought to remove the trial of Klopfer's case to a United States District Court, but on November 17, 1967, the federal court ruled that the North Carolina courts should have the opportunity to dismiss the case. When the case was finally called for trial in the Superior Court of Orange County over two years after it had resulted in a hung jury, Wade Penny's motion to dismiss the charges against Peter Klopfer was accepted by the court.[27]

The criminal-trespass charges against Klopfer were therefore dismissed, but the epitaph for the *Klopfer* case had been written by the editors of the student newspaper at the University of North Carolina, the *Daily Tar Heel*, at the time of the original trials of the Chapel Hill demonstrators. "In the years to come, when all of this is behind us," the *Daily Tar Heel* had said, "UNC instructors William Wynn and Albert Amon, and Duke instructors Frederick Herzog, Robert Osborn, David Smith, Peter Klopfer, and Harmon Smith, will be seen in their true light: Men who braved the winds of near universal disapproval to be true to the ideals of their God and their country, and in so doing, helped the rest of us to ultimately do likewise."[28]

With the incorporation of the Speedy Trial Clause into the Due Process Clause in the *Klopfer* case, the only remaining important part of the Sixth

Amendment that had not been made applicable to the states was the Jury Trial Clause.[29] The Court had, of course, held in *Maxwell* v. *Dow* in 1900 that the Due Process Clause did not impose the Jury Trial Clause of the Sixth Amendment upon the states. The Court's language in "Gunplay" Maxwell's case had also indicated that a jury trial was not considered an essential element of due process of law and that the states were free to abolish jury trials in criminal cases altogether.[30]

The proposition that the states could abolish jury trials in criminal cases without doing violence to the Due Process Clause was occasionally repeated by the Court. Justice Cardozo had thus said in the *Palko* case in reference to the right of jury trial and to indictment by grand jury that few "would be so narrow or provincial as to maintain that a fair and enlightened system of justice would be impossible without them." In subsequent cases, however, the Court began to speak more respectfully of the right to a jury trial. The Court declared in 1961, for example, that "England, from whom the Western World has largely taken its concepts of individual liberty and of the dignity and worth of every man, has bequeathed to us safeguards for their preservation, the most priceless of which is that of trial by jury." And the Due Process Clause, the Court held, required that when a state accorded a defendant a jury trial, the essence of "the right to jury trial guarantees to the criminally accused a fair trial by a panel of impartial, 'indifferent' jurors. The failure to accord an accused a fair hearing violates even the minimal standards of due process."[31]

The Sixth Amendment, of course, also requires a trial by "an impartial jury," and some observers believe that the Court in fact incorporated this requirement of "impartiality" into the Due Process Clause in *Parker* v. *Gladden* in 1966. In the *Parker* case, the Court reversed a murder conviction because a court bailiff, who had been assigned to escort the jury in the case, had made prejudicial remarks to the jurors. "We believe that the statements of the bailiff to the jurors are controlled by the command of the Sixth Amendment, made applicable to the States through the Due Process Clause of the Fourteenth Amendment," the Court said. "It guarantees that 'the accused shall enjoy the right to a . . . trial, by an impartial jury . . . [and] be confronted with the witnesses against him. . . .'" If there had been no further comment by the Court, one could have assumed from this statement that it was intended to incorporate the Sixth Amendment's requirement of an impartial jury into the Due Process Clause. But the Court proceeded to hold that a defendant is entitled to a trial based on the evidence developed on the witness stand in a public courtroom, and in the *Parker* case, the Court said, "there is dispute neither as to what the bailiff, an officer of the State, said nor that when he said it he was not subjected to confrontation, cross-examination or other safeguards guaranteed to the petitioner." It had followed the undeviating rule, the Court concluded, "that the rights of confrontation and cross-examination are among the fundamental requirements of a constitutionally fair trial."[32]

If the statement of the Court regarding the Sixth Amendment was viewed in isolation, it might seem to say that the Jury Trial Clause, including the requirement of impartiality, was incorporated into the Due Process Clause. The Court's further comments, however, indicated that it was reversing the conviction in the *Parker* case primarily on the ground that the defendant had been denied the right of confrontation, and on the additional ground that the bailiff's remarks had rendered an impartial jury impossible. This was clearly the view of Justice Harlan, who in a dissenting opinion said that the "Court finds the bailiff's remarks to be in violation of the Sixth Amendment's confrontation requirement."[33]

It was nonetheless clear that the status of jury trials in criminal cases had been considerably elevated in the eyes of the Court since the decision in *Maxwell* v. *Dow* in 1900. By 1967, the Assistance of Counsel, the Speedy and Public Trial, the Confrontation, and the Compulsory Process Clauses of the Sixth Amendment had all been incorporated into the Due Process Clause, and it seemed only a matter of time until a case raising the question of incorporating the Jury Trial Clause would come before the Court. And *Duncan* v. *Louisiana*, decided by the Court in 1968, turned out to be just such a case.[34]

Justice in Plaquemines Parish: Gary Duncan's Case

Plaquemines Parish, Louisiana, proved to be one of the most obdurate of Southern communities in its resistance to desegregation. The political boss of the parish was Leander H. Perez, Sr., a rabid segregationist and a demagogue of the old school. Perez regarded the civil rights movement to be a "Zionist-Communist" conspiracy, and he adamantly fought any attempt to enforce desegregation or equal rights in Plaquemines Parish. When the federal government began to challenge voting discrimination in 1961, for example, 6,714 of the 8,633 whites in Plaquemines Parish were registered voters, but only 45 of the 2,897 black residents of the parish had succeeded in registering to vote. Anticipating civil rights demonstrations in the parish during the mid-1960s, Perez also prepared Fort St. Philip, built by the Spanish in 1746, as a prison for demonstrators. The powder magazines, some with water standing in them and all harboring swarms of mosquitoes, were converted into cells to hold what Perez called "anarchists, those who come here to overthrow the legally constituted government."[35]

When the Catholic parochial schools in southeastern Louisiana were ordered to desegregate by Church officials in 1962, Perez urged the people of Plaquemines Parish to resist and to cut off contributions to the Church.

Because of his leadership in resisting parochial school desegregation, Perez was excommunicated from the Church, but he continued his defiance. "Our people realize that deep unswerving responsibility to protect their children against the immoral course of forced racial integration," he declared. "I am a life-long Catholic and will continue to be so, regardless of communistic infiltration and the influence of the National Council of Christians and Jews upon our church leadership."[36]

Twelve years after the Supreme Court had declared public school segregation to be unconstitutional, the rigidly segregated Plaquemines Parish public-school system was challenged by the Justice Department in a suit filed in the United States District Court in New Orleans. Leander Perez again fought back with tenacity and addressed meetings throughout the parish urging the establishment of private schools, and the federal court enjoined parish officials to prevent the transfer of public school property to the new private schools. Perez also argued in the federal court that the Fourteenth Amendment had been illegally adopted and was therefore inapplicable to Plaquemines Parish.[37] Desegregation was just like Reconstruction in the South after the Civil War, Perez declared. "During the first Reconstruction period it was the military, now it is the courts hiding behind their dignity and backed up by the military."[38]

Federal Judge Herbert W. Christenberry issued what was, under the circumstances, a rather moderate desegregation decree requiring the immediate desegregation of the Plaquemines Parish public schools in grades one, seven, ten, twelve, and two others to be selected by the school authorities. It is "difficult to understand at this date," Judge Christenberry said, "how anyone can believe that he can operate a segregated school system." Leander Perez nevertheless denounced the court's decision, declaring that when he saw what the Justice Department was demanding in regard to desegregation, "my reaction was, 'My God, we will have to give up our rights of citizenship as Americans.'" The future of Plaquemines Parish, he said, was "not in the lap of the gods, but in the hands of the sadistic mixers."[39]

Given the atmosphere in Plaquemines Parish, the integration of the public schools in the parish was, not unexpectedly, punctuated by racial incidents between blacks and whites attending school together for the first time in the fall of 1966. Harassment by white students, for example, was encountered by Bert Grant and his cousin, Bernard St. Ann, who as black students were attending the parish's formerly all white Boothville-Venice school.

On October 18, 1966, Gary Duncan was driving south on Highway 23 in Plaquemines Parish. Duncan was a nineteen-year-old black who worked on a towboat. In the vicinity of the recently desegregated Boothville-Venice high school, Duncan saw his two cousins, Bert Grant and Bernard

St. Ann, confronted by four white boys beside the highway. Duncan inquired what the trouble was, and his cousins replied that the white boys apparently wanted to fight. Duncan told his cousins to get into his car. What happened next was later a matter of dispute. After an exchange of words with the white boys, Duncan claimed that he told one of them, Herman M. Landry, Jr., to go home and touched him on the elbow. Herman Landry claimed that Duncan slapped him hard on the arm.

P. E. Lathum, the head of a private school established in response to the desegregation of the parish schools, observed the encounter between the white boys and Duncan and called a deputy sheriff. Duncan's car was intercepted by the deputy, but after questioning the boys, the deputy told Duncan that he did not believe that he had assaulted young Landry, and Duncan was released. Nevertheless, three days later, on October 21, Duncan was arrested by Plaquemines Parish authorities and charged with cruelty to juveniles. Bail was set at $1000.[40]

Duncan's parents, Mr. and Mrs. Lambert R. Duncan, apparently felt that their son's arrest was part of the pattern of resistance to civil rights in the parish, and they traveled to New Orleans to contact a representative of the Lawyers Constitutional Defense Committee. The LCDC had been organized in 1964 by such groups as the American Civil Liberties Union, the American Jewish Congress, and the Congress of Racial Equality for the purpose of providing attorneys in civil rights litigation in those areas of the South where attorneys willing to engage in such litigation were few and far between. The LCDC's national office was in New York City, and it deployed volunteer lawyers in Mississippi, Louisiana, and Alabama and eventually established regional offices in Jackson, Mississippi, and New Orleans.[41]

The services of LCDC attorneys were sorely needed in Plaquemines Parish, since there were few if any attorneys there who were willing to engage in civil rights litigation. Yet civil rights attorneys from outside were intimidated when they dared to venture into the parish. In 1961, for example, Plaquemines Parish sheriff's deputies and members of the district attorney's office had raided a black bar in the parish called the Chicken Shack. The telephone was ripped off the wall, and two deputies with machine guns sprayed the bottles and glasses on the bar and on the shelves with bullets. Over one hundred blacks were arrested and charged with disturbing the peace.

Two lawyers representing the NAACP, Earl Amedee and A. M. Trudeau, Jr., had traveled from New Orleans to Plaquemines Parish to represent those arrested at the Chicken Shack. When they arrived at the courthouse at Pointe a la Hache, however, they were confronted by Perez and a group of whites. Perez demanded to know what "you two niggers are doing down here?" The lawyers refused to respond, but Perez told them that they "sure as hell will tell me or you're going to be in for some trouble." Amedee then said, "You know me, Judge. I'm Earl Amedee." But Perez replied, "You're a liar. I don't know any goddamn niggers." He would only tell them, Perez continued, that "those niggers have all pleaded guilty and paid their fines and gone back to their jobs where they should have been that night they were in the Chicken Shack." Fearing for their lives, Amedee and Trudeau quickly left Plaquemines Parish and, as Amedee said later, he had never returned.[42]

Gary Duncan's parents contacted Richard Sobol, who was the chief staff counsel for the LCDC in New Orleans. Born in New York City, Sobol was a graduate of Columbia Law School, where he had been an editor of the *Columbia Law Review* in his senior year. He had clerked for a year for a judge on the United States Court of Appeals for the Second Circuit and had been a staff attorney with the Federal Trade Commission before joining the Washington, D.C., firm of Arnold, Fortas, & Porter. Sobol had given up his position with Arnold, Fortas, & Porter to become a volunteer LCDC lawyer at $2,900 a year.[43]

Sobol and the other LCDC lawyers were at first reluctant to enter the *Duncan* case, since it seemed to be a relatively minor case and was out of the mainstream of their concerns—primarily litigation implementing the Civil Rights Act of 1964. Sobol became convinced, however, that Gary Duncan's case was part of the pattern of anti–civil rights intimidation and harassment in Plaquemines Parish, and he finally agreed with some "trepidation" to represent Duncan.[44]

On November 21, 1966, a hearing was held before Judge Eugene E. Leon, Jr., in the Twenty-Fifth Judicial District Court in Plaquemines Parish on the cruelty-to-juveniles charge against Duncan. Representing Duncan at the hearing, Richard Sobol filed a motion to quash the charge on the ground that such a charge, under Louisiana law, could only be made against a person having some parental control or supervision over the juvenile so abused. Since Duncan occupied no such position in relation to young Landry, Sobol argued that the charge was obviously invalid.

After the hearing at which Sobol made this motion to quash, Assistant District Attorney Daryl Bubrig advised Herman Landry's parents that the cruelty-to-juveniles charge was not going to stick. Mrs. Landry promptly signed an affidavit charging Gary Duncan with simple battery, and on November 25, Duncan was rearrested on the battery charge and bond was set at $1500. Bubrig subsequently *nol-prossed* the cruelty-to-juveniles charge, but Duncan was brought to trial on the battery charge on January 25, 1967.[45]

Again representing Duncan, Sobol filed a demand for a jury trial on the battery count. Noting that the offense of simple battery was punishable in Louisiana by a maximum sentence of two years in prison, Sobol argued that the Sixth Amendment's Jury Trial Clause applied to the states via the Due Process Clause and that jury trials were required where a defendant would be subject to a maximum potential sentence of more than six months in jail. Judge Leon, however, rejected Sobol's demand for a jury trial in the *Duncan* case. "The Court is very familiar with this statute fixing the juries," Leon said. "Misdemeanors are not tried by jury with or without hard labor. It's a five-man jury with hard labor or a twelve-man jury and nine men concurring; capital must be a twelve-man jury, twelve men concurring. These are the requirements under the Louisiana law. The Court is going to deny your request."[46]

Sobol had therefore converted the *Duncan* case into a test of whether the Jury Trial Clause of the Sixth Amendment applied to the states. As Judge Leon had indicated, under Louisiana law all offenses that were punishable by imprisonment but not at hard labor were tried without juries. If imprisonment at hard labor was the possible punishment for an offense, Louisiana law provided for a jury of five and a unanimous verdict. Offenses punishable necessarily by imprisonment at hard labor required a jury of twelve, and the vote of nine jurors was necessary to convict. Only in capital cases did Louisiana law require a jury of twelve and a unanimous verdict. Since the offense of simple battery was classified as a high misdemeanor under Louisiana law, punishable by a maximum of two years in prison but not at hard labor, Judge Leon had denied Sobol's request for a jury trial in the *Duncan* case.

The prosecution of Gary Duncan was handled by District Attorney Leander Perez, Jr., and Assistant District Attorney Darryl Bubrig, while Sobol continued to represent Duncan at the trial. The prosecution called Herman Landry as a witness, and he testified that Duncan had hit him hard on the arm, testimony that was confirmed by two of Landry's companions in the encounter with Duncan. Gary Duncan and his cousins, on the other hand, denied that Duncan had hit young Landry. But P. E. Lathum, the head of the private school who had witnessed the incident, testified that Duncan had "made a pass at the white teenager, hitting him on the arm, knocking his arm up around his shoulders."[47]

After the testimony had been presented, Judge Leon found Duncan guilty of battery. "The Court," he said, "taking into consideration Mr. Lathum's testimony, a man who was not even in the discussion, or whatever we may call it between six boys on the side of the street, and the testimony of the victim himself, Mr. Landry, that this blow was sufficient to sting him, I think the State for those reasons has proved to me beyond a reasonable doubt that the defendant is guilty of simple battery." Duncan was sentenced to pay a fine of $150 and costs and serve sixty days in the parish prison, or an additional twenty days in the event the fine and costs were not paid. Bond for Duncan, pending an appeal, was set by Judge

Leon at $1500. Duncan was rearrested and spent a few hours in jail until money for the bond was raised.[48]

Richard Sobol renewed his jury trial argument in a bill of exceptions filed on February 1, 1967, but Judge Leon again rejected the argument that the trial of a high misdemeanor required a jury. The *Duncan* case was then appealed to the Supreme Court of Louisiana, but that court affirmed Duncan's conviction on February 20, holding in a memorandum opinion that there was no "error of law in the ruling complained of."[49]

On the day following the Louisiana Supreme Court's decision, Sobol telephoned Judge Leon and sought an appointment to arrange for Duncan's bond to remain in effect pending an appeal to the United States Supreme Court. Judge Leon promptly informed Assistant District Attorney Bubrig that Sobol was returning to Plaquemines Parish, and District Attorney Leander Perez, Jr., signed a bill of information charging Sobol with practicing law in Louisiana without a license. Judge Leon then issued a bench warrant for Sobol's arrest, and he was arrested leaving the courthouse in Pointe a la Hache after his appointment with Judge Leon. Sobol was taken to the parish prison, was photographed and fingerprinted, and had his personal belongings seized. He was incarcerated for four hours until his bail, set at $1500, was raised. Meanwhile Judge Leon issued a bench warrant for the arrest of Gary Duncan on the ground that the refusal of the Louisiana Supreme Court to review his case had cancelled his appeal bond. Duncan was arrested again on February 23 and jailed for twenty-four hours before another bond of $1500 could be raised.[50]

After his release from the Plaquemines Parish prison, Sobol filed suit for an injunction and a declaratory judgment against the Louisiana unauthorized-practice statutes in the United States District Court in New Orleans. He charged in his complaint that the enforcement against him of the Louisiana unauthorized-practice statutes violated the First Amendment and the Equal Protection Clause of the Fourteenth Amendment. To prevent his service as a nonresident attorney in association with a member of the state bar in nonfee civil rights suits, Sobol contended, would effectively prevent needy civil rights litigants from obtaining legal assistance.[51]

While this federal suit was pending, Sobol pursued the appeal of *Duncan* v. *Louisiana* to the United States Supreme Court, arguing that the Jury Trial Clause of the Sixth Amendment should be applied to all serious state crimes under the Due Process Clause.[52] The Louisiana attorney general argued, on the other hand, that under the Court's decision in *Maxwell* v. *Dow*, a jury trial was not an essential element of due process of law in a state proceeding.[53]

Opening the oral argument of the *Duncan* case on January 17, 1968, Richard Sobol told the Court that the issue in the case was, "namely, whether the Due Process Clause of the Fourteenth Amendment secures the right to trial by jury in state criminal proceedings." After describing the Louisiana jury system, and noting that Louisiana law did not provide a jury trial in battery cases, he argued that the Court should hold that under the Sixth and Fourteenth Amendments the states were required to afford defendants jury trials in all cases in which the potential maximum sentence was in excess of six months imprisonment.[54]

Justice Fortas interrupted Sobol to ask, "I think it would be easier for me if you tell me what you think we ought to decide. What rule should this Court adopt? What rule are you urging us to adopt?" Sobol replied, "Your Honor, the rule that we are contending for is a rule that would apply the Sixth Amendment right [to a jury trial] in its full force." Fortas inquired what that meant, and Sobol stated that it meant that the states must afford jury trials in all criminal cases in which the potential maximum sentence was in excess of six months, since a test based on actual sentence would be impossible to administer. "In other words," Fortas said, "we ought to lay down a rule that's applicable to all of the states in which we say that if the potential sentence exceeds six months then the jury trial requirement of the Sixth Amendment has to be observed by each state?" Sobol agreed that that was the position he was contending for, but he noted that it would not be necessary for the Court to adopt the six-months rule in the *Duncan* case, since a potential maximum sentence of two years was involved in the case. He suggested that, as in the *Gideon* case, the Court might not want to spell out what was a "serious" offense requiring a jury trial, just as it had not spelled out what the outer limits of the right to counsel were. "You're saying," Fortas again interrupted, "number one, you think it would be nice if we said, if we announce that the six-months rule is applicable to the states; number two, if we don't want to be that bold, we can adopt a *Gideon* approach and leave it for the future. Now I want to ask you one other question, does your analysis mean that the states would have to adopt a twelve-man jury system and a unanimous jury verdict?" Sobol replied in the affirmative, saying that "the Court has so often held that when the Constitution uses the word *jury*" it intended a certain meaning. "You're asking us to overrule precedents, past precedents in this Court?" Justice Harlan asked. "Yes, sir," Sobol replied, and continued to insist that the term *jury* meant a twelve-person jury with a unanimous verdict, and that when the Court applied rights in the Bill of Rights to the states via the Due Process Clause, "it's not the watered down right, . . . it is the full right [and] it means whatever the federal right means." But Justice Brennan noted that the potential maximum sentence that Duncan could have received was two years. "We don't have to decide today, in this case at least, do we," Brennan said, "that that means a twelve-man jury, a unanimous verdict [in] all offenses carrying more than six months, we don't have to reach any of that, do we?"

Still fighting a valiant rearguard action against the incorporationists,

Justice Harlan then challenged Sobol's reliance upon the selective-incorporation approach in the case.

JUSTICE HARLAN: If your thesis is adopted, would not the next logical, if not inevitable, step be also to say that the Seventh Amendment is incorporated to impose a jury trial in every twenty-dollar lawsuit?

MR. SOBOL: No, sir, I don't think that that's the logic of our position.

JUSTICE HARLAN: Then you would incorporate the Sixth Amendment jury-trial provision, but then stop short of incorporating the Seventh Amendment?

MR. SOBOL: Yes, sir. Our position in this case certainly does not involve the logic that the Seventh Amendment necessarily follows. . . .

JUSTICE HARLAN: How do you choose between them? How do you pick and choose among the provisions of the Bill of Rights once you accept the premises of incorporation?

MR. SOBOL: Well, the Court has said, the Court has said recently that the way to pick and choose is by examining the fundamental nature of the right and whether it is essential to a fair trial.

JUSTICE HARLAN: That is the Due Process Clause and not incorporation.

MR. SOBOL: Well, I'm referring to the opinion of the Court in *Washington* v. *Texas*, and to the opinion of the Court where, in discussing the incorporation of the compulsory-process provision, the Court did not say that without implying—I don't believe that every provision of the Bill of Rights applies to the states—that the Court will look to the question of fundamentalness and essentiality. And, I think, in those cases, the Court has put special weight on the criminal trial; I think that while there is great weight to the idea that what the Court has done so far in the criminal-procedure area in incorporating Bill of Rights's protections may well lead you to the conclusion that all of the criminal procedures are incorporated, which is not necessarily our position in this case, I think that the rule in civil cases could well be different. I think there are different considerations that this Court has noted.

JUSTICE HARLAN: How do you get that out of the Constitution? What provision of the Constitution says that some of these provisions of the Bill of Rights go in lock, stock, and barrel to the states and others don't?

MR. SOBOL: Well, none says that. But the Court has interpreted the words *due process* in connection with applying Bill of Rights guarantees. . . .

JUSTICE HARLAN: That's a different concept; that's a different concept. Incorporation is not due process. Incorporation involves, that there's something in the Constitution that despite the language of the Bill of Rights limiting those protections to the federal authority, there's something in the Constitution that brings the Bill of Rights also in its full-blown form into operation against the states. My question to you is, how can you separate one provision of the Bill of Rights from the other under the theory of incorporation?

MR. SOBOL: I would rely, in answer to Your Honor's question, on the decisions of this Court, which have looked to, have made a judgment as to the fundamentalness and the essentiality of the right—*Washington* v. *Texas*, *Pointer* v. *Texas*, *Klopfer* v. *North Carolina*, and, I think, *Gideon*.

At this point in the exchange between Harlan and Sobol, the incorporationists decided to intervene in defense of their approach to the Due Process Clause and the nationalization process.

JUSTICE BLACK: What about *Palko*, and what about *Twining*, and what about *Gideon*?

MR. SOBOL: *Palko* and *Twining* go the other way. . . .

JUSTICE BRENNAN: They applied the selective test, didn't they?

JUSTICE BLACK: Yes.

JUSTICE BRENNAN: Didn't *Palko* introduce the selective test?

MR. SOBOL: And found it not to apply, yes sir.

JUSTICE BRENNAN: As to some, but as to others it found that it did apply, didn't it? Has the Court done anything else but that?

MR. SOBOL: No, sir.

JUSTICE BRENNAN: And isn't there a distinction between the Seventh and Sixth Amendments?

MR. SOBOL: I certainly think that there is a distinction between the Sixth and Seventh. . . .

Incidentally, Justice Brennan continued, "do you get any comfort . . . from our decision last term in *Parker* and *Gladden*?" Sobol replied that he did indeed, and Brennan suggested, "Do you think we crossed that bridge in *Parker* and *Gladden*" in applying the Jury Trial Clause to the states? Sobol replied that the Court appeared in the *Parker* case to be acting on the assumption that the Jury Trial Clause applied to the states, but Justice White interrupted to point out that "there is a confrontation point in that one," and that "as a matter of fact, [the Court] ruled on—the words it used said both [the right to confrontation and to an impartial jury had been violated in the *Parker* case]."

Justice Brennan also continued to insist that the Court need not reach the question of whether a jury was constitutionally required to be composed of twelve persons. "I still don't understand, Mr. Sobol, why we have to reach the question of the twelve man jury . . . ," he said. "It's just not clear to me why we have to reach this question at this time. . . ." Sobol replied that the question was before the Court, and that unless the issue were settled in the *Duncan* case, the issue might well be back before the Court again if Duncan were retried and reconvicted in Louisiana by a jury composed of fewer than twelve persons. Despite their disagreement on this issue, Brennan could be heard whispering to one of his colleagues as Sobol closed his argument, "He did a nice job, didn't he?"

Arguing on behalf of the state of Louisiana, Assistant Attorney General Dorothy D. Wolbrette ran into immediate trouble with her argument that the right to a trial by jury should depend upon the actual sentence given a defendant, rather than upon the potential maximum sentence involved in a case. Since Duncan had received only a sixty-day sentence, she argued, he had not been entitled to a jury trial even if the Jury Trial Clause did apply to the states. Justice Black interrupted at that point and asked, "Are you saying that, you've got to wait about determining whether you have a right to a jury trial until the case is tried and you see how much the judge gives you?" Wolbrette replied that such a position was justified by the Court's decisions. "What I'm asking you," Black persisted, "that you're arguing to us, that a defendant cannot learn whether he's entitled to a jury trial until he's tried by a judge, and convicted and given less than a year?" Receiving another affirmative answer, Black said, "Well, wouldn't that be a very silly ruling . . . ?"

Mrs. Wolbrette insisted that a judge could hear some of the evidence in a case and then determine whether or not the defendant was likely to receive a sufficiently severe sentence that would justify trial by jury. Chief Justice Warren challenged the validity of such a system, noting that it would violate the prohibition against double jeopardy. "How could a judge partially try a man," Warren asked, without putting the defendant in jeopardy? "Well, frankly, Your Honor," Wolbrette replied, "I haven't researched that point. . . ."

Simple battery, the offense with which Gary Duncan had been charged, Mrs. Wolbrette continued, was a typical simple misdemeanor that did not require a jury trial. She noted that at the time of the adoption of the Sixth Amendment, there were numerous much-more-serious offenses that were not tried by juries under the common law. The punishment for simple battery, she also noted, involved a sentence to the parish jail, not the state penitentiary. In response to questions by Justice Marshall, she indicated that there was a "substantial difference" between being sentenced to the parish jail and to the penitentiary—including the lack of hard labor at the jail, the fact that civil disabilities were attached to a conviction for a penitentiary offense, and the fact that it was "certainly a more disgraceful thing" to be sent to the penitentiary than to the parish jail.

"What is the maximum term of imprisonment provided under any of the criminal statutes [in Louisiana] that is not a felony?" Justice Fortas asked. "There is one for three years, which is wearing a hood in the streets, except on Mardi Gras," Wolbrette replied. "How much punishment, how much do they get for wearing it on Mardi Gras?" Fortas inquired. "Nothing. Nothing," Mrs. Wolbrette replied. "You're punished if you don't wear one on Mardi Gras."

The test that should be applied to a state trial, Wolbrette continued, was whether under the Due Process Clause a fair trial had been afforded a defendant, "and a judge could try any case fairly." A state had the right to modify the scope of the right to trial by jury, she said, and since "the *Bar-*

ron decision in 1833, this Court has held in an unbroken line of decisions that the Bill of Rights applies only against the federal government, and not against the states," with the result that "the Sixth Amendment does not apply directly to the states." If the Jury Trial Clause were applied to the states, Wolbrette argued, then each state would necessarily be required to adopt the twelve-person, unanimous jury requirement under the decisions of the Court interpreting the meaning of juries. "Well," Justice White interrupted, "are those decisions any more unchangeable than the ones that the defendant here asks us to overrule about the applicability of the Sixth Amendment [to the states]?"

"It isn't reasonable to argue" that the eighteenth-century common law jury was essential to a fair trial under the Due Process Clause, Mrs. Wolbrette nevertheless argued, and neither "logic nor history" supported the idea that a jury was necessary to a fair trial. Justice Fortas asked if there were not something in the Magna Charta regarding jury trials. "Magna Charta did not guarantee jury trial to anybody," Wolbrette replied, since Parliament had felt free to modify the jury trial right in Great Britain at will. Magna Charta did indicate, Fortas insisted, that "there were some old fellows in the thirteenth century who thought that the jury was a fairly valuable institution," and, although such an indication was not "dispositive," it did indicate an Anglo-American tradition that a jury was important in the administration of criminal justice. The state of Louisiana, Mrs. Wolbrette replied in the conclusion of her argument, did not "deny the value of jury trial, we just say that it may be valuable but it just isn't essential. . . . We just say that value and desirability [are] not constitutional mandate[s]."

If ghosts inhabit the Supreme Court building, those of J. W. N. Whitecotton and "Gunplay" Maxwell must have been in attendance on May 20, 1968, when the decision in *Duncan* v. *Louisiana* was announced, and in an opinion by Justice White, the Jury Trial Clause of the Sixth Amendment was held to apply to the states via the Due Process Clause.[55] White acknowledged that the Court's decision in *Maxwell* v. *Dow* was contrary to the result it had now reached in the *Duncan* case, but he pointed out that the Court's interpretation of the Due Process Clause had shifted dramatically since the decision in the *Maxwell* case.

"In one sense recent cases applying provisions of the first eight Amendments to the States represent a new approach to the 'incorporation' debate," White said. "Earlier the Court can be seen as having asked, when inquiring whether some particular procedural safeguard was required of a State, if a civilized system could be imagined that would not accord the particular protection." In more recent cases, he continued, the Court had "proceeded upon the valid assumption that state criminal processes are not imaginary and theoretical schemes but actual systems bearing virtually every characteristic of the common-law system that has been developing contemporaneously in England and in this country. The question thus is whether given this kind of system a particular procedure is fundamental —whether, that is, a procedure is necessary to an Anglo-American regime of ordered liberty."[56]

In approaching the nationalization of a procedural protection in the Bill of Rights, White said, "it might be said that the limitation in question is not necessarily fundamental to fairness in every criminal system that might be imagined but is fundamental in the context of the criminal processes maintained by the American States. When the inquiry is approached in this way the question whether the States can impose criminal punishment without granting a jury trial appears quite different from the way it appeared in the older cases opining that States might abolish jury trial."[57]

Viewing the right to trial by jury from this standpoint, White said, the Court found that the right reflected a "profound judgment about the way in which law should be enforced and justice administered." Jury trials were thus intended to guard the accused "against the corrupt or overzealous prosecutor and against the compliant, biased, or eccentric judge," while also reflecting a reluctance to "entrust plenary powers over the life and liberty of the citizen to one judge or to a group of judges." The right to trial by jury must, White therefore said, be considered "fundamental to the American scheme of justice," and the Court must hold that "the Fourteenth Amendment guarantees a right of jury trial in all criminal cases which—were they to be tried in a federal court—would come within the Sixth Amendment's guarantee."[58]

Having held that the Jury Trial Clause of the Sixth Amendment was applicable to state criminal proceedings, White turned to the question of whether Gary Duncan had been entitled to a jury trial in his case. Although he acknowledged that the Jury Trial Clause did not require juries in the trial of petty offenses, White held that the Court should look to "the length of the authorized sentence or the seriousness of other punishment" in determining whether a jury trial was required in a given case. He therefore rejected Louisiana's argument that the Court should consider only the actual sentence in determining the applicability of the Jury Trial Clause in a given case. Declining to "settle in this case the exact location of the line between petty and serious offenses," White nevertheless concluded that "a crime punishable by two years in prison is, based on past and contemporary standards in this country, a serious crime and not a petty offense." Gary Duncan was therefore held to have been "entitled to a jury trial, and it was error to deny it."[59]

Justice Fortas concurred in the Court's holding that the states must accord defendants jury trials in serious criminal cases, but he did not agree "that the tail must go with the hide: that when we hold, influenced by the

Sixth Amendment, that 'due process' requires that the States accord the right of jury trial for all but petty offenses, we automatically import all of the ancillary rules which have been or may hereafter be developed incidental to the right to jury trial in the federal courts." Fortas particularly objected to the proposition that the Due Process Clause would require unanimous verdicts and juries of twelve in state criminal trials. "We may well conclude that these and other features of federal jury practice are by no means fundamental—that they are not essential to due process of law—and that they are not obligatory on the States."[60]

Fortas acknowledged that the Court had applied the First and Fourth Amendments and parts of the Fifth and Sixth Amendments to the states in the identical way they applied in federal proceedings, and he conceded that he "need not quarrel with the specific conclusion in these specific instances. But unless one adheres slavishly to the incorporation theory, body and substance, the same conclusion need not be superimposed upon the jury trial right." Without repudiating the incorporation approach to the other rights in the Bill of Rights that the Court had applied to the states, he therefore urged a fair-trial approach in regard to jury trials that would allow the Court to "welcome state variations which do not impair—indeed, which may advance—the theory and purpose of trial by jury."[61]

Many of the questions raised by Justice Fortas, and other questions left unanswered by the Court in the *Duncan* case, were answered by subsequent decisions of the Court. In 1970, the Court thus held that the right to trial by jury applied to all cases involving a potential maximum sentence of more than six months imprisonment, but it also held that juries need not be composed of twelve persons and indeed might be composed of as few as six members. Finally, in 1972, the Court additionally sustained nonunanimous verdicts by twelve-person juries involving votes of ten to two and nine to three. Ironically, the deciding vote in the latter holding was cast by Justice Powell, who, like Justice Harlan before him, adhered to the *Twining* approach to nationalization and believed that the jury-trial requirement was not the same when applied to the states under the Due Process Clause as the Sixth Amendment's Jury Trial Clause. The paradoxical result was that the states may permit nonunanimous verdicts but the federal government may not.[62]

The *Duncan* case also proved to be the occasion for the last full-scale confrontation between Justices Black and Harlan and their fundamentally different approaches to the nationalization of the Bill of Rights. Joined by Justice Douglas in a concurring opinion, Black once again defended the total-incorporation theory that he had advanced more than twenty years earlier in the *Adamson* case. Although he acknowledged that the Court had never accepted total incorporation, Black noted that the Court had accepted a selective-incorporation approach to the Due Process Clause, and that he was "very happy to support this selective process through which the Court has since the *Adamson* case held most of the specific Bill of Rights' protections applicable to the States to the same extent they are applicable to the Federal Government."[63]

Answering the critics of his analysis of the intentions of the framers of the Fourteenth Amendment, Black declared that the total-incorporation theory that he had announced in his *Adamson* dissent had been "the product of years of study and research" in which he had brought to bear his "10 years of legislative experience as a Senator of the United States, not a bad way, I suspect, to learn the value of what is said in legislative debates, committee discussions, committee reports and various other steps taken in the course of passage of bills, resolutions, and proposed constitutional amendments." Black indicated that he had also studied the criticisms of his total-incorporation theory, including those of Professor Charles Fairman, but he nevertheless had "no doubt in my mind that both its sponsors and those who opposed it believed the Fourteenth Amendment made the first eight Amendments of the Constitution (the Bill of Rights) applicable to the States."[64]

Justice Harlan's fair-trial approach to the Due Process Clause, Black charged, allowed judges to read their personal views of morality and ethics into the concept of due process, rather than defining due process within "boundaries fixed by the written words of the Constitution." The fair-trial approach also undermined the principle of federalism, he argued, because it restricted the states to "practices which a majority of this Court is willing to approve on a case-by-case basis" and allowed the Justices "to strike down state laws they do not like."[65]

Black therefore declared that "I believe as strongly as ever that the Fourteenth Amendment was intended to make the Bill of Rights applicable to the States." He was willing to support the majority's selective-incorporation approach, however, because "although perhaps less historically supportable," such an approach did limit the Court "in the Fourteenth Amendment field to specific Bill of Rights' protections only and keeps judges from roaming at will in their own notions of what policies outside the Bill of Rights are desirable and what are not." And, in addition, Black concluded, the selective-incorporation process had "already worked to make most of the Bill of Rights' protections applicable to the States."[66]

Answering Black's opinion, Justice Harlan, joined by Justice Stewart, again defended the *Twining* theory that the Due Process Clause protected rights only similar to those in the Bill of Rights. Black's total-incorporation approach had never been accepted by the Court, Harlan noted, and the "overwhelming historical evidence marshalled by Professor Fairman demonstrates, to me conclusively, that the Congressmen and state legislators who wrote, debated, and ratified the Fourteenth Amendment did not think they were 'incorporating' the Bill of Rights. . . ." Neither "history, nor sense," he declared, "supports using the Fourteenth Amendment to put the States in a constitutional strait-jacket with respect to their own development in the administration of the criminal law."[67]

For one who did not accept Black's total-incorporation theory, Harlan indicated that there was only one "method of analysis that has any internal logic. That is to start with the words 'liberty' and 'due process of law' and attempt to define them in a way that accords with American traditions and our system of government." With this approach, Harlan acknowledged that the Bill of Rights was relevant because the Due Process Clause did impose on the states restrictions "that parallel Bill of Rights restrictions on federal action," and because the Bill of Rights "is evidence, at various points, of the content Americans find in the term 'liberty' and of American standards of fundamental fairness." But when the Court held that the Due Process Clause protected rights similar to those in the Bill of Rights, Harlan continued, "the logically critical thing . . . was not that the rights had been found in the Bill of Rights, but that they were deemed, in the context of American legal history, to be fundamental."[68]

By rejecting Black's theory of total incorporation and instead embracing the selective-incorporation approach, Harlan said, the majority of the Court did not appear to be willing to accept Black's interpretation of the history of the adoption of the Fourteenth Amendment or to be willing to pursue the kind of demanding analysis that the fair-trial approach would require. The majority, he charged, had therefore "compromised on the ease of the incorporationist position, without its internal logic. It has simply assumed that the question before us is whether the Jury Trial Clause of the Sixth Amendment should be incorporated into the Fourteenth, jot-for-jot and case-for-case, or ignored. Then the Court merely declares that the clause in question is 'in' rather than 'out.'"[69]

Harlan argued that, rather than accepting either the total- or selective-incorporation positions, the Court should have inquired in the *Duncan* case whether Louisiana had violated an "element of fundamental procedural fairness." Utilizing this approach, he concluded that juries were not essential elements in fair trials for state criminal defendants. A jury trial, he concluded, was "one means of trying criminal cases; it is a good means, but it is not the only fair means, and it is not demonstrably better than the alternatives States might devise."[70]

Despite Harlan's renewed protest against the incorporation theory, Richard Sobol had succeeded in establishing jury trials as a requirement of the Due Process Clause in the *Duncan* case, and he had in addition successfully challenged the Perez regime in Plaquemines Parish. His suit for a declaratory judgment and an injunction against the Louisiana unauthorized-practice-of-law statutes resulted in the first important federal court challenge to the attempts of the southern states to bar out-of-state attorneys from representing civil rights litigants. In an opinion announced on July 22, 1968, the United States District Court in New Orleans tongue-lashed the Plaquemines Parish authorities and enjoined the application of the unauthorized-practice statutes to Sobol.

Sobol's client, Gary Duncan, had been arrested four times in Plaquemines Parish and required to post $5500 in bail while earning $65 a week and supporting a wife and baby, the court noted. District Attorney Perez, the court also pointed out, had stated in 1965 that "if any known agitator were to appear in Plaquemines Parish, his mere presence would amount to a disturbance of the peace, since he was an outsider." The prosecution instituted by the Plaquemines Parish authorities against Sobol, the court concluded, "was meant to show Sobol that civil rights lawyers were not welcome in the parish, and that their defense of Negroes involved in cases growing out of civil rights efforts would not be tolerated. It was meant also as a warning to other civil rights lawyers and to Negroes in the parish who might consider retaining civil rights lawyers to advance their rights to equal opportunity and equal treatment under the Equal Protection Clause of the Fourteenth Amendment."[71]

Richard Sobol had also petitioned the federal court to enjoin further prosecution of Gary Duncan on the battery charge, but the court ruled that that question had not been raised in Sobol's original complaint and declined to act on the issue. Despite the Supreme Court's decision applying the Jury Trial Clause to the states, therefore, Gary Duncan remained subject to retrial on the battery charge, and District Attorney Leander Perez, Jr., indicated that he would reprosecute the case against Duncan. Lawyers Constitutional Defense Committee attorneys, however, filed suit in the United States District Court in New Orleans for an injunction against a reprosecution of Duncan, and on October 20, 1970, the court granted the injunction.

The court noted that between 1965 and 1970, there had been eighty-four prosecutions for battery in Plaquemines Parish and in only fifteen of those cases were mandatory jail terms imposed, in contrast to the sixty-day sentence given to Gary Duncan. Additionally, in only five of the cases had the sentences exceeded that given to Duncan. The court also noted that after Sobol's arrest for unauthorized practice of the law, Duncan had attempted to post bond pending the appeal of his case to the Supreme Court, but had been assured that the bond posted after his trial and conviction was still in effect. After Sobol filed suit in federal court challenging the unauthorized-practice statutes, however, District Attorney Perez ordered Duncan's bond canceled, and Duncan was arrested late at night and taken to the Pointe a la Hache jail. During the trip to the jail, the court said, Duncan had been "ridiculed, frightened, and insulted" by the arresting officers.

Relatives of Duncan had pledged $1500 worth of property to bail him out of jail, but were informed by the sheriff's office that twice that amount of property would have to be pledged, although Louisiana law provided that property equal to the amount of the bond was sufficient.

The court concluded that the "plaintiff has maintained the heavy burden required for an injunction against a pending state criminal proceeding," since the "proceeding against Duncan in state court is maintained by the defendant in bad faith and for purposes of harassment." There was, the court held, "no legitimate state interest in the reprosecution of Duncan." The alleged violation of the law by Duncan, the court said, "was so slight and technical as to be generally reserved for law school hypotheticals rather than criminal prosecutions." If Duncan were required to face retrial on the battery charge, the court also held, "it would constitute an unmistakable message to Negroes in Plaquemines Parish that it is unprofitable to step outside familiar patterns and to seek to rely on federal rights to oppose the policies of certain parish officials."[72]

The federal court therefore enjoined District Attorney Perez from further prosecution of Gary Duncan on the battery charge. Although this decision was appealed to the United States Court of Appeals for the Fifth Circuit, on June 14, 1971, that court affirmed the district court's issuance of the injunction. [73] The case was then appealed to the Supreme Court, but the Court denied certiorari on November 9, 1971.[74] Gary Duncan was at last, for the first time in five years, free from the threat of prosecution in Plaquemines Parish.

11

The Culmination
of the Nationalization Process
The *Benton* Case

With the Court's decision in the *Duncan* case imposing the Jury Trial Clause on the states, the list of those provisions in the Bill of Rights that had not been applied to the states via the Due Process Clause included relatively few important rights. In his concurring opinion in the *Duncan* case, Justice Black had therefore been correct when he noted that the selective-incorporation process had resulted in making almost all of the Bill of Rights applicable to the states.

By 1968, however, the Court had become the object of a sustained political attack. The Warren Court had offended a wide array of interests with its decisions regarding desegregation, reapportionment, obscenity, school prayer and Bible-reading, and criminal procedure. But it was the Court's criminal-procedure decisions, most of which were based upon the nationalization of the Bill of Rights, that produced the greatest outcry from the Court's critics. *Miranda* v. *Arizona*, requiring the police to warn suspects of their right against self-incrimination and their right to counsel, came to symbolize the charge by the Court's critics that it had "handcuffed" the police.[1] And the eruption of the urban ghettos, the occurrence of campus riots and disorders, mostly related to the Vietnam War, and a rapid rise in the general crime rate all combined to make the 1960s appear to many Americans to be a peculiar time for the Court to be strengthening the rights of criminal defendants.[2]

This popular revulsion against the crime and disorder plaguing American society was fully exploited by the law-and-order appeal of Richard Nixon's campaign for the presidency in 1968. "I pledge that the first civil right of every American," Nixon said during the campaign, "the right to be free from domestic violence, will again be recognized and protected in this great country of ours."[3] And he laid the blame for much of the lawless condition of the country at the doors of the courts, especially the Supreme Court. Some "of our courts and their decisions . . . have gone too far in weakening the peace forces as against the criminal forces in this country," Nixon asserted, and the solution was the strengthening of the "peace forces" against the "criminal forces" by the appointment of "strict con-structionists" to the Supreme Court.[4]

By the time of the 1968 election, it was clear that Nixon would, if elected, have the opportunity to name a new chief justice. Chief Justice Warren, who had led the Court since 1953, announced in 1968 that he would retire as soon as a replacement was appointed and confirmed. Presi-dent Johnson named Justice Abe Fortas as Warren's replacement, but strong opposition in the Senate, Johnson's lame-duck status, and his un-popularity because of the Vietnam War combined to force the withdrawal of Fortas's nomination. The naming of Warren's replacement therefore fell to President Nixon, who requested Warren to serve until the end of the Court's 1968–69 term. In 1969, Warren was finally replaced as chief justice by Judge Warren Earl Burger of the District of Columbia Court of Ap-peals, a leading critic of the Warren Court's criminal-procedure decisions.[5]

During the abortive hearings on his confirmation as chief justice, Jus-tice Fortas's ethics had come under attack because of his acceptance of compensation for off-the-bench activities. After the defeat of his nomina-tion as chief justice, it was revealed that Fortas had agreed to receive $20,000 for life from financier Louis E. Wolfson, who was at the time sub-ject to investigation by the Securities and Exchange Commission. The out-cry that followed this revelation forced Fortas to resign from the Court on May 14, 1969.[6] The Fortas resignation offered President Nixon his second appointment to the Court within his first year in office, but the adminis-tration's bungling and the Senate's reassertion of its role in the appoint-ment process led to the defeat of Nixon's first two nominees to replace Fortas: Judge Clement Haynsworth and Judge G. Harrold Carswell. Judge Harry A. Blackmun of the Court of Appeals for the Eighth Circuit was finally confirmed as Fortas's successor in June of 1970.[7]

A Rogue and Vagabond in Maryland: The *Benton* Case

The Court was therefore on the eve of a major period of transition when the last of the nationalization cases, *Benton* v. *Maryland*, was decided on June 23, 1969. The *Benton* case began when Mr. and Mrs. Marion E. West returned to their home at 4711 Allentown Road in Forestville, Mary-land, on February 4, 1965. The Wests discovered a station wagon backed up to the garage of the house and encountered two men inside, who ripped the telephone from the wall and fled. Missing from the West home was a blender, a toaster, a hydraulic jack, two electric heaters, three cases of whiskey, a fire screen, and a few rare coins.[8]

The Wests subsequently identified John Dalmer Benton as one of the men they had encountered robbing their home. Like many criminal defen-dants, John Benton was not exactly an heroic figure. His criminal record began with a conviction for grand larceny in Washington, D.C., in April of 1938. That conviction was followed by convictions for robbery, violation of parole, contempt of court, and petty larceny between 1940 and 1958 in the District of Columbia. In 1961, Benton was again convicted of grand larceny, this time in the state of Maryland, and he was sentenced to five years in prison. Although he was free again in 1964, the state of Maryland continued to frown upon Benton's activities, and he was convicted of being a "rogue and vagabond" and fined one hundred dollars.[9]

In 1965, Benton was indicted on charges of burglary, common law housebreaking, and larceny in connection with the robbery of the Wests' home. Benton received a jury trial in the Circuit Court of Prince George's County and was convicted of burglary, although the jury acquitted him of larceny and the state abandoned the housebreaking charge at the trial. He was sentenced on August 16, 1965, to serve ten years in the Maryland House of Corrections on the burglary conviction, but his conviction was appealed to the Maryland Court of Appeals, the highest appellate court in Maryland.[10]

While Benton's appeal was pending, the Maryland Court of Appeals decided *Schowgurow* v. *State*, in which it held that article 36 of the Maryland Declaration of Rights was unconstitutional. Article 36 provided that all persons serving on grand or petit (trial) juries in Maryland had to swear to a belief in God as a condition of such service. The court held that this provision required a religious test for a public office or service, a requirement violative of the religious freedom guarantees of the federal Constitution. As a consequence of this ruling, the Maryland Court of Appeals remanded all criminal appeals then pending before it to the trial courts, on the ground that in all such cases either the grand juries or the trial juries or both had been unconstitutionally selected. At the trial-court level, the court said, each defendant should be given the option, on advice of counsel, of either having his conviction vacated and receiving a new trial, or waiving any objections to his original trial and accepting the conviction obtained at the original trial.[11]

This ruling by the Maryland Court of Appeals required extensive reindictments and retrials of criminal defendants in the state. When it decided the *Schowgurow* case, 221 cases were pending before the court, and all were remanded for reindictment and retrial at the option of the defendants. Even more drastic consequences resulted in regard to cases in the process of being tried at the time of the *Schowgurow* decision. Complete statistics are unavailable, but in Baltimore City alone, 1061 reindictments and retrials were required by the decision of the court of appeals.[12]

Since his case was pending before the Maryland Court of Appeals at the time of the *Schowgurow* decision, John Benton was one of the criminal defendants who was given the option of obtaining a new trial or accepting the results of his original trial. Benton opted for a new trial, and his original sentence was accordingly set aside. On June 30, 1966, however, he was again indicted for burglary, larceny, and housebreaking. At the retrial, the state again abandoned the housebreaking charge, but counsel for Benton also objected to his being retried on the larceny count. Benton's counsel pointed out that he had been acquitted of the larceny charge at the original trial and argued that to retry him on that charge would subject him to double jeopardy.

The prosecution, however, argued in Benton's case that the result of the *Schowgurow* decision had been to hold both the indictment and the jury verdict in the original trial to be completely void, since both the grand jurors and the trial jurors had been required to express a belief in God as a condition of service. When Benton opted for a new trial, the prosecution argued, his case could be retried as if the first trial had never occurred, because that trial had been constitutionally defective from the beginning. Benton's acquittal on the larceny charge at the first trial, under this theory, was therefore to be treated legally as a nullity, and he could be retried for both burglary and larceny without doing violence to the concept of double jeopardy.[13]

These arguments were made before Judge Roscoe H. Parker of the Circuit Court of Prince George's County before Benton's retrial began, and Judge Parker sustained the prosecution's argument. Benton was therefore tried again for both burglary and larceny, and this time the jury convicted Benton of both charges. Judge Parker sentenced him to fifteen years in prison on the burglary count and to five years imprisonment on the larceny count, the sentences to run concurrently. By opting for a retrial, Benton had secured for himself a sentence of five more years imprisonment, since his original sentence had been for only ten years.[14]

Benton's counsel again argued in a motion for a new trial that the retrial on the larceny count had constituted double jeopardy. But again the prosecution argued that under the *Schowgurow* decision Benton had "attacked the indictment and attacked the conviction because the Court was illegally constituted. I don't think . . . he can say, 'I think my trial was invalid, the Court lacked jurisdiction, but this part of the trial [the larceny acquittal] was okay. I want to attack this part of the trial.'" Benton was entitled to a new trial, the prosecution argued, "because the Court was without jurisdiction to try him, the grand jury was illegally constituted. But when he attacks the trial, he can't say 'I just want to leave part of it as valid and let me just pick and choose what part I want to say is invalid.' The whole thing is under attack. The whole trial is invalid. The State can certainly reap a little benefit out of that."[15]

Judge Parker stood by his original ruling and denied the motion for a new trial. Benton's counsel then filed an appeal to the Court of Special

Appeals of Maryland, but that court affirmed Benton's conviction on August 17, 1967. The court accepted the theory that the original trial, including the acquittal on the larceny charge, had been a nullity because the original indictment had been invalid. "It is true," the court said, "that the Court of Appeals has held 'that where there has been a regular trial on a valid indictment and a finding of not guilty on a specific offense, the accused cannot thereafter be tried again at the instigation of the State for the same offense. . . . ' But this rule is predicated upon a valid indictment. In the instant case the appellant's original indictment by his election was invalidated." Benton had therefore not been acquitted of larceny at a "regular trial on a valid indictment," the court held, and his retrial on the larceny count had not constituted double jeopardy.[16]

After this affirmation of his conviction by the court of special appeals, Benton appealed his case to the Maryland Court of Appeals, but that court denied review on December 7, 1967.[17] At this stage in the proceedings, Benton had not only exhausted his state remedies but also his funds. The appeal of the double jeopardy question in the *Benton* case to the United States Supreme Court had to proceed *in forma pauperis* and was conducted on behalf of Benton by the Washington, D.C., law firm of Levitan, Ezrin, Cramer, West & Weinstein.

The Supreme Court granted the motion to proceed *in forma pauperis* and the petition for a writ of certiorari in *Benton* v. *Maryland* on June 17, 1968. As it had done in the *Gideon* case, the Court indicated in its order granting certiorari that it would limit its review of the case to two questions. "(1) Is the double jeopardy clause of the Fifth Amendment applicable to the States through the Fourteenth Amendment?" the Court's order asked, and "(2) If so, was the petitioner 'twice put in jeopardy' in this case?"[18]

Counsel in *Benton* v. *Maryland* were therefore put on notice that the Court was prepared to reconsider its ruling in *Palko* v. *Connecticut* that the Fifth Amendment's Double Jeopardy Clause did not apply to the states via the Due Process Clause. As a result, counsel for Benton, M. Michael Cramer, went all out in the attack in his brief on the continuing viability of the *Palko* case. In light of the selective-incorporation approach of the Court during the 1960s, Cramer argued, it was "respectfully submitted that the *Palko* decision lacks vitality in light of subsequent decisions of this Court and, therefore, should not be followed in the instant case." Indeed, in an argument reminiscent of the argument made in the *Palko* case, Cramer argued that the Court should now apply all of the rights in the Bill of Rights to the states.[19]

In urging the reversal of Benton's conviction for larceny, Cramer also relied heavily on the Court's decision in *United States* v. *Ball* in 1896, since the Court had held in the *Ball* case that under the Double Jeopardy

Clause a defendant could not be retried after having been acquitted of a charge, even if the original trial had been based on a defective indictment. If the Double Jeopardy Clause applied to the states, Cramer argued, then the *Ball* case would require the reversal of Benton's larceny conviction, since he had been acquitted of larceny in a first trial held to be defective because of an invalid indictment. The admission of evidence relating to the larceny charge, Cramer additionally argued, had influenced the jury to convict on the burglary charge, and therefore that conviction should be reversed by the Court. And, finally, he argued that the more severe sentence that Benton had received on retrial also constituted double jeopardy and therefore justified the reversal of both the larceny and the burglary convictions.[20]

The Maryland attorney general, on the other hand, urged the Court to approach the *Benton* case under the principles of *Palko* v. *Connecticut* and subsequent cases in which the Court had inquired whether the defendant had been denied fundamental fairness in relation to double jeopardy situations in state cases. "In articulating the 'rationalizing principle' of the due process clause," the attorney general said, "Mr. Justice Cardozo in *Palko* perceived: the due process clause of the Fourteenth Amendment prohibited the states from enforcing their criminal laws at the cost of violating some fundamental precept of justice imposing a 'hardship so acute and shocking that our polity will not endure it.' It is submitted that the criteria to be applied in double jeopardy cases is that 'due process of law' requires only that [Benton] not be denied any element of fundamental procedural fairness."[21]

Applying the standard of fundamental fairness to the *Benton* case, the attorney general argued that since the original indictment had been invalid, Benton's original trial had also been invalid, including the larceny acquittal. It was not, therefore, a denial of "fundamental fairness" to Benton to retry him, at his option, for both burglary and larceny. "When [Benton] exercised his option to void his original indictment within constitutional and procedural safeguards outlined by the Court of Appeals," the attorney general contended, "the indictment became a nullity, and the case proceeded as if the first indictment, trial, conviction, and acquittal had never been had. Said indictment was not *partly valid* and *partly invalid*. Each count of the indictment was invalid. Hence, the conviction and acquittal on the counts were not valid in part and invalid in part." The question in the *Benton* case, the attorney general argued, was whether Benton's reindictment and reconviction for larceny constituted double jeopardy. "On the basis of the historical background of double jeopardy," he said, "the present interpretation of that principle, the facts of the instant case, and the procedural safeguards employed by the courts of Maryland, the answer must be in the negative."[22]

Arguing the case orally before the Court on behalf of Benton, Michael Cramer contended that the Double Jeopardy Clause applied to the states and that Benton's retrial on the larceny count had violated federal double-jeopardy standards. Interestingly enough, however, Cramer did not call for the reversal of *Palko* v. *Connecticut*, as his brief had forthrightly done, but rather he attempted to distinguish *Palko* from the *Benton* case. Such an argument, however, was received with skepticism by the Court.

MR. CRAMER: If it please the Court, it is the petitioner's position that the Double Jeopardy Clause of the Fifth Amendment is a fundamental principle of liberty and justice, and is therefore applicable to the states, either by incorporation in the Fourteenth Amendment, or through the Due Process Clause, in the sense that the procedure here employed by the state was violative of basic fairness.

JUSTICE HARLAN: Does your contention involve overruling *Palko*?

MR. CRAMER: No, sir, because I don't believe that *Palko* sanctioned this type of procedure, sir.

JUSTICE HARLAN: Well, it said that the Double Jeopardy Clause was not carried into the states as such by the Fourteenth Amendment.

MR. CRAMER: Your Honor, I respectfully submit that the Court also carefully set out that in the *Palko* case they were deciding only one issue: Does the state have a right to appeal. And on page 328 of the Court's decision in *Palko* I believe that the Court leaves open the question that's come before the Court today in this case. Of course the state argues—

CHIEF JUSTICE WARREN: In what language did it leave it open? Have you it there before you?

MR. CRAMER: Yes, sir. [Quoting from the Court's opinion in *Palko:*] "What the answer would have to be if the state were permitted after a trial free from error to try the accused over again or to bring another case against him, we have no occasion to consider. We deal with the statute before us and no other."

JUSTICE BLACK: What was the thing [in *Palko*] that they claimed was double jeopardy?

MR. CRAMER: Appeal by the state. The state appealed an alleged error at trial. The case was reversed and a new trial was brought.

JUSTICE BLACK: We limited it to that holding?

MR. CRAMER: Yes, sir. Of course, it's the respondent's position that the Double Jeopardy Clause does not apply, and they pitch that solely on the Court's decision in *Palko* v. *Connecticut*. But as I've stated, Your Honors, we are convinced that *Palko* never sanctioned the type of grossly unfair procedure which was employed by the state in this case.[23]

Despite his disavowal of any contention that *Palko* should be reversed, Cramer nonetheless had to argue not only that the Double Jeopardy Clause did apply to the states but also that the state of Maryland had violated federal double jeopardy standards in the *Benton* case. It did not matter whether the original indictment at Benton's first trial was valid or not, Cramer contended, he had been acquitted of larceny at the first trial, and the state was barred from retrying him on that charge. "It is submitted that the State of Maryland in this case did not adhere to the federal principle for the application of the Double Jeopardy Clause," Cramer said, "and I refer the Court to its decision in *United States* v. *Ball*, which is the most basic type of decision that can be considered on the issue of double jeopardy. There it was held that double jeopardy attached regardless of the validity of the indictment. And that indictment in *United States* v. *Ball* was no more invalid than the indictment in [Benton's] case. We submit, Your Honors, that a faulty indictment constitutes no more than an ordinary trial error. And since the government is unable to undo an acquittal because of an ordinary trial error, we contend that they should not be able to set aside [Benton's] acquittal in this case. For that reason, we ask the Court to reverse this entire case, and remand it for a new trial on the burglary charge alone."

Maryland Assistant Attorney General Edward F. Borgerding defended the state's position before the Court by arguing that (1) Benton had freely and voluntarily agreed to be reindicted and retried on the basis of the conditions laid down by the Maryland Court of Appeals in the wake of the *Schowgurow* decision; and (2) since the indictment that had formed the basis of Benton's first trial had been issued by an invalidly constituted grand jury, his first trial had been void, and his conviction for burglary, as well as his acquittal for larceny, at that trial had been both legally and constitutionally void. Consequently, Borgerding argued, the state could validly retry Benton on both the burglary and the larceny charges without doing violence to the principles of double jeopardy.

Borgerding, however, had a difficult time convincing Chief Justice Warren of the validity of his contentions.

MR. BORGERDING: Our position, the state's position, [is that] when Mr. Benton exercised his right to declare his indictment null and void, the indictment [was] void *ab initio*. It was returned by an illegally or . . . unconstitutional[ly] organized grand jury, and as such, since he exercised that right, an unconstitutionally [constituted] grand jury cannot bring back a valid indictment. And therefore the court had no jurisdiction and he was therefore not placed in jeopardy on his first trial.

CHIEF JUSTICE WARREN: Well, when is . . . a verdict of not guilty final?

MR. BORGERDING: Well, a verdict of not guilty could be final upon it being given, assuming that no one has any right to appeal.

CHIEF JUSTICE WARREN: No, no, a man doesn't ordinarily appeal a verdict of not guilty, does he?

MR. BORGERDING: No, sir, you are correct, he would not.

CHIEF JUSTICE WARREN: Well, when was the verdict of not guilty on the larceny count final in this case?

MR. BORGERDING: I would say it was final on the day it was rendered, Your Honor.

CHIEF JUSTICE WARREN: All right. Then if he takes an appeal from the rest of the judgment, how does he vitiate that?

MR. BORGERDING: Well, we come back to our basic premise that the mere fact that that first indictment was brought by an unconstitutional grand jury that it did not bring back a valid indictment.

CHIEF JUSTICE WARREN: No, I'm assuming that when he was first found not guilty, that was final, wasn't it?

MR. BORGERDING: It was final if the indictment was valid. It was final if the court had jurisdiction over that indictment, yes, I would agree it would be final.

CHIEF JUSTICE WARREN: You mean that in any case, that if a man is acquitted by a jury, and his indictment, the indictment against him was not lawfully drawn, that there was no jeopardy?

MR. BORGERDING: I say in the circumstances of this case, when the court held that the grand jury that brought back this indictment was unconstitutionally organized under the Fourteenth Amendment of the Constitution, that grand jury cannot bring a valid indictment, if that is so. And Mr. Benton made it so by exercising his option. And he was told that the indictment would be null and void. He had the right to exercise, the right either to make it null and void or not, that's true, but once he did, the court had no power to try him on an invalid indictment.

JUSTICE STEWART: Well, aren't you really arguing, because of all this, [an invalid] indictment, [an invalid] first indictment, jeopardy never attached under that indictment. That's what you're arguing?

MR. BORGERDING: Yes, sir.

JUSTICE STEWART: That even though you went all through trial and all through an appeal and everything else, for purposes of the Double Jeopardy Clause that whole proceeding was one in which jeopardy never attached?

MR. BORGERDING: That is correct, Your Honor.

But Borgerding's argument failed to convince Justice Marshall that Benton's acquittal on the larceny charge at the first trial had no legal effect.

JUSTICE MARSHALL: But he was acquitted?

MR. BORGERDING: Yes, sir, he was.

JUSTICE MARSHALL: By a jury?

MR. BORGERDING: Yes, sir.

JUSTICE MARSHALL: And so, now he is reindicted by a [grand] jury?

MR. BORGERDING: Yes, sir.

JUSTICE MARSHALL: For the same thing that he was acquitted for?

MR. BORGERDING: That is correct.

JUSTICE MARSHALL: And you don't see double jeopardy at all? . . . He was never in jeopardy?

MR. BORGERDING: He was never in jeopardy.

JUSTICE MARSHALL: He was just in jail.

MR. BORGERDING: Sir?

JUSTICE MARSHALL: He was just in jail, but never jeopardy.

MR. BORGERDING: That is correct, Your Honor.

In brief concluding remarks, Borgerding made what appeared to be an innocuous statement that on the larceny count, Benton "got a concurrent sentence and in effect was not damaged as such. . . ." Although this was the only reference to the concurrent sentence Benton had received on the burglary and larceny counts, on December 16, the Court announced that the case was being restored to its docket for reargument on March 24, 1969. In setting the case for reargument, the Court indicated that the reargument should be limited to the question of whether the "concurrent sentence" doctrine had continuing validity. The Court also invited the United States solicitor general to file an *amicus curiae* brief expressing his views on the concurrent-sentence question.

The concurrent-sentence doctrine had long been used by the federal courts to avoid ruling on unnecessary questions in appeals in criminal cases. Under the doctrine, for example, if a defendant were convicted of several separate offenses but received equal concurrent sentences for each offense, an appellate court would uphold his conviction if it found his conviction on only one of the offenses valid, since even if the other convictions were invalid, the defendant would still be required to serve the same length of time in prison.

Although the Supreme Court had in the past approved the concurrent-sentence doctrine,[24] in more recent cases, it had recognized that a criminal conviction might have collateral consequences for the defendant in addition to a prison term or other punishment. A criminal conviction might thus bar a person from entrance into many professions or occupations, prevent him from securing certain licenses for operating certain businesses, etc. The Court had therefore tended in more recent cases to ignore the concurrent-sentence doctrine, holding that review of a criminal conviction was necessary to protect a defendant from such collateral effects of an invalid conviction, even if a reversal of the invalid conviction would not decrease the ultimate punishment the defendant would receive.[25]

In the *Benton* case, the question was whether or not the Court should review the validity of the larceny conviction under the Double Jeopardy Clause. Since Benton had received a fifteen-year sentence for burglary and five years for larceny, the sentences to be served concurrently, a reversal of his larceny conviction would not, presumably, have any effect on the ultimate sentence Benton would be required to serve. On the reargument of the *Benton* case, the Maryland attorney general therefore contended that the concurrent-sentence doctrine was derived from Article III of the

Constitution, which limits the Court's jurisdiction to "cases and controversies." Whether Benton's larceny conviction was valid or not would not, the attorney general argued, make any difference in regard to the sentence Benton would serve in prison, since he had received five years on the larceny count to be served concurrently with the fifteen-year sentence he had received on the burglary count. The validity of the larceny count was therefore a hypothetical or theoretical issue, and it did not involve a real "case or controversy" as required by Article III of the Constitution, the attorney general concluded.[26]

Michael Cramer, on the other hand, denied that the validity of the larceny conviction was a moot question and argued that the larceny count had tainted Benton's trial because it allowed evidence otherwise inadmissible to be admitted at the trial, thus contributing to the burglary conviction. Cramer also contended that the larceny conviction would have collateral consequences for Benton, including the possibility that it could be used to impeach his testimony in subsequent cases, the possibility it might hurt his chances for an earlier parole, and the possibility that it might be used to deny him entrance to certain occupations. These possible collateral consequences of the larceny conviction, Cramer argued, made the question of the validity of that conviction a "case and controversy" that was reviewable by the Court.[27]

The solicitor general accepted the Court's invitation and filed an *amicus curiae* brief addressing the concurrent-sentence problem in the *Benton* case. The solicitor general argued that the concurrent-sentence doctrine was not a jurisdictional bar to the Court's reaching and deciding the validity of a conviction, even though such a decision might be unnecessary if the Court upheld the validity of one of several counts involving concurrent sentences. The solicitor general therefore rejected Maryland's argument that the concurrent-sentence doctrine was derived from Article III's provision limiting the Court's jurisdiction to cases and controversies. On the other hand, the solicitor general recommended to the Court that the doctrine be preserved, since it was useful as a tool of judicial efficiency and allowed the courts to avoid deciding unnecessary issues in criminal cases. He especially recommended the use of the doctrine by the courts of appeals, noting that the case loads of those courts were rapidly rising and that the retention of the concurrent-sentence doctrine at the court of appeals level would allow the conservation of judicial resources for the decision of only necessary issues in criminal cases.[28]

Finally, the solicitor general argued that the Court should not assume that a criminal conviction necessarily had collateral consequences for a defendant. The burden of showing such consequences, he said, should be on the defendant when review of a concurrent sentence was sought from the courts. This burden of proof on the defendant would allow the continued application of the concurrent-sentence doctrine where no showing of collateral consequences could be made.[29]

The concurrent-sentence problem was argued in *Benton v. Maryland* on March 24, 1969, and the Court's decision in the case was announced on the last day of the term, on June 23. Justice Thurgood Marshall wrote the opinion of the Court, holding the Double Jeopardy Clause to be applicable to the states and reversing Benton's larceny conviction. Chief Justice Warren and Justices Douglas, Black, and Brennan voted with the majority and Justice White concurred in the result. Justices Harlan and Stewart dissented, while Justice Fortas, of course, did not participate, having resigned from the Court on May 14.

Addressing the problem of the concurrent-sentence doctrine, Justice Marshall concluded that the doctrine was not a jurisdictional bar to the Court's passing upon Benton's challenge to his larceny conviction and that recent cases had made it "perfectly clear that the existence of concurrent sentences does not remove the elements necessary to create a justiciable case or controversy." Benton's larceny conviction might subsequently be used to enhance a sentence against him under a state habitual-criminal statute or to impeach his character at some future trial, Marshall said, and such collateral consequences were sufficient to make his challenge to the larceny conviction justiciable. Although the concurrent-sentence doctrine might, under some circumstances, still be used by federal appellate courts as a rule of convenience, he continued, "there is no jurisdictional bar to consideration of challenges to multiple convictions, even though concurrent sentences were imposed."[30]

Turning to the merits, Marshall noted that the Court had rejected a claim that the Double Jeopardy Clause applied to the states in *Palko* v. *Connecticut* in 1937. But the selective-incorporation decisions of the 1960s, he said, had undermined the viability of the *Palko* case and the fair-trial approach to state criminal procedure it had embraced. The Court found, Marshall said, "that the double jeopardy prohibition of the Fifth Amendment represents a fundamental ideal in our constitutional heritage, and that it should apply to the states through the Fourteenth Amendment. Insofar as it is inconsistent with this holding, *Palko* v. *Connecticut* is overruled." The Court's recent cases, he continued, had "thoroughly rejected the *Palko* notion that basic constitutional rights can be denied by the States as long as the totality of the circumstances does not disclose a denial of 'fundamental fairness.' Once it is decided that a particular Bill of Rights guarantee is 'fundamental to the American scheme of justice,' . . . the same constitutional standards apply against both the State and Federal governments. *Palko's* roots had thus been cut away years ago. We today only recognize the inevitable."[31]

Having held that the Double Jeopardy Clause applied to the states,

Marshall then turned to the question of whether Maryland had violated federal double jeopardy standards by retrying Benton on the larceny count. Relying on *United States* v. *Ball* and cases that had followed it, Marshall held that a defendant could not be retried for an offense of which he had been acquitted, even if the original trial resulting in the acquittal had been based on a defective indictment. Benton's larceny conviction was therefore held to violate federal double jeopardy standards and was reversed.[32]

Michael Cramer had argued that Benton's burglary conviction should also be reversed, since evidence relating to the larceny charge might have prejudiced the jury and contributed to the burglary conviction. The Court, however, declined to reverse the burglary conviction, since in order to evaluate Cramer's claim, it would be required to explore in detail Maryland's rules of evidence and its definitions of larceny and burglary. The Court therefore remanded the *Benton* case to the Maryland courts on this point to allow the state courts an opportunity to determine if Benton had in fact been harmed by the admission of evidence at his trial on the invalid larceny count.[33]

Dissenting from the decision of the Court, Justice Harlan, joined by Justice Stewart, argued that the concurrent-sentence doctrine, properly applied, should have barred the Court from reviewing Benton's larceny conviction, and that the case should therefore have been dismissed. As he had so often done in the past, Harlan also mourned the "complete overruling of one of this Court's truly great decisions" and the fact that the *Palko* case had become "another casualty in the so far unchecked march toward 'incorporating' much, if not all, of the Federal Bill of Rights into the Due Process Clause." Reasserting once again his belief in the fair-trial approach to the Due Process Clause, Harlan evaluated Benton's retrial on the larceny charge under that approach and concluded that his retrial had violated due process standards. Although he believed the Court was barred from hearing the case under the concurrent-sentence doctrine, Harlan nonetheless concluded that on the merits Benton had been subjected to a denial of due process by the state of Maryland.[34]

Whether or not Benton's burglary conviction would be reversed in addition to the larceny conviction had been left by the Court for consideration by the Maryland courts on remand. In December of 1969, the Maryland Court of Special Appeals considered the question of whether Benton's burglary conviction might have been influenced by the admission of evidence at his trial relating to the invalid larceny charge against him. The court concluded that this had not been the case, since no evidence had been admitted at the trial that would not have been admissible if he had been tried on the burglary count alone. The court of special appeals therefore reaffirmed Benton's conviction on the burglary count and his sentence of fifteen years in prison for that offense. Although the Supreme Court had reversed his larceny conviction under the Double Jeopardy Clause, Benton nonetheless still faced the same fifteen-year sentence that he had faced before the Supreme Court's decision.[35]

Benton had, however, attacked his fifteen-year sentence on the burglary count via a petition for a writ of habeas corpus while his appeal of the larceny conviction was pending before the Supreme Court. His counsel in the habeas corpus proceeding argued that since he had received only a ten-year sentence on the burglary count at his original trial, the imposition of a fifteen-year sentence on that count on retrial also violated the Double Jeopardy Clause. On October 18, 1968, the United States District Court for the District of Maryland sustained this argument and held that the increased sentence imposed on Benton for the burglary conviction on retrial had indeed constituted double jeopardy.[36] But the state of Maryland appealed this decision to the United States Court of Appeals for the Fourth Circuit, an appeal that was pending when the Supreme Court decided that the larceny count was invalid in *Benton* v. *Maryland*.[37]

Although the Supreme Court did not decide the question of whether Benton's increased sentence on retrial on the burglary conviction constituted double jeopardy in the *Benton* case, it did subsequently address the problem of increased sentences for defendants who were reconvicted of offenses after having won reversals of original convictions on appeal. In *North Carolina* v. *Pearce*, the Court held that a criminal defendant who was convicted, appealed, and won a reversal of his conviction, must upon retrial and reconviction be given credit against whatever sentence he received on retrial for the time he had served in prison under his original conviction. This requirement was mandated, the Court held, by the Double Jeopardy Clause.

On the other hand, the Court rejected the proposition in the *Pearce* case that a defendant could not be sentenced to a longer period of imprisonment on retrial of an offense after an appeal and reversal of an original conviction. The Double Jeopardy Clause, it held, did not prohibit such stiffer sentences on retrial. However, the Court further held that the imposition of a more severe sentence upon a defendant after an appeal and reversal of an original conviction must be justified by the sentencing judge upon the basis of facts relating to the conduct of the defendant after the original sentencing. Unless such facts could be affirmatively demonstrated by the sentencing judge on retrial and reconviction, the Court held, a more severe sentence after reconviction would violate the Due Process Clause.[38]

In the habeas corpus proceedings initiated by Benton, the United States District Court had been incorrect, therefore, in holding that Benton's more severe sentence of fifteen years rather than the ten years he had originally received on the burglary conviction violated the Double Jeopardy

Clause. But under the principles of the *Pearce* case, the Maryland trial judge was required to justify the more severe fifteen-year sentence by facts relating to Benton's conduct after the original sentence or to face a reversal of the fifteen-year sentence on due process grounds. Such a justification apparently did not exist, since John Benton ultimately had his fifteen-year burglary sentence reduced to ten years imprisonment, the same sentence he had received at his original trial in August of 1965.[39]

The Court's decision in *Benton* v. *Maryland* came close on the heels of the congressional enactment of the Criminal Appeals Act of 1970, which allowed the federal government to take appeals in criminal proceedings when such appeals were not barred by the Double Jeopardy Clause.[40] The Court had long since held that the federal government could not appeal in a criminal case except upon specific statutory authorization by Congress, and Congress had authorized such appeals only in limited circumstances in 1907.[41] As a result of the Criminal Appeals Act of 1970 and the *Benton* decision, the Court thus for the first time had to consider the application of the Double Jeopardy Clause in state proceedings and in many cases involving appeals by the federal government, and in the ten years following the *Benton* case the Court considered more aspects of the Double Jeopardy Clause than it had in its entire previous history.[42]

In applying the Double Jeopardy Clause to the states, the Court thus held that the principle of collateral estoppel was embraced by the Clause and bars repetitive prosecutions of a defendant upon charges growing out of the same criminal transaction when a first trial results in an acquittal and the elements of proof are the same in the subsequent prosecutions.[43] The states were also barred from prosecuting for a greater offense when a defendant has been tried for that offense but convicted of a lesser, included offense. And the same principle applies when a defendant has been convicted of a greater offense and there is an attempt to subsequently prosecute him for a lesser, included offense.[44] The Double Jeopardy Clause has also been held to be applicable to state juvenile-delinquency proceedings,[45] and, in addition, the states have been held to be bound by the federal rule that jeopardy attaches when a jury is impaneled and sworn or when, in nonjury trials, the judge begins to hear evidence.[46]

In construing the Criminal Appeals Act of 1970, the Court has also enunciated double jeopardy principles binding upon the states as well as the federal government, given the "incorporation" of the Double Jeopardy Clause in the *Benton* case. In the Criminal Appeals Act line of cases, the Court has reaffirmed the principle that the government may not appeal an acquittal under the Double Jeopardy Clause.[47] The Court has adhered to the view that the Double Jeopardy Clause "protects against a second prosecution for the same offense after acquittal. It protects against a second prosecution for the same offense after conviction. And it protects against multiple punishments for the same offense."[48] On the other hand, the Court has held that the Double Jeopardy Clause does not bar appeals by the government, "at least when those appeals would not require a new trial." Thus, when a judge rules in favor of a defendant after a verdict of guilty has been rendered, "the Government may appeal from that ruling without running afoul of the Double Jeopardy Clause."[49]

Despite the large number of cases involving the meaning of the Double Jeopardy Clause decided in the wake of the *Benton* decision, the Court has adhered to the principle that a criminal transaction that violates both federal and state law may be prosecuted by both jurisdictions without violating the Double Jeopardy Clause. The Court thus adheres to the position that the same criminal act may constitute two distinct offenses under federal and state law, and that both jurisdictions may subject the offender to prosecution.[50]

The Court's reversal of *Palko* v. *Connecticut* and the application of the Double Jeopardy Clause to the states in the *Benton* case, along with the congressional passage of the Criminal Appeals Act of 1970, has thus led to a proliferation of double jeopardy litigation, the end of which is not yet in sight. *Benton* v. *Maryland*, however, also represented the culmination of the nationalization of the Bill of Rights. The nationalization process had stretched over a hundred years from the adoption of the Fourteenth Amendment in 1868, and the Due Process Clause had in the interim been converted into a guarantee of individual liberties equal to, if not more important than, the Bill of Rights itself.

In addition to being the culmination of the nationalization process, the *Benton* case also marked the end of the series of decisions by the Warren Court that had significantly altered state criminal procedure since the incorporation breakthrough in the early 1960s. It was fitting, therefore, that the date of the *Benton* decision, June 23, 1969, also marked the end of Chief Justice Earl Warren's service on the Court. Indeed, President Nixon was present in the courtroom and heard the *Benton* opinion read by Justice Marshall. After all opinions of the Court had been announced, the President addressed the Court and congratulated Warren on his years of public service. Warren characteristically responded graciously, and then Warren E. Burger took the oath as Chief Justice. The era of the Warren Court had come to an end.[51]

12

The Nationalization of the Bill of Rights in Perspective

The nationalization of the Bill of Rights under the Due Process Clause of the Fourteenth Amendment came to an end with the Supreme Court's decision in *Benton* v. *Maryland*. This was understandably so, since by 1969 only the Second and Third Amendments, the Grand Jury Clause of the Fifth Amendment, the Seventh Amendment and the Excessive Fines and Bail Clause of the Eighth Amendment remained as parts of the Bill of Rights that had not been made applicable to the states in the decisions of the Court. And only the Excessive Fines and Bail Clause appeared to be a likely candidate for future nationalization.[1] The *Benton* case thus marked the end of a remarkable era of constitutional development that had transformed the structure of constitutional protection for political and civil liberties in the United States and had profoundly altered the nature of the federal system.

The Process of Nationalization: An Overview

Viewing the creation of the second bill of rights in perspective, the nationalization process may be viewed as falling into four stages: (1) the period from the decision of the *Slaughter House Cases* in 1873 to the decision in *Twining* v. *New Jersey* in 1908, during which the Court at first seemed to deny the possibility of the nationalization of the Bill of Rights but finally opened the door to that development; (2) the stage of the nationalization of the First Amendment, beginning with *Gitlow* v. *New York* in 1925 and ending with the decision of *Everson* v. *Board of Education* in 1947; (3) the period from the 1930s to 1961 during which the Court approached problems of criminal procedure in state cases under the fair trial rule; and finally, (4) the period of selective incorporationism from 1961 to 1969, during which most of the criminal-procedure provisions of the Bill of Rights were applied to the states.

The first stage of the nationalization process, of course, began with the decisions in the *Slaughter House Cases* (1873) and *Hurtado* v. *California*

(1884) in which the Court enunciated the doctrines of dual citizenship and nonsuperfluousness and thus appeared to doom any prospect that either the Privileges and Immunities Clause or the Due Process Clause of the Fourteenth Amendment might serve as vehicles for the nationalization of the Bill of Rights. It is usual to associate the influential roles of interest groups with constitutional litigation in the twentieth century, but the role played by the railroads in constitutional litigation during the period between the Civil War and the turn of the century may be viewed as rather similar to the roles played by the National Association for the Advancement of Colored People, the American Civil Liberties Union, and other groups familiar to students of more recent constitutional developments.[2] As the nation's first great, modern interstate industry, the railroads were the first nationally organized interest to attempt to use the Fourteenth Amendment as a federal constitutional shield against hostile state policies, and in the process the litigation efforts of the railroads led the Court to at least implicitly repudiate the doctrine of the *Hurtado* case.

In order to successfully convert the Fourteenth Amendment into such a shield for railroad interests, their lawyers had to convince the Court to change the meaning of due process so that it encompassed both substantive rights and corporate interests. The railroad lawyers were eminently successful on both counts: the Court's formal acceptance of substantive due process came in an 1890 railroad case, *Chicago, Milwaukee & St. Paul Railroad* v. *Minnesota*, and the Court had also accepted corporations as "persons" protected by the Due Process Clause in another railroad case, *Santa Clara County* v. *Southern Pacific Railroad*.[3]

The Court's acceptance in these earlier cases of the idea that the Due Process Clause imposed substantive as well as procedural limitations upon exercises of state power paved the way for the Court's 1897 decision in *Chicago, Burlington & Quincy Railroad Co.* v. *Chicago* that just compensation for private property taken for public purposes was required by the Due Process Clause. The railroad lawyers' earlier success in convincing the Supreme Court to accept the concept of substantive due process was of even greater importance to the future of the nationalization of the Bill of Rights, however, than the first nationalization breakthrough in the *Chicago, Burlington & Quincy Railroad Co.* case, for the Court's acceptance of substantive due process laid the necessary groundwork in due process theory for the nationalization of the substantive rights in the Bill of Rights —primarily the rights guaranteed in the First Amendment.

The Court's decision in the *Chicago, Burlington & Quincy Railroad* case, on the other hand, considerably muddled the theory by which the Court was determining the relationship between the Bill of Rights and the Due Process Clause. The Court again relied upon the *Hurtado* case in its *Maxwell* v. *Dow* decision in 1900 that the Due Process Clause did not require jury trials in state criminal proceedings, yet the *Hurtado* doctrine of nonsuperfluousness was logically irreconcilable with the *Chicago, Burlington & Quincy Railroad Co.* holding that the Due Process Clause imposed a just-compensation requirement upon the states.

The Court's rather puzzling reluctance to openly acknowledge that the doctrine of nonsuperfluousness was incompatible with the nationalization of any right in the Bill of Rights continued in the decision of *Twining* v. *New Jersey* in 1908. In *Twining* the Court emphasized the permanence of the doctrine of dual citizenship as a bar to any possible use of the Privileges and Immunities Clause as a vehicle of nationalization, but the Court's interpretation of the Due Process Clause in *Twining* again involved an implicit repudiation of the doctrine of nonsuperfluousness without an open acknowledgment that this was so. For only by holding that the Due Process Clause of the Fifth Amendment protected some rights similar to rights protected by other parts of the Bill of Rights could the Court's concession in *Twining*, that the Due Process Clause of the Fourteenth Amendment might protect certain rights similar to those in the Bill of Rights, be reconciled with the assumption in the doctrine of nonsuperfluousness, that the Due Process Clauses of the Constitution were identical in meaning. Not only would such a holding have been exceedingly peculiar, but it would have contradicted the other assumption in the doctrine of nonsuperfluousness, that there was nothing repetitive or superfluous in the Bill of Rights. Yet the Court did not reverse the *Hurtado* doctrine in the *Twining* case, and the doctrine's official burial did not come until Chief Justice Hughes's cryptic remark in *DeJonge* v. *Oregon* in 1937 that "explicit mention [of a right in the Bill of Rights] does not argue exclusion elsewhere."[4]

During the first phase of the nationalization process, therefore, the Court had laid the theoretical basis for the nationalization of the substantive rights in the Bill of Rights by its acceptance of the concept of substantive due process. In its handling of the relationship of the Due Process Clause to the Bill of Rights, on the other hand, the Court had embraced fundamentally incompatible theories and had made no systematic attempt to untangle the theoretical problems that had resulted. Despite the Court's failure to satisfactorily deal with these problems in *Twining*, however, its statement in that case that the Due Process Clause might guarantee rights similar to some of those in the Bill of Rights did open the door to the nationalization process—a door that had appeared to be firmly shut by the *Slaughter House Cases* and *Hurtado* v. *California*.

The next phase of the nationalization process, of course, involved the nationalization of the First Amendment freedoms, a process that began with the Court's statement of the famous "assumption" in *Gitlow* v. *New York* in 1925 and ended with the nationalization of the Establishment

Clause in *Everson* v. *Board of Education* in 1947. One of the most remarkable aspects of the nationalization of First Amendment freedoms was the fact that each of the leading cases involved in that process reached the Court under the sponsorship of an interest group. The American Civil Liberties Union was the most ubiquitous interest-group participant in the nationalization of First Amendment freedoms, having sponsored the *Gitlow* case while also jointly sponsoring with the International Labor Defense (ILD) the litigation in *Stromberg* v. *California* and *DeJonge* v. *Oregon*. The litigation resulting in the nationalization of freedom of the press in *Near* v. *Minnesota* was sponsored by the American Newspaper Publishers' Association (ANPA), with financing from the Chicago *Tribune*, while the nationalization of the Free Exercise Clause resulted from the Jehovah's Witnesses' sponsorship of *Cantwell* v. *Connecticut*. And, finally, *Everson* v. *Board of Education* came to the Court through the efforts of the Junior Order of United American Mechanics (JOUAM) of New Jersey.[5]

Given this diversity of sponsors, the pattern of interest-group participation in the nationalization of First Amendment freedoms was therefore much less stable and orderly than the pattern noted in other areas of constitutional policy. In his analysis of Establishment Clause litigation from the 1950s to the early 1970s, for example, Frank Sorauf found that three groups, the ACLU, the American Jewish Congress (AJC), and the Americans United for Separation of Church and State (AU), had "imposed an impressive degree of order and stability on church-state litigation."[6] In contrast to the Establishment Clause litigation studied by Sorauf, the nature of the interest-group participation in the nationalization of First Amendment freedoms resulted in both a lack of order and stability in the litigation involved.

The nationalization of the First Amendment, however, involved a multitude of issues—rather than one issue, as in the Establishment Clause litigation—and therefore one should not expect the nationalizing litigation to be dominated by one group or only a few groups. The ACLU was the only group participating in the nationalization process whose goals were sufficiently broad to encompass an interest in the nationalization of all of the First Amendment. However, the ACLU was a sponsor either jointly or alone in only three of the First Amendment cases and also participated as *amicus curiae* in the *Everson* case, and the sponsorship of the remaining First Amendment cases by such diverse groups as the ANPA, the Jehovah's Witnesses, and the JOUAM prevented the kind of order and stability that Sorauf had found in Establishment Clause litigation. An analysis of the interest-group participation in the nationalization of the First Amendment rather confirms Clement Vose's conclusion that the "range in types of voluntary associations having some role in constitutional litigation is remarkable."[7]

Analysts of constitutional litigation have noted in recent years the frequent use of "test case" tactics by interest groups participating in such litigation—tactics that include careful selection of issues to be litigated, recruitment of plaintiffs, deliberate selection of the judicial forums in which to litigate, attempts to control the timing and sequence of litigation, etc.[8] With the exception of the *Everson* case, however, the litigation resulting in the nationalization of First Amendment freedoms did not arise as a result of the use of classic test-case tactics by the interest groups that sponsored the cases, nor were the results achieved in those cases a consequence of any overall, coordinated interest-group strategy.

Instead, the litigation in the *Gitlow, Stromberg, DeJonge,* and *Cantwell* cases was initiated by criminal prosecutions brought by governmental authorities, and there is no evidence that the litigation in these cases was deliberately provoked by the participating interest groups for the purposes of creating test cases. Although it is possible to argue that any case involving the Jehovah's Witnesses during the 1930s and 1940s was a test case because of their policy of appealing all adverse rulings, there is nonetheless no evidence that the *Cantwell* case was deliberately planned by the Witnesses as a vehicle for establishing freedom of religion as a guarantee of the Due Process Clause of the Fourteenth Amendment.

Although *Near* v. *Minnesota* was not a criminal prosecution, the litigation in that case was initiated in a noncriminal injunctive proceeding by the local prosecutor, and it was only after the gag law had been upheld by the Minnesota Supreme Court and the proceedings had temporarily ended that the *Chicago Tribune* and the ANPA intervened. The revival of the proceedings in the *Near* case by the *Tribune* attorneys and the ANPA was clearly designed to obtain a U.S. Supreme Court decision on the free-press issue, and thus, in their second incarnation, the proceedings in the *Near* case did possess some characteristics of a test case. But the *Tribune* and the ANPA had not deliberately planned and organized the *Near* case as a means of obtaining the nationalization of freedom of the press. Rather, the nationalization of freedom of the press in *Near* was the result of the defensive responses of the *Tribune* and the ANPA to hostile governmental action, in much the same way that freedom of religion was nationalized in the *Cantwell* case.

Unlike the other cases resulting in the nationalization of the First Amendment, however, the *Everson* case clearly involved the use of test-case tactics by the JOUAM in the attack on the New Jersey bus law. Nonetheless, the *Everson* case was not designed by Albert McCay and the JOUAM to obtain a holding by the Supreme Court that the Establishment Clause was applicable to the states. Because of his ignorance of the nationalization process, and his belief that the decision in *Cochran* v. *Board of Education* would prevent the successful raising of a Fourteenth Amendment issue in the *Everson* case, McCay had framed the issues in the *Ever-*

son case for the purpose of obtaining a decision by the New Jersey courts that the bus law was invalid under the provisions of the state constitution —adding an allegation that the bus law violated the Fourteenth Amendment almost as an afterthought. Only after the *Everson* case had been lost in the New Jersey Court of Errors and Appeals, and after prodding by the ACLU, did McCay perceive the possibility of an appeal to the Supreme Court on Establishment Clause grounds. Thus, while the *Everson* case was clearly a test case in the classic sense, the policy objective of the JOUAM and Albert McCay had been to obtain the invalidation of the bus law in the state courts on state-law grounds, and the appeal to the Supreme Court on Establishment Clause grounds was decided upon only after the primary objective of the suit met defeat in the New Jersey courts. Although it was a test case, therefore, the *Everson* case—like the other cases involving the nationalization of First Amendment freedoms—was not a carefully planned case that was initiated for the purpose of obtaining the nationalization of a right in the Bill of Rights.

The fact that none of the groups that sponsored the First Amendment nationalizing cases had deliberately planned and initiated the litigation they sponsored does not diminish, however, the crucial contributions those groups made to the nationalizing process. Thus, it would be difficult to exaggerate the importance of the breakthrough accomplished by the ACLU with the Court's statement of the famous "assumption" in the *Gitlow* case that freedom of speech and freedom of the press were protected by the Due Process Clause. And the ACLU, along with the ILD, also made crucial contributions during the 1920s and 1930s to the meager fund of financial resources and legal talent available to the defense of political and civil liberties—as the *Stromberg* and *DeJonge* cases attest.[9]

It is clear that the *Near* case would never have been appealed to the Supreme Court without the intervention of outside forces such as the *Chicago Tribune* and the ANPA, which supplied the legal talent and the finances for an appeal. Similarly, the *Cantwell* case would undoubtedly have remained a run-of-the-mill and unappealed misdemeanor case had not the Cantwells belonged to a group such as the Jehovah's Witnesses, which was ready, willing, and able to challenge prosecutions of its members. And, finally, by financing the *Everson* case, the JOUAM underwrote litigation for a political purpose that was unlikely to be financed by an individual. Although the cost of the *Everson* litigation was modest by modern standards, it was still substantial enough to have been beyond the means of most individuals—particularly for a case promoting a political cause rather than the defense of personal interests.[10]

Thus, although interest-group sponsorship of the First Amendment cases was of crucial importance, the very diversity of the groups participating in the nationalization process involving the First Amendment precluded any centrally orchestrated strategy of litigation that might have resulted in a coordinated theoretical justification of nationalization in the arguments before the Court. Indeed, after Walter Pollak, on behalf of the ACLU and Benjamin Gitlow, persuaded the Court to state its "assumption" in the *Gitlow* case, the attorneys for the appellants in the subsequent First Amendment cases simply took the *Gitlow* assumption as a reality and did not discuss in any systematic way the theoretical question of how, and under what theoretical premises, the freedoms of the First Amendment had become applicable to the states. The group sponsorship of the cases nationalizing the First Amendment therefore did not result in any group formulation of a consistent constitutional theory of nationalization —a circumstance that may occur when only one or a few groups participate in the litigation of more narrow constitutional-policy issues.[11]

If there was to be a theoretical justification of the application of the First Amendment to the states, therefore, such a justification had to come from the Supreme Court itself. During the process of the nationalization of the First Amendment, however, the Court continued the same disregard for the theoretical problems of nationalization that it had evidenced during the first phase of the nationalization process. Since the last major statement by the Court regarding the relationship between the Bill of Rights and the Due Process Clause had been in the *Twining* case, the Court presumably was operating upon the basis of the *Twining* theory at the outset of the nationalization of the First Amendment. But the *Twining* theory— that the Due Process Clause might guarantee certain rights similar but not identical to rights in the Bill of Rights—had clearly been abandoned by the Court as its theory of nationalization by 1940, when the Court began announcing that the First Amendment applied to the states in the identical way that it applied to the federal government.

Typically, the Court did not explain why or when the *Twining* theory had been jettisoned as the theory of nationalization, or, indeed, that the *Twining* theory had ever been the basis of the nationalization process, even at the outset. From the Court's various expressions, during the 1940s, of the view that the First Amendment applied to the states, it would appear that the Court had come to this conclusion for two reasons. First, the post-1937 Court apparently was convinced, at least for a time, that defining the meaning of the Due Process Clause by the specifics of the First Amendment would reduce the judicial discretion in interpreting the clause that had led to the due process mischief of the pre-1937 Court. Second, it appears that the Court's application of the First Amendment to the states was also influenced by the support of a majority on the Court for the concept of "preferred freedoms"—a concept presaged by Chief Justice Hughes's opinions for the Court in the *Stromberg* and *DeJonges* cases, implicit in Justice Cardozo's opinion in the *Palko* case, and finally formalized, at least by a footnote, in Justice Stone's *Carolene Products* (1938) opinion.[12]

These justifications for the nationalization of the First Amendment, however, were never stated by the Court in any systematic theoretical formulation justifying nationalization, but must instead be gleaned from a variety of its opinions. A process that had begun (in the words of Klaus Heberle) as a process of "absent-minded incrementalism" therefore ended essentially as it had begun.[13] The result was clear—by 1947 the First Amendment was considered to be fully applicable to the states—but the Court remained rather uninformative regarding how and upon what theoretical premises that result had been reached.

When the First Amendment had been applied to the states, the nationalization process entered its third phase, which was to last until the incorporation breakthrough of the early 1960s. The central problem of this period was the tension between the Court's application of the First Amendment to the states in the identical way in which it applied to the federal government and the Court's *Twining*-fair trial approach to issues of criminal procedure in state trials. Its resistance to the application of the criminal-procedure provisions of the Bill of Rights to the states in the identical way the First Amendment applied to them appears to have rested upon two foundations.

The first was the view of a majority of the Court—as Justice Cardozo had indicated in the *Palko* case (1937)—that the criminal-procedure provisions of the Bill of Rights were not, at least as they applied in federal proceedings, "of the very essence of a scheme of ordered liberty."[14] On the other hand, the right to a fair trial in state proceedings was considered by the Court to be a fundamental right, and insofar as rights similar but not identical to the procedural protections of the Bill of Rights were essential to a fair trial, the Court was willing to enforce those similar rights in state criminal trials.

The second foundation of the Court's fair trial approach to matters of criminal procedure reflected a respect on its part for the fact that the enforcement of the criminal law was, and remains, a primary responsibility of the states within the federal system; and the Court was therefore reluctant to unduly interfere in this area that had traditionally been the province of the states. Ironically, however, this deference to federalism had not been deemed by the Court to be a sufficient reason not to apply the substantive limitations of the First Amendment to the states.

The dominant episode of this third phase of the nationalization process was undoubtedly the *Adamson* decision (1947), and the impassioned debate between Justices Frankfurter and Black on the relative merits of the fair-trial approach and of Black's total-incorporation position. Although he won the battle with Black in the *Adamson* case, Frankfurter's defense of the fair-trial approach nonetheless added some confusion to the theory of nationalization, which was already hardly a model of clarity. One of his reasons for not applying the Self-Incrimination Clause to the states was that the Due Process Clauses of the Constitution were identical in meaning, but this assertion was simply not true by 1947, when the First Amendment had been fully applied to the states—and indeed had not been true since the *Chicago, Burlington & Quincy Railroad Co.* case in 1897. And Frankfurter's view that the Due Process Clause imposed upon state proceedings the "canons of decency and fairness which express the notions of justice of English-speaking peoples even toward those charged with the most heinous offenses" proved to be an almost unfathomable guide to the meaning of due process—as the Court's subsequent decisions indicated.[15]

The phase of nationalization during the dominance of the fair-trial rule nonetheless produced significant interpretations of the Due Process Clause by the Court. The "core" of the Fourth Amendment was held to be applicable to the states in the *Wolf* case (1949), and the requirement of public trials was held to be a due process requirement in the *Oliver* case (1948), at least as retroactively interpreted by the Court. Perhaps as important, however, was the fact that the due process standards imposed by the Court upon state proceedings were progressively tightened during the regime of the fair-trial rule.

In determining whether "special circumstances" required the appointment of counsel for indigent defendants, for example, the Court in fact reversed after 1950 every state case in which counsel had not been appointed.[16] Similarly, the Court tightened the standards governing the admissibility of coerced confessions in state trials. What had begun in 1936 as a condemnation under due process of the extraction of a confession by especially barbarous methods in *Brown* v. *Mississippi* had become by the early 1960s requirements under the Due Process Clause that rather closely approximated the command of the Self-Incrimination Clause. While still adhering to the fair-trial approach to the Due Process Clause, even Justice Frankfurter thus declared in 1961 that coerced confessions were excluded under the Due Process Clause "not because such confessions are unlikely to be true but because the methods used to extract them offend an underlying principle in the enforcement of our criminal law; that ours is an accusatorial and not an inquisitorial system—a system in which the State must establish guilt by evidence independently and freely secured and may not by coercion prove its charge against an accused out of his own mouth."[17]

The progressive stringency of the due process standards the Court applied to the states under the fair-trial rule thus made the final, incorporationist stage of the nationalization process less of a drastic departure from the established course of constitutional development than it otherwise might have been. Indeed, the incorporationist and fair-trial approaches to the interpretation of the Due Process Clause coalesced in the *Gideon* case in 1963, with the adherents of both approaches agreeing that appointed counsel was required for indigent defendants in all serious state criminal cases. And both the incorporationists and the adherents of the fair trial approach agreed that the Due Process Clause imposed confrontation and compulsory-process requirements upon the states in the *Pointer* (1965) and *Washington* (1967) cases.

As the most staunch defender of the *Twining*-fair trial approach, Justice Harlan of course insisted that the crucial point was that the requirements for counsel, confrontation, and compulsory process that were being recognized by the Court had as their source the Due Process Clause and not the Bill of Rights, and were thus similar, and not identical, to their counterparts in the Bill of Rights. Even if Harlan's views had prevailed in the 1960s, however, it appears that the restrictions imposed by the Due Process Clause upon state criminal trials would have increased, and that those restrictions would have been quite similar to many of the criminal-procedure provisions of the Bill of Rights.

For the selective incorporationists who dominated the last stage of the nationalization process, of course, most but not all of the rights in the Bill of Rights applied to the states via the Due Process Clause, and those rights that did apply were identical to the same rights in the Bill of Rights. Selective incorporationism thus rejected Justice Black's view that all of the Bill of Rights applied to the states, while accepting his view that any right applicable to the states was identical to its counterpart in the Bill of Rights. The selective incorporationists also accepted the view, advanced by Black in the *Adamson* case, that defining the meaning of the Due Process Clause by most of the rights in the Bill of Rights would reduce the discretionary power of the Court in interpreting the Due Process Clause and thus diminish the potential for the sort of judicial abuse of due process that had occurred in the past.[18]

The Due Process Clause has not, however, been confined to serving only as a vehicle for applying most of the Bill of Rights to the states. The Court has held without reference to the specifics of the Bill of Rights, for example, that procedural due process is violated if the state obtains a conviction on the basis of testimony known to be perjured or if the state suppresses evidence favorable to the accused.[19] Due process is also violated, it has been held, if a defendant is convicted and punished without any evidence of guilt.[20]

When the Court faced the question of whether the Due Process Clause protected substantive rights not listed in the Bill of Rights in *Griswold* v. *Connecticut* in 1965, the selective incorporationists also abandoned Justice Black's position that the meaning of the Due Process Clause was supplied by the Bill of Rights and by it alone. Over Black's vigorous protest, the Court thus held that substantive rights beyond those in the Bill of Rights were indeed protected by the Due Process Clause, thus contradicting not only one of Black's justifications for total incorporation but also one of the justifications advanced for selective incorporation. Although Black could ultimately applaud the fact that the process of selective incorporation had resulted in the application of most of the Bill of Rights to the states, he nonetheless failed to ever win a majority on the Court for total incorporation, and he also lost the battle over the future of the Due Process Clause in the *Griswold* case. Neither substantively nor procedurally, therefore, has the meaning of the Due Process Clause been confined to the specifics of the Bill of Rights.[21]

Also inherent in the position of the selective incorporationists was the rejection of the argument, championed by the adherents of the *Twining*-fair-trial approach, that the imposition of the criminal-procedure specifics of the Bill of Rights upon the states would violate the principles of federalism. The selective incorporationists argued, to the contrary, that nebulous due-process standards formulated by the Court under the fair trial rule had led to unpredictable and arbitrary intrusions of federal judicial power in state proceedings, and that the imposition of the specifics of the Bill of Rights would thus, in fact, improve federal-state relations. On this point, the incorporationists had a powerful argument derived from the fair trial approach to the right to counsel in state proceedings. After over thirty years of following the fair trial rule in counsel cases, the Court was requested by the attorneys general of twenty-three states to reverse itself in the *Gideon* case (1963) and to apply the full Sixth Amendment Assistance of Counsel Clause in state proceedings. The *Gideon* case thus represented a major blow to the federalism premises of the fair-trial approach—from which it never recovered—while also supplying the incorporationists with a powerful argument against contentions that selective incorporation violated the premises of federalism.

Although the basic premises of selective incorporationism may be gleaned from the incorporationist decisions of the 1960s, the selective-incorporationist majority never formulated a systematic statement of the theory and justification of its position. The selective incorporationists thus never indicated whether they accepted the overall validity of Black's views as to the intentions of the framers of the Fourteenth Amendment and rejected only the proposition that the framers intended to apply all of the Bill of Rights to the states. Nor did the selective incorporationists ever formulate any precise criteria by which they would determine which rights were worthy of incorporation and which were not. For this inattention to overall theoretical problems, the selective incorporationists, of course, had precedent aplenty from the behavior of the Court throughout the nationalization process. But there was considerable justification for Justice Harlan's charge that the majority of the Court during the 1960s had "compromised on the ease of [Justice Black's] incorporationist position, without its internal logic."[22]

Whatever their theoretical shortcomings may have been, once they had achieved a majority on the Court in the early 1960s the selective incorporationists pursued their objective with determination and what at times appeared to be unseemly haste. The nationalization of the First Amendment had occurred over a period of twenty-two years, but in contrast the nationalization of the criminal-procedure provisions occurred during the relatively short span of eight years, between 1961 and 1969. And although it may be argued that the interest groups that sponsored the First Amendment cases played a considerable part in setting the agenda of nationalization, it was clear during the 1960s that the selective-incorporationist majority of the Court was setting its own agenda for the nationalization of the criminal-procedure provisions. In contrast to the First Amendment cases, the cases nationalizing the criminal-procedure provisions of the Bill of Rights during the 1960s were not sponsored by interest groups—with the lone exception of the Lawyers Constitutional Defense Committee's (LCDC) sponsorship of *Duncan* v. *Louisiana*. The Court's agenda thus was not orchestrated by outside forces during the nationalization of the criminal procedure provisions, but rather the Court itself pushed the nationalization process by reaching out in some cases to nationalize criminal-procedure rights or by directing in other cases that arguments of counsel focus upon the issue of nationalization.

In three of the criminal-procedure cases, for example—*Mapp* v. *Ohio* (1961), *Robinson* v. *California* (1962), and *Pointer* v. *Texas* (1965)—the Court nationalized the Fourth Amendment and the exclusionary rule, the Cruel and Unusual Punishment Clause, and the Confrontation Clause even though those rights had not been the focus of the arguments of counsel involved in those cases. And it could be argued that a Court less intent upon nationalization would have found that the Connecticut courts had applied federal standards of self-incrimination in the *Malloy* case, or that it was unnecessary to reach the double jeopardy claim in the *Benton* case because a reversal of Benton's larceny conviction would not affect his ultimate sentence.

In addition to reaching out for rights to nationalize, the Court also focused the attention of counsel upon nationalization issues by specifically ordering arguments on those issues in its grants of certiorari. The Court thus directed in *Gideon* v. *Wainwright*, *Washington* v. *Texas*, and *Benton* v. *Maryland* that counsel focus their arguments on the question of nationalizing the Assistance of Counsel Clause, the Compulsory Process Clause, and the Double Jeopardy Clause. In the cases nationalizing the criminal-procedure provisions during the 1960s, therefore, the incorporationists on the Court demonstrated that they had not only a policy goal clearly in mind but also a will to pursue that goal with vigor. The result was the completion of the nationalization process upon the basis of incorporationist premises as well as the "revolution in criminal procedure" of the 1960s.

Perhaps the dominant feeling one is left with after an overview of the nationalization process is disappointment that this crucial constitutional development was not more satisfactorily justified by the Court in terms of constitutional theory. Of course this constitutional development occurred in an incremental manner over a span of many years and overlapping the terms of a large number of the members of the Court, and therefore a single, uniformly followed constitutional theory should perhaps not be expected. Eugene Rostow has said, on the other hand, that the "discussion of problems and the declaration of broad principles by the courts is a vital element in the community experience through which American policy is made. The Supreme Court is, among other things, an educational body, and the Justices are inevitably teachers in a vital national seminar."[23] To the extent that rational justification and explanation by the Court is important to the legitimization of constitutional change, it can fairly be said that the Court neglected one of its important functions in regard to the nationalization of the Bill of Rights.

The Nationalization Process and the Federal System

In the course of drastically changing the structure of protection for political and civil liberties in the United States, the nationalization of the Bill of Rights necessarily also altered fundamentally the nature of the federal system. At the time of the Civil War, the Bill of Rights was applied only to exercises of federal power and as such was the subject of almost no litigation in the Supreme Court. For the protection of their basic substantive rights, such as freedom of speech and of religion, as well as for criminal-procedure protections, citizens had to depend upon the provisions of the laws and constitutions of their respective states. And with the exception of the Commerce Clause, the Contract Clause, and the Supremacy Clause, the hand of the federal Constitution lay very lightly upon the states in terms of restricting the exercise of their powers. It was this pre–Civil War federal system that the Supreme Court sought to preserve in its decisions in the *Slaughter House Cases* and the *Hurtado* case—despite the ratification of the Fourteenth Amendment—and it was this federal system that the nationalization process altered so fundamentally.

Although the nationalization process thus involved a basic change in the relationship between the federal and state governments within the federal system, it is one of the more remarkable aspects of the nationalization of the First Amendment that counsel representing state interests in that litigation did not more vigorously resist the nationalization process. In the breakthrough case of *Gitlow* v. *New York*, for example, one brief on behalf of New York essentially conceded that freedom of speech was guaranteed by the Due Process Clause of the Fourteenth Amendment and another only rather perfunctorily disputed that point. And, just as the appellants in the subsequent cases nationalizing the First Amendment took the *Gitlow* assumption to be a matter of fact counsel for the states in the subsequent cases behaved similarly, recording only sporadic and anemic denials that First Amendment rights applied to the states. Given the momentous significance the nationalization of the First Amendment had for the nature of the federal system and for the status of the states within that system, it is indeed singular that counsel for the states did not initiate a great debate before the Court on the nationalization of the First Amendment.[24]

In the litigation nationalizing the criminal-procedure provisions of the Bill of Rights, counsel for the states did, of course, mount strenuous opposition to the claims of the appellants in most cases. The resistance of counsel for Texas, in the *Pointer* and *Washington* cases, however, was notably half-hearted, and Texas counsel in the *Washington* case conceded that the Compulsory Process Clause applied to the states. Counsel for North Carolina in the *Klopfer* case (1967) also essentially confessed error in his argument before the Court on the issue of the applicability of the Speedy Trial Clause to the states.

By the time of the incorporation breakthrough of the 1960s, legal representatives of the states had created national organizations such as the National Association of State Attorneys General (NASAG) and the National District Attorneys Association (NDAA), through which a defense of state interests could be articulated. It is ironic, however, that the most significant intervention in the nationalization litigation by such organizations came with the intervention of the attorneys general of twenty-three states in the *Gideon* case, supporting the reversal of *Betts* v. *Brady* (1942) and the application of the Assistance of Counsel Clause to the states. Only the attorneys general of Alabama and North Carolina, on the other hand, supported the retention of the *Betts* regime. The National District Attorneys Association also filed an *amicus* brief in *Malloy* v. *Hogan* (1964), but that brief focused upon the need to retain the validity of state grants of immunity from prosecution and was not directed to an argument against the applicability of the Self-Incrimination Clause to the states. In the remaining cases nationalizing the criminal-procedure provisions, there were only sporadic *amicus* interventions by representatives of state interests, such as the *amicus* intervention by the New York attorney general in the *Duncan* case and by the California attorney general in the *Malloy* case.

It is possible that there was not more opposition to the nationalization of the criminal-procedure provisions by the organized legal representatives of state interests because in at least some of the nationalizing cases, the Court unexpectedly reached out to decide cases on issues that had not appeared to be the primary issues in those cases. This was notably true of *Mapp* v. *Ohio*, in which the central issue appeared to be a First Amendment issue but which resulted in the Court's application of the Fourth Amendment and the exclusionary rule to the states. It is highly likely that if the search-and-seizure issue had appeared to be the central issue in the *Mapp* case, the National District Attorneys Association almost certainly would have intervened as *amicus curiae* in opposition to the nationalization of the Fourth Amendment and the exclusionary rule, since after the Court's decision in the *Mapp* case was announced, the NDAA joined the state of Ohio in a rather angry petition for rehearing.

Similarly, the bases upon which the Court decided both the *Robinson* and the *Pointer* cases—the Cruel and Unusual Punishment Clause and the Confrontation Clause—could not have been easily predicted. Groups alert to the protection of state interests would have needed to possess prophet-like qualities to have predicted that the *Mapp*, *Robinson*, and *Pointer* cases would have resulted in the decisions that they ultimately produced.

To some extent, the array of *amicus* participants in cases may furnish cues to the Court indicating the relative support for or opposition to its decisions; it must nevertheless be concluded that there were few such cues indicating significant opposition by organized representatives of state interests to the nationalization of the criminal-procedure provisions. On the contrary, the most important *amicus* intervention in the nationalizing cases by representatives of state interests—the *amicus* intervention by the twenty-three state attorneys general in *Gideon*—pointed the other way and suggested that the nationalization of at least some of the criminal-procedure rights would be welcomed by the representatives of state interests.

The behavior of the representatives of state interests in the cases nationalizing the criminal-procedure provisions may thus be contrasted with their behavior in other cases in which important state interests have been at stake. When the Court came to apply the principles of the *Gideon* and *Malloy* cases to the question of custodial interrogations in *Miranda* v. *Arizona* in 1966, for example, both the NDAA and the attorneys general of twenty-eight states and two commonwealths filed *amici* briefs opposing the result the Court ultimately reached.[25] Similarly, when the Court had under consideration the question of what standard the Equal Protection Clause imposed upon state legislative apportionment systems in *Reynolds* v. *Sims* and companion cases in 1963, the attorneys general of fifteen states intervened as *amici* to urge that at least one house of a state legislature be allowed to deviate from a strict population standard of apportionment.[26] In both the *Miranda* and Apportionment cases, therefore, the Court was provided with important cues that there was significant opposition to, and indeed potential resistance to, its decisions in those cases in contrast to the nationalizing cases. In the cases nationalizing the criminal-procedure provisions of the Bill of Rights, on the other hand, few such cues were provided to the Court by the representatives of state interests.

Of course, avenues of protest against or resistance to the decisions of the Supreme Court exist outside the process of litigation that produces decisions by the Court, and there were protests against the course of the Court's decisions by state interests outside the litigation process. Interestingly enough, however, the most dramatic protest against the Court for allegedly undermining the federal system came in the 1950s, before the Court began the process of selective incorporation of the criminal-procedure provisions of the Bill of Rights. This protest occurred in 1958, when the Conference of State Chief Justices voted overwhelmingly in favor of a resolution criticizing the Supreme Court for promoting "an accelerating trend towards increasing power of the national government and correspondingly contracted power of the state governments." The principles of federalism were endangered, the state chief justices asserted, by "the extent of the control over the actions of the states which the Supreme Court exercises under its views of the Fourteenth Amendment."[27]

Although the action of the state chief justices aroused considerable attention and comment,[28] nothing concrete came of it. That the state chief justices' resolution was evidence of a continuing feeling of resentment on the part of state authorities, however, was indicated in 1962 when the General Assembly of the States adopted a resolution supporting a constitutional amendment that would create a "Court of the Union." The Court of the Union, it was proposed, would be composed of the chief justices of the state supreme courts and would be empowered to "reverse decisions of the United States Supreme Court relating to rights reserved to the states or to the people under the Constitution." Along with the Court of the Union proposal, the General Assembly of the States also proposed that Article V of the Constitution be amended to allow the proposal of constitutional amendments by two-thirds of the state legislatures and that a constitutional amendment be adopted eliminating the jurisdiction of the federal courts over cases challenging state legislative apportionment systems.[29]

Although the Court of the Union proposal was in part an expression of state officials' resentment of the Court's decision in *Baker* v. *Carr* in 1962 opening the doors of the federal courts to suits challenging state-apportionment systems,[30] the proposal undoubtedly also reflected a broader resentment of the Court's use of the Fourteenth Amendment to impose increased restrictions upon state power, including restrictions on the conduct of state criminal trials. As one legislator who supported the resolutions of the General Assembly of the States said, the Tenth Amendment "has been raped twice a day for ten years."[31]

Some state legislatures adopted resolutions petitioning Congress to call a constitutional convention to consider some or all of the proposals of the General Assembly of the States, but speeches by Chief Justice Warren and other members of the Court drew attention to the drastic changes in the Constitution the adoption of the proposals would entail, and other national leaders, including President Kennedy, spoke out against the proposals. The Conference of State Chief Justices failed to endorse the proposals in its 1963 meeting, and support for the proposals by state legislatures also diminished. Like the protest of the Conference of Chief Justices in 1958, the proposals of the General Assembly of the States thus ultimately came to naught.[32]

Perhaps the most concrete resistance by state authorities to the expansion of federal judicial power under the Fourteenth Amendment came with their attack upon the habeas corpus jurisdiction of the federal courts. As the Due Process Clause was being interpreted to impose increased restrictions upon state criminal proceedings, the Court also liberalized the availability of the writ of habeas corpus in the federal courts to state prisoners challenging their convictions on federal constitutional grounds.[33] The result was that the number of petitions for writs of habeas corpus filed by state prisoners attacking their convictions skyrocketed during the 1950s and 1960s. There were 541 such petitions filed by state prisoners in 1952, but the number rose to 1,020 in 1961 and to 9,063 in 1970.[34]

Federal habeas corpus proceedings in which state prisoners attacked their convictions as being violative of the federal Constitution thus became one of the most visible manifestations of the increasing restrictions imposed upon state criminal proceedings via the Fourteenth Amendment, and the habeas corpus jurisdiction of the federal courts therefore became a focus of the resentment felt by state judges and officials toward the increased federal role in state criminal proceedings. In addition to resentment against expanding federal intrusion in state proceedings, state supreme court judges not unnaturally felt an institutional hostility toward the idea of federal district court judges reviewing in habeas proceedings, and occasionally reversing, convictions that had been reviewed and affirmed by the state supreme courts. And both state judges and state officials objected to the fact that state prisoners could attack their convictions through successive petitions for writs of habeas corpus in the federal courts, thereby destroying any finality to state criminal proceedings.

"Every conscientious state court judge is irked," one former state judge said, "by the covert suggestion that he needs to be watched closely lest he deviously steal away the citizen's rights." And as early as 1952, the Conference of State Chief Justices had complained about the habeas corpus jurisdiction of the federal courts and had argued that orderly "procedure under our dual system of government should require that a final judgment of a state's highest court be subject to review or reversal only by the Supreme Court of the United States."[35] Over ten years later, during the heyday of selective incorporationism, the state chief justices were still reported to be concerned "about the use of habeas corpus proceedings, as a means of obtaining review, in Federal District Courts, of state court convictions in criminal cases. The Chief Justices, along with the Attorneys General of the states and the District Attorneys, believe that the lack of finality of decisions in criminal cases is a threat to our system of law."[36]

Interestingly enough, however, the most concentrated attack upon the habeas corpus jurisdiction of the federal courts by state interests came, not during the 1960s, but in the 1950s. At that time proposals to drastically curtail the habeas corpus jurisdiction of the federal courts were considered by Congress, but in the end they were rejected.[37] While the number of habeas corpus petitions by state prisoners as well as the number of federal rights enforceable through such petitions increased dramatically during the 1960s, no further serious threats to the habeas corpus jurisdiction of the federal courts were mounted by state interests. The result was that most of the rights nationalized by the Court in the 1960s remained enforceable not only by the Court on direct review of state court proceedings but also by the federal courts through their habeas corpus jurisdiction.[38] While the Supreme Court's conversion of the Due Process Clause into a code of federal criminal procedure applicable to the states thus aroused vocal criticism and some significant resistance on the part of state authorities, both the criticism and the resistance proved to be largely ineffectual, and, paradoxically, such criticism and resistance appeared to have been greater during the 1950s than during the period of selective incorporationism of the 1960s.

Historically, assertions of authority by the Supreme Court that have affected state interests have also led on occasion to defiance of the Court's authority by the state judiciaries, and this might have been a part of a pattern of resistance to the Court's nationalization decisions.[39] Such a pattern did not emerge, however, with regard to the decisions of the Court nationalizing the Bill of Rights.

Regarding the First Amendment cases, the Court of course affirmed decisions of the state courts in the *Gitlow* and *Everson* cases, thus providing no occasion for evasion or defiance. And in the *Stromberg, Near, Cantwell,* and *DeJonge* cases, there is no evidence that the state courts acted to defy or evade those decisions, despite the fact that the Court both reversed state court decisions and invalidated state policies in those cases.

The outcomes in the criminal-procedure cases were similar. The results of the Court's decisions in *Mapp, Malloy, Washington,* and *Klopfer* on remand were that the charges were dropped by state authorities or dismissed by the state courts, and in response to *Robinson* v. *California*, the local police were immediately ordered to cease enforcement of the law invalidated in that case. Both Clarence Earl Gideon and Bob Granville Pointer were retried after the Court reversed their convictions; Gideon was acquitted and Pointer was reconvicted, but in both cases the state courts were careful to protect the right to counsel and the right of confrontation the Court's decisions had mandated in those cases.[40]

In *Benton* v. *Maryland*, the Maryland courts ruled on remand that Benton's larceny conviction had not affected his burglary conviction, and thus they reaffirmed his fifteen-year sentence for burglary. This would not appear to have been an evasion of the Court's ruling in the *Benton* case, since the effect of the larceny conviction upon the burglary conviction was left open by the Court, and the case was specifically remanded to the Maryland courts for them to make that determination. The Maryland courts also subsequently followed the Supreme Court's due process rulings affecting stiffer sentences on retrial and reduced Benton's sentence to ten years imprisonment.

Finally, in the *Duncan* case, the Court of course ruled that Gary Duncan was entitled to a jury trial, and therefore the threat of the Plaquemines Parish authorities to retry Duncan was not technically in defiance of the Court's decision. Their purpose was clearly to harass Duncan, however, and their behavior, until enjoined by the federal district court, was therefore undoubtedly directed at discouraging blacks from appealing for protection from the federal courts. While not directly defiant of the Court's decision in the *Duncan* case, the subsequent behavior of the Plaquemines Parish officials was expressive of an overall defiance of the intrusion of federal authority into parish affairs, and may be interpreted as at least a part of a pattern of resistance to federal authority—including that of the Court—in the parish. This behavior thus comes as close to defiance of the Court's authority as any evidenced in the cases nationalizing the Bill of Rights.

With the possible exception of the Plaquemines Parish authorities, one therefore finds no twentieth-century Spencer Roanes defying the mandates of the Court among the state judges and officials affected by the litigation nationalizing the Bill of Rights. More-generalized studies of the reactions of the state courts to the Warren Court's decisions, on the other hand, indicate that many state judges did indeed engage in their share of vocal and at times vituperative denunciations of the nationalization of the criminal-procedure provisions and the application of those provisions in subsequent cases such as *Miranda* v. *Arizona*. Typical of such denunciations was one that came from a judge of the Utah Supreme Court, who declared in 1968 that the "United States Supreme Court, as at present constituted, has departed from the Constitution as it has been interpreted from its inception and has followed the urgings of social reformers in foisting upon this Nation laws which even Congress could not constitutionally pass. It has amended the Constitution in a manner unknown to the document itself."[41] And a Maryland judge similarly accused the Court of making "fantastic new law" in its "inexorable march toward complete federalization of the criminal law."[42]

In an analysis of the reactions of the state courts to *Mapp* v. *Ohio*, as well as to the *Miranda, Escobedo,* and *Gault*[43] decisions (which involved extensions of the principles established in the nationalizing cases), Bradley Canon found that such strong verbal criticism of the Supreme Court's nationalizing decisions and their extensions was rather widespread among the state supreme courts. One or more of the decisions Canon studied were "negatively evaluated" by thirty-two of the fifty state supreme courts. The cases in which such negative evaluations occurred, however, were few in number, since they were found in only 5 percent of the cases in which the state courts had been called upon to implement the policies in the Supreme Court's decisions surveyed.[44]

In *Mapp* v. *Ohio*, and in the extension of the principles of the *Gideon* and *Malloy* cases in *Miranda* v. *Arizona*, the Court was also attempting not just to affect the conduct of trials in the state courts but to influence the behavior of the police and prosecutors. And it is clear that the Court's policy in the *Mapp* and *Miranda* cases met with mixed results at best.[45] Thus, while there was no evidence of outright defiance of the Court in the litigation involving the nationalization of the Bill of Rights, it seems clear that in cases implementing the policies of some of those decisions there was both vociferous criticism by the state courts and—in regard at least to the *Mapp* and *Miranda* decisions—substantial evasion of the policy of the Court.

The nationalization process therefore met with a variety of forms of resistance from representatives of state interests. At no time, however, did the opposition to the process of nationalization seriously threaten to mount a direct attack upon the Court itself, such as withdrawing appellate jurisdiction from the Court or reversing the Court via constitutional amendment. Since the nationalization of the Bill of Rights entailed a fundamental alteration of the federal system and of the status of the states within that system, it is not surprising that there was criticism and some resistance by state interests and officials to that process. What is surprising in retrospect is that there was not more criticism and resistance than there appears to have been.

The Second Bill of Rights and the Constitutional System

The creation of a second bill of rights through the Due Process Clause of the Fourteenth Amendment established a new system of constitutional protection for basic individual rights in the United States. Whereas, prior to the adoption of the Fourteenth Amendment and the nationalization process that followed, the basic rights of the individual were almost exclusively dependent upon state law for their protection, the nationalization process has resulted in a dual system of constitutional protection for those rights. The nationalization process, of course, insured that basic individual rights would henceforth be protected by the federal Constitution from invasion by either the national or the state governments. But the rights thus protected are also protected by bills of rights in the constitutions of the states, which guarantee rights either identical or parallel to those guaranteed in the federal Bill of Rights and the Fourteenth Amendment.

The nationalization of the Bill of Rights has not, therefore, reduced the state courts to the status of being mere transmitters of Supreme Court decisions interpreting federal constitutional rights; instead, the state courts retain considerable leeway for creativity regarding the interpretation of their own state bills of rights. The state courts thus retain the power to interpret state bills of rights more broadly than the Supreme Court may interpret the rights guaranteed by the Fourteenth Amendment, and indeed this has occurred on numerous occasions.

During the period from 1949 to 1961, for example, the Supreme Court adhered to the view that while the "core" of the Fourth Amendment applied to the states via the Due Process Clause, the federal rule, requiring the exclusion of illegally seized evidence, did not. During this period, however, an increasing number of state supreme courts adopted an exclusionary rule as a means of enforcing their own state constitutions' prohibitions of unreasonable searches and seizures. Similarly, the Supreme Court did not require under the Fourteenth Amendment the appointment of counsel in all serious state noncapital cases from 1932 to 1963, but by the time of the *Gideon* case in 1963, most of the state courts had already required the appointment of counsel in such cases under state law. And although the Supreme Court approved publicly financed transportation for parochial school students under the Establishment Clause in the *Everson* case, most state courts have invalidated similar laws in accordance with provisions in their own state constitutions that guarantee separation of church and state.

The state courts thus retain a residual power of creativity in constitutional interpretation through the construction of their own state constitutions, and interests that perceive themselves as disadvantaged by the Supreme Court's interpretation of the federal Constitution may find refuge in state-court interpretations of state constitutions. Following the Supreme Court's renunciation of its role as censor of socioeconomic policy after 1937, for example, conservative economic interests found themselves stripped of the federal constitutional protections they had previously enjoyed. Conservative spokesmen, particularly members of the bar, therefore argued that the best litigation strategy for seeking protection of economic rights was to invoke the provisions of state constitutions without reference to the federal Constitution.[46]

It is one of the ironies of American constitutional development that when in the 1970s the Burger Court began to construe more conservatively the rights guaranteed by the Fourteenth Amendment—especially criminal-procedure protections—liberals adopted the same tactic that conservative spokesmen had previously urged after 1937. There was thus a liberal rediscovery of the state courts and state constitutions in the 1970s, led in part by Justice Brennan, a leading architect of the selective incorporationism of the 1960s, who pointedly noted both in his opinions on the Court and in a law-review article that the state courts were free to interpret their state constitutions more liberally than the Court was interpreting the Fourteenth Amendment. And some state supreme courts did indeed construe the criminal-procedure provisions of their state constitutions as prohibiting practices that would have been upheld by the Supreme Court under the Fourteenth Amendment.[47] While the nationalization of the Bill of Rights imposed significant new restrictions upon the state judiciaries and increased federal judicial power, the state judiciaries were nonetheless not reduced to impotence by that process, but rather retained considerable power to play an independent role in the protection of political and civil liberties.

In addition to its impact upon the federal system and the state judiciaries, the nationalization of the Bill of Rights also changed the agenda of litigation encountered by the Supreme Court. Prior to the adoption of the Fourteenth Amendment, litigation requiring the interpretation of the Bill of Rights by the Supreme Court had to involve challenges to exercises of federal power. Such challenges based upon the provisions of the Bill of Rights had been almost nonexistent prior to the Civil War, and indeed throughout the nineteenth century, with the result that the Court was not a significant source of civil and political liberties policy until the twentieth century. There were also only a very limited number of important criminal-procedure decisions rendered by the Supreme Court during the nineteenth century, primarily because of the limited criminal jurisdiction then being exercised by the federal government and because appeals to the Supreme Court in federal criminal cases was highly restricted until almost the turn of the century.[48]

As a consequence, modern constitutional law governing political and civil liberties has largely been the product of Supreme Court decisions rendered in the twentieth century, and the nationalization of the Bill of Rights was a leading reason why that has been the case. Rather than being confined to litigation raising issues under the Bill of Rights involving the federal government, as a result of the nationalization process the docket of the Court was opened to litigation challenging an almost unlimited array of state and local policies that had previously been insulated from attack on the basis of the Bill of Rights. The result was that the Court was called upon to render more significant interpretations of political and civil liberties than ever before, and in almost every field from freedom of speech to criminal procedure, a majority of the cases in which the Court rendered decisions on civil and political liberties were cases challenging state policies under the Fourteenth Amendment.[49]

In his speech introducing the constitutional amendments that were to become the Bill of Rights, James Madison took special note of his proposal that the states also be prohibited from invading the rights of conscience, freedom of the press, and trial by jury in criminal cases. This proposed amendment, he said, was "of equal, if not greater importance" than the other proposed amendments restricting the powers of the national government. Despite his belief that "the State Governments are as liable to attack these invaluable privileges as the General Government is, and therefore ought to be as cautiously guarded against," Madison failed in his attempt to include a restriction on the powers of the states in the Bill of Rights.[50]

Through the nationalization of the Bill of Rights via the Due Process Clause of the Fourteenth Amendment, the Supreme Court more than made up for Madison's failure on this score, and while most Americans undoubtedly believe that the Bill of Rights is the most important source of their liberties, the fact is that when fundamental liberties are tested in Supreme Court litigation, the Constitution is most often interpreted on the basis of the Due Process Clause of the Fourteenth Amendment as it applies most of the Bill of Rights to the states. It is therefore no exaggeration to say that the process of nationalization has transformed the Due Process Clause of the Fourteenth Amendment into our second bill of rights, a bill of rights more salient to the liberty of the average American than the original document authored by Madison and ratified by the states in 1791.

Reference Matter

Notes

A Note on Sources

I have relied heavily upon the records and briefs filed with the United States Supreme Court in the analysis of the litigation covered herein. In analyzing the early nationalization cases, I relied on the briefs and records of Supreme Court cases available in the Law Library of the Library of Congress and the Law Library of the U.S. Supreme Court, while I relied on the microcard edition of Supreme Court briefs and records produced by Information Handling Services in analyzing the more recent cases. I have also drawn some data regarding the early nationalizing cases from the Correspondence Files of Appellate Cases that are located in the National Archives. References to these data in the notes are accompanied by the letters *NA*. In studying the nationalizing cases decided by the Court after 1955, I have used the tape recordings of the oral arguments obtained from the Audio-Visual Division of the National Archives. References in the notes to these tape recordings follow the citation system used by the National Archives in cataloging the recordings. The Archives of the American Civil Liberties Union in the Seeley G. Mudd Manuscript Library at Princeton University were also the source of considerable information regarding some of the cases covered in this work. References to data from these archives are identified in the notes by "ACLU Archives." Finally, in regard to *Everson* v. *Board of Education* (330 U.S. 1 [1947]), the source of much of the information regarding the background of that case was the legal file of Albert C. McCay on the *Everson* case. This file is in the possession of the law firm of Parker, McCay & Criscuolo in Mt. Holly, New Jersey. References to data from this file are identified in the notes by "McCay File."

CHAPTER 1

1 In art. 1, secs. 9 and 10, the original Constitution did, of course, prohibit both the states and the national government from enacting bills of attainder and ex post facto laws. Art. 1, sec. 9, also provided that the writ of habeas corpus "shall not be suspended, unless when in Cases of Rebellion or Invasion the public Safety may require it." Art. 3 additionally provided for jury trials in all criminal cases except impeachments and narrowly defined treason against the United States, a definition designed to prevent the use of charges of treason as weapons against legitimate dissent.

2 See *The Federalist*, no. 84 (New York: Modern Library, 1941), pp. 555-61; Robert Allen Rutland, *The Birth of the Bill of Rights* (New York: Collier Books, 1962), p. 136.

3 Quoted in Rutland, *The Birth of the Bill of Rights*, p. 120.

4 Ibid., chapter 7, "The Ratification Struggle," pp. 130-62.

5 Quoted in Saul K. Padover, *Thomas Jefferson on Democracy* (New York: Mentor Books, 1958), p. 47.

6 Rutland, *The Birth of the Bill of Rights*, chapter 9, "The Campaign Pledge Fulfilled," pp. 194-221.

7 Quoted ibid., p. 212.

8 *Barron* v. *Baltimore*, 7 Pet. 243 (1833).

9 7 Pet. 243, 249-50.

10 *Permoli* v. *New Orleans*, 3 How. 589, 609 (1845).

11 For a comprehensive analysis of the Fourteenth Amendment's impact on the constitutional system, see Bernard Schwartz, ed., *The Fourteenth Amendment: A Century in American Law and Life* (New York: New York University Press, 1970).

12 U.S. Congress, Senate, *Globe*, 39th Cong., 1st sess. (1865-66), p. 2765.

13 Charles Fairman, "Does the Fourteenth Amendment Incorporate the Bill of Rights: The Original Understanding," *Stanford Law Review*, 2 (1949): 5-139. For contrary views, see Justice Black's dissenting opinion and appendix in *Adamson* v. *California*, 332 U.S. 46 (1947), and also Horace Edgar Flack, *The Adoption of the Fourteenth Amendment* (1908; reprint ed., Gloucester, Mass.: Peter Smith, 1965).

14 *Slaughter House Cases*, 16 Wall. 36 (1873).

15 The best and most thorough analysis of the *Slaughter House Cases* is found in Charles Fairman, *Reconstruction and Reunion, 1864-1888*, Oliver Wendell Holmes Devise History of the Supreme Court of the United States, vol. 1, pt. 1 (New York: Macmillan, 1971), pp. 1320-63. See also, Charles Warren, *The Supreme Court in United States History* (Boston: Little, Brown, 1922), 2:533-50.

16 *Slaughter House Cases*, 16 Wall. 36, 61 (1873).

17 16 Wall. 36, 72.

18 See Fairman, *Reconstruction and Reunion*, pp. 1348-49.

19 *Slaughter House Cases*, 16 Wall. 36, 76 (1873).

20 16 Wall. 36, 79-80.

21 16 Wall. 36, 74-80.

22 16 Wall. 36, 80-81.

23 16 Wall. 36, 96, 118-19, 129.

24 See C. Vann Woodward, *Reunion and Reaction* (New York: Doubleday, Anchor, 1956).

25 *Slaughter House Cases*, 16 Wall. 36, 78, 82 (1873).

26 John W. Burgess, *Political Science and Comparative Constitutional Law* (Boston: Ginn and Co., 1890), 1: 228-30.

27 The quote is from Erwin N. Griswold, "Due Process Problems Today in the United States," in Schwartz, ed., *The Fourteenth Amendment*, p. 164.

CHAPTER 2

1 *Hurtado* v. *California*, 110 U.S. 516 (1884).

2 In the Record, p. 1, *Hurtado* v. *California*, 110 U.S. 516 (1884), Estuardo's name is listed as "Stuardo." The Sacramento *Daily Bee*, however, consistently listed the name as "Estuardo," and I have followed the newspaper's spelling here.

3 The description of the Estuardo murder is drawn from "Dark Deed of Blood," Sacramento *Daily Bee*, Feb. 7, 1882, p. 3, since the Record in the *Hurtado* case contains few details of the crime. The *Daily Bee*, as far as I could determine, did not have numbered pagination; page references were therefore determined by counting the pages from page one of the newspaper.

4 Ibid., Feb. 6, 1882, p. 2, and Feb. 7, 1882, p. 3.

5 Ibid., Feb. 7, 1882, p. 3.

6 The provision of the California Constitution was art. 1, sec. 8; the legislation implementing this provision was secs. 809 and 888 of the California Penal Code (1880).

7 Sacramento *Daily Bee*, Feb. 15, 1882, p. 3. The information is in the Record, p. 1, *Hurtado* v. *California*.

8 Sacramento *Daily Bee*, May 2, 1882, p. 3, May 4, 1882, p. 3, and May 6, 1882, p. 3.

9 Ibid., May 8, 1882, p. 3, and June 6, 1882, p. 4; Record, pp. 18–19, *Hurtado* v. *California*.

10 *People* v. *Hurtado*, 63 Cal. 288 (1883).

11 Record, p. 36, *Hurtado* v. *California*.

12 This decision is unreported; it is printed ibid., p. 34.

13 Ibid., p. 36.

14 *Murray's Lessee* v. *Hoboken Land and Improvement Co.*, 18 How. 272, 277, 280 (1856).

15 *Davidson* v. *New Orleans*, 96 U.S. 97 (1878).

16 96 U.S. 97, 103-4.

17 96 U.S. 97, 102.

18 96 U.S. 97, 105.

19 Brief of the Plaintiff in Error, pp. 28, 33, *Hurtado* v. *California*, 110 U.S. 516 (1884).

20 Ibid., pp. 42-43.

21 *Walker* v. *Sauvinet*, 92 U.S. 90 (1876); *United States* v. *Cruikshank*, 92 U.S. 542 (1876).

22 Brief for Defendant in Error, pp. 1-2, *Hurtado* v. *California*, 110 U.S. 516 (1884).

23 Ibid.

24 Ibid., pp. 5-9, 16-20.

25 *Hurtado* v. *California*, 110 U.S. 516 (1884).

26 110 U.S. 516, 529.

27 110 U.S. 516, 530.

28 110 U.S. 516, 534-35.

29 110 U.S. 516, 535-38.

30 On the first Harlan's career on the Court, see F. B. Clark, *The Constitutional Doctrines of Justice Harlan* (Baltimore: Johns Hopkins University Press, 1915). See also, Henry J. Abraham, "John Marshall Harlan: The Justice and the Man," *Kentucky Law Journal* 46 (1958): 448–74.

31 *Civil Rights Cases*, 109 U.S. 53 (1883).

32 *Hurtado* v. *California*, 110 U.S. 516, 541 (1884).

33 110 U.S. 516, 547. The phrase *doctrine of nonsuperfluousness* is my own, and it will be used herein to characterize the logic of the Court in the *Hurtado* case in denying that any right in the Bill of Rights could be applicable to the states via the Due Process Clause.

34 110 U.S. 516, 558.

35 Sacramento *Daily Bee*, March 4, 1884, p. 3, and April 4, 1884, p. 3.

36 John T. Carey to James H. McKenney, Clerk of the U.S. Supreme Court, April 6, 1884, Correspondence File, *Hurtado* v. *California*, NA.

37 *Presser* v. *Illinois*, 116 U.S. 252 (1886); *Spies* v. *Illinois*, 123 U.S. 131 (1887). On Tucker, see Arnold Paul, *Conservative Crisis and the Rule of Law* (New York: Harper & Row, 1969), pp. 76–77.

38 *In re Kemmler*, 136 U.S. 436 (1890); *McElvaine* v. *Bush*, 142 U.S. 155 (1891); *O'Neil* v. *Vermont*, 144 U.S. 323 (1892).

39 *O'Neil* v. *Vermont*, 144 U.S. 323, 361, 370.

40 *Santa Clara County* v. *Southern Pacific Railroad*, 118 U.S. 394 (1886). See also Andrew C. McLaughlin, "The Court, the Corporation, and Conkling," *American Historical Review*, 46 (1940): 45–63; Howard J. Graham, "The Conspiracy Theory of the Fourteenth Amendment," *Yale Law Journal*, 47 (1938): 371–403.

41 *Chicago, Milwaukee & St. Paul Railroad* v. *Minnesota*, 134 U.S. 418 (1890). See also Edward S. Corwin, "The Doctrine of Due Process of Law before the Civil War," *Harvard Law Review*, 24 (1911): 366–85; Edward S. Corwin, "The Supreme Court and the Fourteenth Amendment," *Michigan Law Review*, 7 (1909): 643–72; and Walton H. Hamilton, "Property—According to Locke," *Yale Law Journal*, 41 (1932): 64–80. For judicial biographies covering justices whose tenures on the Court spanned these years, see C. Peter Magrath, *Morrison R. Waite: The Triumph of Character* (New York: Macmillan, 1963); Willard L. King, *Melville Weston Fuller* (New York: Macmillan, 1950); Charles Fairman, *Justice Miller and the Supreme Court* (Cambridge, Mass.: Harvard University Press, 1939); and Carl Brent Swisher, *Stephen J. Field* (Washington, D.C.: Brookings, 1930). Although these biographical studies are helpful for background, they provide little information on the litigation involved in the nationalization of the Bill of Rights.

42 *Allgeyer* v. *Louisiana*, 165 U.S. 578, 589 (1897).

43 *Lochner* v. *New York*, 198 U.S. 45 (1905). For the role of liberty of contract in constitutional litigation up to the 1930s, see Richard C. Cortner, *The Wagner Act Cases* (Knoxville: University of Tennessee Press, 1964), especially chapters 1 and 2.

44 Some of those who accept the "incorporationist" interpretation of the relationship of the Due Process Clause to the Bill of Rights, particularly those who believe the intentions of the framers of the Fourteenth Amendment were

to make the Bill of Rights applicable to the states, would reject my reasoning at this point. The substantive guarantees of the Bill of Rights apply to the states, they would argue, because it was the intent of the framers to do so, and thus their application to the states is a development wholly apart from the development of substantive due process. It is nonetheless difficult for me to perceive how the Due Process Clause could have come to guarantee such substantive rights as freedom of speech and of the press if it had remained an essentially procedural guarantee. On this point, compare the concurring opinions of Justice Douglas in *Roe* v. *Wade*, 410 U.S. 113, 209–21 (1973), especially n. 4, and of Justice Stewart, 410 U.S. 113, 167–71 (1973).

45 *Chicago, Burlington & Quincy Railroad Co.* v. *Chicago*, 166 U.S. 226 (1897).

46 Brief of the Chicago, Burlington & Quincy Railroad Co., pp. 1–3, *Chicago, Burlington & Quincy Railroad Co.* v. *Chicago*, 166 U.S. 226 (1897). Record, pp. 1–6, 146, 153, *Chicago, Burlington & Quincy Railroad Co.* v. *Chicago*, 166 U.S. 226 (1897). The *Chicago, Burlington & Quincy Railroad Co.* cases were tried before juries; in the *Chicago & Northwestern Railroad Co.* case, a jury was waived.

47 *Chicago & Northwestern Railroad Co.* v. *Chicago*, 140 Ill. 309 (1892); *Chicago, Burlington & Quincy Railroad Co.* v. *Chicago*, 149 Ill. 457, 149 Ill. 464 (1894).

48 Record, p. 196, *Chicago, Burlington & Quincy Railroad Co.* v. *Chicago*.

49 *Chicago & Northwestern Railroad Co.* v. *Chicago*, 164 U.S. 454 (1896).

50 Brief of the Chicago, Burlington & Quincy Railroad Co., pp. 46–47, *Chicago, Burlington & Quincy Railroad Co.* v. *Chicago* (italics in the original omitted).

51 Ibid., pp. 46–86; an equal-protection claim was also raised by the railroad, but it is not discussed here.

52 Brief for Defendant in Error, pp. 8–18, *Chicago, Burlington & Quincy Railroad Co.* v. *Chicago*, 166 U.S. 226 (1897).

53 Ibid., p. 24.

54 Ibid., pp. 25–43.

55 *Chicago, Burlington & Quincy Railroad Co.* v. *Chicago*, 166 U.S. 226, 241 (1897).

56 166 U.S. 226, 242–58.

57 166 U.S. 226, 259–63. The Illinois Supreme Court's decision in the second *Chicago, Burlington & Quincy Railroad Co.* case—166 U.S. 258 (1897)—was affirmed by the Court on the basis of the reasoning in the first case.

58 William D. Guthrie, *Lectures on the Fourteenth Article of Amendment to the Constitution of the United States* (1898; reprint ed., New York: Da Capo Press, 1970).

59 Paul, *Conservative Crisis and the Rule of Law*, p. 173 n. 42. See also Benjamin R. Twiss, *Lawyers and the Constitution* (Princeton: Princeton University Press, 1942). The *Income Tax Case* was *Pollock* v. *Farmers' Loan and Trust Co.*, 158 U.S. 601 (1895).

60 Guthrie, *Lectures on the Fourteenth Amendment*, pp. 60–65. To the extent that Senator Howard's statement reflected the intentions of the framers of the Fourteenth Amendment, it had been called to the attention of the Court in the *Slaughter House Cases*, 16 Wall. 36 (1873). See Charles Fairman, *Recon-*

struction and Reunion, 1864–1888, Oliver Wendell Holmes Devise History of the Supreme Court of the United States, vol. 1, pt. 1 (New York: Macmillan, 1971), pp. 1348–49.

61 See especially the briefs in *Twining* v. *New Jersey*, 211 U.S. 78 (1908), and *Maxwell* v. *Dow*, 176 U.S. 581 (1900).

62 *Brown* v. *New Jersey*, 175 U.S. 172, 174 (1899).

63 *Maxwell* v. *Dow*, 176 U.S. 581 (1900).

64 The jury had, of course, become generally defined as being composed of twelve persons sometime in the fourteenth century. The Sixth Amendment was held to require twelve jurors in criminal cases in *Thompson* v. *Utah*, 170 U.S. 34 (1898), and this ruling was followed in such cases as *Rasmussen* v. *United States*, 197 U.S. 516 (1905), and *Patton* v. *United States*, 281 U.S. 276 (1930). Similarly, the Seventh Amendment requirement of a jury trial was held to require a twelve-person jury in *Capital Traction Co.* v. *Hof*, 174 U.S. 1 (1899), and *American Publishing Co.* v. *Fisher*, 166 U.S. 464 (1897). The Supreme Court held in *Williams* v. *Florida*, 399 U.S. 78 (1970), however, that under the Sixth and Fourteenth Amendments, juries could be composed of fewer than twelve persons. Although unanimous verdicts had also been indicated as a requirement of the constitutional protection of a jury trial in *American Publishing Co.* v. *Fisher*, 166 U.S. 464 (1897), in *Johnson* v. *Louisiana*, 406 U.S. 356 (1972), and *Apodaca* v. *Oregon*, 406 U.S. 404 (1972), the Court held that verdicts by juries in criminal cases tried in state courts by votes of nine to three and ten to two were valid under the Fourteenth Amendment.

65 See *Williams* v. *Florida*, 399 U.S. 78, 98 n. 45 (1970).

66 *American Publishing Co.* v. *Fisher*, 166 U.S. 464, 468 (1897). The Utah Territorial Supreme Court upheld the less-than-unanimous civil-jury verdicts in *Hess* v. *White*, 9 Utah 61 (1893). The U.S. Supreme Court held the practice invalid in *American Publishing Co.* v. *Fisher*, 166 U.S. 464 (1897), and *Springville* v. *Thomas*, 166 U.S. 707 (1897). *Walker* v. *Sauvinet* was decided by the Court in 1876 (92 U.S. 90).

67 *State* v. *Thompson*, 15 Utah 488 (1897).

68 *Thompson* v. *Utah*, 170 U.S. 343, 349 (1898).

69 *Salt Lake Tribune*, June 23, 1898, p. 7.

70 Ibid., May 29, 1898, pp. 1, 2.

71 Ibid.

72 Ibid., May 31, 1898, p. 8.

73 Ibid., June 26, 1898, p. 7.

74 Ibid., May 29, 1898, p. 2. See also ibid., May 30, 1898, p. 8, and May 31, 1898, p. 8; Charles Kelley, *The Outlaw Trail* (New York: Devin-Adair, 1959), pp. 150–51, 181–82.

75 Record, pp. 6–9, *Maxwell* v. *Dow*, 176 U.S. 581 (1900). *Salt Lake Tribune*, Sept. 20, 1898, p. 7.

76 *In re Maxwell*, 19 Utah 495, 503–4 (1899). See also *In re McKee*, 19 Utah 23 (1899), and Record, pp. 1–9, *Maxwell* v. *Dow*.

77 J. W. N. Whitecotton to James H. McKenney, Clerk of the U.S. Supreme Court, July 26, 1899, Correspondence File, *Maxwell* v. *Dow*, NA.

78 McKenney to Whitecotton, July 31, 1899, Correspondence File, *Maxwell* v. *Dow*, NA. For a good summary of the Supreme Court's contemporary *in forma pauperis* rules, see Robert L. Stern and Eugene Gressman, *Supreme Court Practice* (Washington, D.C.: Bureau of National Affairs, 1969), chapter 8.

79 Whitecotton to McKenney, Aug. 21, 1899, Correspondence File, *Maxwell* v. *Dow*, N.A. See also McKenney to Whitecotton, July 19, 1900, Correspondence File, *Maxwell* v. *Dow*, NA.

80 Whitecotton to McKenney, Aug. 29, 1899, Correspondence File, *Maxwell* v. *Dow*, NA.

81 Plaintiff's Brief, pp. 5-6, 20-21, *Maxwell* v. *Dow*, 176 U.S. 581 (1900).

82 Ibid., pp. 9-18, 24, 30-33.

83 Brief of the Defendant in Error, pp. 7-11, 17-19, 21-23, 31-40, *Maxwell* v. *Dow*, 176 U.S. 581 (1900).

84 Ibid., p. 5.

85 *Maxwell* v. *Dow*, 176 U.S. 581 (1900).

86 176 U.S. 581, 585-86.

87 176 U.S. 581, 602.

88 176 U.S. 581, 602.

89 176 U.S. 581, 602-3.

90 176 U.S. 581, 612.

91 176 U.S. 581, 614.

92 *Salt Lake Herald*, Feb. 27, 1900, p. 8, and Feb. 28, 1900, p. 5.

93 Kelley, *The Outlaw Trail*, p. 185.

94 *Twining* v. *New Jersey*, 211 U.S. 78 (1908).

CHAPTER 3

1 The account in this paragraph and the following two paragraphs is drawn from a description of the events in the *New York Times*, Feb. 14, 1903, p. 3.

2 Vreedenberg's name is variously spelled throughout the Record, *Twining* v. *New Jersey*, 211 U.S. 78 (1908), and in the contemporary newspaper accounts. I have arbitrarily selected this spelling from among the many variations because this is the spelling adopted by the U.S. Supreme Court in its opinion in the *Twining* case. Vreedenberg's first name was also reported at times as "James."

3 *New York Times*, Feb. 15, 1903, p. 13.

4 Ibid., Feb. 14, 1903, p. 3, lists the officers and directors of both the First National Bank and the Monmouth Trust Company.

5 Ibid., June 17, 1905, p. 2, Feb. 17, 1903, p. 3, and Feb. 18, 1903, p. 5.

6 Ibid., Feb. 18, 1903, p. 5.

7 Ibid.

8 Ibid.

9 Ibid. The First National Bank stock purchase is reported ibid., Feb. 20, 1903, p. 2. Twining's assets were revealed when he assigned them to an attorney to satisfy his creditors. See also, ibid., April 10, 1903, p. 1, Feb. 26, 1903, p. 1, and Feb. 28, 1903, p. 2.

10 *State* v. *Twining*, 71 N.J.L. 388 (1904); the conviction of Twining and Cor-

nell is reported in the *New York Times*, Jan. 8, 1904, p. 14. Twining was also subjected to at least one civil action arising from the collapse of the Monmouth Trust Company. See *Lanning* v. *Johnson*, 75 N.J.L. 259 (1906).

11 *New York Times*, Jan. 31, 1905, p. 11, and Feb. 5, 1905, p. 1.

12 *Twining* v. *United States*, 141 F. 41 (3rd Cir., 1905).

13 The minutes of the alleged board of directors meeting are reprinted in the Record, pp. 123-24, *Twining* v. *New Jersey*.

14 The motives behind the bank-stock deal are not apparent either from the Record in the *Twining* case or the contemporary newspaper accounts. The best explanation of the transaction I have found is contained in the opinion of the Supreme Court of New Jersey sustaining the convictions of Twining and Cornell on the exhibition of false-papers charges. See *State* v. *Twining*, 73 N.J.L. 3 (1905).

15 Record, pp. 7-11, *Twining* v. *New Jersey*. The statute under which Twining and Cornell were indicted was section 17 of the Trust Company Act of 1899, N.J. Laws of 1899, p. 450.

16 Record, pp. 34-105, *Twining*, v. *New Jersey*.

17 Ibid., pp. 127-33.

18 Ibid., pp. 139-45.

19 Ibid., p. 145.

20 Ibid., p. 15.

21 In many jurisdictions, however, the defendant was allowed to make an unsworn statement to the court and jury.

22 *Wilson* v. *United States*, 149 U.S. 60 (1893), interpreting 20 Stat. 30, 18 U.S.C. 3481. A good review of the movement to make defendants competent witnesses is contained in the Court's opinion in *Ferguson* v. *Georgia*, 365 U.S. 570 (1961).

23 The New Jersey act was section 8 of the Act Concerning Evidence, 2 N.J. General Statutes, p. 1398. The leading cases interpreting this statute were *Parker* v. *State*, 61 N.J.L. 308 (1898), *aff'd* upon the opinion of the Supreme Court by the Court of Errors and Appeals, *Parker* v. *State*, 62 N.J.L. 801 (1899); *State* v. *Wines*, 65 N.J.L. 31 (1900); *State* v. *Zdanowicz*, 69 N.J.L. 619 (1903).

24 *State* v. *Twining*, 73 N.J.L. 683, 692 (1906), affirming *State* v. *Twining*, 73 N.J.L. 3 (1905).

25 See Brief for the Plaintiff in Error, p. 21, *Twining* v. *New Jersey*, 211 U.S. 78 (1908), and Supplemental Brief for Defendant in Error, *Twining* v. *New Jersey*, 211 U.S. 78 (1908).

26 Brief for the Plaintiff in Error, pp. 49-50, 60, *Twining* v. *New Jersey*.

27 Ibid., pp. 29-43. Ultimately, however, six states—California, Connecticut, Iowa, New Jersey, New Mexico, and Ohio—permitted comment on the failure of a defendant to testify. See *Griffin* v. *California*, 380 U.S. 609, 611 n. 3 (1965).

28 Ibid., p. 48. The fact that Twining had a prior criminal record at the time of his trial, which could have been revealed had he taken the stand, was apparently overlooked by the Court in later years. In *Adamson* v. *California*, 332 U.S. 46, 56-58 (1947), the Court apparently felt that the fact of Adamson's

prior criminal record, and the possible revelation of it if he testified, presented a somewhat different factual situation than that which had been presented in *Twining*. This of course was incorrect. See also Justice Frankfurter's concurring opinion in *Adamson*, 332 U.S. 46, 60.

29 Brief for David C. Cornell, pp. 37–38, *Twining* v. *New Jersey*, 211 U.S. 78 (1908). Fully nine pages of the brief were composed of quotations from Guthrie's *Lectures*.

30 Brief for the State of New Jersey, pp. 52–55, *Twining* v. *New Jersey*, 211 U.S. 78 (1908).

31 *Twining* v. *New Jersey*, 211 U.S. 78 (1908).

32 211 U.S. 78, 96–99.

33 211 U.S. 78, 99.

34 211 U.S. 78, 97–106.

35 211 U.S. 78, 91–93.

36 211 U.S. 78, 105–6. The accuracy of the Court's historical analysis in *Twining* has been seriously questioned. See Leonard W. Levy, *Origins of the Fifth Amendment* (New York: Oxford University Press, 1968), preface and pp. 334–35.

37 211 U.S. 78, 110–14.

38 211 U.S. 78, 119.

39 Albert C. Twining to James H. McKenney, Clerk of the U.S. Supreme Court, March 22, 1908, Correspondence File, *Twining* v. *New Jersey*, NA.

40 *Adamson* v. *California*, 332 U.S. 46, 59 (1947).

41 *Malloy* v. *Hogan*, 378 U.S. 1 (1964). Comment was also held to violate the Fifth and Fourteenth Amendments in *Griffin* v. *California*, 380 U.S. 609 (1965).

42 A deviation occurred in *Colgate* v. *Harvey*, 296 U.S. 404 (1935), a deviation soon repudiated in *Madden* v. *Kentucky*, 309 U.S. 83 (1940).

43 On the Red Scare generally, see Julian F. Jaffe, *Crusade against Radicalism: New York during the Red Scare, 1914–1924* (Port Washington, N.Y.: Kennikat Press, 1972); on Palmer's role in the Red Scare, see Stanley Coben, *A. Mitchell Palmer: Politician* (New York: Columbia University Press, 1963). The enactment of criminal syndicalism legislation is described in Eldridge Foster Dowell, *A History of Criminal Syndicalism Legislation in the United States* (Baltimore: Johns Hopkins University Press, 1939). The impact of the Red Scare on civil liberties is well covered in Zechariah Chafee, Jr., *Free Speech in the United States* (Cambridge, Mass.: Harvard University Press, 1954), and in Paul L. Murphy, *The Meaning of Freedom of Speech* (Westport, Conn.: Greenwood Publishing Co., 1972).

44 A good description of Gitlow's early career is found in Theodore Draper, *The Roots of American Communism* (New York: Viking Press, 1957), pp. 139–41; see also Gitlow's autobiography, Benjamin Gitlow, *I Confess* (New York: E. P. Dutton, 1940).

45 *New York Times*, Nov. 11, 1919, p. 2.

46 Gitlow, *I Confess*, p. 60.

47 *New York Times*, Nov. 12, 1919, pp. 1, 3, and Nov. 15, 1919, p. 2.

48 The Brief for the State of New York, pp. 13–14, *Gitlow* v. *New York*, 268

U.S. 652 (1925), contains a description of the reasons for the adoption of the Criminal Anarchy Act.

49 The "Left Wing Manifesto" is reprinted in part in *Gitlow* v. *New York*, 268 U.S. 652, 656 n. 2 (1925).

50 Ibid.

51 Record, pp. 13-14, 48-49, *Gitlow* v. *New York*, 268 U.S. 652 (1925). See also, *New York Times*, Nov. 20, 1919, p. 7, and Nov. 27, 1919, p. 3; Gitlow, *I Confess*, p. 70.

52 Gitlow, *I Confess*, p. 71.

53 Ibid., p. 72.

54 Ibid., p. 73; *New York Times*, Feb. 6, 1920, p. 17.

55 *New York Times*, Feb. 7, 1920, p. 10, editorial, "A Criminal Anarchist."

56 Gitlow, *I Confess*, p. 128.

57 *People* v. *Gitlow*, 195 N.Y.App.Div. 773, 790-92 (1921).

58 *People* v. *Gitlow*, 234 N.Y. 132, 136; 158 (1922).

59 Gitlow, *I Confess*, pp. 140-52; Donald Johnson, *The Challenge to American Freedoms* (Lexington: University of Kentucky Press, 1963), chaps. 1, 5; Roger Baldwin to Ms. Edwinna L. Klee, April 9, 1923, and Baldwin to Mrs. Elizabeth Glendoner Evans, April 13, 1923, vol. 244, ACLU Archives.

60 Baldwin to State Senator John Hastings, Jan. 15, 1923, vol. 244, ACLU Archives.

61 Alpheus T. Mason, *William Howard Taft: Chief Justice* (New York: Simon and Schuster, 1964), pp. 213-15. On the Taft Court generally, see Henry F. Pringle, *The Life and Times of William Howard Taft*, 2 vols (New York: Farrar & Rinehart); and Joel F. Paschal, *Mr. Justice Sutherland: A Man against the State* (Princeton: Princeton University Press, 1951).

62 See, for example, *Bailey* v. *Drexel Furniture Co.*, 259 U.S. 20 (1922); *Adkins* v. *Children's Hospital*, 261 U.S. 525 (1923); and *Wolff Packing Co.* v. *Industrial Court*, 262 U.S. 522 (1923).

63 *Meyer* v. *Nebraska*, 262 U.S. 390 (1923); *Pierce* v. *Society of Sisters*, 268 U.S. 510 (1925).

64 See Alexander M. Bickel, *The Supreme Court and the Idea of Progress* (New York: Harper & Row, 1970), pp. 24-29.

65 *Patterson* v. *Colorado*, 205 U.S. 454, 462 (1907).

66 *Fox* v. *Washington*, 236 U.S. 273 (1915); *Gilbert* v. *Minnesota*, 254 U.S. 325 (1920).

67 *Prudential Insurance Co.* v. *Cheek*, 259 U.S. 530, 538, 543 (1922).

68 Brief for the Plaintiff in Error, pp. 11, 18, *Gitlow* v. *New York*, 268 U.S. 652 (1925).

69 Ibid., pp. 20-21, 102.

70 *Schenck* v. *United States*, 249 U.S. 47, 52 (1919).

71 Chafee, *Free Speech in the United States*, p. 319.

72 *Abrams* v. *United States*, 250 U.S. 616 (1919).

73 Brief for the State of New York, p. 7, *Gitlow* v. *New York*.

74 Ibid., pp. 13-14.

75 Brief for Defendant in Error, p. 9, *Gitlow* v. *New York*, 268 U.S. 652 (1925).

76 Ibid., pp. 11-28.

77 *Gitlow* v. *New York*, 268 U.S. 652 (1925). The *United States Reports* indicate that Justice Stone participated in the decision of the *Gitlow* case, but the *Reports* are in error. See Alpheus T. Mason, *Harlan Fiske Stone: Pillar of the Law* (New York: Viking Press, 1956), p. 518.

78 268 U.S. 652, 666.

79 268 U.S. 652, 665-66.

80 268 U.S. 652, 671.

81 268 U.S. 652, 668-71.

82 268 U.S. 652, 669-70.

83 268 U.S. 652, 672.

84 268 U.S. 652, 673.

85 *New York Times*, Dec. 12, 1925, p. 1; Gitlow, *I Confess*, pp. 284-86.

86 Theodore Draper, *American Communism and Soviet Russia* (New York: Viking Press, 1960), pp. 422-30.

87 *New York Times*, July 20, 1965, p. 33; Draper, *American Communism and Soviet Russia*, p. 430.

CHAPTER 4

1 Roger Baldwin to Mrs. Henry Moskowitz, July 22, 1925, vol. 288, ACLU Archives.

2 *Whitney* v. *California*, 274 U.S. 357 (1927); *Burns* v. *United States*, 274 U.S. 328 (1927). Under 16 U.S.C. 57-58, Congress provided that if any offense were committed in Yosemite National Park that was not prohibited by the laws of the United States, the offender could be prosecuted in federal court under applicable California laws. Burns solicited fellow employees of a lumber company in Yosemite to join the Industrial Workers of the World (IWW) and was thus tried and convicted in a U.S. district court of violating the California Criminal Syndicalism Act. The *Burns* case was jointly sponsored and financed on appeal to the Court by the California branch of the IWW General Defense Committee and the ACLU. See Peter Stone to Roger Baldwin, Dec. 2, 1924; R. W. Henderson to Baldwin, Dec. 16, 1924; Baldwin to Henderson, Feb. 24, 1925—all in vol. 284A, ACLU Archives.

The ACLU entered the *Whitney* case after the California courts had upheld the validity of the criminal syndicalism act. The case was financed jointly by the ACLU and Charlotte Anita Whitney's California counsel, Walter Neylan, who was also publisher of the *San Francisco Call*. See Neylan to Forrest Bailey, Jan. 4, 1926; Bailey to Neylan, Jan. 9, 1926; Neylan to Bailey, Feb. 2, 1926; Bailey to Neylan, Feb. 8, 1926; Neylan to Bailey, Feb. 13, 1926—all in vol. 305, ACLU Archives.

3 *Whitney* v. *California*, 274 U.S. 357, 371, (1927).

4 274 U.S. 357, 373, 379-80. See also, Alexander M. Bickel, *The Supreme Court and the Idea of Progress* (New York: Harper & Row, 1970), p. 26.

5 Memorandum on *Whitney* v. *California*, by Walter Pollak, n.d., vol. 324, ACLU Archives.

6 *Lyons* (Kansas) *Daily News*, July 3, 1923, p. 1, hereinafter cited as *Lyons Daily News*. Record, pp. 7-22, *Fiske* v. *Kansas*, 274 U.S. 380 (1927).

7 The preamble of the IWW constitution is printed in the Record, pp. 7–8, *Fiske* v. *Kansas*, 274. U.S. 380 (1927).

8 See the *One Big Union Monthly* 2, no. 3 (Aug. 1920): 16, and 3, no. 1 (Jan. 1921): 56. On the IWW General Defense Committee, see John S. Gambs, *The Decline of the IWW* (New York: Columbia University Press, 1932), pp. 56–60.

9 Memorandum of National Bail Fund on bail securities furnished to Chas. L. Carroll, April 12, 1928, vol. 340, ACLU Archives; *Lyons Daily News*, Sept. 17, 1923, p. 1, and Sept. 18, 1923, p. 1.

10 Author's interview with Charles L. Carroll, Great Bend, Kansas, July 17, 1976.

11 *Lyons Daily News*, Sept. 19, 1923, p. 1, and Sept. 20, 1923, p. 1.

12 A. M. Harvey to ACLU, Feb. 27, 1928, vol. 344, ACLU Archives; *State* v. *Fiske*, 117 Kan. 69 (1924).

13 ACLU press release, Dec. 18, 1924, vol. 259, ACLU Archives; memorandum re Fiske supersedeas bond by Forrest Bailey, n.d., vol. 340, ACLU Archives; A. M. Harvey to ACLU, Feb. 27, 1928, vol. 344, ACLU Archives. The ACLU ultimately experienced serious difficulties with Charles Carroll in the *Fiske* case, since it appears that Carroll allowed the appeal bond to be kept by the Harveys in partial payment of their fees and also failed to pay back other funds loaned to him by the ACLU for bail and bonds in the *Fiske* and other cases. See the Bailey memorandum cited in this note. Because of his conduct in the *Fiske* case, Carroll was at one time described by a member of the National Bail Fund as a "crook." See Kathryn Fenn to Roger Baldwin, Feb. 26, 1929, vol. 373, ACLU Archives.

14 Brief for the Plaintiff in Error, p. 27, *Fiske* v. *Kansas*, 274 U.S. 380 (1927).

15 Brief for the Defendant in Error, pp. 20–25, *Fiske* v. *Kansas*, 274 U.S. 380 (1927).

16 *Fiske* v. *Kansas*, 274 U.S. 380, 387 (1927). There has been considerable difference of opinion regarding the significance of the *Fiske* case. These differences will be discussed later in this chapter, at the conclusion of the analysis of the *Stromberg* and *Near* cases. As I shall indicate there, I do not agree that the *Fiske* case made freedom of speech clearly applicable to the states. Cf. Zechariah Chafee, Jr., *Free Speech in the United States* (Cambridge, Mass.: Harvard University Press, 1954), p. 352.

17 Memorandum on *Whitney* v. *California*, by Walter Pollak, n.d., vol. 324, ACLU Archives.

18 Record, pp. 10–15, 52–57, *Near* v. *Minnesota*, 283 U.S. 697 (1931). *New York Times*, Sept. 7, 1934, pp. 1, 18.

19 *New York Times*, Sept. 7, 1934, p. 18; Record, p. 46, *Near* v. *Minnesota*.

20 Record, pp. 74, 132–40, 160–62, 188, 223, 332, *Near* v. *Minnesota*.

21 Ibid., pp. 269, 328–29.

22 Ibid., pp. 321–27.

23 Ibid., pp. 4–9.

24 See *Editor & Publisher*, 62, no. 49 (1930): 140. The gag law was chapter 285 of the 1925 Minnesota Session Laws.

25 Record, pp. 355–65, *Near v. Minnesota*.

26 *State ex rel. Olson* v. *Guilford*, 174 Minn. 457, 463-64 (1928).
27 Carol Weiss King to Forrest Bailey, June 22, 1928, vol. 346, ACLU Archives.
28 King to Bailey, June 22, 1928, and June 25, 1928, vol. 346, ACLU Archives.
29 Bailey to J. M. Near, June 27, 1928, vol. 346, ACLU Archives.
30 Near to Bailey, July 2, 1928, vol. 346, ACLU Archives.
31 George B. Leonard to Bailey, July 3, 1928, vol. 346, ACLU Archives.
32 Bailey to Near, July 3, 1928, vol. 346, ACLU Archives.
33 Near to Bailey, July 13, 1928, vol. 346, ACLU Archives.
34 Near to Bailey, Aug. 9, 1928; Roger Baldwin to Near, Aug. 13, 1928; Carol Weiss King to Near, Aug. 14, 1928—all in vol. 346, ACLU Archives.
35 Telegram, T. E. Latimer to ACLU, Nov. 30, 1928, vol. 346, ACLU Archives.
36 J. M. Near to Carol Weiss King, Dec. 9, 1928, vol. 346, ACLU Archives.
37 Forrest Bailey to the *Chicago Tribune*, Dec. 20, 1928, vol. 346, ACLU Archives.
38 E. S. Beck to Bailey, Jan. 11, 1929, vol. 374, ACLU Archives; Bailey to *Chicago Tribune*, Jan. 9, 1930; Weymouth Kirkland to Bailey, Jan. 27, 1930; Bailey to Kirkland, Feb. 28, 1930—all in vol. 425, ACLU Archives.
39 Quoted in *Editor & Publisher*, 62, no. 46 (1930): 5.
40 *State ex rel. Olson* v. *Guilford*, 179 Minn. 40, 41 (1929).
41 Quoted in *Editor & Publisher*, 62, no. 46 (1930): 5.
42 Quoted ibid., 62, no. 50 (1930): 3.
43 Record, pp. 24-25, *Stromberg* v. *California*, 283 U.S. 359 (1931).
44 The Red flag law is printed in Brief for Appellant, p. 4, *Stromberg* v. *California*, 283 U.S. 359 (1931); Paul L. Murphy, *The Meaning of Freedom of Speech* (Westport, Conn.: Greenwood Publishing Co., 1972), p. 245.
45 Record, p. 1, *Stromberg* v. *California*.
46 Telegram, Clinton P. Taft to Forrest Bailey, Aug. 5, 1929, vol. 371, ACLU Archives.
47 Theodore Draper, *American Communism and Soviet Russia* (New York: Viking Press, 1960), pp. 180-82.
48 See Dan T. Carter, *Scottsboro* (Baton Rouge: Louisiana State University Press, 1969), pp. 169-73; Herbert B. Ehrmann, *The Case That Will Not Die* (Boston: Little, Brown, 1969); Richard H. Frost, *The Mooney Case* (Stanford: Stanford University Press, 1968), pp. 427-46.
49 Telegram, ACLU to Clinton P. Taft, Aug. 6, 1929, vol. 371, ACLU Archives. The ILD initially retained Leo Gallagher, also a member of the California CLU State Committee, and Gallagher and Beardsley jointly represented the defendants in the Red flag case at their preliminary hearing. Beardsley then assumed sole responsibility for the defense in the case. See John Beardsley to Forrest Bailey, Feb. 5, 1930, vol. 371, ACLU Archives.
50 Record, p. 25, *Stromberg* v. *California*; Brief of Appellant, p. 10, *Stromberg* v. *California*, 283 U.S. 359 (1931).
51 Record, pp. 2-3, *Stromberg* v. *California*.
52 Ibid., pp. 2-4, 26. *The California Red Flag Case* (ACLU pamphlet, April 1930), in vol. 371, ACLU Archives.
53 Undated news account, vol. 417, ACLU Archives.
54 ILD press release, Nov. 5, 1929, vol. 371, ACLU Archives.

55 Telegrams, Clinton Taft to Forrest Bailey, Oct. 10, 1929, and Bailey to Taft, Oct. 11, 1929—both in vol. 371, ACLU Archives.

56 Taft to Roger Baldwin, Nov. 5, 1929, vol. 371, ACLU Archives.

57 Baldwin to Taft, Nov. 11, 1929, vol. 371, ACLU Archives.

58 John Beardsley to Baldwin, Nov. 16, 1929, vol. 371, ACLU Archives.

59 Ibid.

60 Ibid.

61 Forrest Bailey to Arthur Garfield Hays, Nov. 29, 1929; Hays to Bailey, Dec. 6, 1929—both in vol. 371, ACLU Archives.

62 Roger Baldwin to John Beardsley, Nov. 19, 1929, vol. 371, ACLU Archives.

63 Beardsley to Baldwin, Aug. 19, 1930; Forrest Bailey to George Mauer, Assistant Secretary, ILD, Jan. 28, 1930—both in vol. 416, ACLU Archives; Samuel A. Darcy, ILD, to ACLU, Sept. 8, 1930; Bailey to Beardsley, Feb. 2, 1931; memorandum, "Cost Red Flag Case," n.d.—all in vol. 417, ACLU Archives.

64 *People* v. *Mintz*, 106 Cal.App. 725, 734 (1930).

65 Roger Baldwin to John Beardsley, July 7, 1930; Beardsley to Baldwin, July 9, 1930; July 18, 1930—all in vol. 416, ACLU Archives. The conspiracy charges against all of the defendants were dismissed in the San Bernardino County Superior Court on September 15, 1930. *Open Forum*, published by the Southern California branch CLU, n.d., vol. 416, ACLU Archives.

66 Telegrams, Baldwin to Beardsley, July 28, 1930, and Beardsley to Baldwin, July 29, 1930, vol. 416, ACLU Archives.

67 Beardsley to Baldwin, July 30, 1930, vol. 416, ACLU Archives.

68 Beardsley to George Mauer, Feb. 27, 1930, vol. 416, ACLU Archives.

69 Forrest Bailey to Beardsley, Feb. 1, 1930; Beardsley to Bailey, Feb. 5, 1930—both in vol. 416, ACLU Archives.

70 Bailey to George Mauer, Jan. 28, 1929; Mauer to Bailey, Jan. 31, 1929; Bailey to Mauer, Feb. 1, 1930—all in vol. 416, ACLU Archives.

71 Samuel A. Darcy, Assistant Secretary, ILD, to Roger Baldwin, Sept. 2, 1930, vol. 416, ACLU Archives; John Beardsley to Forrest Bailey, Jan. 20, 1931, vol. 478, ACLU Archives.

72 Beardsley to Roger Baldwin, March 16, 1931, vol. 478, ACLU Archives.

73 Telegram, Forrest Bailey to Beardsley, March 20, 1931, vol. 478, ACLU Archives.

74 Roger Baldwin to Mrs. Kate Crane-Gartz, April 8, 1931, vol. 478, ACLU Archives.

75 Appellant's Brief, p. 47, *Near* v. *Minnesota*, 283 U.S. 697 (1931); Brief for Appellant, p. 14, *Stromberg* v. *California*, 283 U.S. 359 (1931).

76 Brief for Appellee, p. 6, *Near* v. *Minnesota*, 283 U.S. 697 (1931).

77 Ibid., pp. 7-13, 32.

78 Brief for Appellant, p. 22, *Stromberg* v. *California*, 283 U.S. 359 (1931).

79 Brief for Appellant, pp. 20-30, *Stromberg* v. *California*.

80 Brief of Appellee, pp. 4-10, 23-27, *Stromberg* v. *California*, 283 U.S. 359 (1931).

81 Henry F. Pringle, *The Life and Times of William Howard Taft* (New York: Farrar & Rinehart, 1939), 2: 967, 1047.

82 Ibid., p. 1044.
83 Alpheus T. Mason, *The Supreme Court from Taft to Warren* (New York: Norton, 1964), pp. 70–74.
84 *Stromberg* v. *California*, 283 U.S. 359, 368 (1931).
85 283 U.S. 359, 368–69.
86 *Near* v. *Minnesota*, 283 U.S. 697, 707 (1931).
87 283 U.S. 697, 713–19.
88 283 U.S. 697, 721.
89 *Stromberg* v. *California*, 283 U.S. 359, 371–76 (1931).
90 *Near* v. *Minnesota*, 283 U.S. 697, 723–24 (1931).
91 *Labor Defender*, 6, no. 6 (June 1931): 112. *Labor Defender* was the official publication of the ILD; its name was subsequently changed to *Equal Justice* in 1937.
92 *New York Times*, Sept. 7, 1934, pp. 1, 18, Sept. 8, 1934, p. 30, and April 19, 1936, sec. 2, p. 10.
93 See Klaus H. Heberle's excellent article, "From Gitlow to Near: Judicial Amendment by Absent-Minded Incrementalism," *Journal of Politics*, 34 (1972): 458–83.
94 For example, Chafee, *Free Speech in the United States*, p. 352, argued that the *Fiske* case nationalized freedom of speech. Henry J. Abraham, *Freedom and the Court* (New York: Oxford University Press, 1972), p. 54, agrees with Chafee. Others are doubtful; see Heberle, "From Gitlow to Near," pp. 458, 477.
95 Quoted in Heberle, "From Gitlow to Near," p. 470 n. 37.
96 David J. Danelski and Joseph S. Tulchin, eds., *The Autobiographical Notes of Charles Evans Hughes* (Cambridge, Mass.: Harvard University Press, 1973), appendix 3, p. 341.
97 *Near* v. *Minnesota*, 283 U.S. 697, 723–24 (1931).
98 *Grosjean* v. *American Press Co.*, 297 U.S. 233, 244 (1936).
99 297 U.S. 233, 243.
100 *DeJonge* v. *Oregon*, 299 U.S. 353 (1937).
101 Oregon Code of 1930, section 14–3112, as amended by chapter 459 of the Oregon Laws of 1933. Eldridge Foster Dowell, *A History of Criminal Syndicalism Legislation in the United States* (Baltimore: Johns Hopkins University Press, 1939), pp. 118–22, covers some earlier prosecutions under the Oregon act.
102 *Labor Defender*, 10 (Dec. 1936): 16.
103 Record, p. 7, *DeJonge* v. *Oregon*, 299 U.S. 353 (1937).
104 Ibid., p. 7; Portland *Oregon Journal*, Oct. 3, 1934, p. 7.
105 Gus Solomon to Emily Nunn, Nov. 15, 1934; Solomon to Lucille B. Milner, Nov. 22, 1934—both in vol. 753, ACLU Archives.
106 Portland *Oregon Journal*, Oct. 30, 1934, p. 1; Portland *Oregonian*, Oct. 30, 1934, p. 18.
107 Portland *Oregon Journal*, Oct. 31, 1934, p. 6, and Nov. 7, 1934, p. 13.
108 The corruption of Doyle and of members of the Portland police department was subsequently revealed in the Record, pp. 514–21, 553–58, *Bridges* v. *Wixon*, 326 U.S. 125 (1944). See also *New York Times*, July 12, 1939, p. 3, July 13, 1939, p. 3, and July 14, 1939, p. 20.

109 Quoted in *State* v. *DeJonge*, 152 Ore. 315, 347 (1935).
110 Portland *Oregon Journal*, Nov. 23, 1934, p. 2.
111 Portland *Oregon Journal*, Nov. 21, 1934, p. 10, and Nov. 22, 1934, pp. 1, 8.
112 Gus Solomon to Lucille Milner, Nov. 22, 1934, vol. 753, ACLU Archives.
113 Portland *Oregonian*, Nov. 27, 1934, p. 1; Portland *Oregon Journal*, Nov. 26, 1934, pp. 1, 2.
114 Roger Baldwin to Solomon, Dec. 21, 1934; see also Solomon to Lucille Milner, Dec. 15, 1934—both in vol. 753, ACLU Archives.
115 *State* v. *DeJonge*, 152 Ore. 315 (1935).
116 *Labor Defender*, 10 (May 1936): 19, and 10 (Dec. 1936): 16.
117 Gus Solomon to ACLU, Dec. 6, 1935; Samuel Paul Puner to Solomon, Dec. 21, 1935; telegram, ACLU to Solomon, Dec. 10, 1935—all in vol. 855, ACLU Archives.
118 Gus Solomon to ACLU, Oct. 22, 1936; Solomon to ACLU, Jan. 25, 1936—both in vol. 947, ACLU Archives.
119 Lucille Milner to Gus Solomon, Jan. 28, 1936, vol. 947, ACLU Archives.
120 *Labor Defender*, 10 (Dec. 1936): 16.
121 Lucille Milner to Osmond Fraenkel, Jan. 28, 1936; Fraenkel to Milner, Jan. 28, 1936; Milner to Gus Solomon, Jan. 29, 1936; Fraenkel to Solomon, March 10, 1936—all in vol. 947, ACLU Archives.
122 Gus Solomon to ACLU, Oct. 22, 1936, vol. 947, ACLU Archives.
123 Ibid.
124 Harry A. Poth, Jr., to Gus Solomon, Oct. 27, 1936, vol. 947, ACLU Archives.
125 Solomon to ACLU, Oct. 27, 1936; Poth to Solomon, Oct. 29, 1936—both in vol. 947, ACLU Archives.
126 Brief for Appellant, pp. 5-6, *DeJonge* v. *Oregon*, 299 U.S. 353 (1937).
127 Ibid., p. 8.
128 Ibid., p. 12.
129 Ibid., p. 13.
130 Appellee's Brief, p. 29, *DeJonge* v. *Oregon*, 299 U.S. 353 (1937).
131 Ibid., pp. 29-30.
132 Lucille Milner to Osmond Fraenkel, Dec. 9, 1936, vol. 947, ACLU Archives.
133 "Notes Taken by Osmond Fraenkel during Argument of *DeJonge* v. *Oregon*," n.d.; Osmond Fraenkel to ACLU, Dec. 10, 1936; Roger Baldwin to Fraenkel, Dec. 14, 1936—all in vol. 1056, ACLU Archives.
134 *DeJonge* v. *Oregon*, 299 U.S. 353, 364 (1937).
135 299 U.S. 353, 365.
136 299 U.S. 353, 365-66.
137 *Labor Defender*, 10 (Dec. 1936): 16-17, and 10 (Feb. 1936): 15.
138 DeJonge's appearance before the Committee on Un-American Activities is reported in U.S. Congress, Committee on Un-American Activities, House of Representatives, 84th Cong., 2d sess., 1957, pt. I, pp. 6976-77.
139 Carlton E. Spencer, "Criminal Syndicalism: *DeJonge* v. *Oregon*," *Oregon Law Review*, 16 (1937): 278-85.
140 *Labor Defender*, 11 (April 1937): 17-18.
141 Edward D. Tittmann to Roger Baldwin, Feb. 26, 1937; Edward Fuhlbruegge to Baldwin, March 1, 1937—both in vol. 1056, ACLU Archives.

142 See Richard C. Cortner, *The Wagner Act Cases* (Knoxville: University of Tennessee Press, 1964), chap. 7.

143 Hughes's language in his opinions in the *Stromberg* and *Near* cases, and especially in his opinion in the *DeJonge* case, was strikingly like the language he used in defense of the New York Socialists. See Merlo J. Pusey, *Charles Evans Hughes* (New York: Macmillan, 1952), 1: 391–93.

CHAPTER 5

1 *Meyer* v. *Nebraska*, 262 U.S. 390, 399 (1923); *Hamilton* v. *Board of Regents*, 293 U.S. 245, 262, 265 (1934).

2 *Cantwell* v. *Connecticut*, 310 U.S. 296 (1940). Some observers believe that the *Hamilton* case read religious liberty into the Due Process Clause. For example, Henry J. Abraham expresses that view in *Freedom and the Court* (New York: Oxford University Press, 1972, pp. 55–56). In his opinion in *Palko* v. *Connecticut* (302 U.S. 319, 324 [1937]), Justice Cardozo also cited the *Hamilton* case to the same effect. Arthur A. North in *The Supreme Court: Judicial Process and Judicial Politics* (New York: Appleton-Century Crofts, 1966, p. 144) and C. Herman Pritchett in *The American Constitution* (New York: McGraw-Hill, 1968, p. 553), on the other hand, appear to believe that the *Cantwell* case, rather than *Hamilton*, read religious liberty into the Due Process Clause. Although there is thus considerable room for dispute on this point, my own view is that the *Hamilton* case went no further than what the Court had said in *Meyer* v. *Nebraska* in 1923; yet no one appears to suggest that religious freedom was read into the Due Process Clause in *Meyer*. I have therefore resolved the conflict on this point in favor of the *Cantwell* case.

3 The description of the Jehovah's Witnesses in this paragraph and the three that follow is drawn from David Manwaring, *Render Unto Caesar* (Chicago: University of Chicago Press, 1962), pp. 17–34.

4 Record, pp. 18–36, 80–84, *Cantwell* v. *Connecticut*, 310 U.S. 296 (1940).

5 Ibid., pp. 1–4.

6 Ibid., pp. 11–14.

7 Ibid., pp. 40–42.

8 Ibid., pp. 80–84.

9 Ibid., pp. 64–78.

10 Ibid., pp. 95–96.

11 *Connecticut* v. *Cantwell*, 126 Conn. 1, 5–8 (1939).

12 *Cantwell* v. *Connecticut*, 309 U.S. 626 (1940). See also Manwaring, *Render Unto Caesar*, p. 121.

13 Appellants' and Petitioners' Brief, pp. 13–18, *Cantwell* v. *Connecticut*, 310 U.S. 296 (1940).

14 Ibid., p. 20.

15 Ibid., pp. 39–40.

16 Appellee's and Respondent's Brief, pp. 4–10, *Cantwell* v. *Connecticut*, 310 U.S. 296 (1940).

17 Ibid., p. 19.

18 *Cantwell* v. *Connecticut*, 310 U.S. 296, 303 (1940).

19 310 U.S. 296, 305–7.

20 310 U.S. 296, 310–11.

21 *Minersville School District v. Gobitis*, 310 U.S. 586 (1940), the first Flag Salute case, was reversed in the *Barnette* case, 319 U.S. 624 (1943); see Manwaring, *Render Unto Caesar*.

22 Marley Cole, *Jehovah's Witnesses* (New York: Vantage Press, 1955), p. 113.

23 Milton R. Konvitz, *Expanding Liberties* (New York: Viking Press, 1967), p. 14.

24 Quoted in Cole, *Jehovah's Witnesses*, pp. 113–14, 122–23.

25 *Douglas v. Jeannette*, 319 U.S. 157, 162 (1943); for similar statements, see *Minersville School District v. Gobitis*, 310 U.S. 586, 593 (1940); *Murdock v. Pennsylvania*, 319 U.S. 105, 108 (1943); *West Virginia Board of Education v. Barnette*, 319 U.S. 624, 639 (1943); and *Thomas v. Collins*, 323 U.S. 516, 530–31 (1945).

26 *Everson v. Board of Education*, 330 U.S. 1 (1947).

27 Cases rejecting the child-benefit theory were *Judd v. Board of Education*, 273 N.Y. 200 (1938); *State v. Brown*, 36 Del. 181 (1934); *Gurney v. Ferguson*, 190 Okla. 254 (1941); *Mitchell v. Consolidated School District*, 17 Wash.2d 61 (1943); *Williams v. Board of Trustees*, 173 Ky. 708 (1917); *Sherrard v. Jefferson County Board of Education*, 294 Ky. 469 (1941); *Van Shaten v. Milquet*, 180 Wis. 109 (1923). Cases upholding the child-benefit theory were *Chance v. Mississippi State Textbook Board*, 190 Miss. 543 (1941); *Board of Education v. Wheat*, 174 Md. 314 (1938); and *Adams v. County Commissioners*, 180 Md. 550 (1942).

28 *Judd v. Board of Education*, 278 N.Y. 200, 211–12 (1938).

29 *New York Times*, Oct. 13, 1938, p. 19, Oct. 27, 1938, p. 8, Nov. 5, 1938, p. 18, and Nov. 9, 1938, pp. 1, 18.

30 N.J. Public Laws, p. 581 (1941).

31 Assembly Public Hearing on Senate Bill no. 152, Assembly Chamber, State House, Trenton, N.J. (April 21, 1941), in McCay File.

32 Albert McCay to Challen B. Ellis, Nov. 14, 1946, McCay File.

33 Roscoe Walker to Powell & Parker of Mt. Holly, N.J., Sept. 4, 1942, McCay File. In 1942, Albert McCay was a member of the firm of Powell & Parker; he subsequently became a partner in the firm, and its name is presently Parker, McCay and Criscuolo.

34 Walker to McCay, Dec. 15, 1942, McCay File.

35 Record, pp. 11–26, *Everson v. Board of Education*, 330 U.S. 1 (1947).

36 *Ward v. Keenan*, 3 N.J. 298, 307 (1949). On the New Jersey certiorari practice, see Louis L. Jaffe, *Judicial Control of Administrative Action* (Boston: Little, Brown, 1965), pp. 170, 467–68.

37 Record, p. 1, *Everson v. Board of Education*.

38 Ibid., pp. 11–23.

39 *Cochran v. Board of Education*, 281 U.S. 370, 375 (1930).

40 McCay to Clifford Forster, Staff Counsel for the ACLU, July 6, 1943, McCay File.

41 Record, pp. 8–9, *Everson v. Board of Education*.

42 Clifford Forster to McCay, July 29, 1943, and McCay to Forster, Sept. 2, 1943, McCay File.

43 *Everson* v. *Board of Education*, 132 N.J.L. 98, 39 A.2d 75, 76–77 (1944).

44 Roscoe Walker to McCay, Sept. 21, 1944, McCay File.

45 *Everson* v. *Board of Education*, 133 N.J.L. 350, 44 A.2d 333, 337 (1945). While the *Everson* case was pending in the court of errors and appeals, *amicus curiae* briefs were filed in the case by the attorney general of New Jersey and by an attorney representing Protestant parochial schools, both defending the bus law's validity.

46 Letter, William Abbotts to the author, Dec. 13, 1972.

47 In his correspondence with the author, William Abbotts strongly hinted that this was the case, without confirming it absolutely. Abbott's memory of the details of the *Everson* case was vague on some points, however, and not entirely reliable.

48 Clifford Forster to McCay, Oct. 16, 1945, McCay File.

49 McCay to Forster, Oct. 17, 1945, McCay File.

50 Forster to McCay, Oct. 26, 1945, McCay File.

51 McCay to Roscoe Walker, Dec. 1, 1945, McCay File.

52 McCay to Challen B. Ellis, Dec. 8, 1945, McCay File.

53 Ellis to McCay, Dec. 13, 1945, McCay File.

54 McCay to Ellis, Jan. 14, 1946, McCay File.

55 Ellis to McCay, Jan. 16, 1946, McCay File.

56 Excerpt of minutes of joint meeting of the Board of Managers and State Council Legislative Committee, JOUAM, Jan, 28, 1946, McCay File.

57 Record, p. 70, *Everson* v. *Board of Education*.

58 McCay to Clifford Forster, Jan. 26, 1946, and Forster to McCay, May 7, 1946, McCay File.

59 McCay to Mr. Altmark, American Jewish Congress, Oct. 17, 1946, McCay File.

60 McCay to Milton Lasher, Nov. 10, 1946, McCay File.

61 *Loan Association v. Topeka*, 20 Wall. 655 (1875). Brief for Appellant, pp. 6–11, *Everson* v. *Board of Education*, 330 U.S. 1 (1947).

62 Letter, Porter R. Chandler to the author, June 15, 1973. For more information on Chandler, see Richard E. Morgan, *The Supreme Court and Religion* (New York: Free Press, 1972), p. 91.

63 Appellee's Brief, pp. 9–10, *Everson*, v. *Board of Education*, 330 U.S. 1 (1947).

64 Brief for Appellant, p. 11, *Everson* v. *Board of Education*.

65 Ibid., p. 16.

66 Appellee's Brief, p. 35, *Everson* v. *Board of Education*.

67 J. Woodford Howard, *Mr. Justice Murphy: A Political Biography* (Princeton: Princeton University Press, 1968), pp. 448–50; Fowler V. Harper, *Justice Rutledge and the Bright Constellation* (New York: Bobbs-Merrill, 1965), pp. 67–73. See also, J. Woodford Howard, "On the Fluidity of Judicial Choice," *American Political Science Review*, 62 (March 1968): 43–56.

68 *Everson* v. *Board of Education*, 330 U.S. 1, 15–16 (1947).

69 330 U.S. 1, 18.
70 330 U.S. 1, 19.
71 330 U.S. 1, 59.
72 330 U.S. 1, 63.
73 See David Fellman, *Religion in American Public Law* (Boston: Boston University Press, 1965), p. 83.
74 Harper, *Mr. Justice Rutledge*, pp. 76–77. A good survey of the newspaper reaction to the *Everson* case may be found in "Forceful Editorial Comment by some Well-Known Journals on the New Jersey Bus Case," *Liberty*, 42, no. 3 (1947): 19–26.
75 *New York Times*, Feb. 12, 1947, p. 27.
76 "Adventists Oppose Free Transportation of Parochial School Pupils," *Liberty*, 42, no. 4 (1947): 23–24.
77 Leo Pfeffer and Anson P. Stokes, *Church and State in the United States*, rev., 1 vol. ed. (New York: Harper & Row, 1964), pp. 346–47.
78 Quoted in Morgan, *The Supreme Court and Religion*, p. 93.
79 *Newark Star-Ledger*, Feb. 11, 1947, pp. 1, 5, and Feb. 12, 1947, p. 1.
80 McCay to Challen Ellis, Feb. 13, 1947, and Ellis to Charles H. Michaelson (who had succeeded Roscoe Walker as State Council Secretary of the JOUAM), March 13, 1947, McCay File.
81 McCay to Ellis, Feb. 15, 1947, McCay File.
82 *Newark Evening News*, Oct. 10, 1947, p. 25; *New York Times*, Oct. 23, 1947, p. 27.
83 *New York Times*, Oct. 23, 1947, p. 27; *Newark Evening News*, Oct. 16, 1947, p. 15.
84 *New York Times*, Nov. 5, 1947, pp. 1, 6, and Nov. 6, 1947, p. 18.
85 The provision of the 1947 New Jersey Constitution providing for free transportation of both private and parochial school students was art. 8, sec. 4, para. 3. The legislature's implementation of this provision was challenged subsequently in the New Jersey courts, but to no avail. See *Fox* v. *Board of Education*, 93 N.J. Super. 544 (Law Div., 1967); *McCanna* v. *Sills*, 103 N.J. Super. 480 (Ch. Div., 1968); *Board of Education* v. *Gateway Regional High School*, 104 N.J. Super. 76 (Law Div., 1968); *West Morris Regional Board of Education* v. *Sills*, 58 N.J. 464 (1971), *cert. denied*, 404 U.S. 986 (1971).

CHAPTER 6
1 *Powell* v. *Alabama*, 287 U.S. 45 (1932).
2 287 U.S. 45, 66–67.
3 287 U.S. 45, 66–68.
4 Palko's last name was misspelled in the proceedings against him. Its correct spelling was "Palka," but because he has gone into the history of constitutional litigation as "Palko," I shall use the latter spelling. On the correct spelling of Palko's name, see Brief for the Appellant, p. 3, *Palko* v. *Connecticut*, 302 U.S. 319 (1937). Record, p. 11, *Palko* v. *Connecticut*, 302 U.S. 319 (1937); *New York Times*, Sept. 30, 1935, p. 3.
5 The facts of Palko's first trial are most fully reported in *State* v. *Palko*, 121 Conn. 669 (1936).

6 The charge to the jury is quoted in *State* v. *Palko*, 121 Conn. 669 (1936).
7 121 Conn. 669, 676-77, 681-82.
8 Record, p. 1, *Palko* v. *Connecticut*.
9 *State* v. *Palko*, 122 Conn. 529, 538-42 (1937).
10 Horace Edgar Flack, *The Adoption of the Fourteenth Amendment* (1908; reprint ed., Gloucester, Mass.: Peter Smith, 1965), p. 94.
11 Brief for the Appellant, pp. 31, 48, 68-69, *Palko* v. *Connecticut*.
12 Brief for the State of Connecticut, pp. 1-6, 36, *Palko* v. *Connecticut*, 302 U.S. 319 (1937).
13 *Palko* v. *Connecticut*, 302 U.S. 319, 323-24 (1937).
14 302 U.S. 319, 324-25.
15 302 U.S. 319, 325-26.
16 302 U.S. 319, 327.
17 302 U.S. 319, 328.
18 302 U.S. 319, 327. See *Betts* v. *Brady*, 316 U.S. 455 (1942); *Gideon* v. *Wainwright*, 372 U.S. 355 (1963).
19 *DeJonge* v. *Oregon*, 299 U.S. 353, 364 (1937).
20 *Palko* v. *Connecticut*, 302 U.S. 319, 327.
21 *United States* v. *Carolene Products Co.*, 304 U.S. 144 (1938). See also, George D. Braden, "The Search for Objectivity in Constitutional Law," *Yale Law Journal*, 57 (1948): 571-94; Alpheus T. Mason, *Harlan Fiske Stone* (New York: Viking, 1956), p. 516.
22 *West Virginia Board of Education* v. *Barnette*, 319 U.S. 624, 639 (1943).
23 319 U.S. 624, 639. It should be noted that Jackson later revised his views and decided that at least the freedom of expression protected by the Due Process Clause was not identical with the freedom of expression protected by the First Amendment. See his dissenting opinion in *Beauharnais* v. *Illinois*, 343 U.S. 250, 287-305 (1952).
24 *Cantwell* v. *Connecticut*, 310 U.S. 296, 303 (1940).
25 See *Douglas* v. *Jeanette*, 319 U.S. 157, 162 (1943); *Murdock* v. *Pennsylvania*, 319 U.S. 105, 108 (1943); *Thomas* v. *Collins*, 323 U.S. 516, 530-31 (1945).
26 *Powell* v. *Alabama*, 287 U.S. 45 (1932); *Brown* v. *Mississippi*, 297 U.S. 278 (1936).
27 297 U.S. 278, 285-86.
28 *Johnson* v. *Zerbst*, 304 U.S. 458 (1938); *Betts* v. *Brady*, 316 U.S. 455 (1942).
29 *Malinski* v. *New York*, 324 U.S. 401, 416-17 (1945).
30 J. Woodford Howard, *Mr. Justice Murphy: A Political Biography* (Princeton: Princeton University Press, 1968), pp. 428 n. c, 431-32.
31 *Chambers* v. *Florida*, 309 U.S. 227, 235 n. 3 (1940).
32 *Betts* v. *Brady*, 316 U.S. 455, 474-75 (1942).
33 316 U.S. 455, 474 n. 1, 475.
34 *Malinski* v. *New York*, 324 U.S. 401, 414-15 (1945).
35 Fowler V. Harper, *Justice Rutledge and the Bright Constellation* (New York: Bobbs-Merrill, 1965), p. 214.
36 See Frankfurter's concurring opinion in *Louisiana* v. *Resweber*, 329 U.S. 459, 467 (1947).

37 *Los Angeles Times*, July 26, 1944, pt. I, p. 5.
38 Record, pp. 124–28, *Adamson* v. *California*, 332 U.S. 46 (1947).
39 Ibid., pp. 45–48.
40 Ibid., pp. 164–70, 299–305.
41 Ibid., pp. 309–11.
42 Ibid., pp. 238–60.
43 Ibid., pp. 182–90, 314–15.
44 Article 1, sec. 13, had been adopted as an amendment to the California Constitution in 1934.
45 Record, pp. 334–79, *Adamson* v. *California*.
46 Ibid., pp. 331–34.
47 *People* v. *Adamson*, 27 Cal.2d 478, 487 (1946).
48 27 Cal.2d 478, 485–92.
49 Reply Brief for Appellant, pp. 2–3, *Adamson* v. *California*, 332 U.S. 46 (1947).
50 Ibid., pp. 54–55, 63–64.
51 Appellee's Brief, pp. 15, 27–28, *Adamson* v. *California*, 332 U.S. 46 (1947).
52 Harper, *Mr. Justice Rutledge*, p. 215; Howard, *Mr. Justice Murphy*, p. 440.
53 *Adamson* v. *California*, 332 U.S. 46, 54 (1947).
54 332 U.S. 46, 54–59.
55 332 U.S. 46, 70–72; the appendix to Black's opinion is at 332 U.S. 46, 92–124.
56 332 U.S. 46, 75.
57 332 U.S. 46, 89.
58 332 U.S. 46, 124.
59 See *Griswold* v. *Connecticut*, 381 U.S. 479 (1965); Howard, *Mr. Justice Murphy*, pp. 439–43; Richard C. Cortner, *The Supreme Court and Civil Liberties Policy* (Palo Alto: Mayfield, 1975), pp. 31–33.
60 *Adamson* v. *California*, 332 U.S. 46, 62.
61 332 U.S. 46, 62–64.
62 332 U.S. 46, 66–68.
63 332 U.S. 46, 66.
64 Charles Fairman, "Does the Fourteenth Amendment Incorporate the Bill of Rights: The Original Understanding," *Stanford Law Review*, 2 (1949): 2, 5.
65 For a sample of the ongoing debate, see J. B. James, *The Framing of the Fourteenth Amendment* (Urbana: University of Illinois Press, 1956), pp. 85, 130ff.; Alfred H. Kelley and Winfred A. Harbison, *The American Constitution: Its Origins and Development*, 4th ed. (New York: Norton, 1970), p. 463; Louis Henkin, "Selective Incorporation in the Fourteenth Amendment," *Yale Law Journal*, 73 (1963): 74–88; Frank H. Walker, "Constitutional Law —Was It Intended that the Fourteenth Amendment Incorporates the Bill of Rights?" *North Carolina Law Review*, 42 (1964): 925–36; William W. Crosskey, "Charles Fairman, 'Legislative History,' and the Constitutional Limitations on State Authority," *University of Chicago Law Review*, 22 (1954): 1–143; Charles Fairman, "A Reply to Professor Crosskey," *University of Chicago Law Review*, 22 (1954): 144–56; John R. Green, "The Bill of Rights, the Fourteenth Amendment and the Supreme Court," *Michigan Law Review*, 46

(1948): 869–910; Felix Frankfurter, "Memorandum on 'Incorporation' of the Bill of Rights into the Due Process Clause of the Fourteenth Amendment," *Harvard Law Review*, 78 (1965): 746–83.

66 See Leonard Levy, Introduction to *The Fourteenth Amendment and the Bill of Rights: The Incorporation Theory* (New York: Da Capo, 1970), pp. vii–xxv.

67 *Duncan* v. *Louisiana*, 391 U.S. 145, 171 (1968); that case is analyzed in depth later in this study. On Black's judicial philosophy, see Hugo L. Black, *A Constitutional Faith* (New York: Knopf, 1968); "The Bill of Rights and the Federal Government," in Edmond Cahn, ed., *The Great Rights* (New York: Macmillan, 1968). See also, "Symposium on Mr. Justice Black," *Yale Law Journal*, 65 (1956): 449–528.

68 The late Helen Shirley Thomas in her *Felix Frankfurter: Scholar on the Bench* (Baltimore: Johns Hopkins University Press, 1960, p. 155), said this of Frankfurter's position on this point: "The paradox is that, in practice, Frankfurter himself has elaborately rejected such an identification [of the due process clauses]."

69 In an article published posthumously, Frankfurter acknowledged that an important question in the nationalization of the Bill of Rights was "how to fit the First Amendment into the virtually uniform pattern, at least until *Mapp* v. *Ohio*, 367 U.S. 643 [1961], of rejection by this Court of explicit application of Bill of Rights specifics to the States." But Frankfurter's article still does not satisfactorily reconcile the applicability of the rights of the First Amendment to the states with his use of the language of nonsuperfluousness in *Malinski* and *Adamson*. See Felix Frankfurter, "Memorandum on 'Incorporation' of the Bill of Rights into the Due Process Clause of the Fourteenth Amendment," *Harvard Law Review*, 78 (1965): 746–83.

70 *Haley* v. *Ohio*, 332 U.S. 596, 603 (1948); *Solesbee* v. *Balkcom*, 339 U.S. 9, 16 (1950); *Irvine* v. *California*, 347 U.S. 128, 144 (1954); *Rochin* v. *California*, 342 U.S. 165, 172 (1952).

71 Carl B. Swisher, *The Supreme Court in Modern Role* (New York: New York University Press, 1958), p. 55.

72 Record, p. 32, *Palko* v. *Connecticut*, 302 U.S. 319 (1937); Palko's execution was confirmed in a letter from his lawyer, David Goldstein, to the author, Dec. 15, 1972.

73 *Adamson* v. *California*, 332 U.S. 784 (1947).

74 *Adamson* v. *California*, 333 U.S. 831 (1947).

75 *Ex parte Adamson*, 167 F.2d 996 (9th Cir., 1948), *cert. denied, Re Adamson*, 334, U.S. 834 (1948).

76 Letter, Lee E. DeBord, Information Officer, California State Prison at San Quentin, to the author, June 13, 1973.

77 *Malloy* v. *Hogan*, 378 U.S. 1 (1964).

78 *Griffin* v. *California*, 380 U.S. 609 (1965).

CHAPTER 7

1 *In re Oliver*, 333 U.S. 257 (1948).

2 Glenn R. Winters, "The Michigan One-Man Grand Jury," *Journal of the American Judicature Society*, 28 (1945): 137–51; William Henry Gallagher,

"The One-Man Grand Jury—A Reply," *Journal of the American Judicature Society*, 29 (1945): 20–24. Further background material on the Michigan one-man grand jury system may be found in Brief for the Detroit Chapter, National Lawyers' Guild, as *Amicus Curiae*, pp. 12–18, *In re Oliver*, 333 U.S. 257 (1948); and in Brief for the State of Michigan, pp. 3–6, 31–34, *In re Oliver*, 333 U.S. 257 (1948).

3 Brief for the State Bar of Michigan as *Amicus Curiae*, pp. 16–17, *In re Oliver*, 333 U.S. 257 (1948).

4 Gallagher, "The One-Man Grand Jury—A Reply," p. 24. See also *In re Slattery*, 310 Mich. 458 (1945), *cert. denied*, 325 U.S. 876 (1945); *Slattery* v. *MacDonald*, 151 F.2d 326 (7th Cir., 1945), *cert. denied*, 326 U.S. 787 (1946).

5 See Clifford Forster to W. H. Gallagher, April 26, 1946; ACLU *Bulletin* no. 1218, Feb. 18, 1946; W. H. Gallagher to Roger Baldwin, Jan. 15, 1946—all in vol. 2753, ACLU Archives.

6 *Detroit Free Press*, Sept. 12, 1946, p. 6.

7 Ibid., Sept. 14, 1946, p. 4; Brief in Answer to the Brief of the Michigan State Bar, pp. 17–18, *In re Oliver*, 333 U.S. 257 (1948).

8 "Report of the Special Committee to Study and Report upon the One-Man Grand Jury Law," *Michigan State Bar Journal*, 26 (1947): 55–62.

9 "Minority Report," *Michigan State Bar Journal*, 26 (1947): 62–67.

10 See Brief for the State Bar of Michigan as *Amicus Curiae*, pp. 3–5, *In re Oliver*.

11 Petition for a Writ of Certiorari, Deposition of William D. Oliver, pp. 1–2, *In re Oliver*, 333 U.S. 257 (1948).

12 Record, pp. 11–14, *In re Oliver*, 333 U.S. 257 (1948).

13 Ibid., pp. 14–16.

14 Ibid., p. 6.

15 Ibid., pp. 8–15.

16 *In re Oliver*, 318 Mich. 7, 14 (1947).

17 318 Mich. 7, 15–20. See also *In re Hartley*, 317 Mich. 441 (1947), and the *Detroit Free Press*, Sept. 15, 1946, pt. I, p. 8.

18 Letter, William Henry Gallagher to the author, July 21, 1973.

19 Reply Brief for Petitioner, p. 5, *In re Oliver*, 333 U.S. 257 (1948). Brief in Answer to the Brief of the Michigan State Bar, p. 28, *In re Oliver*.

20 Brief for the State Bar of Michigan as *Amicus Curiae*, pp. 12–13, *In re Oliver*.

21 Brief for the State of Michigan, pp. 12–17, *In re Oliver*.

22 Brief for the Detroit Chapter, National Lawyers' Guild, as *Amicus Curiae*, pp. 25–32, *In re Oliver*.

23 *In re Oliver*, 333 U.S. 257, 266–70 (1948).

24 333 U.S. 257, 270–73.

25 333 U.S. 257, 273.

26 333 U.S. 257, 275–78.

27 333 U.S. 257, 278–82.

28 Quoted in Fowler V. Harper, *Justice Rutledge and the Bright Constellation* (New York: Bobbs-Merrill, 1965), pp. 207–8.

29 *Detroit Free Press*, March 9, 1948, pp. 1, 2.

30 Ibid., pp. 1, 2.
31 Ibid., pp. 1, 2.
32 Ibid., March 10, 1948, p. 6.
33 "Report of the Special Committee to Study and Report upon the One-Man Grand Jury Law," *Michigan State Bar Journal*, 27 (1948): 60-68.
34 See *Michigan State Bar Journal*, 28 (1949): 69-73.
35 "Report of the Special Committee to Study and Report upon the One-Man Grand Jury Law," *Michigan State Bar Journal*, 28 (1949): 63-78. The Michigan one-man grand jury system was subsequently revived, however, and in 1955 the U.S. Supreme Court was constrained to hold that for grand jurors to preside over the contempt trials of witnesses they themselves had cited for contempt violated the Due Process Clause. See *In re Murchison*, 349 U.S. 133 (1955).
36 The *Oliver* case has been so interpreted in *Duncan* v. *Louisiana*, 391 U.S. 145, 148 n. 10 (1968); *Washington* v. *Texas*, 388 U.S. 14, 18 n. 11 (1967). Henry J. Abraham, *Freedom and the Court* (2d ed. [New York: Oxford University Press, 1972], p. 62), agrees with this view. See also, "Comment Note —What Provisions of the Federal Constitution's Bill of Rights are Applicable to the States," 23 L.Ed.2d 383, 393 (1969).
37 Record, pp. 10-24, *Wolf* v. *Colorado*, 338 U.S. 25 (1949).
38 *Denver Post*, April 29, 1944, p. 5.
39 Record II, p. 5, *Wolf* v. *Colorado*. Wolf was tried in two cases, and the pagination of the record begins anew with the second case. I shall therefore indicate the record of the second case as Record II.
40 Record, pp. 5-41, *Wolf* v. *Colorado*; Record II, pp. 15-66, *Wolf* v. *Colorado*.
41 Record, pp. 15-17, *Wolf* v. *Colorado*; Record II, pp. 8-11, *Wolf* v. *Colorado*.
42 *Weeks* v. *United States*, 232 U.S. 383 (1914).
43 *Massantonio* v. *People*, 77 Col. 392 (1925).
44 *Wolf* v. *People*, 117 Col. 279, 281-83 (1947).
45 *Wolf* v. *Colorado*, 333 U.S. 879 (1948).
46 Brief of Petitioner, p. 24, *Wolf* v. *Colorado*, 338 U.S. 25 (1949).
47 Ibid., p. 38.
48 Brief of Respondent, pp. 25-26, *Wolf* v. *Colorado*, 338 U.S. 25 (1949).
49 Ibid., pp. 12-13.
50 Ibid., pp. 33-34.
51 Brief of the New York County Criminal Courts Bar Association as *Amicus Curiae*, pp. 4-9, *Wolf* v. *Colorado*, 338 U.S. 25 (1949).
52 *Wolf* v. *Colorado*, 338 U.S. 25, 26-27 (1949).
53 338 U.S. 25, 27-28.
54 338 U.S. 25, 33.
55 338 U.S. 25, 39-40.
56 338 U.S. 25, 46.
57 338 U.S. 25, 47-48.
58 338 U.S. 25, 48. See *Harris* v. *United States*, 331 U.S. 145 (1947); *Marron* v. *United States*, 275 U.S. 192 (1927).

59 Letter, Philip Hornbein, Jr., to the author, July 24, 1973.

60 Record, pp. 9-31, *Rochin* v. *California*, 342 U.S. 165 (1952).

61 *People* v. *Mayen*, 188 Cal. 237 (1922). Record, pp. 88-154, *Rochin* v. *California*.

62 *People* v. *Rochin*, 101 Cal.App.2d 140, 143 (1950).

63 101 Cal.App.2d 140, 144-45.

64 *Rochin* v. *California*, 342 U.S. 165, 171 (1952).

65 342 U.S. 165, 170-72.

66 342 U.S. 165, 172-73.

67 342 U.S. 165, 174-79.

68 *Irvine* v. *California*, 347 U.S. 128 (1954). For a fuller discussion of the litigation in the *Irvine* case, see Alan F. Westin, "Bookies and Bugs in California," in Westin, ed., *The Uses of Power* (New York: Harcourt, Brace & World, 1962), pp. 117-71.

69 347 U.S. 128, 132.

70 347 U.S. 128, 132-34.

71 347 U.S. 128, 138-39.

72 347 U.S. 128, 143-49.

73 *Breithaupt* v. *Abram*, 352 U.S. 432, 435 (1957).

74 352 U.S. 432, 442.

75 On Justice Brennan, see his "The Bill of Rights and the States," in Edmond Cahn, ed., *The Great Rights* (New York: Macmillan, 1963), pp. 67-86.

76 On Justice Harlan, see Norman Dorsen, "The Second Mr. Justice Harlan: A Constitutional Conservative," *New York University Law Review*, 44 (1969): 249-71; Norman Dorsen, "Mr. Justice Black and Mr. Justice Harlan," *New York University Law Review*, 46 (1971): 649-52; J. Edward Lumbard, "John Harlan: In Public Service, 1925-71," *Harvard Law Review*, 85 (1971): 372-76; Henry J. Friendly, "Mr. Justice Harlan, As Seen by a Friend and Judge of an Inferior Court," *Harvard Law Review*, 85 (1971): 382-89.

77 *Ohio ex rel. Eaton* v. *Price*, 364 U.S. 263, 274-75 (1960).

78 See the posthumously published article by Frankfurter, "Memorandum on 'Incorporation' of the Bill of Rights into the Due Process Clause of the Fourteenth Amendment," *Harvard Law Review*, 78 (1965): 746, 747-49.

79 On Harlan's view that the First Amendment's guarantee of freedom of expression did not apply identically to the states and to the federal government, see his dissenting opinion in *Roth* v. *United States* and *Alberts* v. *California*, 354 U.S. 476, 503-8 (1957); see also, *Smith* v. *California*, 361 U.S. 147, 169-72 (1959). This ultimately had been the view of Justice Jackson also; see *Beauharnais* v. *Illinois*, 343 U.S. 250, 288 (1952).

80 *New State Ice Co.* v. *Liebmann*, 285 U.S. 262, 311 (1932).

81 The James Madison Lecture by Brennan is republished as "The Bill of Rights and the States," in Edmond Cahn, ed., *The Great Rights*, pp. 67-86.

82 Ibid., p. 80-81.

CHAPTER 8

1 *Mapp* v. *Ohio*, 367 U.S. 643 (1961).

2 *Gideon* v. *Wainwright*, 372 U.S. 335 (1963).

3 See *Weeks* v. *United States*, 232 U.S. 383, 398 (1914); *Byars* v. *United States*, 273 U.S. 28, 33 (1927); *Feldman* v. *United States*, 322 U.S. 487, 492 (1944); and *Gambino* v. *United States*, 275 U.S. 310 (1927). For a comprehensive analysis of the law of search and seizure, see Jacob W. Landynski, *Search and Seizure and the Supreme Court* (Baltimore: Johns Hopkins University Press, 1966).

4 *Elkins* v. *United States*, 364 U.S. 206, 213, 224 (1960).

5 364 U.S. 206, 219, 224-25.

6 *People* v. *Cahan*, 44 Cal.2d 434, 445-47 (1955).

7 *Rios* v. *United States*, 364 U.S. 206, 238, (1960). The *Rios* case was a companion case to the *Elkins* case.

8 364 U.S. 206, 238.

9 364 U.S. 206, 239-40.

10 Record, p. 81, *Mapp* v. *Ohio*, 267 U.S. 643 (1961).

11 *Ohio* v. *Mapp*, 170 Ohio St. 427, 430-34 (1960).

12 The *Lindway* case is reported at 131 Ohio St. 166 (1936); Record, pp. A-C, 16-53, *Mapp* v. *Ohio*.

13 Record, p. 81, *Mapp* v. *Ohio*.

14 *Ohio* v. *Mapp*, 170 Ohio St. 427, 430.

15 170 Ohio St. 427, 431.

16 170 Ohio St. 427, 430-34.

17 Brief of the Ohio and American Civil Liberties Unions as *Amici Curiae*, p. 14, *Mapp* v. *Ohio*, 367 U.S. 643 (1961).

18 Brief of Appellee, p. 3, *Mapp* v. *Ohio*, 367 U.S. 643 (1961).

19 Brief of Appellant, p. 18, *Mapp* v. *Ohio*, 367 U.S. 643 (1961).

20 The description of and excerpts from the oral argument in *Mapp* v. *Ohio* in the paragraphs that follow are based on the tape recording of the argument before the Court on March 29, 1961, which is listed in the audiovisual division of the National Archives as no. 236, 267-317.

21 *Washington Post*, June 20, 1961, pp. 1, A4, reported that Kearns had informed the Court during the oral argument that he had never heard of the *Wolf* case. Although it was obvious during the oral argument that Kearns had not heard of the *Wolf* case, he did not make the statement attributed to him in the *Post*.

22 The Court was, of course, bound by the construction that the Ohio Supreme Court had placed upon the statute, and it was a major error for Mrs. Mahon to raise this point before the Court.

23 *Mapp* v. *Ohio*, 367 U.S. 643, 654-55 (1961).

24 367 U.S. 643, 655-57.

25 367 U.S. 643, 658-60.

26 367 U.S. 643, 661-66.

27 367 U.S. 643, 686.

28 367 U.S. 643, 673-86.

29 An angry petition for a rehearing was filed by the state of Ohio in the *Mapp* case, alleging that the Court had decided the case on a point that had gone unargued. This petition was supported by *amicus* briefs on behalf of the National District Attorneys' Association and the state of California. See Petition

for a Rehearing on Behalf of the State of Ohio, *Mapp* v. *Ohio*, and the *Amicus Curiae* briefs on Behalf of the National District Attorneys' Association and the State of California in Support of the Petition for a Rehearing, *Mapp* v. *Ohio*, 367 U.S. 643 (1961).

30 *Cleveland Plain Dealer*, June 20, 1961, pp. 1, 5; *Stanley* v. *Georgia*, 394 U.S. 557 (1969).

31 *New York Times*, June 20, 1961, p. 1, and June 21, 1961, p. 21. For an excellent discussion of the significance of *Mapp*, see Francis A. Allen, "Federalism and the Fourth Amendment: A Requiem for Wolf," in Philip B. Kurland, ed., *The Supreme Court Review: 1961* (Chicago: University of Chicago Press, 1961), pp. 1–48.

32 *New York Times*, April 6, 1962, p. 1, and March 30, 1962, p. 1.

33 See Justice White's opinion in *Duncan* v. *Louisiana*, 391 U.S. 145 (1968), and Justice Goldberg's concurring opinion in *Pointer* v. *Texas*, 380 U.S. 400, 410–14 (1965). The addition of White and Goldberg to the Court was also crucial in other areas of constitutional development. See Richard C. Cortner, *The Apportionment Cases* (New York: Norton, 1972), pp. 143–44.

34 Record, pp. 16–27, *Robinson* v. *California*, 370 U.S. 660 (1962).

35 Ibid., pp. 5–26.

36 Ibid., pp. 5–6, 27–81.

37 The decision of the appellate department is unreported; it appears ibid., pp. 111–12; the common-drunk ruling of the California Supreme Court was *In re Newbern*, 53 Cal.2d 786 (1960).

38 See Appellant's Opening Brief, p. 2, *Robinson* v. *California*, 370 U.S. 660 (1962).

39 Ibid., pp. 10–40.

40 Ibid., pp. 13–19.

41 Ibid., pp. 29–30.

42 The excerpts from the oral argument quoted in this paragraph and the four that follow are from the tape recording of the oral argument in *Robinson* v. *California* on April 17, 1962, which is listed in the audiovisual division of the National Archives as no. 554, 267–384.

43 *Robinson* v. *California*, 370 U.S. 660, 666 (1962).

44 370 U.S. 660, 666.

45 370 U.S. 660, 667.

46 370 U.S. 660, 679.

47 370 U.S. 660, 679–85, 686.

48 Petition for a Rehearing, p. 8, appendix B, *Robinson* v. *California*, 370 U.S. 660 (1962).

49 *Robinson* v. *California*, 371 U.S. 905 (1962).

50 *New York Times*, June 26, 1962, pp. 1, 18.

51 See, for example, *Powell* v. *Texas*, 392 U.S. 514, 532, 558–59 (1968); *Pointer* v. *Texas*, 380 U.S. 400, 412, (1965); *Gideon* v. *Wainwright*, 372 U.S. 335, 342 (1963). See also Michael Meltsner, *Cruel and Unusual: The Supreme Court and Capital Punishment* (New York: Random House, 1973), pp. 179–80.

52 Anthony Lewis, *Gideon's Trumpet* (New York: Random House, 1964), pp. 65-66, 98.
53 Record, pp. 5-41, *Gideon* v. *Wainwright*, 372 U.S. 335 (1963).
54 Ibid., pp. 45-47.
55 *Betts* v. *Brady*, 316 U.S. 455 (1942). On the right-to-counsel issue generally, see Yale Kamisar, "The Right to Counsel and the Fourteenth Amendment: A Dialogue on 'the Most Pervasive Right of an Accused,'" *University of Chicago Law Review*, 30 (1962): 1-77; William M. Beaney, *The Right to Counsel in American Courts* (Ann Arbor: University of Michigan Press, 1955); Charles F. Allen, "The Supreme Court and State Criminal Justice," *Wayne Law Review*, 4 (1958): 191-204.
56 Lewis, *Gideon's Trumpet*, pp. 7-8, 37-38.
57 *Gideon* v. *Cochran*, 370 U.S. 908 (1962). Fortas was, of course, ultimately appointed to the Court by President Johnson in 1965 and was nominated to succeed Chief Justice Warren in 1968. Opposition in the Senate forced the withdrawal of the latter nomination, and Fortas was subsequently forced to resign from the Court for improper conduct, the first such occasion in our history. For an account of the Fortas tragedy, see Robert Shogan, *A Question of Judgment* (New York: Bobbs-Merrill, 1972).
58 Brief for Petitioner, p. 7, *Gideon* v. *Wainwright*, 372 U.S. 335 (1963).
59 Ibid., p. 32.
60 Ibid., pp. 8-12.
61 Lewis, *Gideon's Trumpet*, pp. 141-48; Brief for the State Governments as *Amici Curiae*, *Gideon* v. *Wainwright*, 372 U.S. 335 (1963); *Amicus Curiae* Brief for the State of Alabama, *Gideon* v. *Wainwright*, 372 U.S. 335 (1963).
62 Brief for the State Governments as *Amici Curiae*, p. 12, *Gideon* v. *Wainwright*.
63 Ibid., pp. 19, 24-25.
64 Brief of the American Civil Liberties Union and the Florida Civil Liberties Union, *Amici Curiae*, p. 38, *Gideon* v. *Wainwright*, 372 U.S. 335 (1963).
65 Ibid., appendix 2, pp. 47-57. The reversal of Gideon's conviction was also urged upon the Court by an *amicus* brief filed by the state of Oregon. See Brief for the State of Oregon as *Amicus Curiae*, *Gideon* v. *Wainwright*, 372 U.S. 335 (1963).
66 Quoted in Lewis, *Gideon's Trumpet*, p. 156.
67 Brief for the Respondent, pp. 18-29, *Gideon* v. *Wainwright*, 372 U.S. 335 (1963).
68 Ibid., p. 56.
69 The reader may notice that the quotations from the oral argument contained herein differ somewhat from the language quoted in Lewis, *Gideon's Trumpet*, pp. 170-81. The quotations in this paragraph and the six that follow are drawn from the tape recording of the argument in the *Gideon* case, Jan. 15, 1963, which is listed as no. 155, 267-418 in the audiovisual division of the National Archives.
70 *Gideon* v. *Wainwright*, 372 U.S. 335, 339 (1963).
71 372 U.S. 335, 342.
72 372 U.S. 335, 344-45. Twenty-three states had intervened as *amici* urging the

reversal of the *Betts* case, but New Jersey had been inadvertently left off the list of states signing the brief *amici curiae* of the states.

73 Lewis, *Gideon's Trumpet*, pp. 223-38.
74 Ibid., p. 203.
75 *New York Times*, May 18, 1965, p. 38; Anthony Lewis, "Gideon: An Epitaph," *New York Times*, Feb. 12, 1972, p. 29: *Argersinger* v. *Hamlin*, 407 U.S. 25 (1972).
76 *Gideon* v. *Wainwright*, 372 U.S. 335, 345-47 (1963).
77 372 U.S. 335, 349-51.
78 372 U.S. 335, 352.
79 Quoted in Lewis, *Gideon's Trumpet*, p. 222.
80 Brief for the State Governments as *Amici Curiae*, p. 19, *Gideon* v. *Wainwright*.
81 Lewis, *Gideon's Trumpet*, p. 172.
82 Archibald Cox, *The Warren Court: Constitutional Decision as an Instrument of Reform* (Cambridge, Mass.: Harvard University Press, 1968), p. 74.

CHAPTER 9

1 The incorporationists indicated a willingness to reverse *Twining* in *Cohen* v. *Hurley*, 366 U.S. 117, 131-60 (1961). For an excellent analysis of the history of the right against self-incrimination, see Leonard W. Levy, *Origins of the Fifth Amendment* (New York: Oxford University Press, 1968); for a useful analysis of self-incrimination problems in regard to confessions of guilt, see Otis Stephens, Jr., *The Supreme Court and Confessions of Guilt* (Knoxville: University of Tennessee Press, 1973).
2 Record, pp. 6-8, *Malloy* v. *Hogan*, 378 U.S. 1 (1964).
3 Letter, Harold Strauch to the author, July 19, 1973.
4 Record, pp. 8-10, *Malloy* v. *Hogan*. John Bergoti was never identified in the record, briefs, or the oral argument of the *Malloy* case.
5 *Hartford Courant*, Jan. 26, 1961, p. 5, and Jan. 27, 1961, p. 5. Record, p. 10, *Malloy* v. *Hogan*.
6 Record, p. 1, *Malloy* v. *Hogan*.
7 Memorandum of Decision, Feb. 7, 1961, ibid., pp. 6-13.
8 *Malloy* v. *Hogan*, 150 Conn. 220, 224-26 (1963).
9 150 Conn. 220, 226.
10 150 Conn. 220, 226-31.
11 150 Conn. 220, 231-32.
12 *Malloy* v. *Hogan*, 373 U.S. 943 (1963).
13 Brief of Petitioner, pp. 6-8, *Malloy* v. *Hogan*, 378 U.S. 1 (1964).
14 Ibid., pp. 13-14.
15 Ibid., p. 15.
16 Brief of Respondent, pp. 10-12, *Malloy* v. *Hogan*, 378 U.S. 1 (1964).
17 Ibid., pp. 14-24.
18 Brief of the State of California as *Amicus Curiae*, pp. 2-3, *Malloy* v. *Hogan*, 378 U.S. 1 (1964).
19 See the Brief of the American Civil Liberties Union as *Amicus Curiae* and the Brief of the National District Attorneys' Association as *Amicus Curiae*, *Malloy* v. *Hogan*, 378 U.S. 1 (1964).

20 The discussion, in this paragraph and the seven that follow, of the oral argument in *Malloy* v. *Hogan* is drawn from the tape recording of the argument on March 4, 1964, which is listed in the audiovisual division of the National Archives as no. 110, 267-485.

21 Malloy v. Hogan, 378 U.S. 1, 6-8 (1964).

22 378 U.S. 1, 11.

23 378 U.S. 1, 11-14.

24 378 U.S. 1, 15.

25 378 U.S. 1, 32-33.

26 378 U.S. 1, 37.

27 *Reynolds* v. *Sims*, 377 U.S. 533 (1964); see Richard C. Cortner, *The Apportionment Cases* (New York: Norton, 1972).

28 *Griffin* v. *California*, 380 U.S. 609 (1965).

29 *Miranda* v. *Arizona*, 387 U.S. 436 (1966). See Richard C. Cortner and Clifford M. Lytle, "Rape in the Desert," pp. 158-98, in *Modern Constitutional Law* (New York: Free Press, 1971); see also, Stephens, *The Supreme Court and Confessions of Guilt*, chapters 6, 7.

30 Letter, Harold Strauch to the author, July 19, 1973.

31 *Pointer* v. *Texas*, 380 U.S. 400 (1965).

32 Record, pp. 17-42, *Pointer* v. *Texas*, 380 U.S. 400 (1965). *Houston Post*, June 18, 1962, sec. 1, p. 7.

33 Record, pp. 44-50, *Pointer* v. *Texas*.

34 Ibid., pp. 12-37, 40-60.

35 *Pointer* v. *Texas*, 375 S.W.2d 293, 295 (1963).

36 Brief for Petitioner, p. 2, *Pointer* v. *Texas*, 380 U.S. 400 (1965).

37 Ibid., pp. 10-11; *Hamilton* v. *Alabama*, 368 U.S. 52 (1961); *White* v. *Maryland*, 373 U.S. 59 (1963).

38 Brief for Petitioner, pp. 11-12, *Pointer* v. *Texas*.

39 Brief for Respondent, pp. 7-9, *Pointer* v. *Texas*, 380 U.S. 400 (1965).

40 The excerpts from the oral argument contained in this paragraph and the seven that follow are drawn from the tape recording of the argument on March 15, 1965, which is listed in the audiovisual division of the National Archives as no. 577, 267-536.

41 *Pointer* v. *Texas*, 380 U.S. 400, 405-6 (1965).

42 380 U.S. 400, 407-8.

43 380 U.S. 400, 409-10.

44 380 U.S. 400, 408.

45 380 U.S. 400, 408-9.

46 380 U.S. 400, 410-14.

47 This account of the proceedings in the *Pointer* case after the Supreme Court's decision is based on a letter from C. C. Divine to the author, Dec. 18, 1972. Divine was one of the attorneys for Pointer at his original trial.

48 The facts in the *Washington* case are recounted in the opinion of the Texas Court of Criminal Appeals, *Washington* v. *Texas*, 400 S.W.2d 756 (1966).

49 Record, p. 2, *Washington* v. *Texas*, 388 U.S. 14 (1967).

50 Ibid., p. 3.

51 Ibid., pp. 9-14.

52 Ibid., pp. 4-5.
53 *Washington* v. *Texas*, 400 S.W.2d 756, 759 (1966).
54 *Washington* v. *Texas*, 385 U.S. 812 (1966).
55 The excerpts from the oral argument contained in this paragraph and the seven that follow are drawn from the tape recording of the argument on March 15 and 16, 1967, which is listed in the audiovisual division of the National Archives as no. 649, 267-630-631.
56 While the *Washington* case was pending before the Court, the Texas legislature repealed the statutes prohibiting co-defendant testimony. See Brief for Petitioner, p. 10, *Washington* v. *Texas*, 388 U.S. 14 (1967).
57 *Washington* v. *Texas*, 388 U.S. 14, 19 (1967).
58 388 U.S. 14, 22-23.
59 388 U.S. 14, 23-25.
60 See Justice Brennan's discussion in *Malloy* v. *Hogan*, 378 U.S. 1, 4-7 (1964). For contemporary commentary on the selective-incorporation approach, see Alex B. Lacy, "The Bill of Rights and the Fourteenth Amendment: The Evolution of the Absorption Doctrine," *Washington and Lee Law Review*, 23 (1966): 37-65; Louis Henkin, "Selective Incorporation in the Fourteenth Amendment," *Yale Law Journal*, 73 (1963): 74-88; and Frank H. Walker, Jr., "Constitutional Law—Was It Intended that the Fourteenth Amendment Incorporates the Bill of Rights?" *North Carolina Law Review*, 42 (1964): 925-36.
61 See Chief Justice Warren's opinion in the *Washington* case, 388 U.S. 14, 17-18 nn. 6-11.
62 Letter, Charles W. Tessmer to the author, May 18, 1971.

CHAPTER 10

1 *Brown* v. *Board of Education*, 347 U.S. 483 (1954). See also, Daniel M. Berman, *It is So Ordered* (New York: Norton, 1966), and Albert P. Blaustein and Clarence C. Ferguson, *Desegregation and the Law* (New York: Vintage Books, 1962).
2 *NAACP* v. *Alabama*, 357 U.S. 449 (1958); *NAACP* v. *Button*, 371 U.S. 415 (1963); *New York Times* v. *Sullivan*, 376 U.S. 254 (1964).
3 *Klopfer* v. *North Carolina*, 386 U.S. 213 (1967); *Duncan* v. *Louisiana*, 391 U.S. 145 (1968). The *Klopfer* case was decided on March 13, 1967, two months before the Court's decision in *Washington* v. *Texas* on June 12. I have reordered the sequence of these cases for topical purposes.
4 John Ehle, *The Free Men* (New York: Harper & Row, 1965), pp. 152-53. For further background on the *Klopfer* case, see Daniel H. Pollitt, "Legal Problems in Southern Desegregation: The Chapel Hill Story," *North Carolina Law Review*, 43 (1965): 689-767.
5 Ehle, *The Free Men*, p. 145.
6 Ibid., pp. 146-69.
7 Record, pp. 1-8, *Klopfer* v. *North Carolina*, 386 U.S. 213 (1967).
8 Quoted in Ehle, *The Free Men*, p. 271.
9 Record, p. 8, *Klopfer* v. *North Carolina*.

10 Ibid., pp. 9–10; *Heart of Atlanta Motel* v. *United States*, 379 U.S. 241 (1964); *Katzenbach* v. *McClung*, 379 U.S. 294 (1964).

11 *Hamm* v. *Rock Hill*, 379 U.S. 306, 308 (1964).

12 Record, pp. 9–10, *Klopfer* v. *North Carolina*.

13 Ibid., pp. 11–12.

14 Ibid., p. 12.

15 *State* v. *Klopfer*, 266 N.C. 349, 350–51 (1966).

16 *Klopfer* v. *North Carolina*, 384 U.S. 959 (1966).

17 Brief for Petitioner, p. 13, *Klopfer* v. *North Carolina*, 386 U.S. 213 (1967).

18 Ibid., p. 18.

19 Brief of the American Civil Liberties Union and the North Carolina Civil Liberties Union as *Amici Curiae*, p. 26, *Klopfer* v. *North Carolina*, 386 U.S. 213 (1967).

20 Brief of Respondent, pp. 5–7, *Klopfer* v. *North Carolina*, 386 U.S. 213 (1967).

21 Ibid., pp. 5–7.

22 The excerpts from the oral argument in this paragraph and the seven that follow are from the tape recording of the argument on Dec. 8, 1966, which is listed in the audiovisual division of the National Archives as no. 100, 267–612.

23 *Klopfer* v. *North Carolina*, 386 U.S. 213, 216 (1967).

24 386 U.S. 213, 219–26.

25 386 U.S. 213, 226–27.

26 Ehle, *The Free Men*, p. 293.

27 William S. Geimer, "Effect of the Right to Speedy Trial on Nolle Prosequi," *North Carolina Law Review*, 46 (1968): 387–92; letter, Peter H. Klopfer to the author, Sept. 19, 1973.

28 Quoted in Ehle, *The Free Men*, p. 243.

29 The *Oliver* case had been subjected to the retroactive-incorporation process and was now considered to have incorporated the Public Trial Clause. The Sixth Amendment also requires that a criminal defendant be "informed of the nature and cause of the accusation." The Court had held as well in the *Oliver* case that adequate notice of the charges against a defendant was a requirement of the Due Process Clause. Since the requirement of notice has traditionally been regarded as an essential element of due process, it is clear that notice is a requirement of the Due Process Clause with or without the incorporation of the specific language of the Sixth Amendment in that regard.

30 *Maxwell* v. *Dow*, 176 U.S. 581, 602–3 (1900).

31 *Palko* v. *Connecticut*, 302 U.S. 319, 325 (1937); *Irvin* v. *Dowd*, 366 U.S. 717, 721–22 (1961). See also, *Turner* v. *Louisiana*, 379 U.S. 466 (1965).

32 *Parker* v. *Gladden*, 385 U.S. 363, 364–65 (1966).

33 385 U.S. 363, 367. The much-respected Henry J. Abraham indicates in his *Freedom and the Court* (3d ed. [New York: Oxford University Press, 1977], p. 88) that the result of *Parker* v. *Gladden* was to incorporate the Sixth Amendment's standard of impartiality in regard to jury trials into the Due Process Clause. As my discussion of the *Parker* case indicates, I do not agree

with that conclusion. The language of the Court, and that of Justice Harlan in dissent, indicates, I think, that the case was considered to be primarily a confrontation case, including the additional factor of fairness in jury-trial proceedings required of the states by the Due Process Clause independent of Sixth Amendment. If this view is rejected, however, and the Court's comments on the applicability of the Sixth Amendment to the states in *Parker* are viewed in isolation from the Court's subsequent comments, it seems to me that a literal reading of the Sixth Amendment comments would require the conclusion that the Court not only incorporated the Sixth Amendment's requirement of impartiality in the *Parker* case but also its requirement of jury trials, since the Court quoted not just the part of the Sixth Amendment requiring impartiality but rather the whole Jury Trial Clause. Professor Abraham, however, concedes that the Jury Trial Clause was not incorporated until *Duncan* v. *Louisiana*, 391 U.S. 145 (1968) (Abraham, *Freedom and the Court*, pp. 90–93). The Court's listing of the rights in the Bill of Rights that had already been incorporated into the Due Process Clause in the *Duncan* case does not include the Sixth Amendment's standard of impartiality, nor does it cite the *Parker* case to that effect. (See 391 U.S. 145, 148 nn. 4–12.) This, it seems to me, is understandable, since it would have been peculiar for the Court to incorporate the word *impartial* before it incorporated the requirement of jury trials in state cases, especially in light of the fact that the Due Process Clause standing alone had already been held to require impartial jurors in state criminal cases. With due deference to my colleague Abraham's opinion, therefore, I have concluded that he is incorrect on this point. In support of his view, however, see "Comment Note—What Provisions of the Federal Constitution's Bill of Rights are Applicable to the States" (18 L.Ed.2d 1388, 1409).

34 *Duncan* v. *Louisiana*, 391 U.S. 146 (1968). For a previously published account of the *Duncan* case, see Richard C. Cortner, *The Supreme Court and Civil Liberties Policy* (Palo Alto: Mayfield Publishing Co., 1975), pp. 6–30.

35 James Conaway, *Judge: The Life and Times of Leander Perez* (New York: Knopf, 1973), pp. 118–19, 142–43.

36 *New York Times*, April 17, 1962, pp. 1, 16. For an account of Perez's role in the resistance to public school desegregation, see Jack Peltason, *Fifty-Eight Lonely Men* (New York: Harcourt, Brace & World, 1961), pp. 233, 240–41.

37 New Orleans *Times-Picayune*, Aug. 6, 1966, pp. 1, 3.

38 Ibid., Aug. 13, 1966, p. 27.

39 Ibid., Aug. 16, 1966, p. 1, and Aug. 27, 1966, p. 1.

40 Record, pp. 42–48, 63, *Duncan* v. *Louisiana*, 391 U.S. 145 (1968).

41 New Orleans *Times-Picayune*, Jan. 25, 1968, sec. 2, p. 4, and Jan. 30, 1968, sec. 1, p. 17; *Law Quadrangle Notes* (University of Michigan Law School official publication), 13, no. 2 (spring 1969): 9–10.

42 Conaway, *Judge*, pp. 119–21. This incident is also reported in New Orleans *Times-Picayune*, Feb. 1, 1968, sec. 1, p. 6.

43 New Orleans *Times-Picayune*, Jan. 31, 1968, sec. 3, p. 2; *Law Quadrangle Notes*, 13, no. 2 (spring 1969): 9–10.

44 New Orleans *Times-Picayune*, Jan. 31, 1968, sec. 3, p. 2.

45 See *Sobol* v. *Perez*, 289 F.Supp. 392, 397 (E.D.La., 1968).

46 Record, pp. 4, 18-19, *Duncan* v. *Louisiana*.

47 Ibid., pp. 42-72.

48 Ibid., p. 73.

49 *Duncan* v. *Louisiana*, 250 La. 258 (1967).

50 *Law Quadrangle Notes*, 13, no. 2 (spring 1969): 9-10; Conaway, *Judge*, pp. 173-77.

51 *Sobol* v. *Perez*, 289 F.Supp. 392 (E.D.La., 1968); New Orleans *Times-Picayune*, Feb. 23, 1967, sec. 1, p. 25 and Jan. 28, 1968, sec. 1, p. 10.

52 Brief for Appellant, pp. 9-11, *Duncan* v. *Louisiana*, 391 U.S. 145 (1968).

53 Brief for Appellee, pp. 64-68, *Duncan* v. *Louisiana*, 391 U.S. 145 (1968). An *amicus curiae* brief was also filed by the attorney general of New York opposing the application of the Jury Trial Clause to the states. See Brief of the State of New York as *Amicus Curiae*, *Duncan* v. *Louisiana*, 391 U.S. 145 (1968).

54 The excerpts of the oral argument in this paragraph and the eleven that follow are drawn from the tape recording of the argument on Jan. 17, 1968, which is listed in the audiovisual division of the National Archives as no. 410, 267-668.

55 *Duncan* v. *Louisiana*, 391 U.S. 145 (1968).

56 391 U.S. 145, 149-50 n. 14.

57 391 U.S. 145, 150 n. 14.

58 391 U.S. 145, 149, 156.

59 391 U.S. 145, 159-62.

60 Fortas's concurring opinion was recorded in a companion case to *Duncan*, *Bloom* v. *Illinois*, 391 U.S. 194, 213-15 (1968).

61 391 U.S. 194, 213-15.

62 The six-months rule was adopted by the Court in *Baldwin* v. *New York*, 399 U.S. 66 (1970), while the six-member-jury ruling came in *Williams* v. *Florida*, 399 U.S. 78 (1970). The Court has subsequently held, however, that a five-person jury violates the Sixth and Fourteenth Amendments. See *Ballew* v. *Georgia*, 435 U.S. 223 (1978). The nonunanimous-verdict rulings came in *Apodaca* v. *Oregon*, 406 U.S. 404 (1972), and *Johnson* v. *Louisiana*, 406 U.S. 356 (1972). See Justice Powell's concurring opinion at 406 U.S. 356, 366; it should be noted that presently only three members of the Court appear to adhere to Justice Powell's view of the right to trial by jury under the Due Process Clause. See the concurring opinion by Justice Powell in *Ballew* v. *Georgia*, 435 U.S. 223, 245-46 (1978), which was joined by Chief Justice Burger and Justice Rehnquist.

63 *Duncan* v. *Louisiana*, 391 U.S. 145, 164 (1968).

64 391 U.S. 145, 164-65.

65 391 U.S. 145, 168-71.

66 391 U.S. 145, 171.

67 391 U.S. 145, 174-75.

68 391 U.S. 145, 177-79.

69 391 U.S. 145, 180-81.

70 391 U.S. 145, 193.

71 *Sobol* v. *Perez*, 189 F.Supp. 392 (E.D.La., 1968), 401-2.

72 *Duncan* v. *Perez*, 321 F.Supp. 181 (E.D.La., 1970), 182–85.
73 *Duncan* v. *Perez*, 445 F.2d 557 (5th Cir., 1971).
74 *Perez* v. *Duncan*, 404 U.S. 940 (1971).

CHAPTER 11

1 On this point, see Richard C. Cortner, *The Apportionment Cases* (New York: Norton, 1972), pp. 222–26.
2 On reactions to the Warren Court's criminal-procedure decisions, see Fred P. Graham, *The Self-Inflicted Wound* (New York: Macmillan, 1970); for a scholarly criticism of these decisions, see Henry J. Friendly, "The Bill of Rights as a Code of Criminal Procedure," *California Law Review*, 53 (1965): 929–56.
3 Quoted in James F. Simon, *In His Own Image: The Supreme Court in Richard Nixon's America* (New York: David McKay, 1973), p. 74.
4 Quoted in Graham, *The Self-Inflicted Wound*, p. 15.
5 See Simon, *In His Own Image*, pp. 74–96.
6 For a fuller discussion, see Robert Shogan, *A Question of Judgment* (New York: Bobbs-Merrill, 1972).
7 See Simon, *In His Own Image*, pp. 97–124. On the defeat of the Carswell nomination, see Richard Harris, *Decision* (New York: Ballantine Books, 1971).
8 These facts are related in *Benton* v. *State*, 8 Md.App. 388, 260 A.2d 86, 87–88 (1969).
9 Benton's criminal record was revealed in the Respondent's Supplemental Brief, p. 20 n. 6, *Benton* v. *Maryland*, 395 U.S. 784 (1969).
10 Record, p. 1, *Benton* v. *Maryland*, 395 U.S. 784 (1969).
11 *Schowgurow* v. *State*, 240 Md. 121 (1965).
12 See the Respondent's Brief, p. 22, *Benton* v. *Maryland*, 395 U.S. 784 (1969).
13 Record, pp. 3–4, *Benton* v. *Maryland*.
14 Ibid., p. 5.
15 Ibid., p. 7.
16 *Benton* v. *State*, 1 Md.App. 647, 232 A.2d 541, 543 (1967).
17 Brief for the Petitioner, p. 2, *Benton* v. *Maryland*, 395 U.S. 784 (1969).
18 *Benton* v. *Maryland*, 392 U.S. 925 (1968).
19 Brief for the Petitioner, pp. 7–8, 11–12, *Benton* v. *Maryland*.
20 Ibid., pp. 14–22; *United States* v. *Ball*, 163 U.S. 662 (1896).
21 Respondent's Brief, p. 14, *Benton* v. *Maryland*.
22 Ibid., pp. 23, 16.
23 The excerpts from the oral argument of December 12, 1968, in this paragraph and the five that follow are drawn from the tape recording of that argument, which is listed in the audiovisual division of the National Archives as no. 201, 267–719. A reargument of the *Benton* case was ordered by the Court on December 16, 1968; see *Benton* v. *Maryland*, 393 U.S. 994 (1968).
24 A leading case was *Hirabayashi* v. *United States*, 320 U.S. 81 (1943).
25 Cases recognizing collateral effects of criminal convictions were *Ginsberg* v. *New York*, 390 U.S. 629 (1968); *Peyton* v. *Rowe*, 391 U.S. 54 (1968); *Carafas* v. *LaVallee*, 391 U.S. 234 (1968); and *Sibron* v. *New York*, 392 U.S. 40 (1968).
26 Supplementary Brief for Respondent, p. 8, *Benton* v. *Maryland*, 395 U.S. 784 (1969).

27 Supplementary Brief for Petitioner, pp. 3-9, *Benton* v. *Maryland*, 395 U.S. 784 (1969).

28 Memorandum of the United States as *Amicus Curiae*, pp. 6-8, 20-23, *Benton* v. *Maryland*, 395 U.S. 784 (1969).

29 Ibid., pp. 18-20.

30 *Benton* v. *Maryland*, 395 U.S. 784, 790-91 (1969).

31 395 U.S. 784, 794-95.

32 395 U.S. 784, 796-97.

33 395 U.S. 784, 797-98.

34 395 U.S. 784, 801-13.

35 *Benton* v. *State*, 8 Md.App. 388 (1969).

36 *Benton* v. *Copinger*, 291 F.Supp. 141 (D.Md., 1968).

37 See *Benton* v. *Maryland*, 395 U.S. 784, 786, n. 1.

38 *North Carolina* v. *Pearce*, 395 U.S. 711 (1969). Due process, however, does not prohibit the imposition of an increased sentence by a jury, rather than a judge, upon a retrial in these circumstances. See *Chaffin* v. *Stynchcombe*, 412 U.S. 17 (1973).

39 Letter, M. Michael Cramer to the author, Sept. 21, 1973.

40 18 U.S.C. sec. 3731; see *United States* v. *Wilson*, 420 U.S. 332 (1975).

41 *United States* v. *Sanges*, 144 U.S. 310 (1892); Criminal Appeals Act, 34 Stat. 1246 (1907).

42 See *United States*, v. *Scott*, 437 U.S. 82 (1978).

43 *Ashe* v. *Swenson*, 397 U.S. 436 (1970). See also *Simpson* v. *Florida*, 403 U.S. 384 (1971); *Harris* v. *Washington*, 404 U.S. 55 (1971); *Turner* v. *Arkansas*, 407 U.S. 366 (1972). The *Ashe* case, in effect, reversed *Hoag*. v. *New Jersey*, 356 U.S. 464 (1958).

44 *Price* v. *Georgia*, 398 U.S. 323 (1970); *Jeffers* v. *United States*, 432 U.S. 137 (1977); *Brown* v. *Ohio*, 432 U.S. 161 (1977); *Harris* v. *Oklahoma*, 433 U.S. 682 (1977).

45 *Breed* v. *Jones*, 421 U.S. 519 (1975); *Swisher* v. *Brady*, 438 U.S. 204 (1978).

46 *Crist* v. *Bretz*, 437 U.S. 28 (1978); *Serfoss* v. *United States*, 420 U.S. 377 (1975).

47 *United States* v. *Linen Supply Co.*, 430 U.S. 564 (1977); *Burks* v. *United States*, 437 U.S. 1 (1978); *Sanabria* v. *United States*, 437 U.S. 54 (1978).

48 *North Carolina* v. *Pearce*, 397 U.S. 711, 717 (1969).

49 *United States* v. *Wilson*, 420 U.S. 332 (1975). See also, *United States* v. *Morrison*, 429 U.S. 1 (1976); *United States* v. *Rose*, 429 U.S. 5 (1976); *United States* v. *Sanford*, 429 U.S. 14 (1976); *United States* v. *Kopp*, 429 U.S. 121 (1976).

50 *Bartkus* v. *Illinois*, 359 U.S. 121 (1959); *United States* v. *Wheeler*, 435 U.S. 313 (1978).

51 The proceedings are reprinted in 23 L.Ed.2d xli-xlv. See also, the *Washington Post*, June 24, 1969, pp. 1, 13A.

CHAPTER 12

1 See *Schilb* v. *Kuebel*, 404 U.S. 357, 365 (1971); Henry J. Friendly, *Federal Jurisdiction: A General View* (New York: Columbia University Press, 1973), p. 18 n. 17.

2 See Clement E. Vose, *Caucasians Only* (Berkeley: University of California Press, 1959) and *Constitutional Change* (Lexington, Mass.: Lexington Books, 1972).

3 *Chicago, Milwaukee & St. Paul Railroad* v. *Minnesota*, 134 U.S. 418 (1890); *Santa Clara County* v. *Southern Pacific Railroad*, 118 U.S. 394 (1886).

4 *DeJonge* v. *Oregon*, 299 U.S. 353, 364 (1937).

5 While I do not regard *Fiske* v. *Kansas*, 274 U.S. 380 (1927), as having nationalized freedom of speech, it should nevertheless be noted that the *Fiske* case was sponsored by the General Defense Committee of the Industrial Workers of the World (IWW).

6 Frank J. Sorauf, *The Wall of Separation* (Princeton: Princeton University Press, 1976), p. 59.

7 Vose, *Constitutional Change*, p. 331.

8 See Richard C. Cortner, "Strategies and Tactics of Litigants in Constitutional Cases," *Journal of Public Law*, 17 (1968): 287–307.

9 It is interesting to recall in this regard that the *Stromberg* case almost did not make it to the Supreme Court because the ACLU and the ILD were unable to raise $2500 for John Beardsley's fee.

10 From the evidence in the McCay file, the *Everson* case appears to have cost between $7000 and $8000.

11 Compare the deliberate assault of the NAACP upon the separate-but-equal doctrine through the formulation of an expanding theory of equal protection. Vose, *Caucasians Only*, pp. 30–73; Daniel M. Berman, *It Is So Ordered* (New York: Norton, 1966), pp. 28–32. See also, Sorauf, *The Wall of Separation*, pp. 91–129, on the attempts of the ACLU, AJC, and AU to control the framing of issues in Establishment Clause litigation.

12 See Alpheus T. Mason, *Harlan Fiske Stone* (New York: Viking Press, 1956), pp. 512–15; *United States* v. *Carolene Products Co.*, 304 U.S. 144 (1938).

13 Klaus H. Heberle, "From Gitlow to Near: Judicial 'Amendment' by Absent-Minded Incrementalism," *Journal of Politics*, 34 (1972): 458–83.

14 *Palko* v. *Connecticut*, 302 U.S. 319, 325 (1937).

15 *Malinski* v. *New York*, 324 U.S. 401, 416–17 (1945).

16 See Anthony Lewis, *Gideon's Trumpet* (New York: Random House, 1964), p. 114.

17 *Rogers* v. *Richmond*, 365 U.S. 534, 540–41 (1961).

18 The best statement by a selective incorporationist on this point is by Justice Goldberg in his concurring opinion in *Pointer* v. *Texas*, 380 U.S. 400, 410–14 (1965).

19 *Mooney* v. *Holohan*, 297 U.S. 103 (1935); *Brady* v. *Maryland*, 373 U.S. 83 (1963).

20 *Thompson* v. *Louisville*, 362 U.S. 199 (1960); *Garner* v. *Louisiana*, 368 U.S. 157 (1961).

21 *Griswold* v. *Connecticut*, 381 U.S. 479 (1965). For an in-depth analysis of the litigation in the *Griswold* case, see Richard C. Cortner and Clifford M. Lytle, *Modern Constitutional Law* (New York: Free Press, 1971), "The Connecticut Birth Control Case," pp. 77–111.

22 *Duncan* v. *Louisiana*, 391 U.S. 145, 181 (1968).

23 Eugene V. Rostow, *The Sovereign Perogative* (New Haven: Yale University Press, 1962), pp. 167-68.

24 By ignoring the overall significance of the cases in which they were involved, and instead focusing upon the merits of each case, counsel for the states in the First Amendment cases closely resemble Jonathan D. Casper's description of the "Advocate." Advocates, Casper has said, "are typically not concerned with (and may not even be aware of) the broader implications of the litigation in which they become involved" (*Lawyers before the Warren Court* [Urbana: University of Illinois Press, 1972], p. 96).

25 See Cortner and Lytle, *Modern Constitutional Law*, p. 176.

26 See Richard C. Cortner, *The Apportionment Cases* (Knoxville: University of Tennessee Press, 1970), p. 209 n. 62.

27 *Report of the Committee on Federal-State Relationships as Affected by Judicial Decisions* (Chicago: Conference of State Chief Justices, 1958).

28 See Paul Oberst, "The Supreme Court and States' Rights," *Kentucky Law Journal*, 48 (1959): 63-89; John D. O'Reilly, Jr., "The Spencer Roanes of 1958," *Villanova Law Review*, 4 (1958-59): 92-116; William B. Lockhart, "Response to the Conference of State Chief Justices," *University of Pennsylvania Law Review*, 107 (1958-59): 802-10.

29 *State Government*, 36 (1962): 186.

30 *Baker* v. *Carr*, 369 U.S. 186 (1962).

31 *Congressional Quarterly* 21 (1963): 662-63. See also, Alexander M. Bickel, "Curbing the Union," chapter 11 in *Politics and the Warren Court* (New York: Harper & Row, 1965); Paul Oberst, "The Genesis of the Three States-Rights Amendments of 1963," *Notre Dame Lawyer*, 39 (1964): 644-58.

32 See Oberst, "The Genesis of the Three States-Rights Amendments of 1963," 653-55; Cortner, *The Apportionment Cases*, pp. 222-23.

33 *Brown* v. *Allen*, 344 U.S. 443 (1953); *Fay* v. *Noia*, 372 U.S. 391 (1963); Friendly, *Federal Jurisdiction*, p. 18.

34 These figures may be found in the *Annual Reports* of the Administrative Office of the United States Courts, Washington, D.C., for the relevant years.

35 Fred P. Graham, *The Self-Inflicted Wound* (New York: Macmillan, 1970), p. 110. See also, "Report of the Committee on Habeas Corpus of the Conference of Chief Justices," *State Government*, 26 (1953): 241.

36 *State Government*, 38 (1965): 67.

37 Louis H. Pollack, "Proposals to Curtail Federal Habeas Corpus to State Prisoners: Collateral Attack on the Great Writ," *Yale Law Journal*, 66 (1956): 50-66.

38 For an excellent summary of the development of the federal writ of habeas corpus, see "Developments in the Law of Federal Habeas Corpus," *Harvard Law Review*, 83 (1970): 1038-1280. When an unlawful search-and-seizure claim has been given a full and fair hearing in the state courts, the Court ruled in 1976, the search-and-seizure claim may not be subsequently raised on petition for a federal writ of habeas corpus. See *Stone* v. *Powell*, 428 U.S. 465 (1976). The Court further restricted the availability of the federal writ of habeas corpus in *Francis* v. *Henderson*, 425 U.S. 536 (1976). In addition to these restrictions upon the availability of the writ of habeas corpus, it should

be noted that the failure of state interests to mount further attacks upon the habeas corpus jurisdiction of the federal courts may be attributable to the very small number of state prisoners whose convictions are overturned by the federal courts after habeas hearings. Also, the number of habeas petitions filed by state prisoners in the federal courts leveled off and declined somewhat in the early 1970s. From a peak of 9,063 petitions in 1970, the number declined to 7,949 in 1972.

39 For early examples, see Charles Warren, *The Supreme Court in United States History* (Boston: Little, Brown, 1922), vol 1, chaps. 8, 13; for more modern examples, see Stephen L. Wasby, *The Impact of the United States Supreme Court* (Homewood, Ill.: Dorsey Press, 1970), pp. 196–203.

40 One standard by which evasion of Supreme Court mandates is measured in some studies is the extent to which the prevailing party in the Supreme Court also prevails in subsequent proceedings in the lower courts. I have obviously not adhered to this standard, since by its terms, the Florida courts in *Gideon* would not be counted as evading the Supreme Court's decision, while the Texas courts in *Pointer* would be so counted. In fact, the courts of both states fully complied with the Court's mandates in the *Gideon* and *Pointer* cases.

41 Quoted in Bradley C. Canon, "Organizational Contumacy in the Transmission of Judicial Policies: The *Mapp, Escobedo, Miranda*, and *Gault* Cases," *Villanova Law Review*, 20 (1974): 50, 68.

42 Quoted in Bradley C. Canon, "Reactions of State Supreme Courts to a U.S. Supreme Court Civil Liberties Decision," *Law and Society Review*, 8 (1973): 109, 110.

43 *Escobedo* v. *Illinois*, 378 U.S. 478 (1964); *In re Gault*, 387 U.S. 1 (1967).

44 Canon, "Organizational Contumacy," pp. 70, 78. The extent of outright evasion of the decisions of the Warren Court between 1959 and 1969, on the other hand, appears to be a disputed matter. See Jerry K. Beatty, "State Court Evasion of the United States Supreme Court Mandates During the Last Decade of the Warren Court," *Valparaiso University Law Review*, 6 (1972): 260–85; Ronald Schneider, "State Court Evasion of United States Supreme Court Mandates: A Reconsideration of the Evidence," *Valparaiso University Law Review*, 7 (1973): 191–95; Jerry K. Beatty, "Reconsideration of the Evidence: A Rebuttal," *Valparaiso University Law Review*, 7 (1973): 198–200.

45 See Wasby, *The Impact of the United States Supreme Court*, pp. 147–69.

46 John R. Schmidhauser, *The Supreme Court* (New York: Holt, Rinehart and Winston, 1961), pp. 80–88.

47 See Brennan's opinions in *United States* v. *Miller*, 425 U.S. 435, 454 (1976); *Michigan* v. *Mosley*, 423 U.S. 96, 120–21 (1975). The state cases construing state constitutional provisions more liberally than the Supreme Court has construed the federal Constitution are listed in William J. Brennan, "State Constitutions and the Protection of Individual Rights," *Harvard Law Review*, 90 (1977); 489–504. See also, Donald E. Wilkes, Jr., "The New Federalism in Criminal Procedure: State Court Evasion of the Burger Court," *Kentucky Law Journal*, 62 (1974): 421–51; "More on the New Federalism in Criminal Procedure," *Kentucky Law Journal*, 63 (1975): 873–94; Project Report, "To-

ward an Activist Role for State Bills of Rights," *Harvard Civil Rights-Civil Liberties Law Review*, 8 (1973): 271–350.

48 Felix Frankfurter and James M. Landis, *The Business of the Supreme Court* (New York: Macmillan, 1928), p. 109.

49 In the field of freedom of expression, for example, of the 175 cases decided by the Court with opinions between 1931 and 1970, 70 percent involved challenges to state policies under the Fourteenth Amendment; similarly, 85 percent of the right-to-counsel cases decided by the Court between 1963 and 1970 arose under the Fourteenth Amendment.

50 Quoted in Marvin Meyers, ed., *The Mind of the Founder: Sources of the Political Thought of James Madison* (New York: Bobbs-Merrill, 1973), pp. 217–26.

Index of Cases

General Index

Cross-references to the Index of Cases appear in boldface type.

Abbotts, William, 111, 114
ACLU. SEE American Civil Liberties
 Union
Adamson, Admiral Dewey, 139-44, 150-
 51. SEE ALSO *Adamson* v. *California*
Agricultural Workers Industrial Union.
 SEE Industrial Workers of the World
AJC. SEE American Jewish Congress
Allen, Joseph W., 32
Allison, Charles L., 75
Amedee, Earl, 248-49
American Association of University
 Women, 109
American Civil Liberties Union, 63-65,
 109, 153, 156, 181, 183-84, 210-11,
 238-39, 248, 280, 282, 284-85; Florida
 Civil Liberties Union, 201; New Jersey
 Civil Liberties Union, 110; North Caro-
 lina Civil Liberties Union, 238-39; Ohio
 Civil Liberties Union, 181, 183-84;
 Portland (Ore.) Civil Liberties Union,
 88-91, 93-94; Southern California Civil
 Liberties Union, 74, 76
—role of: in *DeJonge* case, 88-96; in
 Everson case, 113-15, 117; in *Gitlow*
 case, 54-55, 61; in *Near* case, 69-72;
 in *Stromberg* case, 74-80
American Committee for the Protection
 of the Foreign Born, 97
American Jewish Congress, 117, 248,
 282
American Legion, 73, 76, 89-90
American Newspaper Publishers' Asso-
 ciation, 72-73, 282-84
American Union against Militarism, 54

Americans United for Separation of
 Church and State, 282. SEE ALSO Prot-
 estants and Other Americans United for
 Separation of Church and State
Amicus curiae briefs, 92, 153, 210-11, 282,
 292-94; in *Benton* case, 272-74; in
 Everson case, 113, 117; in *Gideon* case,
 196-97, 199-201, 203-4; in *Klopfer*
 case, 238-39; in *Mapp* case, 181, 183-
 84; in *Oliver* case, 156-57; in *Wolf* case,
 165
Amon, Albert, 235, 244
ANPA. SEE American Newspaper Pub-
 lishers' Association
Appellate Division of New York Supreme
 Court, 53-54
Article III, 29, 272-73
Article V, 294
Aschen, Charles S., 55
Assembly and petition, freedom of. SEE
 Freedom of assembly and petition
Assistance of Counsel Clause, 24, 135-38,
 161, 174-75, 177, 204, 214, 216, 218-
 23, 228, 232, 246, 263, 288-90, 292; in
 Gideon case, 194-204

Bailey, Forrest, 79-80
Baldwin, Mathias, 69
Baldwin, Roger N., 54-55, 63, 71, 76-80,
 91, 96, 98
Banks, Charles, 188
Baptist Joint Conference Committee on
 Public Relations. SEE Joint Baptist
 Conference Committee on Public Rela-
 tions

351

Near, J. M., 66–72, 81, 85. SEE ALSO
  Near v. Minnesota
NCLB. SEE National Civil Liberties
  Bureau
Nelles, Walter, 55
New Haven County (Conn.) Court of
  Common Pleas, 102–3
New Jersey bus law, 109–23
New Jersey Civil Liberties Union. SEE
  American Civil Liberties Union
New Jersey Council of Churches, 109
New Jersey Court of Errors and Appeals,
  44, 114, 119, 284
New Jersey Education Association, 109
New Jersey Federation of District Boards
  of Education, 109
New Jersey League of Women Voters, 109
New Jersey Supreme Court, 44, 111, 113–
  114
New Jersey Taxpayers Association, 109–10
New Jersey Taxpayers Association for
  Separation of Church and State, 123
New Republic, 56
New York County Criminal Courts Bar
  Association, 165
New York County Supreme Court, 72
New York Court of Appeals, 53–54
New York Criminal Anarchy Act, 51, 53–
  54, 57–60, 82
New York Times, 53, 109, 187
Nixon, Richard M., 263–64, 278
Nol. pros. SEE *Nolle prosequi*
Nolle prosequi, 236–44
Nonsuperfluousness, doctrine of. SEE
  Doctrine of nonsuperfluousness
North Carolina Civil Liberties Union.
  SEE American Civil Liberties Union
North Carolina Supreme Court, 238, 243
Northfield News, 68

Oakland County (Mich.) Circuit Court,
  154–55
O'Brien, Clifford, 89
Ohio Civil Liberties Union. SEE American
  Civil Liberties Union
Ohio Supreme Court, 180–81
Oliver, William D., 155–59. SEE ALSO
  Oliver, In re
Olson, Floyd, 67–68, 70–71
One-man grand jury. SEE Michigan one-
  man grand jury

Orange County (N.C.) Superior Court,
  236–37, 244
Oregon Criminal Syndicalism Act, 87–
  97
Osborn, Robert, 235, 244

Packard, A. O., 31
Palka, Frank Jacob. SEE Palko, Frank
  Jacob
Palko, Frank Jacob, 126–31, 150–51. SEE
  ALSO *Palko v. Connecticut*
Palmer, A. Mitchell, 50, 52
Parker, John J., 83
Parker, Roscoe H., 266–67
Parker, William, 193
Patriotic Order of Americans, 110
Peckham, Rufus W., 35–36
Pena, Gilbert J., 220–23
Penny, Wade H., Jr.: role in *Klopfer*
  case, 236–40, 244
Perez, Leander H., Jr., 250–51, 261–62
Perez, Leander H., Sr., 246–49
Phillips, Juanita Lavon, 217
Phillips, Kenneth W., 217–18, 220–23,
  225
Picano, Eugene, 206, 216
Pointer, Bob Granville, 217–26, 297. SEE
  ALSO *Pointer v. Texas*
Polashian, George, 206, 216
Pollak, Walter H., 64, 66, 71, 85, 285;
  role in *Gitlow* case, 54–55, 57–59
Pontiac Amusement Company, 155
Portland (Ore.) Civil Liberties Union. SEE
  American Civil Liberties Union
Portland *Oregon Journal*, 90
Poth, Harry, 93–94
Pound, Cuthbert, 54
Powell, Lewis F., Jr., 258
Preferred freedoms, doctrine of. SEE Doc-
  trine of preferred freedoms
Preservation, 101
Press, freedom of. SEE Freedom of the
  press
Prince George's County (Md.) Circuit
  Court, 265–66
Prior restraint, 81–84
Protestants and Other Americans United
  for Separation of Church and State,
  121
Public Trial Clause, 175, 232, 246, 287;
  in *Oliver* case, 157–58, 161

GENERAL INDEX

JACKET DESIGNED BY GARY G. GORE
COMPOSED BY METRICOMP
GRUNDY CENTER, IOWA
MANUFACTURED BY CUSHING MALLOY, INC.
ANN ARBOR, MICHIGAN
TEXT AND DISPLAY LINES ARE SET IN BODONI

Library of Congress Cataloging in Publication Data
Cortner, Richard C
The supreme court and the second Bill of Rights.
Includes bibliographical references and index.
1. United States. Constitution. 1st-10th amendments.
2. United States. Constitution. 14th amendment.
3. Civil rights—United States. 4. Due process of
law—United States. 5. United States. Supreme Court.
I. Title.
KF4749.C66   342.73′085   80-5112
ISBN 0-299-08390-X

Date Due